The Book in Society

THE BOOK IN SOCIETY

AN INTRODUCTION TO PRINT CULTURE

SOLVEIG C. ROBINSON

broadview
press

Library and Archives Canada Cataloguing in Publication

Robinson, Solveig C., 1962–, author
  The book in society : an introduction to print culture / Solveig C. Robinson.

Includes bibliographical references and index.
ISBN 978-1-55481-074-1 (pbk.)

  1. Books—History. I. Title.

Z4.R62 2013   002   C2013-906598-9

Broadview Press is an independent, international publishing house, incorporated in 1985.

We welcome comments and suggestions regarding any aspect of our publications— please feel free to contact us at the addresses below or at broadview@broadviewpress.com.

North America
PO Box 1243, Peterborough, Ontario, Canada K9J 7H5
2215 Kenmore Ave., Buffalo, New York, USA 14207
Tel: (705) 743-8990; Fax: (705) 743-8353
email: customerservice@broadviewpress.com

UK, Europe, Central Asia, Middle East, Africa, India, and Southeast Asia
Eurospan Group, 3 Henrietta St., London WC2E 8LU, United Kingdom
Tel: 44 (0) 1767 604972; Fax: 44 (0) 1767 601640
email: eurospan@turpin-distribution.com

Australia and New Zealand
NewSouth Books
c/o TL Distribution, 15-23 Helles Ave., Moorebank, NSW, Australia 2170
Tel: (02) 8778 9999; Fax: (02) 8778 9944
email: orders@tldistribution.com.au

www.broadviewpress.com

Edited by Michel Pharand

This book is printed on paper containing 100% post-consumer fibre.

PRINTED IN CANADA

For Rosemary VanArsdel

CONTENTS

Acknowledgments 13
Introduction 15

PART ONE
THE HISTORY OF THE BOOK

Chapter One Origins 21

Writing and Writing Systems: Moving from Signs to Words 22
Egypt and Mesopotamia 23
    Egyptian Hieroglyphic 24
    ≡ *The Rosetta Stone 25*
    ≡ *The Book of the Dead 27*
    Cuneiform 28
    Semitic Writings 31
    ≡ *The Torah 32*
    Parchment 33
    ≡ *The Dead Sea Scrolls 34*
China 35
    Other Asian Writing Systems 38
    Paper 39
Mesoamerica 40
    Mesoamerican Codices 41
    ≡ *Mayan Codices 42*
    Incan Quipus 43
Ancient Greece 44
Selected Bibliography 46

Chapter Two Scribal Culture and the Codex 49

Books and the Roman Empire 51
    Writing at the Center: Rome 51
    Writing in the Provinces: Vindolanda 53
Books of the Jewish Diaspora 55
    Jewish Codices 56

Islam and the Book   57
   ≡ *The Qur'an*   58
   Bookmaking in the Muslim World   60
Christianity and the Codex   61
   The Development of the Christian Bible   62
Book Production in the Middle Ages   64
   The Monastic Scriptorium   65
   ≡ *The Book of Hours*   66
The Renaissance   69
   Universities   71
Selected Bibliography   72

Chapter Three The Printing Revolution   75

Early Printing in Asia   76
   Printing in China   77
   ≡ *The Diamond Sutra*   80
   Printing in Japan and Korea   81
Early Printing in Europe   82
   Gutenberg   82
   ≡ *The Biblia Pauperum*   83
   ≡ *Type Design*   86
   The Common Press   88
   ≡ *The Gutenberg Bible*   91
The Press and the Reformation   93
   Printing and the Protestant Churches   94
   Printing and the Catholic Church   96
The Expansion of Print Culture   97
   ≡ *The Officina Plantiniana*   98
   Printing and the Enlightenment   99
   Encylopedists and Lexicographers   100
   ≡ *L'Encylopédie*   101
   ≡ *Johnson's Dictionary*   102
Printing in the Industrial Age   104
   Developments in the Printing Trades   105
   Wood-Pulp Paper   106
   Mechanized Typesetting   108
   The Book Arts Revival   111
Selected Bibliography   113

Chapter Four Modern Times: From Paperbacks to e-Books 115

Education, Literacy, and Mass Readerships 116
    Periodicals 118
    ≡ *The Saturday Evening Post* 119
The Paperback Revolution 120
    Penguins and Pockets 121
    ≡ *Penguin Books* 123
    Popular Genres 124
    Mass Market versus Quality 124
The Digital Revolution 125
    Gutenberg and the Internet 127
    ≡ *Wikipedia* 128
    e-Readers 131
The Future of the Book 134
Selected Bibliography 135

Selected Activities and Resources for Part One 137

PART TWO
THE BOOK CIRCUIT: AUTHORS, AUTHORITIES, PUBLISHERS, READERS

Chapter Five Authors 145

The Rise of the Modern Author 146
    Anonymous and Pseudonymous Publishing 149
    ≡ *William Shakespeare* 150
Author by Profession 155
    ≡ *The Royal Literary Fund* 156
    Subscription Publication 157
    From Profit Sharing to Royalties 159
    Copyright and Contracts 160
Literary Agents and Professional Societies 162
    ≡ *Eudora Welty and Diarmuid Russell: An Author and Her Agent* 163
    Authors' Associations 164
    ≡ *PEN International* 166
Translation, Adaptation, and Other Transformations 168
Self-Publishing 170
    ≡ *Bapsi Sidhwa and the Self-Publishing Springboard* 172
Selected Bibliography 173

Chapter Six States and Censors 177

Regulating Print 178
    Trade Associations 180
Censorship 181
    ≡ *Book Bans and Challenges 182*
    Censorship and the Inquisition 183
    State Censorship 185
    ≡ *Obscenity Legislation and Lady Chatterley's Lover 186*
    Censorship and the Third Reich 188
    Censorship in the Modern Era 190
Promoting Print 192
    Freedom of the Press 193
    ≡ *The Danish Cartoons Controversy 194*
    The History of Copyright 195
    International Copyright Protections 198
    Limits on Copyright: Fair Use 200
    Copyright Law Today 201
    Copyright and Copyleft 203
Harnessing Print 204
    Propaganda and War 205
Selected Bibliography 208

Chapter Seven Publishers 211

The Professionalization of Publishing 212
    ≡ *Geraldine Jewsbury: A Publisher's Reader 213*
    An Explosion of Publishing Ventures 215
    Multinationals 217
    ≡ *Pearson 219*
Specialized Publishers: Educational Presses 221
    Textbook Publishing 222
    ≡ *Readability 224*
    University Presses 226
The Publishing Process 229
Acquisitions and Development 230
    Acquisitions 230
    ISBNs and CIP Data 232
    Development 233
    ≡ *Max Perkins: A Literary Editor 234*

Production   235
   Copyediting   235
   ≡ *Misguided Editing: Bowdlerization*   237
   Design   238
   Typesetting, Printing, and Binding   241
Selected Bibliography   243

Chapter Eight Booksellers   245

Independent Booksellers   246
   Independents Today   246
   ≡ *The Strand Book Store*   248
   Used and Antiquarian Booksellers   250
   ≡ *Powell's Books*   252
Bookstore Chains   253
   ≡ *Glorious Chain Stores*   254
The Superstores   256
   ≡ *Foyles: A Legendary Superstore*   256
   ≡ *Barnes & Noble*   260
Online Booksellers   261
   The Internet Superstore: Amazon.com   262
   Other Internet Booksellers   264
Distributors and Wholesalers   264
Book Fairs   266
   ≡ *The Frankfurt Book Fair*   267
Selected Bibliography   269

Chapter Nine Libraries   271

The Evolution of the Library: Ancient Greece to the Renaissance   272
   ≡ *The Vatican Library*   274
Modern Libraries   276
The Public Library Movement   277
   ≡ *Mudie's Select Library*   278
   ≡ *Chetham's Library*   280
   The Library Builders: John Passmore Edwards and Andrew Carnegie   282
   ≡ *The Tacoma Public Library*   285
   Grand Public Libraries   286
   Public Libraries Today   288
National Libraries   290

The First National Libraries   290
        The British Library   291
        ≡ *The Private Case*   294
        The Bibliothèque Nationale   296
        The Library of Congress   298
Modern National Libraries   300
Librarianship   302
        Cataloguing Systems   303
        Specialization   306
Conservation and Preservation   307
        Emergency Preparedness   307
        Brittle Books   308
        Space   310
Selected Bibliography   311

Chapter Ten Readers   313

Literacy   314
        ≡ *George Dawson: Late-Life Literacy*   315
        Aliteracy   317
Tools for Reading   318
        Aids to Vision   319
        Devices for Readers   322
Reading Communities   324
        The Book-of-the-Month Club   326
        Book Clubs of the Air   328
Special Books for Special Readers   330
        ≡ *J.K. Rowling: The Magic of Harry Potter*   332
        Romance   334
        ≡ *Nora Roberts: Queen of Romance*   335
        Action/Adventure and Suspense   336
        ≡ *Stieg Larsson: Scandinavian Crime Success*   337
Selected Bibliography   339

Selected Activities and Resources for Part Two   341

Glossary   349
Landmarks in the History of the Book   361
Index   367

ACKNOWLEDGMENTS

Thanks are due to many organizations and individuals for research assistance and encouragement. I would especially like to thank my colleagues at Pacific Lutheran University for their support, and the library staffs at Pacific Lutheran University, the British Library, and the John Rylands Library in Manchester for their help in locating source materials. Further thanks are due to friends and colleagues in the Research Society for Victorian Periodicals (RSVP), the Victorian Interdisciplinary Studies Association of the Western United States (VISAWUS), and the Society for the History of Authorship, Reading, and Publishing (SHARP). I am also grateful to my many Publishing & Printing Arts (PPA) students at Pacific Lutheran University, especially those in the January 2012 and Fall 2012 "Book in Society" classes, whose input was invaluable. Special thanks go to Bradford Andrews and Donald Ryan, Pacific Lutheran University, for help with early writing systems; to Megan Benton and Jessica Summers, my book artist colleagues; to Joanne and David for hospitality; and to Peter for everything.

What exactly is a "book"? Who produces it, who reads it, and why? What effect have books had on the societies into which they have been introduced, and how have those societies in turn shaped the kind of books produced in them?

The Book in Society: An Introduction to Print Culture will examine the origins and development of one of the most important inventions in human history—indeed, the invention that is instrumental to the definition and preservation *of* human history. After writing systems were developed in ancient Mesopotamia, China, and Mesoamerica, the tools were in place for the emergence of texts of all kinds: records of agricultural seasons and triumphs in war, books of prophecy and divination, and finally works of imagination and pleasure. Along the way, rules emerged about who was allowed access to the written word, and under what circumstances. In a rich symbiosis that expressed itself differently at different times and places, recorded words shaped and reflected the cultures that in turn shaped and reflected them, driving (or arresting) changes in both the world and the texts.

All of these factors have coalesced into modern societies' conceptions of what a book is and what it does. Whether its intention is to inform, entertain, inspire, irritate, liberate, or challenge readers; whether its format is tangible and traditional, like a printed hardcover, or virtual and transitory, like a screen-page of a cell-phone novel, a book offers its readers a chance to step outside themselves and (however briefly) enter into the thoughts of another.

DEFINING THE BOOK

The term *book* encompasses a variety of texts, from handwritten to print, short to multivolume. Some countries and organizations simply define books in terms of page counts, enabling them to more easily track particular data, such as sales of certain kinds of texts, or the number of readers. The United Nations Educational, Scientific and Cultural Organization (UNESCO), for example, at one point specified that to qualify as a book, a text required a minimum of forty-nine pages, not including the covers. But this statistical approach clearly is at odds with most readers' and writers' notions of what a "book" is. Length is just one quality that inheres in books, and particular page or word counts only give us a sense of how much paper might be required to produce such a text, or how much time might be required to read it.

Others have approached the book as a cultural artifact, a material object that carries in its form and design some clues about a culture's values and organization. This approach underpins the science and art of *bibliography*. Bibliography is concerned with the detailed description of books, especially with the details that help reveal the transmission of texts over time. Although it is familiar to most readers through its application in library catalogues, bibliography at its most engrossing entails working out the entire production and history of individual, particular copies of books. As publishing scholar Eli MacLaren observes: "Every object bears witness to a process of production. Everything is, in its being, a trace of its own creation; its mere existence is proof of its having been made." This approach also underlies the study of the *history of the book*, sometimes called the *history of print culture*. Cultural historian Leslie Howsam (b. 1946) notes that historians of print culture emphasize the importance of books in and to history, pointing to them "as the material and commercial and cultural artefacts" that support and surround ideas, experiences, and relationships in almost any era. One of the pioneers of the field, Elizabeth Eisenstein (b. 1923), explained that her interest in the technology of printing was based on the "special effects" it had on society: "As *an* agent of change, printing altered methods of data collection, storage and retrieval systems, and communication networks used by learned communities throughout Europe." Thus, the close study of a book can yield a wealth of information about its creation, and also about the world in which it was created.

Still others concentrate on the book as a container of ideas. Literary studies, history, and many other disciplines have traditionally approached the book this way. From this perspective, books are vessels for conveying what is known about the world, and for appreciating the rich variety of interpretations and expressions of our experiences with and in it. Books disseminate ideas, reveal secrets, move us to laughter and tears. Depending on what we want from books—information, entertainment, solace, aesthetic experience—we approach them differently. And even when seeking a particular kind of content from a particular genre, individual readers will interact in unique ways with those books. English novelist Virginia Woolf (1882–1941) encapsulated this wonderful idiosyncrasy in her essay "How Should One Read a Book?" She declared: "Even if I could answer the question for myself, the answer would apply only to me and not to you. The only advice, indeed, that one person can give another about reading is to take no advice, to follow your own instincts, to use your own reason, to come to your own conclusions."

In *The Book Revolution*, French scholar Robert Escarpit (1918–2000) declared: "Like anything that lives, the book is not to be defined.... When we hold it in our hands, all we hold is the paper: the *book* is elsewhere. And yet it is in the pages as well, and the thought alone without the support of the printed words could not make a book. A book is a reading-machine, but it can never be used mechanically. A book is sold, bought, passed from hand to hand, but it cannot be treated like an ordinary commercial commodity, because it is, at once, multiple and unique, in ample supply yet precious." In keeping with Escarpit's sentiments and the general consensus of contemporary book historians, *The Book in Society* therefore uses the word *book* in the broadest possible sense.

THE STRUCTURE OF THIS BOOK

The Book in Society is organized into two main sections. *Part One: The History of the Book* provides an overview of the rise of the modern book and of the publishing and bookselling industries. It explores the evolution of written texts from early forms to contemporary formats, the interrelationship between literacy and technology, and the status of—and prospects for—the book in the electronic age. Especially over the past decade or so, myriad essays and articles have appeared with titles such as "Final Chapter?" or "Digitization and Its Discontents." While some have predicted that the long-heralded "paperless society" is finally coming to pass and that we will soon see the "death of the book," others have suggested more soberly that print and digital books will coexist far into the future. "When our descendants take their summer holidays in 100 years time," *Observer* columnist James Robinson muses, "they are still likely to be reading the latest airport thriller on the beach, even if they ordered it online." The historical framework offered in Part One provides a context for thoughtfully considering the future of the book—in any or all forms.

Part Two: The Book Circuit: Authors, Authorities, Publishers, Readers examines the processes by which books migrate from the minds of authors to the minds of readers. Based loosely on publishing historian Robert Darnton's (b. 1939) concept of a book publishing "communication circuit," the chapters in this section look at the rise of the modern notion of the author, the roles of states and others in promoting or restricting the circulation of books, various modes of reproducing and circulating texts, and how readers' responses to various kinds of books help shape what is made available to them.

SELECTED BIBLIOGRAPHY

Eisenstein, Elizabeth L. *The Printing Revolution in Early Modern Europe*. Cambridge: Cambridge UP, 1983.

Escarpit, Robert. *The Book Revolution*. London: Harrap and UNESCO, 1966.

Glaister, Geoffrey Ashall. *Encyclopedia of the Book*. 2nd ed. New Castle, DE: Oak Knoll, 1996.

Grafton, Anthony. "Future Reading: Digitization and Its Discontents." *New Yorker*, 5 November 2007.

Howsam, Leslie. *Old Books and New Histories: An Orientation to Studies in Book and Print Culture*. Toronto: U of Toronto P, 2006.

MacLaren, Eli. "The Place of Bibliography in the Academy Today." *SHARP News* 16.4 (2007): 3–4.

Robinson, James. "Final Chapter?" *Observer*, 27 July 2008.

Williams, W.P., and C.S. Abbott. *Introduction to Bibliographical and Textual Studies*. 2nd ed. New York: MLA, 1989.

Woolf, Virginia. "How Should One Read a Book?" *The Second Common Reader: First and Second Series*. New York: Harcourt, 1948. 281–95.

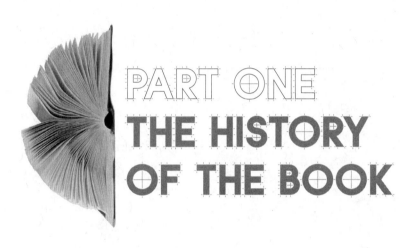

PART ONE
THE HISTORY
OF THE BOOK

CHAPTER ONE

ORIGINS

What is the most important technological development in human history? The candidates that most commonly spring to mind are the harnessing of fire, the invention of the wheel, or the discovery of penicillin. But the invention of writing systems may claim pride of place on that list, because it is writing that has enabled theorists, inventors, and practitioners in all spheres of human endeavor across time and space to share, challenge, and refine one another's ideas. Writing systems enabled early cultures to record their daily activities and elaborate their beliefs about humankind's relations to one another and to the world beyond. Many of our earliest examples of written communications are very simple records and exchanges of information. But there are also glimpses of more complex texts, texts that we today would identify as "books," even if their material forms do not resemble contemporary formats.

Writing systems—and eventually books—emerged in three distinct times and places in the ancient world. The first emergence was in Egypt and Mesopotamia, sometime around 3700 BCE. The Egyptians developed a system of *hieroglyphs*, or picture-writing, that remained in use for nearly four millennia. Nearby, several centuries later, the Akkadians developed a system of writing on clay tablets, *cuneiform*, that was adopted and refined by various peoples in the region, including the Sumerians, Assyrians, Babylonians, Hittites, and Persians. The origins of an alphabetic writing system emerged somewhat later, sometime between 2000 and 1200 BCE, with the Semitic peoples in the Mediterranean. Their invention in turn led to perhaps the most important development in the Western world, when in about 900 BCE the Greeks adapted a consonant-based Semitic alphabet by adding letters to represent vowel sounds. The resulting twenty-four-letter alphabet, rooted in the representation of *phonetics* (speech-sounds), enabled writers to more directly move from speech to written text, or from oral to literate culture. Significantly, this more speech-mimicking writing system also helped drive an increase in overall literacy and a cultural flourishing that influenced subsequent eras.

The second emergence of writing systems occurred in China. The earliest examples, which date from about 1200 BCE, are records of consultations with diviners, or fortune-tellers. Inscribed on animal shells and bones, the writing indicates the date of the consultation (and sometimes the seeker's or diviner's identities), what was predicted, and in some cases whether the prophecy came true. Unlike Western writing, which culminated in largely phonetic-based alphabetic systems, writing in China developed around a *logographic*, or word-based, system, with signs (*characters*) representing either whole words or concepts or—more commonly—the syllabic components of those words or concepts. The Chinese system of writing spread Chinese culture and influence throughout Asia, where it was adapted to create writing systems specific to other Asian languages and traditions. In addition to a writing system, the Chinese also invented paper and printing.

The third major writing system developed in Mesoamerica, probably sometime in the first millennium BCE. Somewhat like Egyptian hieroglyphic, Mesoamerican writing combined pictorial components (*glyphs*) with some phonetic components. Although most of what still exists of Mesoamerican writing are the monumental inscriptions, the cultures also produced written books. However, in one of the more horrific episodes in the history of the book, nearly all of these were ordered destroyed by the Inquisition in the sixteenth century. Only a handful survived.

This chapter will explore the emergence of the book in the ancient world, up to about the time of the Common Era. It will examine some of the key innovations that contributed to the origins of the book, including the invention of writing systems and the concurrent development of writing tools, most notably ink, papyrus, paper, and parchment.

WRITING AND WRITING SYSTEMS: MOVING FROM SIGNS TO WORDS

In order to understand the significance of writing systems that have had a direct impact on the history of the book, it may be helpful to have a basic overview of writing systems more broadly. Humans in various times and places have devised many written systems of communication, but not all of those systems work in the kind of close collaboration with specific languages that we usually mean when we think of "writing." For example, there have been numerous systems for notating music—for showing the duration and relationship between pitches—through the ages. The music notation system most commonly in use today arranges notes ♪ on grids of five lines that are marked for voice (*treble clef* for higher voices, and *bass clef* for lower voices), key (the number of *flats* ♭ or *sharps* ♯), and duration (the *time signature* specifies the number of beats per measure and which kind of note gets one beat). Although Italian is often used to provide further indicators about other aspects of the music, such as *tempo* (speed), knowledge of the Italian language is not essential to decoding and performing from a musical score. A musician who knows no Italian but can read music can still reproduce the sounds intended by the composer.

Another commonly used written communication system that is uncoupled from a specific language is mathematics. When we learn basic arithmetic (1 + 1 = 2), we also learn a symbolic system of communication that can become so deeply internalized that we forget that *numerals* themselves—1, 2, 3, and so on—are symbols of concepts related to quantity. Some mathematical symbols may derive their names from Greek letters, but the meaning of, say, π (*pi*) in a mathematical context is understood to be distinct from its meaning in a portion of a text by Plato, or on a street-sign in Athens.

More recently, our increased use of various kinds of keyboards and electronic devices has resulted in further systems of written communication. *Emoticons* have evolved from keyboard-derived winking faces [;-)], designed to take the edge off a message that might otherwise be misunderstood, to the ubiquitous ♥ for *love*. Both to save space and to avoid the difficulties of marketing specific gadgets to different language communities, various software and hardware manufacturers have relied increasingly on *icons*, pictorial images that quickly convey information to users: an image of a file folder signals where a document can be saved or retrieved, while an image of a lidded rubbish bin signals where a file may be discarded.

Each of these systems can quickly communicate particular kinds of information to those who know how to read them. But the kinds of information they convey are also very restricted: musical notation only conveys information about music; mathematical notations only convey information about mathematical theory and calculation. These written systems are *semasiographic*, or based on signs that are not derived from speech. By contrast, *lexigraphic* systems are based on words—they derive from the basic building blocks of language. As a result, they are much more flexible and expansive, enabling their users to capture the full range of human thought.

It is lexigraphic writing systems that have literally defined the contours of human history, by enabling us to recreate the worlds and ideas of cultures far remote from our own. We may be able to deduce something of a long-lost people from close observation of its remaining monuments, but it is only when we are able to read the people's words that we can enter into their beliefs and customs and truly come to know them. Not surprisingly then, it is those cultures who invented and passed down lexigraphic writing systems that have had the greatest influence on the history of the book.

EGYPT AND MESOPOTAMIA

Supported by the great rivers of the Nile, Tigris, and Euphrates, several early civilizations in the Middle East grew to a size and complexity that required special innovations for administration and record keeping. The general scholarly consensus is that this is what spurred the development of writing in ancient Egypt and Mesopotamia. The history of the book begins here.

Egyptian Hieroglyphic

If you ask an ordinary person on the street to name an ancient writing system, he or she will probably come up with hieroglyphic. The pictorial symbols that decorated Egyptian tombs and monuments, and that were used to record some of the world's most ancient surviving books, are distinctive, thanks to an ongoing popular fascination with mummies and pyramids. Visitors to Egypt can purchase customized *cartouches* or "name rings" (so called because of the circles around the hieroglyphs) that purport to spell out the buyer's name in hieroglyphs; armchair travelers can take advantage of websites that offer to translate their text into hieroglyphs. Yet another sign of the enduring popularity of Egyptian writing is the name of a popular line of language software, which evokes the story of the translation of the texts on the Rosetta Stone, the first great breakthrough in reading hieroglyphic.

But despite its compelling visual aspects and long duration, the ancient Egyptian writing system ultimately proved a dead end. Developed before the unification of Egypt's Upper and Lower Kingdoms (which occurred in about 3000 BCE), some form of hieroglyphic writing was in almost continual use in the region for nearly four millennia. The form known as *Middle* or *Classical Egyptian* first appeared in writing in about 2100 BCE, and it is the system used for most surviving ancient Egyptian writing. Although vestiges of the ancient Egyptian language endured into the eleventh century in the sacred writings and liturgy of the Coptic church (modern Egyptians now speak and write Arabic), the hieroglyphic writing system itself fell out of use before the Common Era, and soon even scholars in the region could no longer read texts written in it.

Like other ancient writing systems, hieroglyphic probably developed primarily to allow for record keeping. To a certain degree, hieroglyphic was a writing system based on *ideograms*, or "idea-signs." A hieroglyph that represented a waterbird or a reed, for example, probably originally implied that there was a one-to-one relationship between the thing depicted and its sign. If the primary purpose of a particular Egyptian text was, say, to enumerate the amount of grain in a given storehouse, then drawing a given number of representations of grain would quickly convey this information. Even a simplified and stylized version of the item being depicted would have the same effect for a reader: so many pictures of a grain sheaf, so many bundles in the storehouse.

But this assumption that there was a one-to-one relationship between sign and object is one of the things that stood in the way of translating hieroglyphic for so many centuries after the writing system had fallen out of use: simply adding up the images didn't render the inscriptions meaningful. As it happens, the Egyptian system wasn't strictly semasiographic, or based on signs unconnected from speech and language. Something else was involved.

What had been lost through the ages, and what the French Egyptologist Jean-François Champollion (1790–1832) established in the early nineteenth century, when he finally worked out how to translate the hieroglyphic text on the Rosetta Stone, was that Egyptian hieroglyphic worked on two interacting levels. Champollion's great insight was to see that in addition to hieroglyphs' symbolic value, they also had a phonetic, or sound-based, component. Champollion figured out that in addition to the logographic level, where particular symbols did in fact represent the items they depicted, hieroglyphs also worked on a phonographic level: they represented sounds in the Egyptian language. So while the image of a reed might represent a reed, it also might

THE ROSETTA STONE

By the beginning of the Common Era, Egyptian hieroglyphic was becoming unintelligible. The phonetic component of the hieroglyphs was forgotten, and Greek and Roman writers began to ascribe esoteric meanings to the increasingly mysterious symbols. Although a fifth-century work entitled *Hieroglyphica* included accurate translations of many hieroglyphs, it also offered bizarre allegorical explanations for them, and the more fanciful aspects of the work were what endured in subsequent readers' imaginations. This fundamental misunderstanding of the Egyptian writing system persisted for the next thousand years.

The key to understanding hieroglyphic writing again was discovered in 1799, when French soldiers at a fortress in the Egyptian port city of Rosetta uncovered a triangular monument, with inscriptions in Greek, demotic, and hieroglyphic. The Greek inscription on the Rosetta Stone was easily read: it proclaimed a decree in honor of the boy king Ptolemy Epiphanes (c. 204–181 BCE). Working on the assumption that the other two inscriptions contained the same text, interested scholars focused their attention on deciphering the demotic, and several were eventually able to figure out the symbols that represented proper names.

However, it was Jean-François Champollion who ultimately solved the puzzle of both the demotic and the fragmentary hieroglyphic inscriptions. A talented linguist, Champollion had learned Hebrew, Arabic, and Coptic (among many other languages) before the age of eighteen, when he became a professor at the university of Grenoble. He suspected that at least some of the hieroglyphs might be read phonetically, and he guessed that the ancient Egyptian phonemes might be related to those in Coptic. Working from copies of the inscriptions on the Rosetta Stone, as well as copies of inscriptions from Egyptian temples, Champollion deciphered the royal names of Ptolemy, Cleopatra, and Ramses in the monument's cartouches. The announcement of his discovery, on September 29, 1822, marks the beginning of modern Egyptology.

Because of its significance to unlocking the mystery of ancient Egyptian texts, the term Rosetta stone has come to be used for any key essential to the understanding of a particular subject—making it a natural choice for the name of a popular language-learning program.

serve as a *rebus*, a graphic symbol encoding a recognizable speech sound. For example, the hieroglyph of a folded piece of linen cloth,

∩

appeared to represent the phoneme /s/. Working from his study of ancient history and his knowledge of Greek and Coptic, Champollion was able to determine the phonetic value of many of the known hieroglyphs, and his announcement of his discovery in 1822, followed by the publication in 1824 of his *Précis du système hiéroglyphique*, marks the beginning of modern Egyptology.

Building on Champollion's groundbreaking work, Egyptologists rapidly refined their understanding of Egyptian writing. Egyptian hieroglyphs not only function as ideograms and phonograms, but they can also function as *determinatives*, or signs that indicate that the other symbols are meant as phonograms or that indicate a general idea of the word intended. Unlike most modern writing systems, which can only be written and read in one direction (for example, in rows from left to right, as in English), hieroglyphs can be written and read in both rows and columns, and from either left to right or right to left. They are also typically grouped, with taller signs (like the folded cloth shown previously) standing alone, but shorter signs arranged in squares or rectangles. This flexibility in ordering enabled Egyptian scribes to produce inscriptions that were symmetrically pleasing and added an additional aesthetic element to the overall effect.

Once the key to the hieroglyphs had been provided, Egyptologists made rapid headway in reading the many inscriptions, paintings, and papyrus texts that nineteenth- and early twentieth-century archaeologists brought to light. Among the documents that were now readable again after so many millennia were the collections of texts found in many tombs and known as the *Book of the Dead*. Not so much a "book" as an assortment of spells and hymns combined in different ways, the various texts that make up the *Book of the Dead* describe the course of the afterlife from judgment to eternity and offer guidance or protection to the deceased. Texts from the *Book of the Dead* were often inscribed on tomb walls and sarcophagi, so their survival into the modern age is not entirely surprising. However, some were also inscribed on the significantly more fragile medium of papyrus, the oldest of which date to the Eighteenth Dynasty, about 1,500 to 1,300 years before the Common Era. That so many of these texts have come down to us is probably due to two factors: first, the tombs protected the fragile papyrus from the extremes of weather (both heat and rain); and second, unlike those grave goods that could be readily sold (if made of precious metals and stones) or even reused (if made of wood or cloth), papyrus scrolls appear to have been relatively unattractive to untold generations of grave robbers.

As a writing medium, papyrus offered many advantages to the ancient world. Besides endurance, it was also readily renewable, pliable, relatively easy to write on, and relatively easy to store. Its importance to cultural history is encapsulated in the fact that the word *papyrus* is the origin of many modern words for both *paper* (*Papier, papel, papier*, from the Greek and Latin *papuros*

THE BOOK OF THE DEAD

One of the best-known texts of ancient Egypt is the *Book of the Dead*, a collection of spells or incantations and hymns found in most tombs of royal or otherwise prosperous persons. The number of spells varies from version to version, but the most complete versions, dating from the Ptolemaic period (c. 300–30 BCE), can have as many as 200 spells. The spells relate to the journey of the soul into the afterlife, and they describe the burial processes, prepare the soul for its ordeal, and seek to propitiate gods and spirits as the soul proceeds. Some versions of the *Book of the Dead* also include hymns to Ra and Osiris, the sun god and god of the underworld, respectively.

The earliest versions of the *Book of the Dead*, dating from about 2400 BCE, were inscribed on coffins, while later versions were written on papyrus and on the walls of the burial chambers. Those from the New Kingdom period were often especially lavishly written and illustrated. For example, the papyrus *Book of the Dead* of Hunefer, from about 1300 BCE in Thebes, includes a striking image of the mummy of Hunefer being supported by the god Anubis, while his wife and children mourn and priests carry out the burial rituals. The foreground shows the various tools required for the "opening of the mouth" ritual—which enabled the mummy to breathe, speak, and eat—and preparations for an animal sacrifice.

Here is a translation of an "opening of the mouth" spell from the *Book of the Dead*, translated in 1895 by Egyptologist E.A. Wallis Budge:

> May Ptah open my mouth, and may the god of my town loose the swathings, even the swathings which are over my mouth.
> Moreover, may Thoth, being filled and furnished with charms, come and loose the bandages, the bandages of Set which fetter my mouth;
> and may the god Tmu hurl them at those who would fetter [me] with them, and drive them back. May my mouth be opened, may my mouth be unclosed by Shu
> with his iron knife, wherewith he opened the mouth of the gods. I am Sekhet, and I sit upon the great western side of heaven.
> I am the great goddess Sah among the souls of Annu. Now as concerning every charm and all the words which may be spoken against me,
> may the gods resist them, and may each and every one of the company of the gods withstand it them.

and *papyrusi*), and *book* or *library* (*Buch, biblioteca, bibliothèque*, from the Greek *bubloi*, or inner fiber of the papyrus plant, and the Latin *biblia*, or writings on papyrus sheets). One of the best-known accounts of how to prepare papyrus was provided in the first century by Pliny the Elder (23–79), who described the process in his *Naturalis historia*. Other evidence suggests the process did not change appreciably over the millennia. The reeds were cut and peeled,

cut down to approximately one-foot (30 cm) lengths, and then pounded until flat, which left the sheets with a natural ribbing that is helpful for aligning rows of text. Two such sheets were then laid crosswise to one another (the ribs running horizontally on one sheet, and vertically on the other) and pounded together to make a complete, two-sided writing surface.

To create a scroll, as many as twenty of these two-sided sheets were laid side-by-side and pounded together at the edges. The scrolls could then be written on with black or red ink, which the Egyptians and other ancient peoples in the region made from carbon (black) and iron oxide (red). The ink was stored in small boxes, recon-

Seated statue of an Egyptian scribe found in the Western cemetery at Giza; 5th dynasty. Photograph by Jon Bodsworth.

stituted on a palette, and applied with a small reed brush. Representations of these tools formed one of the Egyptian hieroglyphs for *scribe*. Complete papyrus scrolls would be rolled and tied, and perhaps marked with a clay seal to show ownership. They would then be stored in boxes or jars.

Cuneiform

Egyptian hieroglyphic writing endured for nearly four millennia, but it was so intricately tied into the culture that created it that it did not survive ancient Egypt's final collapse. As the spoken language evolved, so did the written language. A form of hieroglyphic that was easier to write, *hieratic*, was in use from very early on, primarily for letters and accounts. By about 650 BCE, hieratic had been largely replaced by *demotic* (Greek for "popular") script, which no longer resembled hieroglyphic. By the time of the Ptolemies (c. 332–330 BCE), it is likely that only priests were still able to read and write hieroglyphic. Greek was both easier to read and write, and it was also more widely understood throughout the Mediterranean region. When the last remnants of ancient Egyptian culture finally succumbed to Roman influence under Cleopatra's reign (51–30 BCE), the Egyptian system of writing did, too. The Egyptians who adopted Christianity after the first century CE eschewed demotic for their translations of scripture, and they developed a Greek-based script, *Coptic*, for their writings. Coptic was the last vestige of the venerable Egyptian language, which finally died out completely in the first millennium.

But alternative writing systems had arisen in other parts of the ancient Middle East. Unlike hieroglyphic, which was largely picture-based, some of the other systems sought to more directly represent speech. These systems had the advantage of some built-in flexibilities: because they represented not just words or concepts but the speech sounds that expressed those words or concepts, the writing systems could be more easily adapted and redeployed as languages—and cultures—evolved.

The oldest decipherable lexigraphic writing system in the world arose in the region that is now modern Iraq, around 3400 BCE. First used by the Akkadians, and later by the Sumerians, Babylonians, and others, *cuneiform* was a wedge-shaped form of writing that was incised into clay with a stylus made of reed or wood or, for more monumental texts, carved into rock with chisels. The importance of writing to the Akkadians and their successors is suggested by its place in their creation stories. For example, in Sumerian and Babylonian mythology, Asuru (later Marduk) created both the world and human beings. His son Nebo (or Nabu) was the god of wisdom and the inventor of the alphabet, while the goddess Nisaba invented the art of writing. That writing and alphabets were considered divine gifts—and ones that were given fairly early in the cultures' history, as well—signals how the ability to communicate through written texts was recognized as a distinct cultural advantage.

The earliest examples of cuneiform tend to be records of one sort or another. According to Sumerologist Christopher Woods, curator of a 2011 exhibit at the Oriental Institute of the University of Chicago about the origins of writing, about 90 per cent of the earliest Mesopotamian writings were administrative documents. The texts might indicate quantities of various agricultural goods, such as grain, and were probably used to keep track of inventories or trading transactions, or for taxation purposes. Later examples of cuneiform include more diversified kinds of texts, including letters, records of historical events, and laws. The clay tablets used for cuneiform writing were usually rectangular in shape and ranged from a mere one-quarter inch square (about 6.35 mm) to as large as 18 x 12 inches (45 x 30 cm). The text was inscribed in lines from left to right, parallel to the shortest side of the tablet, and could be continued on to the reverse of the tablet. Space at the end of the last column of text was often used for a *colophon*, which indicated who had written the text; if the text ran to multiple tablets, the colophon would also note how many tablets were involved and the title of the whole. While the clay was still pliable, errors could be smoothed from the tablet's surface with the edge of the stylus, or the entire tablet could be wiped clean with a damp cloth.

While some historians maintain that cuneiform had pictorial origins, by the time it was in full use as a writing system, it was already a largely abstract system of signs: the things that the various symbols represented were no longer readily visible in the written signs themselves. Cuneiform's abstraction may have rendered it more difficult to learn, but the writing system still offered some practical advantages. Unlike Egyptian hieroglyphs, cuneiform characters were fairly simple to produce, so it was probably comparatively easier to master the art of writing. Sumerian cuneiform documents include numerous examples of exercises used to train scribes. Although only the practice clay tablets have survived, apprentice scribes also may have incised their exercises on wax tablets fixed in a wooden frame, a form of temporary writing surface that existed well into the Middle Ages. Like their clay counterparts, the wax tablets could be wiped clean and corrected or reused.

Cuneiform synonym list tablet from the Library of Ashurbanipal. Neo-Assyrian period (934–608 BCE). Photograph by Fae.

As it turns out, the primary writing medium used by the Akkadians and their successors was critical to preserving their texts for later ages. Not only did the clay tablets stand up to the hot, dry climate but, ironically, they also thwarted attempts by their cultures' enemies to eliminate all traces of them. Some of the largest caches of clay tablets have been discovered in the remains of burned-out ruins: the fires that destroyed the buildings also fixed the tablets in a more permanent form, just as firing in a kiln hardens and fixes pottery.

Historian Steven Fischer attributes the world's earliest "literary" texts to the Sumerians, most notably the *Epic of Gilgamesh*, which was probably first composed around 2700 BCE and written down centuries later. The epic ran to some twelve tablets, which were found in the library of the Assyrian king Ashurbanipal (c. 668–627 BCE). It tells the story of Gilgamesh, an ancient king of Uruk, and Enkidu, who was created by the gods to try to rein in some of Gilgamesh's more outrageous behavior. After many adventures together, Enkidu dies at the decree of the gods, and Gilgamesh, overcome by grief, embarks on a quest to try to escape from—but ultimately to reconcile himself to—his own mortality. Another major Sumerian text was the *Enuma Anu Ellil*, a series of astrological omens that ran to about 8,000 lines of text over seventy-one tablets. Such multi-tablet texts were usually stored in wooden or clay boxes or jars, or in reed baskets, with an affixed label summarizing their contents.

Another notable contribution to the history of the world in cuneiform was Hammurabi's Code, one of earliest existing examples of a systematized code of law. Hammurabi (c. 1795–1750 BCE) was an ancient Babylonian ruler who probably constructed his code by pulling together and reorganizing existing laws. His code, inscribed on a massive black stone, spelled out the consequences for different kinds of wrongdoing, ranging from bad construction practices to false testimony to murder. Most of the punishments prescribed for various crimes were proportionately retaliatory—an early example of the "eye for an eye" notion of justice—but wrongdoers were also given the alternative of throwing themselves into the Euphrates River. If the accused survived the water, he or she was deemed to be innocent, while drowning was a sign of guilt.

Semitic Writings

Cuneiform was not the only lexigraphic writing system that emerged in the ancient Middle East. Various *Semitic* scripts were devised in the region as well, the most important of which was that used by the Phoenicians in the fifteenth century BCE. By the tenth century BCE, Phoenician script had given rise to Aramaic, the source of both Hebrew and Arabic, and possibly the ancestor of many of the scripts used on the Indian Subcontinent as well. Semitic scripts are important to the history of the book because of their use by three distinctive "peoples of the book": the Jews, the Christians, and the Muslims.

The original script of the ancient Hebrews is no longer extant, but there are so many references to writing in the earliest books of the Bible that scholars suspect that there was a long written culture preceding the earliest examples of Semitic script. Biblical scholars have estimated that at the time of Moses (c. late thirteenth to early twelfth centuries BCE), the Hebrews were speaking at least eight different languages and using five different writing systems. However, a distinctive Hebrew script was in use by at least 1000 BCE. The oldest example of that script is in the Gezer Calendar, a limestone tablet dating to the time of Saul and David that lays out agricultural seasons and associated farming tasks. Another ancient example of the script was discovered in the first decade of the twenty-first century, on a stone found at Tel Zayit, near ancient Judah. Dating from the tenth century BCE, it appears to be the oldest known *abecedary*, or alphabet table.

Writing and literacy became central to the ancient Hebrews, the first "people of the book." With the bequest to Moses of the Ten Commandments, the Jewish religion coalesced around written texts. The most important texts were the *Torah* or *Pentateuch*, the first five books of the Hebrew Bible (also known as the Books of Moses or the Books of Law). In time, to these were added prophetic books and other kinds of writings, including hymns and moral precepts.

By the third or second centuries BCE, a variety of Aramaic script known as *square Hebrew*—so called because its letters were regularized into a square frame—had emerged. Because of its importance to the sacred Jewish texts, the script's form was largely fixed by the first century of the Common Era. Formal rules about the script's *calligraphy* (style of handwriting and letter shapes) and spelling were laid down by the *Talmud*, the authoritative body of Jewish teachings and tradition that grew up around the reading and interpretation of the Torah. Square Hebrew was the script used in the Dead Sea Scrolls.

The square Hebrew script features twenty-two alphabet letters, all consonants. The first two letters were *aleph* and *beth*, which gave their names (via the Greek *alpha* and *beta*) to the word *alphabet*. Although Semitic writing

THE TORAH

The Torah consists of the first five books of the Hebrew Bible: *Bereshit* (Genesis), *Shemot* (Exodus), *Vayikra* (Leviticus), *Bamidbar* (Numbers), and *Devarim* (Deuteronomy). These five books, also known as the *Pentateuch* or the Books of Moses, are the core of Jewish scripture. They tell the story of the Jewish people from the creation of the world until the death of Moses, and they are believed to have been given by God to Moses during the time that the Israelites were wandering the Sinai desert after their escape from Egypt, in about the thirteenth century BCE. The Torah lays out the relationship, or covenant, between the Jewish people and God, including the rules governing daily life and religious practice.

Because of their centrality to Jewish history and religious faith, the copying and maintenance of Torah scrolls, or *Sifrei Torah*, has long been dictated by scripture and tradition. The scrolls contain the name of God, so they are deemed holy and treated with great care. Torah scrolls are written on parchment made from the skins of kosher (ritually fit for use) animals. Many sheets of parchment are sewn together to make one continuous scroll, and each page of the scroll contains forty-two lines of Hebrew text. The meticulous process of creating a new copy can take upwards of a year, and if any mistake or smudge is made, the imperfect page must be destroyed and the scribe must begin the page anew. Although in traditional practice each adult Jewish male was expected to copy a Torah scroll once during his lifetime, this work is more often undertaken by professional scribes, or *sofers*.

To protect them, Torah scrolls are usually carefully wrapped in special covers, and some are additionally ornamented with special scroll crowns and shields. The ornaments and wrapping are removed when the scroll is removed from the ark (a special cabinet used to house Torahs in synagogues) to be read. Typically, a pointer, or *yad*, is used by readers to trace their way in the text, so that they can avoid soiling the parchment. When a Torah scroll becomes worn or damaged in any way, it is no longer deemed kosher and is removed from use. Retired scrolls are usually removed to a *genizah*, a special storage room or area for sacred documents no longer in use, and then eventually buried. However, not all *genizot* are regularly emptied: one of the most famous, that of the Ben Ezra Synagogue in Old Cairo, was found in the 1890s to contain over 200,000 scroll fragments and other objects, some dating as far back as the tenth century, and it became an invaluable resource for texts and information about Judaism over the previous millennium.

systems generally don't have vowels, four of the letters in square Hebrew are used to represent long vowels, especially at the ends of words. In addition, square Hebrew borrowed from Aramaic the use of *diacritics*, dot and dash notation marks used to denote long, short, or semivowels, as well as word tone and stress. These additional marks were required as the ancient form of the spoken language gradually fell out of use, and readers began to need additional cues to help them to read and explain the Torah correctly.

The second important descendant of Aramaic writing was Arabic script, which is currently the second most widely used script in the world. The youngest member of the Aramaic family, a form of Arabic script had already been developed by the fourth century CE. After the rise of Islam in the seventh century, Arabic script's importance and endurance was ensured. Two distinctive forms of Arabic script developed. The first, *Kufic*, was devised in the mid-seventh century in what is now Iraq and was used for theological writings. In the eighth century, Kufic was appointed as the only script acceptable for copying the *Qur'an*, the sacred writings of Islam, and it continued to be preferred until the twelfth century by Muslims in Andalusia and northern Africa. The second form of Arabic script, *Naskhi*, also arose in Iraq in the early tenth century. Naskhi came to be preferred for Qur'an copying in the eastern Islamic countries. (The role of Islam in the history of the book is discussed in more detail in Chapter 2.)

Parchment

After papyrus, the second most important form of writing material in the ancient world was *parchment*, a thin and pliable writing surface made from the skins of animals, primarily sheep or goats, but also calves. Although examples of animal skins used as writing materials date back to at least 2500 BCE, and parchment itself was probably in use as early as 1500 BCE, parchment's invention has been attributed to a second-century BCE king of Pergamum, a kingdom in Asia Minor in what is now modern Turkey. At the time, Egypt controlled the production of papyrus, and the development of a parchment industry in Pergamum was probably at least in part an effort to break Egypt's monopoly over a key element of book production.

Parchment is made from the inner lining of the skin of a suitable animal. (The outer skin is used for leather.) The skin is first washed and rubbed with lime, which renders a more paper-like surface and texture than ordinary tanning would do. Then all the hair is removed through careful scraping and washing again. The cleaned skin is then stretched with leather thongs on a wooden frame, continuing to be scraped until the surface is completely smooth and even. Finally, it is dusted with chalk and rubbed with fine pumice. When the processing is complete, the parchment is cut into sheets of the desired size. Before being written on, the sheets or scrolls are typically scored with a sharp implement to indicate rows and columns and guide the scribe's hand. It can then be written on with ordinary carbon-based inks. Parchment of a particularly fine quality is known as *vellum*.

Parchment was vitally important to the Hebrews, as custom dictated that Torah scrolls must be made of it. To make a scroll, individual sheets of parchment were sewn together, and a handle sheet was attached to one end, which would be at the beginning of the text (and on the outside of the scroll). However, parchment also proved to be a perfect medium for another book format that took hold at the turn of the Common Era: the codex. A *codex* is a book with folded and sewn-together sheets that form *leaves*, with pages on each side—the format still most common today. Parchment was more pliable than papyrus and more amenable to folding. When the codex was adopted as the preferred form for early Christian texts, its influence throughout the Roman world was almost assured.

THE DEAD SEA SCROLLS

The Dead Sea Scrolls are a collection of over 800 *manuscripts*, or handwritten texts, in Hebrew, Aramaic, and Greek, mostly on parchment (a few are on papyrus), dating from the beginning of the Common Era and discovered hidden in caves near the ruins of Qumran. The scrolls were stored in the caves by members of a Jewish Essene sect that had retreated to the Judean desert. Political strife under Roman rule and disagreements about religious practices may have led the Qumranis to withdraw from mainstream society in Judea; scholars are less certain about what led them to conceal their archive and why and under what circumstances they departed from Qumran. Some of the scrolls were carefully wrapped in linen and stored in sealed pottery jars, which suggests that they were secreted away before a planned departure, but others were simply left on shelves, as if unintentionally abandoned.

The Dead Sea Scrolls constitute the most extensive trove of religious documents from the period immediately predating the rise of both rabbinical Judaism and Christianity. As such, they are an invaluable source of information about the origins of various beliefs and practices in both religions, as well as a repository of fascinating texts that anticipate, confirm, and challenge assumptions about scripture. Only about 15 of the scrolls have survived intact; the remainder of the archive is in fragments that have had to be painstakingly pieced together. An international, interfaith scholarly effort has made all of the surviving texts available in digital form and in translation, so that historians and theologians throughout the world can now read and investigate them.

Although some early scholars assumed that the scrolls had been produced by the Qumranis, closer investigation has suggested that most were simply gathered by the residents of Qumran. The texts share some characteristics: many are critical of the religious authorities of the time and are concerned with matters of purity, and many others are concerned with what was believed to be the imminent end of the world. About a quarter of the scrolls are copies of texts from the Hebrew Bible, comprising some of the oldest copies of Bible books in existence, and another quarter, the "sectarian texts," have to do with the Essene sects, of which Qumran was one. The last and largest category of scrolls are comprised of other kinds of Jewish literature, most of which was previously unknown to scholars. Differences in script styles and *orthography* (spelling) among the scrolls suggest that they may span as much as a 300-year period, but carbon dating has been inconclusive.

The largest group of scrolls—over 500 fragmentary manuscripts—were discovered in what is known as Cave 4, which was the closest cave to Qumran and may have served as a library for the community. Unfortunately, the Cave 4 scrolls were also among the least well preserved, so it took a full half-century to reconstruct and publish them. Some of the most interesting documents among the Dead Sea Scrolls are the "Rules Scroll," which provides clues about how the Qumran community was formed and conducted itself; the "Copper Scroll," a list of concealed treasures, presumably from the Jerusalem Temple, inscribed on two long rolls of copper; the "Psalms Scroll," a collection of psalms by David arranged in a different order than the traditional one, and including some psalms never before known in Hebrew; and the "Great Isaiah Scroll," the oldest existing copy of the book of Isaiah (c. 100 BCE), whose textual differences have already been incorporated into modern Bible translations.

CHINA

Sometime between the fourteenth and eleventh centuries BCE, the second great writing system arose in China. Still in use after more than 3,000 years, and employed by more than a quarter of the world's population, the Chinese writing system remains powerfully influential today. Over the centuries it has also been adapted by other Asian cultures. For example, although both Japanese and Korean have distinctive writing systems, they also both incorporate some imported Chinese characters, which are known in Japanese as *kanji* and in Korean as *hanji*, for "Chinese writing."

While writing systems in the West eventually became grounded in alphabets, which represented phonetic aspects of speech, Chinese writing took another path altogether. The symbols or characters that make up Chinese writing are *logograms*, or "word-signs": the Chinese system is thus a full-fledged *logography*, or word-based writing system. There are two kinds of Chinese characters: "simple" and "complex." Simple characters, which make up only about 10 per cent of the total 50,000-plus signs in Chinese writing, consist of *radicals*, which represent a word or concept directly, or *phonetics*, which give some indication of the sound intended. For example, one of the simplest characters is *rén*:

人

Comprised of just two strokes that evoke legs, the character means "person" or "human." Another fairly simple character is *guó*, which means "country" or "kingdom":

This character combines the character for "jade," a precious stone, with an enclosing box. The remaining 90 per cent of Chinese characters are complex, consisting of a radical plus a phonetic marker made up of additional strokes that give a hint about the sound of the word intended.

Chinese characters are read by discerning the radical first, then the number of additional strokes needed to add the phonetic. Because the strokes are added in a particular order, they provide an additional scaffolding for the process of learning to read or write Chinese. They also serve as one of the organizational principles for Chinese dictionaries, which are organized first by radical, and then by the number of strokes required to determine the phonetic.

Although some scholars claim that Neolithic sites (dating as far back as c. 4000 BCE) include some signs that may be forerunners of Chinese script, most agree that the oldest examples of Chinese writing date to the late Shang dynasty, from about 1200 BCE. These early examples are records of prophecies, inscribed on specially prepared turtle shells and animal bones (usually cattle shoulder bones, or scapulae, but sometimes the bones of pig, sheep, or deer). The prepared shells and bones were known as *oracle-bones*. Members of the nobility would consult fortune-tellers about matters ranging from the weather and agricultural forecasts, the significance of dreams, the outlook for matters of war and diplomacy, and the birth of royal children. When consulted for advice, a fortune-teller would subject an oracle-bone to heat, which would cause it to crack in particular ways, and the cracks would then be interpreted to provide answers to the seeker. In some cases, particular oracle-bones might be heated several times to refine the answer to the question; in other cases, a series of oracle-bones might be required. These "oracle inscription sets" could be strung together in a kind of book.

The inscriptions on the oracle-bones typically include two (but sometimes as many as four) types of information. First, the "preface" includes the date and the identity of the questioner. Second, the "charge" includes the question being posed. If the question was posed more than once, with the oracle-bone heated each time, the questions and subsequent scorching and cracks would be carefully numbered to indicate the order in which the answers were provided. In some instances, a third kind of information, the "prognostication" or prediction, is also recorded on the oracle-bone. Finally, and more rare, there might also be a "verification," or record of whether the prediction came true. For example, at least one oracle-bone reveals that a member of the royal household consulted the fortune-tellers about the sex of her unborn child. The marked turtle shell reveals her name and date of consultation, the question, the numbering of the cracks and scorches that provided the answers, and the prediction that her child would be born under propitious circumstances—in other words, would be a boy. It also reveals that the prediction proved false: the child was a girl.

Along with the fortune consultations themselves, the oracle-bones provide some other kinds of records as well, including accounts of historical events and descriptions of rituals. These historical records are known as the "Heavenly Stems and Earthly Branches," and they seem to have functioned as a kind of calendar, marking events such as wars and hunting parties, or the proper times to sacrifice to ancestors or gods. From the inscriptions related to the oracle-bones' use, we know that turtle shells were an important kind of tribute, and that they needed to be collected in autumn, cleaned and prepared in spring, and stored in a special "turtle chamber" until required. We also know that when the oracle-bones were no longer needed for consultation, they were to be buried. It was the burial that resulted in their preservation through the ages—although that preservation certainly was not ensured.

The oracle-bones were first rediscovered in 1899, when a Chinese official, Wáng Yiróng (1845–1900), discovered that the fragments of turtle shell in his fever-reducing concoction had recognizable inscriptions on them. Consulting his medical practitioner, Wáng learned that the turtle shells deemed most effective for fever remedies had inscriptions on them—as did the "dragon bones" that were highly sought after for use in other traditional Chinese medicines. Wáng's inquiries led to the first significant recovery of a cache of oracle-bones. (Predictably, because of oracle-bones' instant value on the antiques market, the discoveries also led to some major forgeries and frauds, as well.)

The Chinese writing system has changed in important ways since its origins in the Shang dynasty. The script used on the oracle-bones was continued in the subsequent Zhou dynasty, which began in about 1100 BCE, where the script was used for official purposes and for writing histories. The only remaining examples of Zhou texts were written on bamboo strips near the end of the dynasty, and they are evidently copies of earlier forms. Therefore, because of the greater fragility of the writing medium, we are not able to trace the precise evolution of the characters: while some Shang characters persisted, many were lost. In the third century BCE, the emperor Qín Shǐ Huángdì (259–210 BCE), perhaps best known in the West for the terracotta warriors created for his tomb, took steps to harmonize what were by then a variety of script and character styles into one standardized set of approximately 3,300 characters. The standardized form became known as the *small seal* script style. This standardization effort not only led to the production of the first Chinese dictionary, but it also set the stage for significant efficiency gains in the administration of the expanding Chinese empire. Unfortunately, it also contributed in 213 BCE to the destruction of many previously existing Chinese books, both to ensure the dominance of the new writing system and because the emperor wanted to efface the records of his predecessors.

Changes in writing materials resulted in some further modifications of the Chinese script style, but by the early centuries of the Common Era, the *clerical* style had become dominant. It continued relatively unchanged until the middle of the twentieth century and continues to serve as the basis for Chinese writing today—with a few qualifications. In the People's Republic of China in the 1960s, efforts were made to modernize and simplify some 2,200 characters. While the intention of making it easier to learn to read and write Chinese was a worthy one, one consequence of this modernization effort was that it has rendered not only historic Chinese writing, but also many texts written by Chinese elsewhere around the world, unintelligible to readers within the People's Republic—and vice versa.

Other Asian Writing Systems

Over the centuries, the influence of Chinese language and culture spread throughout Asia. As a result, variants of the Chinese writing system can be found throughout the region. For example, in Japan, Chinese characters were incorporated into a particularly elaborate hybrid writing system. Japanese combines a syllabary (sound characters) of *hiragana*, or "ordinary signs," with imported Chinese logograms (*kanji*, or "Chinese writing"). Modern Japanese also makes extensive use of *katakana*, a syllabary used primarily for transliterating foreign and loan words and for scientific or technical terminology. The resulting writing system is regarded by many scholars as one of the most complex in the world, but despite its challenges, it underpins one of the highest literacy rates in the modern world.

The Korean writing system also adopted Chinese characters, even though the writing system did not entirely suit the needs of the culture or the phonetic basis of the Korean language. Initially, Korean simply used Chinese characters, or *hanji*. However, in the 1440s, king Sejong (1397–1450) promoted the development of a specifically Korean writing system, one that incorporated phonetics and that simplified the shapes of the characters. The resulting *Hangul* system was a unique innovation: its original twenty-eight characters (only twenty-four are still used today) not only represented consonants and vowels, thus making it a phonetic, alphabetic system like those in the West, but the shapes of the characters also represented the ways in which the sounds would be produced in the mouth. In effect, each character was based on the position of the mouth and tongue during the articulation of the represented sound.

One fortuitous result of the Hangul system was that the unified sizes and shapes of the characters and their restricted number meant that it was relatively easy to create movable, reusable type for printing purposes. As a result, Korea was one of the first countries in the world to exploit the advantages of printing.

Paper

In addition to inventing one of the major writing systems in the world, the Chinese invented one of the most important tools for the dissemination of written works: paper. And, as one of the many offshoots of the invention of paper, the Chinese also invented printing, although some of the earliest important innovations in printing were to happen in Japan and Korea.

Among all the materials that have been used for writing throughout the ages, paper has two major claims to significance. First, it is the only writing material that is almost wholly manufactured: though derived from natural fibers, even handmade paper involves processes that fundamentally transform the original materials into a wholly new substance. Second, paper is wonderfully adaptable: it can be made from a variety of raw materials and a number of processes, and it can be created in an almost infinite number of sizes, colors, textures, and qualities. This adaptability led to paper's being the perfect medium for printing, and thus for the spread of book culture.

Although a number of materials look like and act like paper, *true* paper is a substance that is made of beaten plant or cloth fibers that have been mixed with water, sieved on a screen until they form into a mat, and then dried. Paper was first described in China in CE 105 by Cài Lún (c. 50–121), who reported the substance to the emperor, and the earliest surviving examples of paper have been found near the Great Wall. Prior to the invention of paper, Chinese scribes, like their counterparts elsewhere in the world, used strips of wood or bark, leaves, or pieces of cloth for writing. Originally made from rags, later papers also frequently incorporated bark fibers, especially mulberry bark. In the earliest days, papermakers would beat the fibers with a mortar and pestle, but technological advances soon included foot-operated wooden hammers and, eventually, water-powered hammers to speed up the macerating process.

In the eighth century, papermaking spread across Asia and into the Middle East due to both peaceful and bellicose means. Papermaking was most likely introduced to other Asian countries by Buddhist monks, who carried with them sacred texts written on paper and the techniques for making the new writing material. For example, Dōkyō (c. 700–770), a Buddhist monk and physician to the Japanese Empress Shōtoku (or Kōken, 718–770), was credited with bringing papermaking to Japan, and by the early ninth century, papermaking workshops and communities had already spread across the country. The first recorded instance of waste paper being recycled into new paper is from Japan, dating from 1031. The account notes that the recycled paper was gray in tone because of the presence of the ink from previous writings.

While religion seems to have disseminated papermaking in the Far East, war was responsible for its dissemination in the Middle East. Although earlier samples of paper likely came west to the Mediterranean along various trade routes, the taking of Chinese papermakers as prisoners of war in Samarkand (modern Uzbekistan) in 751 marks the true beginning of the papermaking trade in the Middle East. From Samarkand it quickly spread to Baghdad, Damascus, Egypt, and Morocco, all of which became important papermaking centers.

MESOAMERICA

Writing also appears to have developed independently in the Western hemisphere, probably sometime in the first millennium BCE, although some scholars speculate that it may have come to the New World from Asia. Like the writing system invented by the Egyptians, the writing systems invented by Mesoamerican cultures had a strong pictorial component, and this led early scholars to make some of the same erroneous assumptions about how the systems worked as they had made about ancient Egyptian texts. As a result of those misperceptions, many of the texts of Mesoamerican culture—most of which exist only as inscriptions on temples and other buildings—are only now being deciphered and translated.

The greatest number of surviving Mesoamerican texts are those of the Mayan peoples, who flourished in southeastern Mesoamerica (in what is now part of Mexico down through Central America) from about 2000 BCE, until the waves of fifteenth-century European explorers decimated their populations through conquest and disease. The origins of the Mayan writing system can be traced in that of the Olmecs (c. 1200–400 BCE), and there are also possible links between Mayan writing and that of the Zapotec peoples (c. 600–400 BCE). Distinctively Mayan texts date back to as early as 200 BCE, although the earliest decipherable text, carved on a piece of jade, dates to about 50 BCE. Glyphs discovered in the early twenty-first century on a ruined pyramid in Guatemala and radiocarbon dated to about 300 BCE also appear to be Mayan, but the script so far predates any deciphered Mayan text that archaeologists are not yet able to read it with confidence.

Mayan glyphs are *logophonetic*: in addition to logograms or word-signs, they also include *syllabograms* or sound-signs. The syllabograms provide clues about how the logograms are to be pronounced. The glyphs are read from top to bottom, and within each column of text, combinations of glyphs are read from left to right. Approximately 800 Mayan glyphs have been identified to date, but in most circumstances scribes probably only required between 200 and 300. Most surviving Mayan inscriptions deal with matters relating to the birth, death, heirs, and achievements of the ruling dynasties. Mayan scribes were part of the ruling classes whose doings they chronicled, and presumably the ruling elites could read about themselves, but scholars are divided about how literate the general Mayan population may have been. On the one hand, the pictorial quality and sheer repetitiveness of the monumental inscriptions probably enabled ordinary people to discern their meaning. On the other hand, Steven Fischer points out that while there is a single word for *write* in the Mayan language, there are multiple, mostly post-Conquest words for *read*, suggesting that widespread reading only came about at the end of the Mayan era.

The fact that Mayan writing uses pictorial glyphs meant that for many years scholars made the same mistake about it that they had made about Egyptian hieroglyphic: that there was no phonetic component to the writing system. However, as early as the sixteenth century there was evidence that Mayan writing did have a phonetic element. In his 1566 manuscript book, *Relación de las Cosas de Yucatán*, Diego de Landa Calderón (1524–79), Bishop of Yucatan, noted some aspects of the Mayan language. Among other things, he assigned some alphabet letters and phonetic-linked syllables to particular Mayan glyphs. But it was not until the middle of the twentieth century that Russian scholar Yuri Knorosov (1922–99), a student of Egyptian hieroglyphs, Japanese, and Arabic, discerned that the Mayan glyphs likely worked in a similar manner to the Egyptian ones: while they sometimes functioned as logograms, they could also function as phonograms. This was the insight required to decipher the ancient texts. Working from their knowledge of surviving Mayan languages, Knorosov and other scholars were then able to begin translating the glyphs and once more read the accounts of warfare, tribute, and sacrifice that had been silent for five centuries.

Mesoamerican Codices

In addition to the many inscriptions on temples, other buildings, and monuments, the Mayans also wrote books. Contemporary historical accounts indicate that books were kept by priests and scribes throughout the Mayan empire, and many of these are thought to have been calendars, works of astronomy and religion, and histories. However, out of what may have been hundreds, thousands, or even hundreds of thousands of books, only a handful remain. Under the influence of the Inquisition, in 1562 Diego de Landa—ironically, the same individual who preserved important clues about the workings of the Mayan writing system—ordered the destruction of all of the books that could be acquired, so that these pagan texts would no longer be able to influence (and pollute) the populations that he was trying to Christianize. Only four Mayan codices, along with twenty or so Mixtec and Aztec books, survived the conflagration.

The surviving *codices* (the plural of *codex*, or paged book) are, for the most part, made of the inner bark of mulberry or fig trees. (Some are made of hide.) To prepare it for writing, the bark would be stripped, boiled, pounded and smoothed until flat, and then dried. It would then typically be coated with a mixture of lime and water, which rendered the surface white, and then painted with figures and characters. Individual pages were combined into long, accordion-folded volumes that were read in a *boustrophedon* or back-and-forth pattern. While each individual page is within the range of standard sheets of contemporary paper, when stretched out the codices can be as many as 12 yards (11 meters) long. To modern eyes, portions of these codices may resemble

MAYAN CODICES

Although Mesoamerica was one of the sites of the origins of writing, our knowledge about pre-Conquest books is severely restricted because of their wholesale destruction by the Inquisition during the sixteenth century. Only a handful of Mesoamerican books have survived, at least some of which are post-Conquest copies. Because the original creators and owners of the codices have been lost to history, the Mesoamerican codices are known by the names of their owners, many of which are museums.

Maya stucco glyphs displayed in the Museum at Palenque, Mexico.

From the Mayan culture, which was established about 2000 BCE and flourished from the third century of the Common Era until the Conquest, four codices are known to exist, the most recent (and contested) having been rediscovered only in the 1970s. The surviving works are concerned with astronomy, the calendar, divination, and religious rituals, and they are all boustrophedon (accordion-folded) books written on *amatl*, or bark, paper.

The oldest and most beautiful surviving Mayan codex is the *Codex Dresdensis*, which dates from about CE 1200. It is made of thirty-nine sheets of paper and is about 12 feet (3.5 meters) long. Judging from the style of scripts and illustrations, the codex was probably created by a number of different scribes. A work concerned with astronomy and divination, the *Dresden Codex* is particularly noteworthy for its detailed tables depicting the cycles of the moon and of the planet Venus. Unfortunately, the codex was damaged during the firebombing of Dresden in World War II, so some of the glyphs are now illegible.

The other surviving Mayan codices are the *Codex Tro-Cortesianus* (also known as the *Madrid Codex*), which probably dates from the 1600s, and the *Codex Peresianus* (or *Paris Codex*), whose dates are uncertain. The *Madrid Codex* is about 112 pages long. Thought to have been created by one scribe, its text and illustrations show definite influences of the Spanish occupation. It is believed to have been sent back to Spain by the explorer Hernán Cortés, who completed the overthrow of the Aztec Empire and secured Mexico for Spain. The *Paris Codex*, much shorter than the others and less imposing, was lost in the French *Bibliothèque Nationale* for some of the nineteenth century and now exists only in fragments. Like the *Codex Dresdensis*, it is concerned with prophecy and astronomy, and it is remarkable for its depiction of the Mayan zodiac. The last surviving Mayan manuscript, the *Grolier Codex*, is also only partial, and its authenticity is doubted by some Mayan scholars. While its eleven-page fragment contains nothing that is not also in the *Codex Dresdensis*, the illustrations of gods or heroes are intriguing.

the paneling of comic books or manga, as vertical and horizontal rules are used to help guide the eye to the next section of the text.

Incan Quipus

The Mayan writing system was not only lexigraphic, which increased its utility, but it was also employed in the largest geographic territory and thus has had the most enduring influence on the history of the book in the Americas. However, one other New World system for creating texts merits a mention here. The Incas, who lived in what is now Peru and flourished from the twelfth century until the Conquest, developed a culture whose complexity and longevity suggested that they must have had some written communication system, even though no clear evidence of one had come to light.

However, in recent years some scholars have suggested that we haven't found examples of Incan texts because we haven't been seeing what was before us. While there is no evidence of an Incan writing system that followed the conventional practice of making marks on a surface, there are many examples of Incan records created by a system that involved making knots in carefully arranged strings. These knotted strings, called *quipus* or *khipus*, had existed in Mesoamerica and elsewhere for many centuries. They are generally believed to have been a means of calculation or statistical record keeping—a kind of abacus that uses knots instead of balls or tokens on spindles. Indeed, their presumed function as calculators may have helped save them from the fires of the Inquisition.

Some Incan scholars have begun to explore the possibility that the knots in the quipus signify more than just calculations. These scholars have suggested that the way the strings are tied—the order in which the strings are passed over one another, and the size and complexity of the resulting knots—may represent words and syntax, and that in turn, the ordering of the strings along their connecting crosspiece may represent a more elaborate narrative structure. Anthropologist Gary Urton has recently published a study that breaks down the quipu knots into their "grammatical" constituents, and he has established a database to help analyze the quipus. According

Incan quipus. From *The Chronicle of Good Government* by Guaman Poma de Ayala, 1615–16.

to Urton, the quipus may have begun, like cuneiform, as a kind of accounting device. However, he suggests that by the time of Francisco Pizarro's conquest of Peru in the 1530s, the quipus had already evolved into an elaborate textile code, with the weavers making binary yes-no choices about wool or cotton, spin or ply of thread, and the direction of knots. The result of these choices was a possible 1,536 distinct knotted signs, a number that compares favorably with the 1,000 to 1,500 cuneiform signs and that is nearly double the 600 to 800 known Egyptian and Mayan glyphs. If Urton is right, and if the quipu knots prove to be a kind of three-dimensional Braille that can be deciphered, we may be able to learn a great deal more about Incan culture.

ANCIENT GREECE

Unlike most of the other cultures discussed so far in this chapter, the ancient Greeks did not invent a writing system. Instead, in the tenth to ninth centuries BCE, they borrowed and combined elements of preexisting writing systems. However, the Greeks added a key innovation that provided greater ease of use and flexibility of expression. Their refinement of the alphabetic system that they adapted from Semitic scripts formed the basis for all subsequent alphabetic systems. Concurrently, the refined writing system fostered a culture of written expression that first underpinned their military and political influence in the ancient Mediterranean and then endured far and long beyond it, becoming one of the primary sources of Western culture.

As noted above, the alphabetic systems developed by the Semitic peoples included symbols that represented the phonemes of consonant sounds, but they largely omitted vowel sounds. For native speakers of these languages, this omission probably was not perceived as a difficulty: since they knew what the intervening sounds would be, they could tacitly supply the missing sounds and recreate the complete words in their minds. Numerous jokes and puzzles available online and elsewhere show that this is a fairly easy task for most readers to perform:

VN WTHT TH VWLS, THS PHRS CN B RD.

The vowel-less phrase above clearly suggests that the first word should be *even*, but out of context, it is less clear which first word is intended in the following:

VN FRD VGTBLS TST GD. ·

Even fried vegetables—in comparison, say, to boiled or baked? Or *oven* fried vegetables—as opposed to deep-fat fried? The major Greek innovation in alphabetic writing was to devise symbols for vowel sounds, which eliminated any ambiguity about what word was intended, whatever the context. For the first time, writers could easily generate words that they had never seen written before.

The Ionic form of the Greek alphabet, consisting of twenty-four letters, was officially adopted in Athens in 403 BCE. It replaced all previous variants and helped ensure a uniformity of spelling and script styles that furthered the cause of literacy in Greek culture. Scribes—and other writers—gradually developed standardized, easily written and read scripts, especially uncial, a combination of capital and small letters that came to be used for classical Greek codices, and a cursive hand that gave rise to the primary book script just before the Common Era. Equally exciting, readers could, with confidence, sound out words that they had never encountered in script before and discern what was intended, a development that opened up a much larger potential reading audience and contributed to increasing literacy rates.

The logic and ease of the new Greek writing system enabled an explosion of new vocabulary in lyric poetry and in tragedy, the first categories of Greek literature that were composed in writing, rather than deriving from the oral tradition. While a comprehensive analysis of ancient Greek literature is beyond the scope of this volume, its influence on the history of the book cannot be overemphasized. In the West, both before and after the Dark Ages, Greek literature and language was at the very heart of both secular and religious education. Homer's great epics, the *Iliad* (c. 759 BCE) and the *Odyssey* (c. 725 BCE), have continued to shape readers' ideas of human nature and of literary structure over three millennia. Over the course of several centuries, Greek poets and playwrights laid down models that influenced the themes and styles of their European successors. The various forms of lyric (from the Greek for "lyre") poetry practiced by Pindar, Sappho, and Anacreon, and the tragedies and comedies of Sophocles, Aeschylus, and Aristophanes were anatomized in later eras by Aristotle (384–322 BCE) and others, who sought to explain how literature worked and to hold up the highest models for emulation. Thus Greece was not only responsible for an extraordinary flowering of literary arts, but also for the critical theory that enabled both readers and practitioners to analyze and understand that literature.

Greek works of rhetoric, politics, mathematics, astronomy, music, and medicine became the groundwork for what there was to know of the world. Efforts to collect and copy works by Greek authors led to the establishment of the first libraries, helpful reading features in books such as indexes, and the birth of the fields of bibliography and library science. For centuries, readers and writers sought to compare and improve their copies of the original texts, to emulate the ancient models in modern works, and to thereby add to the sum of the world's knowledge. While Greek influence on secular education was incalculable, its importance for religious education was also immense. Since the New Testament was written in a form of Greek (Aramaic), Church scholars and theologians who wished to better understand the scriptures turned to the original language for insights. Thus, copying and refining Greek grammars and dictionaries was a significant undertaking throughout the succeeding centuries.

Ironically, however, ancient Greece exerted its greatest influence over the world from a position of relatively little power. After the Battle of Corinth in 146 BCE, Greece was essentially a province of Rome, finally quelled for good in the first decades of the Common Era. Yet despite being a captive state, Greece was greatly admired by the Romans, who adapted its religion and emulated its literature, art, and architecture. Thus, via the expanding Roman empire, a core of Greek education, values, and models for book culture were spread throughout Europe and into Asia Minor.

SELECTED BIBLIOGRAPHY

Ackroyd, P.R., and C.F. Evans, eds. *The Cambridge History of the Bible. Vol. 1: From the Beginnings to Jerome.* Cambridge: Cambridge UP, 1970.

Allen, James P. *Middle Egyptian: An Introduction to the Language and Culture of Hieroglyphs.* Cambridge: Cambridge UP, 2000.

Budge, E.A. Wallis. *The Book of the Dead: The Papyrus of Ani in the British Museum.* [London]: British Museum, 1895. http://www.sacred-texts.com/egy/ebod/.

Chabad-Lubavitch Media Center. http://www.chabad.org/.

Coe, Michael D., and Mark Van Stone. *Reading the Maya Glyphs.* 2nd ed. London: Thames and Hudson, 2005.

Davies, Philip R., George J. Brooke, and Phillip R. Callaway. *The Complete World of the Dead Sea Scrolls.* London: Thames and Hudson, 2002.

Fabrikant, Geraldine. "Hunting for the Dawn of Writing, When Prehistory Became History." *New York Times,* 20 October 2010.

Fischer, Steven Roger. *A History of Writing.* [London]: Reaktion Books, 2005.

Gardiner, Alan. *Egyptian Grammar: Being an Introduction to the Study of Hieroglyphs.* 3rd ed. Oxford: Griffith Institute, Ashmolean Museum, 1957.

Gnanadesikan, Amalia E. *The Writing Revolution: Cuneiform to the Internet.* Chichester: Wiley-Blackwell, 2009.

Hunter, Dard. *Papermaking: The History and Technique of an Ancient Craft.* 2nd ed. London: Cresset, 1957.

Kott, Ruth E. "The Origins of Writing." *University of Chicago Magazine* (Jan.–Feb. 2011): 38–41.

Mann, Charles C. "Appendix B: Talking Knots." In *1491: New Revelations of the Americas Before Columbus.* New York: Random House, 2005.

Maugh, Thomas H., II. "Now They Know Their Ancient Hebrew ABCs." *Tacoma News Tribune,* 13 November 2005.

The Maya Hieroglyphic Codices. http://www.mayacodices.org/Madcod.asp.

Mroczek, Eva. "Thinking Digitally About the Dead Sea Scrolls: Book History Before and Beyond the Book." *Book History* 14 (2011): 241–69.

Powell, Barry B. *Writing: Theory and History of the Technology of Civilization.* Chichester: Wiley-Blackwell, 2009.

Selin, Helaine, ed. *Encyclopedia of the History of Science, Technology and Medicine in Non-Western Cultures.* 2nd ed. 2 vols. Berlin: Springer, 2008.

Society for Anglo-Chinese Understanding. http://www.sacu.org/china.html.

University of Arizona Library, Special Collections. Mesoamerican Codices. http://www.library.arizona.edu/exhibits/mexcodex/intro.htm.

Wilford, John Noble. "Symbols on the Wall Push Maya Writing Back by Years." *New York Times*, 10 January 2006.

Xu, Yahui. *Ancient Chinese Writing: Oracle Bone Inscriptions from the Ruins of Yin*. Trans. Mark Caltonhill and Jeffrey Moser. Taiwan: National Palace Museum, 2002.

CHAPTER TWO

SCRIBAL CULTURE
AND THE CODEX

By the time of the Common Era, writing had already existed for nearly four millennia, and the many texts being generated and amassed in parts of the ancient world bore testimony to writing's vital contribution to human development. Writing had proved its value as a medium for communicating near and far: it allowed individuals and cultures to trade and to document their goods and populations, to sing the praises of the divine and of humanity, to share and further wisdom, and to provide pleasure and ease. As the reach of writing increased, so too did the pressure to experiment with and improve the technologies for generating and circulating texts.

This chapter will explore one of the key innovations that took place around the dawn of the Common Era: the emergence of the *codex*, or paged book, as the primary physical format for texts. Previously, most texts had existed either as separate tablets or leaves—whether made of wax, bark, leaves, wood, skins, or paper—that might be hinged or tied together in some manner, or combined in scrolls or *boustrophedon* (accordion-folded) collections. Writing surface materials that were malleable enough to be easily combined into scrolls or boustrophedons offered obvious advantages to writers and copiers over less flexible materials: not only could the writer of a longer text proceed with fewer interruptions, but the component pieces of the text were less likely to become separated or shuffled into the wrong order. Texts in these formats were also advantageous to readers: they offered readers greater confidence in the reliability of the text that had been transmitted, and the longer formats also enabled them to more easily immerse themselves in their reading.

But scrolls and boustrophedons also had their disadvantages. To begin with, reading a scroll is a two-handed operation: one hand must always be unrolling the text, while the other is always rolling it up. And both scrolls and boustrophedons make it very difficult for readers to compare passages: readers must constantly roll and unroll or fold and unfold the text to find the desired sections. Especially if the two passages are quite distant from one other, this can be very inconvenient. Furthermore, both scrolls and boustrophedons tend to be somewhat unwieldy. You need space to lay them out and manipulate them. While storing either format in a library is fairly straightforward, if you wish to transport them somewhere else, you need to devise covers for them, and in the case of scrolls, those covers must be fully detachable.

The codex rather neatly solved most of the unwieldiness problems presented by scrolls and boustrophedons. Comprised of sheets that were folded, cradled together, and then bound through their folded or hinged side, the pages of the codex could be turned with just one hand, leaving the other hand free to take notes, to use some kind of magnifying crystal or glass to increase the word size, or perhaps to shade the eyes from the sun or other light source. Pages could also be quickly turned to allow the comparison of passages, and those passages could also be easily marked without necessarily defacing the text itself. More beguiling still, the codex could be devised with permanently affixed protective covers in a size that was convenient for personal use. The very nature of the codex made it easier for individuals to own and to transport books.

These perceived advantages probably account for the codex's rapidly becoming the format of choice for books of all kinds, secular and sacred. New texts in science, medicine, philosophy, history, and the arts were generated in the new format, and old ones were regularly copied into it. The codex was also quickly embraced by the early Christians for the copying and dissemination of their sacred texts, and it became and remained the dominant format for Christian writings to the present era. As the advantages of the format became apparent, the codex also became the preferred format for many Judaic books, including the books of commentary collectively known as the Talmud, and the book that explained and celebrated the Passover Seder, the Haggadah. (The Torah continued to be produced in scroll form, as prescribed in the scriptures themselves.) When the Qur'an and other Islamic religious texts finally came to be written down, the codex also became the standard book format for the Muslim world.

Scribal culture (so called to distinguish it from the later *print culture*) continued well into the fifteenth century and beyond. During that time, however, the center of gravity of scribal culture shifted significantly. The Romans carried scribal culture to the furthest outposts of their empire, and Christianity helped spread literacy and book production throughout the Roman world. However, when the Roman Empire collapsed, the civilization that writing had helped to foster was fundamentally disabled, and literacy was pushed to the margins of Europe. It endured in isolated monastic communities, especially in Celtic countries, and in those regions where the newer religion of Islam held sway. The knowledge preserved in those enclaves would prove an invaluable source of wisdom and replenishment for the West in the fourteenth- through seventeenth-century Renaissance, a time of rebirth and learning that would be helped along by the invention and dissemination of yet another crucial technology: the printing press.

BOOKS AND THE ROMAN EMPIRE

By the second century BCE, the Romans had absorbed many aspects of Greek culture and civilization, including its well-established educational traditions. The Romans also adapted the Greek alphabet, adding and modifying characters to suit the phonemes of the Latin language. The resulting twenty-three-letter Latin alphabet was not only well-suited for Roman monumental inscriptions (with regularized letter shapes that were both relatively easy to chisel and easy to read from a distance), but because of the reach of the Roman Empire throughout Europe and the Near East, it also became the foundation alphabet for many modern languages.

Roman fresco from Pompeii, c. 50 CE.

Literacy rates in ancient Greece and in the Roman Empire are difficult to assess accurately. However, evidence suggests that there were fairly high levels of literacy among males in Athens and in other Greek cities that provided elementary education (girls were also educated, but not at the same levels), and that this pattern continued in Roman cities. The spread of reading and writing was driven by practicalities. Thus, there is evidence that many Roman slaves were literate, as their duties required them to undertake correspondence for their masters.

In fact, the practical need to communicate is probably what drove an overall increase in literacy at all levels of society throughout the Roman Empire. In many respects, the Roman Empire was an administrative miracle. Stretching across most of modern Europe, Egypt, North Africa, and into Asia, the vast territory was held together for some 500 years by a complex combination of military force, compelling innovations in agriculture and urban development, vast trading networks, and a governmental system that culturally tied myriads of physically isolated local administrators back into the central workings of Rome. This would have been virtually impossible without a huge and reliable communication system. The extensive network of well-constructed and well-maintained roads and garrisons throughout the Empire ensured that both troops and information could be directed wherever they were required.

Writing at the Center: Rome

The capital was an important center for cultural developments of all kinds during the Roman era. Wealthy citizens employed Greek tutors to teach their

A bilingual papyrus of Cicero, In Catilinam 2.15. A.S. Hunt. *Catalogue of the Greek Papyri in the John Rylands Library: Volume I* (Manchester University, 1911).

children, and fee-paying elementary schools existed from as early as the third century BCE. By the dawn of the Common Era, centers of higher education offering instruction in the especially important skill of *rhetoric* (oratory and persuasion) were well established. The works of Cicero (106–43 BCE) and Quintilian (35–100) were particularly influential. Between the first and third centuries of the Common Era, schools of law and of philosophy had also been founded. The status of educators increased during this period, and the best might even seek the endowed chairs that were established by the emperor Vespasian (7–79) at Rome and by Marcus Aurelius (121–180) at Athens.

Because Roman ideals of education and literature were based on their Greek predecessors, aspects of classical Roman scholarship hinged on the challenges of investigating and properly imitating those earlier models. For example, Roman scholars understood the difficulties of working with *manuscript*, or handwritten, texts, versions of which could vary, sometimes in significant ways. Following Greek scholarly models, one line of Roman scholarship was devoted to gathering and comparing texts, thereby arriving at the most accurate and reliable versions. Another line of scholarship was devoted to compiling manuals of correct style and usage, so that modern writers could imitate their forebears. Further lines of scholarship focused on commentary and interpretation. Notable commentaries for which we also know something about the original authors include Pomponius Porphyrio's commentary on the works of Horace (c. second or third century), Aelius Donatus' commentaries on the poets Terence and Virgil (c. mid-fourth century), and Priscian's commentaries on Virgil—and on his predecessor Donatus (c. late fifth century).

The centrality of literacy to Roman culture supported a significant book copying and production industry, most of which was centered in the capital. However, as populations and demand increased, book markets could be found in other Roman cities as well. Although individual scholars might copy books for themselves, or rely on their slaves to do so, there are also accounts of Roman booksellers who had entire staffs of slaves who copied books for sale. The most popular works were Greek scrolls, especially the epics of Homer, and volumes of Virgil (70–19 BCE). Roman booksellers advertised their wares in posters and flyers and displayed them on racks to would-be buyers. Because complete books remained extremely expensive, it is unlikely that individuals amassed very many complete scrolls or volumes; instead, they probably copied excerpts or shorter texts, perhaps in the popular small papyrus notebooks of the era. When longer texts were to be copied, they were most likely divided into manageable portions (segments of scrolls, and *gatherings* or *quires* of paged volumes) and doled out to a number of scribes. The finished texts would be reassembled and checked for accuracy before being disseminated.

Writing in the Provinces: Vindolanda

The importance of education and writing in the Roman Empire was not restricted to more high-cultural literary or scholarly productions, nor to the capital. Many of the surviving documents from the Roman era are more mundane writings: administrative reports, dispatches, and personal letters. One extraordinary cache of such Roman documents was discovered in one of the furthest outreaches of the empire: Vindolanda, a settlement in Britain along Hadrian's Wall. In the 1970s, a series of excavations uncovered a large collection of over 1,600 handwritten texts from the first century, written on folded wooden tablets that had been discarded in the straw flooring of the Roman barracks and gradually buried (and thus preserved) in the clay soil.

The Vindolanda tablets fundamentally changed our knowledge of writing materials in the Roman world, and also of the extent and uses of literacy during that period. Before the Vindolanda discoveries, the Romans were believed to have used only the writing materials known in the ancient world, scrolls and wax-filled tablets, plus their apparent innovation of small folded papyrus codices. The Roman historian Herodian (c. 170–240) had mentioned one other option, writing tablets made of thin slices of folded lime-wood, known as *tilia* (for "lime tree"). However, because virtually none of these *tilia* had survived, they were not considered to be an important writing medium in the Roman world. Even when the Vindolanda tablets were found and analyzed, the fact that they were made of birch and alder meant that, at least initially, scholars continued to regard them as a unique innovation, rather than as representative of another important category of writing material.

The Vindolanda tablets were made of very thin slivers of native British wood. Most were 1 to 2 millimeters thick, but some were even thinner. Because they were cut from very young trees, they were probably very supple when new, and the inner surface that was used for writing was also very smooth and fine-grained. Most of the tablets ranged from about 6 to 8 inches (16–20 cm) by 2.5

to 3.5 inches (6–9 cm), about the size of a modern postcard. If the tablet was to be used for a letter, the broadest edge would be at the top, so that when the wood was scored and folded at the middle, it would form a small booklet with two interior columns for text. When the booklet was folded closed, the address could be written on the outside cover. Some letter tablets have notches, where they were probably tied closed with string. If the tablet was to be used for another purpose, such as accounts, it would be oriented with the narrow edge at the top, which allowed for longer columns of figures or other information. There are a few examples of multi-leaved tablets, which were punched and bound together at the outside edges, in a zigzag or *concertina* format.

Relief from a scribe's tomb found in Flavia Solva. Photograph by Hermann A.M. Mucke.

The fragility of the Vindolanda tablets makes their discovery and preservation over the millennia quite extraordinary. When the first batches of tablets were found, the excavators weren't entirely certain what they were, as they initially appeared to be some kind of organic rubbish. It was only when one archaeologist discerned what appeared to be writing in black ink that the investigators became excited—and that excitement quickly turned to despair when, exposed to air after so many centuries, the markings quickly faded. Fortunately, however, because the ink was carbon-based, the inscriptions could still be read with infrared photography. Digital imaging has rendered them even more legible.

According to experts, the wooden tablets look very much like Roman papyrus tablets and were written on in the same manner, with reed pens and ink made from carbon, gum arabic, and water. The scripts used were also very similar to a common business script used in other parts of the Roman world, a script known as *Old Roman cursive*. The tablets were composed by over 100 different individuals from all over Britain and possibly from Gaul (northern France), with most of the texts written by clerks or *amanuenses* who were probably working from dictation. Individual senders usually added a line or two of closing in their own hands. The similarities in the forms of address, content, grammar, and writing itself confirm that the Latin language and scripts used throughout the Roman Empire were strikingly consistent, and they suggest that the levels of educational and literary standards in the first century were fairly high.

The letters include details about all aspects of running the Empire, including information about workshops, the building of forts, and accounts of food purchases and ration disbursements. They also include many more personal details. For example, one letter appears to have accompanied a care package to a Roman stationed at this very remote British outpost, with the sender noting: "I have sent you … pairs of socks from Sattua, two pairs of sandals and two pairs of underpants." Another letter, a birthday invitation, is the earliest known example of female writing in Latin. From Claudia Severa to Suplicia Lepidina, the invitation for a celebration "on the third day before the Ides of September" is mostly written in a clerk's hand, but Claudia Severa added in her own hand: "I shall expect you, sister. Farewell, sister, my dearest soul, as I hope to prosper, and hail."

The Vindolanda tablets bear witness to the fact that even at the outermost edges of the empire, writing and literacy flourished under the Romans.

BOOKS OF THE JEWISH DIASPORA

From the destruction of the Temple in Jerusalem in 70 BCE through the first two centuries of the Common Era, Roman rule was largely disastrous for the Jews in ancient Palestine. Political upheaval has been offered as one possible explanation for the abandonment of the Essene community at Qumran, where the Dead Sea Scrolls were collected, and it was responsible for a further scattering of Jews throughout the Middle East and into Europe and Asia. What provided continuity for the Jews during the *Diaspora*, or dispersal, was a consciousness that they were "people of the book"; the centrality of Jewish scripture and a continued emphasis on distinctively Jewish learning meant that Jews were able to preserve a core identity, even while they were adopting the languages and customs of their new home cultures.

Over the next centuries, several centers of Jewish culture and learning were established. In Mesopotamia, important Jewish schools were founded in Sura and Pumbeditha after the third century. These schools' work gradually coalesced around the creation and refining of the body of work known as the *Talmud* ("teaching"), a collection of law, customs, and commentary that shaped the interpretation of the Hebrew Bible and provided guidance for daily life. Efforts to compile a definitive version of the Babylonian Talmud were begun by *rabbis*, or teachers, in the sixth century, and the work continued for nearly 200 years. Once completed, the Babylonian Talmud was circulated widely among the various Diaspora communities, where it was carefully studied and became an authoritative guide to Jewish thought and culture.

In post-Roman Europe, Jews in different areas had different experiences. In the Mediterranean area, many Jews lived under Muslim rule from the eighth through the eleventh centuries. Jewish culture in Moorish North Africa and Spain was particularly vibrant. Among these *Sephardic* communities (from the Hebrew name for Spain) were many scholars and artisans involved in the book trades. Moses Maimonides (1135–1204), a talented linguist, was one of the many Jewish scholars who helped keep the classical Greek and Roman literature alive for subsequent generations, by translating these works from the original languages or from Arabic into European vernaculars. Jews were noted for their skills in calligraphy and bookbinding, as well, especially in

Seville and Cordoba, which were major centers for book production. Thus, their handiwork can be seen not only in Jewish books of that era, but also in Muslim and Christian ones. However, after the Christian reconquest of Spain, an increased regulation of the book trades eventually meant that only coreligionists of any individual faith could work on their particular scriptures, out of fear that members of other religions might (intentionally or unintentionally) defile the books. The so-called "Hebrew Golden Age" ended with the expulsion of the Jews from Catholic Spain, and their persecution under the Inquisition.

For the most part, Jews who settled in northern Europe had a more difficult time than those who settled in the south. From the outset, the *Ashkenazim* (from the Hebrew for Germany) communities were subject to a greater degree of anti-Jewish prejudice from their Christian neighbors than were the Jews in Muslim-ruled regions. Although large communities of Jewish traders and scholars were established throughout what is now Germany and France, and even in the British isles, from the eleventh century they were increasingly subject to *pogroms*, or organized persecutions and executions. Nevertheless, there were important centers of Jewish life in many cities, especially those along the Rhine River. Forced expulsions in the thirteenth and fourteenth centuries pushed many Jews further east, into what is now Hungary, Poland, and Lithuania, where the resulting Yiddish-speaking communities forged their own traditions of scholarship and culture. By the sixteenth century, Poland had become the proverbial "heaven for Jews," with the Jewish community accorded a great deal of autonomy, including a Chief Rabbinate and a noted *yeshiva*, a religious academy dedicated to the study of the Torah and Talmud.

Jewish Codices

While the Torah continued to be produced in scroll form, other Jewish books were increasingly produced in the codex format. Codex versions of the Hebrew Bible, which include the five books that make up the Torah, were probably being created as early as the second century, although there are few extant examples until the ninth century. One distinction between the text in a Torah and in a Hebrew Bible is that the latter includes both vowel notations and punctuation. These notations were regularized by scribes in eighth- and ninth-century Palestine who specialized in copying biblical texts, the *Masoretes*. According to historian Leila Avrin, the Masoretes wanted to ensure that not a single word of the scripture was lost. When tenth- and eleventh-century masoretic books, such as the Leningrad Codex or the Aleppo Codex, are compared with similar texts from the Dead Sea Scrolls, the consonant shapes and placement are extraordinarily close. The care these scribes took with their work meant that a millennium of copying—potentially more than 30 generations—introduced virtually no errors into the texts.

Medieval Jewish book production involved divisions of labor. When copying Hebrew Bibles, for example, one scribe would typically copy the consonantal text, another would add the vowel and punctuation marks, and a third would add the *Masora*, additional word lists and counts that served as a kind of index, to the margins. Colophons would identify each scribe or, in the rare case when one scribe had completed all the tasks, would note that extraordinary feat. Because they were originally based on scroll texts, many Hebrew codices closely resembled the layout of a scroll page, usually incorporating three columns of text with regular margins and spacing between words and columns. As many as ten scribes might work on one manuscript in order to produce it more quickly, and an individual scribe could produce between six and sixteen pages per day, usually working for six or seven hours if the light and demands of the project allowed.

Scribes, especially those who copied religious texts, were respected specialists, and as such were relatively well paid. Avrin reports that they could be paid as much as three gold dinars for a large codex of more than 500 pages, at a time when the average monthly income of a family was about two dinars. Patrons typically provided the materials for the book, and the scribe might be invited to live at the home of the patron while working on the project. Torahs could only be produced by men, but there is some evidence that women worked as scribes as well, especially if they came from scribal families.

Medieval Jewish codices were sometimes lavishly ornamented, and the designs depended very much on where they were produced. In Moorish Spain and North Africa, and in other Islamic areas, Jewish manuscript illustration was very similar to that employed in Muslim books of the region. Many were decorated with abstract geometric designs, rather than with representative figures. In Christianized parts of Europe, Jewish books displayed a greater range of illumination. One particular kind of book, the *Haggadah*, which depicts the events of the Exodus and is used in Jewish homes during the Passover Seder, could be quite lavishly illustrated, with scenes not only of the events being described, but also of contemporary Jewish life, especially the preparations for the Passover. For example, the *Golden Haggadah*, dating from early fourteenth-century Barcelona and now at the British Library, features fifty-six miniatures and an abundance of gold leaf. At least two artists created the book, whose illustrations are strongly influenced by French and Italian illuminations of the period.

ISLAM AND THE BOOK

The Prophet Muhammad (569–632), founder of the religion of Islam, received his first revelations at the age of forty, and began preaching and gathering followers a few years later. The continuing body of revelations that the Prophet had received over twenty-one years formed the foundation text of the new faith: the *Qur'an*, or "recitation." The chapters or *suras* that make up the Qur'an were memorized and recited by the earliest converts to Islam, a fundamental act of piety that would continue even after the suras were written down in the years after the Prophet's death—initially, to ensure that the revelations would not be lost if the populations that had memorized them were eliminated through warfare or other disasters.

Although Muhammad and most of his first converts were illiterate, literacy soon became an important part of Islam. Indeed, the imperative to read and recite the texts is laid out in various suras, which use the image of the pen as a powerful metaphor for the means by which God's will had been revealed. When the Qur'an was first written down in the late seventh century, it was not as a scroll, but as a codex. The Caliph Abu Bakr (c. 573–634) was credited with first gathering together the then-extant versions of the Qur'an and having them checked by a scholarly committee against the memorized suras. His early, personal copy of the Qur'an later served as the basis for the authoritative and

THE QUR'AN

The central religious text of Islam, the Qur'an is comprised of 114 chapters or *suras* and is a compilation of the revelations received by the Prophet Muhammad. Originally memorized and transmitted orally, the revelations were codified and written down after the Prophet's death.

The first Muslim political and religious leaders, or *caliphs*, attempted to gather the suras, but it wasn't until CE 653 that the first standardized version of the Qur'an was produced under the authorization of the third caliph, Uthman. Although the canonization of the Uthmanic Qur'an was a source of contention for some Shi'ite Muslims (the second largest sect of Islam), who claimed that certain elements had been forgotten or omitted, for nearly every Muslim today, the Arabic Uthmanic text is the sole source for all transla-

Sultan Baybar's Qur'an, Add. MS 22406, folio 74. Copyright © The British Library Board.

tions. The earliest extant copy dates from the late seventh to early eighth century.

Unlike the scriptures of many other religious traditions, the Qur'an contains no hymns, elegies, or other overtly poetic texts. However, it is a complex and eloquent text that employs a variety of narrative and dramatic techniques. Believers seek to memorize the entire text, and its recitation in Arabic underscores the inherent rhythm and rhyme in the suras.

widely disseminated edition that was established by the third Caliph, Uthman ibn Affan (c. 579–656). Because of its importance to the transmission and practice of the Muslim faith, the structure and appropriate *calligraphy* (handwriting) for the Qur'an were codified fairly quickly. The proper use of diacritics, punctuation, and ornamentation, including the use of gold and silver to decorate particular headings and verse marks, were all carefully specified.

Once written down and disseminated, the Qur'an served as the basis for a significant and widespread rise in literacy in all of the areas under the influence of Islam. By the eleventh century, this included most of the Middle East, other parts of the Mediterranean (most notably what is now southern Spain), and the northern half of Africa. Arabic became the *lingua franca*, or common language, of the Muslim world, and children and adults learned Arabic language and grammar in order to read the Qur'an, but also to aid their correct memorization and recitation of the text. Copying of the Qur'an, like reciting it, was an act of religious devotion, and the more carefully and beautifully it was copied, the more deeply felt was the religious experience for both the scribe and future readers.

While the rapid spread of literacy in the Muslim world might logically be expected to have inspired a concurrent increase in the number and variety of books, this did not immediately happen. In the first place, the very importance of the Qur'an raised the question of whether anything else *should* be written down. As late as the thirteenth century, the Muslim theologian al-Dhahabi (1274–1348) observed that one sign of holiness was to never use written material other than the Qur'an. This attitude would surely have inhibited some would-be writers and readers. However, permission to write down other works was gradually extended to religious literature and eventually to other kinds of texts as well. Thus, by the ninth century, authors with significant bodies of work were emerging throughout the Arab world. For example, the Persian scholar Jabir ibn Hayyan (d. c. 815) was credited with writing some 300 or more pamphlets about topics ranging from grammar to astronomy to alchemy. (Some accounts attribute more than 3,000 works to his name, although most of those were probably compilations or simply misattributions.)

The first major Islamic libraries were amassed at this time as well. Among the most important was the library of al-Ma'mun (786–833), in what is now Iraq. The library's patrons helped to make Baghdad one of the premier centers of learning in the world, where scholars gathered to translate major works of knowledge into Arabic and Persian. Many classical Greek and Latin texts were preserved in this way. Another major library was founded by al-Hakam II of Spain (915–976) in Cordoba. Al-Hakam amassed thousands of books and also sponsored the translation of classical works into Arabic. The Fatimid caliph al-Hakim (996–1021) is credited with founding the Fatimid library and university in Egypt. The Fatimid library constituted a collection of books so vast that it was considered one of the wonders of the world. All of these rulers had extensive staffs to translate, copy, illuminate, bind, and repair the books in their collections.

Many individuals of means also had private libraries. Ibn Killis (930–991), an official in Cairo, reportedly spent 1,000 dinars per month on authors, copyists, and bookbinders for his library. Historian Frank Kilgour reports that another official, Al-Sahib ibn Abbad (d. 995), turned down a promotion to prime minister of another region, on the grounds that it would require 400 camels to transport his books to the new locale. Books were highly valued in this era. The authors of a study of Islamic bookmaking note that in tenth-century Cordoba, books had become an important means of displaying one's cultural achievements and position at court, and this belief appeared to become widespread in the Muslim world, so much so that some collectors were accused of amassing books merely for vanity's sake. For example, in the fifteenth century, the Tunisian historian Ibn Khaldun (1332–1406) complained about losing an auction to someone who was bidding on a book just to fill an empty space in his library.

Graziano Krätli and Ghislaine Lydon report that in the Sahara and surrounding regions, books functioned as trade goods, serving as a kind of currency in themselves and also being exchanged for gold and even horses. While many of the books were produced in major cities such as Baghdad, Cairo, Mecca, and Fez, secondary book markets and copying centers sprang up in a number of different regions, including Marrakesh and Timbuktu. Along the trade routes, some oasis towns came to be known for the calligraphic skills of their inhabitants. All of these developments point to the continued importance of books in the Muslim world.

Bookmaking in the Muslim World

The preferred format for Muslim books was the codex. Many of the codices were perforated, sewn-together sheets of papyrus or, from the tenth century, paper, often described in library catalogues of the time as pamphlets. There were also many more substantial, leather-bound volumes. (In the first four centuries of Islam, a small number of codices were also made from parchment.) Islamic books gradually shifted in orientation from a vertical (portrait) format to a horizontal (landscape) format in the eighth century, and then back again by the tenth. Depending on the religious practices and cultural traditions of the particular region, some books were strictly text- and calligraphy-only, with no representations whatsoever of living creatures. To decorate and beautify such texts, elaborate geometric patterns and colors were used, as well as exuberantly abstracted and ornamented calligraphic scripts. Such books frequently also used colored papers, with particular colors associated with certain qualities, such as blue for mourning or red for celebration or high rank. Other books, particularly those in Persian regions or in areas that showed an influence of Byzantine or Mongol art and culture, included beautifully detailed illustrations, or *miniatures*.

(Despite the name, miniatures could be of any size, from tiny initial letters to full-page illustrations.)

It was largely thanks to Muslim artisans that papermaking was introduced into the West. The paper trade spread outwards from Samarkand and Baghdad from the second half of the eighth century, and it was well established throughout the territories under Muslim influence by the tenth. Islamic paper was made from flax that was soaked in quicklime to whiten it, then pounded with mortars (and later trip-hammers), and dried on straw moulds. Islamic papers were *sized*—smoothed and sealed to prepare them for ink—with vegetable starch or gum, which was applied either by soaking the paper in a vat or by spreading the size on as a paste or powder. The surface

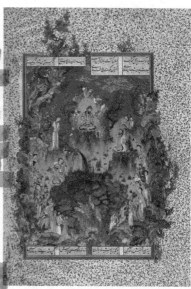

Sultan Muhammad, *The Court of Gayumars*. Iran, c. 1525–35.

was then *burnished*, or polished, with wood or glass tools. The resulting paper had the general appearance of parchment and could be written on with the same inks and pens, but it was whiter and—crucially—much less expensive to produce. From the eleventh century until the fourteenth, the Islamic world produced most of the paper used in the Byzantine Empire and other parts of Europe.

CHRISTIANITY AND THE CODEX

One major innovation in book culture during the Roman era was the development of the codex, a format quickly adopted by the early Christians. In the first centuries of the Common Era, Christianity was a minority sect, subject to persecution by religious and civil authorities. But it was also a religion whose adherents were expected to seek converts. It was incumbent upon believers to study and to spread the *gospel* (good news) of their faith, and thus circulating the four gospels and various *epistles* (letters) that laid out the doctrine of this new religion was of critical importance.

There are a few descriptions of codices being used by the Romans prior to the Christian age. For example, Julius Caesar (100–44 BCE) used folded sheets of papyrus to send dispatches, and the poet Martial (c. 40–103 CE) commented on how much more space-efficient codices were than scrolls. By contrast, there are virtually no descriptions or extant examples of papyrus codices in Syrian or

Egyptian culture until the third and fourth centuries. Since the early Christians had already adopted the codex for most of their sacred writings by the middle of the second century, the Syrian and Egyptian codices are probably evidence that the format had caught on and was now being employed more generally throughout the literate world.

Scholars are divided about exactly why the early Christians rejected scrolls in favor of codices. One proposed explanation is that the format was more economical: unlike scrolls, it was not only easier to write on and read both sides of a page, but more text could be fitted on to each leaf, and thus into each individual volume. However, early examples of codices are not particularly laden with text: they feature well-spaced pages that carry a comparable quantity of words to contemporary scrolls of similar length. Other scholars have suggested that the codex was more convenient for travelers and missionaries. Not only would their numbered pages and more compact shape make them more efficient as reference tools, but they would also be easier to transport and—if necessary—to conceal from the authorities. However, Jewish teachers and missionaries did not abandon the scroll format, and neither did most pagan scholars. One last explanation rests in the Roman origins of the codex format and the Roman influence on many of the peoples who converted to Christianity. Perhaps the early converts and church leaders were already familiar with the codex and with hinged wax tablets, so the format was simply a comfortable convenience for them.

In any event, the codex became what the editors of the *Cambridge History of the Bible* have called the "almost exclusive choice" for the Christian Bible, and all of the very earliest Christian manuscripts are papyrus codices. Even one of the oldest fragments of the Christian Bible, a brief excerpt from the Gospel of St. John dating from about CE 125 and now preserved in the Rylands Library in Manchester, consists of text written on both sides of a piece of papyrus. The layout of the text makes it clear that it was originally part of a paged book, rather than part of a scroll.

The Development of the Christian Bible

The earliest examples of Christian manuscript books are not uniform, and they mostly do not seem to be the productions of professional scribes. Instead, they appear to be personal items that were created for individuals among the early communities of believers. There are no standard sizes, but most of the early codices are about twice as high as they are wide. Although the pages are numbered, the number of lines per page varies, and the writers do not seem to have planned the layout of the books before they began. They simply copied the text as it fit into the pages they had available and continued to the end.

The importance of the written text to early Christianity probably derives from the significance of the holy books in Judaism. Since many of the earliest converts came out of the Jewish traditions, early Christians viewed books as an essential part of religious practice. The Christians adopted the Jewish sacred books, which became the *Old Testament* of the Christian Bible. They also added other texts—the *New Testament*—that interpreted those older scriptures in a Christian context and brought the story forward to incorporate the new communities of believers. The *gospels* and *Acts* included stories of the life of Christ and the early church; the *epistles*, texts that combined letters and literature, offered guidance to far-flung communities seeking to understand how to organize themselves and their faith; and the last book, *Revelation*, was a book of prophecy.

As the Christian religion spread outward from the Mediterranean, it was embraced in different ways by different populations. Local religious communities and leaders interpreted the texts in terms that were determined by their own past experiences and present values, and they also emphasized different aspects of doctrine and of worship practice. The almost inevitable result was that some versions of the circulating texts were elevated or deemphasized (or even rejected) by certain Christian communities, and some practices and beliefs fell into disfavor. Although the Old Testament remained stable, because of its basis in established Jewish tradition, there was disagreement about the value and authority of some of the possible New Testament texts. By the third century, church leaders began sifting through and rejecting certain texts because they seemed to conflict with teachings in books that were universally accepted. As a result, the texts known as the Gnostic gospels, some books of revelation, and a handful of other texts were set aside as non-authoritative. By the fourth century, these judgments were formalized, first by individual bishops and later by *synods* or councils.

The recto of Rylands Library Papyrus P52 from the Gospel of John. Manuscript held by the John Rylands Library.

In 367, the church father Athanasius (c. 293–373) specified the twenty-seven *canonical* books of the New Testament, those that would from then on be regarded as authoritative books of scripture. Besides a general harmony with other accepted books, Athanasius' primary criterion for determining whether texts were canonical seems to have been whether they were written by or described the actions of early believers, notably the twelve original disciples, or *apostles*, of Christ and the early and influential convert Paul (c. 5–67). The canonical books of the Old Testament were generally accepted to be those in the *Septuagint*, a Greek version of the Hebrew scriptures that had been collated in the second and third centuries.

The most comprehensive formalization of the Christian scriptures came soon after Athanasius' declaration. In about 383, Pope Demasus I (c. 305–384) commissioned Jerome (c. 347–419), one of the most-respected biblical scholars of his age, to prepare an authoritative, standard Latin edition of the Bible. Jerome's edition became known as the *Vulgate*, the official Latin version of the Bible approved by the Roman Catholic Church. For the Old Testament,

Jerome returned to the Jewish scriptures, examining both the Greek-language Septuagint and eventually the original Hebrew texts. In his *Prologus Galeatus*, which was published with the first section of his translation of the Old Testament, Jerome carefully explained how he went about collating what he regarded as authoritative texts. As the project continued, he also denoted those books that were deemed unambiguously authoritative or canonical, and those that were of a different status, or *apocryphal*. Most of the fifteen apocryphal books were written in the 300 or so years before and after the turn of the Common Era, and depending on the interpreter, they were either held to contain esoteric knowledge that needed to be kept from ordinary readers (*apocryphal* means "hidden"), or they were regarded as spurious and heretical—not texts that should be regarded as part of scripture. Jerome did not actually try to determine which interpretation applied: he simply followed Jewish tradition in marking these books as special. As a result, the Apocrypha was included in the Vulgate and continued to be regarded as part of authoritative Christian scripture until the Middle Ages.

Despite Jerome's efforts to explain his methods, his edition of the Bible was not universally welcomed. Fourth-century readers who were familiar with, and therefore comfortable with, the Septuagint resisted his new translations from the original Hebrew texts. In fact, it was not until the eighth century—some 400 years later—that the Vulgate Bible became generally popular. Even then, the Eastern or Byzantine branch of the early church, which was based in Constantinople, continued to give priority to the Septuagint and disallowed some of the apocryphal books, and when the two branches of the church separated in the eleventh century, the Vulgate remained the official Bible only of the Western, or Roman Catholic, branch. It was not until the mid-sixteenth century that the Vulgate was again revised, when the Council of Trent (1545–63) met to shape the official Catholic responses to the Reformation. New revisions of the Vulgate were subsequently issued in 1590 and 1594 under Popes Sixtus V (1520–90) and Clement VIII (1536–1605); the latter revision remained in use in the Catholic Church until the twentieth century.

BOOK PRODUCTION IN THE MIDDLE AGES

Between the fall of the Roman Empire after CE 476 and the gradual Christianization of Europe, scribal culture, and literacy more broadly, receded. With no more empire to administer from afar, there was less need for written communication, and reading and writing—never universal skills—fell out of use among most segments of the population. Entire swathes of the European continent were subsumed by invaders from the north and east whose societal and religious structures were less dependent on written forms, or whose writing systems were so different from the Latin alphabet that they were mutually unintelligible. This period of steep decline in literacy, accompanied in most of

Europe by an overall plummeting in living conditions and life expectancy, is sometimes referred to as the Dark Ages.

Where scribal culture continued, in those parts of Europe that already were or became Christian, it increasingly became the purview of specialized religious orders within the Church. Until the reawakening of interest in classical learning that came with the Renaissance, book culture in Europe depended primarily on clerics in far-flung monastic communities, where books continued to be copied or at least preserved. Even then, the safety of the written treasures contained in monastery libraries was not always assured, as the cautionary tale of the *Book of Kells* reveals.

Evangeliary of Henry II, Echternach Scriptorium. Ottonian, c. 1020. Bremen, University Library Ms. 216, folio 124v.

The Monastic Scriptorium

The Church gradually became the center for virtually all aspects of literate culture in Europe, from education to book production. In order to supply the Church's own need for books of liturgy and theology, as well as the needs of patrons and scholars, many religious communities established workshops to copy and produce manuscript books. Several monastic orders, including the Benedictines, even mandated the copying of books, viewing it as a good and useful devotional practice—and also as a way to avoid the idleness that might distract a monk from his responsibilities.

Managed for the most part by monks, but sometimes by nuns, these workshops, or *scriptoria*, varied in size and specialization, but between them they produced a majority of the books in Europe between the sixth and the thirteenth centuries. While many of the books were quite utilitarian—simple copies of texts for use by clerics and scholars—others were extraordinary works of art and religious devotion. The calligraphy, illustrations, and bindings of the more elaborately and exuberantly produced books make them some of the treasures of the age. For example, many medieval *Books of Hours*, devotional texts that contained calendars of religious feasts and festivals, psalms, prayers, and other aids to meditation and reflection, frequently included splendid illustrations. The distinctive artistry involved in their production has enabled scholars to trace them to particular monasteries or convents, and sometimes even to particular individuals within a scriptorium.

Among the more renowned illuminated manuscripts of the medieval period is the *Book of Kells*, a set of the gospels (the Gospel of John is incomplete) produced sometime around 800, probably at a monastery on Iona, one of the western islands off Scotland. The island of Iona was plundered by Viking raiders at about this period, and the *Book of Kells* was moved to Kells Abbey in County Meath, Ireland, probably for safekeeping. However, Kells itself was raided in the early eleventh century, and the book was stolen, stripped of its jeweled cover, and left in the dirt. Even without its cover, the *Book of Kells* is an extraordinary work of art: the text is interspersed with full-page illuminations of stylized, geometric letter shapes and fantastic animals, characteristic of the Celtic style of the region. The *Lindisfarne Gospels* are another example of

THE BOOK OF HOURS

One popular and widely produced medieval text was the *Book of Hours*, a Christian devotional aid devised in the thirteenth century. Members of medieval religious orders were enjoined to pray at certain times of the day, and the timing and specific content of their devotional practices were laid out in *breviaries*, which marked the particular scriptural passages and prayers that were designated for each date and time. Increasingly, pious laypeople wished to emulate the example of the clerics, but the breviary was a bit too complicated for most believers. The Book of Hours was the solution: it typically contained a liturgical calendar, showing the feast days of the Church, excerpts from the gospels, and sets of prayers dedicated to the Virgin Mary, the "Hours of the Virgin." A Book of Hours might also include Hours of the Cross, of the Holy Spirit, and of the Passion or a specific saint; most also contained the Office of the Dead, which was said the night before a burial, and additional psalms, *litanies* (prayers of supplication), and prayers to saints.

The Latin text of the Book of Hours indicated the timing and content of prayers appropriate for different times of the day throughout the church year. But for at least some of the owners of Books of Hours, the illustrations may have been more important as a devotional aid. Medieval Christians memorized the Latin of the mass and scriptures from daily exposure, so they were able to recite the prayers and psalms, but this did not necessarily mean they knew how to read Latin. And although the lavish nature of many Books of Hours indicates that they were commissioned by wealthy patrons, wealth did not always equate to literacy. Rather than "reading" the calendar and prayers, then, at least some owners of Books of Hours likely used the illustrations as an aide-mémoire, turning the pages for reminders about which prayers were appropriate for the particular feast and hour.

Some Books of Hours were produced in vernacular languages in the sixteenth century, although vernacular versions were only very popular in the Netherlands. In England, Books of Hours came to be known as "primers," and they were used to teach children. The Book of Hours gradually fell out of favor in the sixteenth century, as saying prayers with the use of a *rosary* (string of beads used for counting prayers) came into practice. However, the beauty of the books caused many of them to be saved even when they were no longer used for religious purposes.

the Celtic style of book illustration from that period.

Monastic scriptoria might vary significantly according to time, place, and religious order, but the work of each was organized around some common practices. Because book copying involved expensive and flammable materials, the managers of scriptoria were always wary of introducing live flames (either for candles or for warming fires) into the workshops. Therefore, the scriptorium was always sited in a portion of the church or its surrounding precincts that provided good natural light. Especially in colder climates, the scriptorium was also, ideally, adjacent to some heat source. For example, the scriptorium at the Cathedral in Chester, England, was situated on a courtyard next to the monastery kitchens, so that the heat from the cooking fires carried through the walls to warm the workshop. The reliance on natural light probably meant that workdays in a typical scriptorium rarely extended longer than six hours, and in more northern countries during the winter, there were likely days when no work could be done at all.

Detail from the *Book of Kells*, c. 800. Folio 292r. Trinity College Library, Dublin.

Within a scriptorium, book production was typically broken down into component tasks. In most scriptoria, the greatest number of monks or nuns would be engaged in copying the *exemplar*, or original book's text, letter-for-letter in black ink. Others worked as *rubricators*, adding not only the red-letter text (*rubrics*) that indicated the beginnings of sections or sometimes the names of the Trinity, but also other important design elements in the text, such as titles or the enlarged initial capital letters (*incipits*) that marked the beginnings of major passages. Still others specialized in adding various kinds of graphic and pictorial decorations to the pages, including *illuminations*, the gold, silver, or brilliantly colored graphic features that surrounded the text, and *miniatures*, the illustrations that augmented, pointed to, or commented on the text. Others worked as *correctors*, checking the copies against the exemplar to make sure the transcription was accurate.

Depending on the size of the scriptorium and the extent of its production operations, other tasks might have been performed inside the religious order or outside of it. Some scriptoria produced books on a relatively large scale, copying works such as Bibles and Books of Hours that were always in demand, and allowing clients to request various kinds of customization of the final product— extra rubrication or gold leaf, for example. Some even provided catalogues or portfolios of their work to prospective customers. A given religious house might produce its own parchment for book-making, or it might contract out for it. Preparing sufficient parchment for a major book was a significant undertaking, with many skins required to produce just one volume. (For example, historians have estimated that a single copy of the Gutenberg Bible printed on parchment would have required the skins of 300 sheep. Since the forty-two-line Bible consisted of 643 folio leaves in two volumes, that would have worked out to just over two parchment leaves per sheep. The cost of keeping and slaughtering that many animals, even without the subsequent costs of preparing the skins for writing, helps to explain the expense of parchment books.)

Producing a book from an exemplar required careful planning. In many instances, the goal was to create as close a copy of every aspect of the original book as possible. In other instances, the goal would be to produce a copy that rendered the *text* accurately, but whose final physical dimensions and degree of decoration (or plainness) were determined by the patron, perhaps so that the new book would match others in an existing library.

In either case, one of the first tasks would be to carefully analyze the exemplar to determine how much parchment was required for the copy, and then to prepare the parchment to ensure that each finished page would be uniform in dimensions and layout. This was done by trimming the sheets to the final page size, and then *ruling* or *lining* them to indicate margins and lines of text. In most cases, a pattern sheet would be created first. Using the pattern sheet, several sheets of parchment would be laid on top of each other and then pricked through with an awl at the beginning and end of each line of text. This would ensure that the entire set of pages were all in proper alignment. Next, each sheet would be lightly scored across from hole to hole, using a metal straightedge, or lightly lined with a lead point. Various tools also allowed scribes to rule multiple lines at a time: some looked like forks with tines at fixed intervals, and others were like stiff wires or guitar strings set in a block of wood. The tools would be dragged across the surface of the page to produce lines. If the parchment to be used was very fine, an inked guide-sheet could be prepared and laid underneath the page, so that the lines showed through for the scribe doing the copying.

In most cases, the exemplar would be unbound, so that the copying work could be parceled out to a number of scribes who would work simultaneously. Again, this required very careful planning, to ensure that the copied pages were prepared in the optimal order for assembling the finished book—and to ensure that the pages of the exemplar were reassembled properly. When an exact line-for-line copy was being made, individual scribes would regularly begin and end copying in the middle of passages, or even in the middle of words. When a freer copy was being made, individual scribes might work on more extended passages, fitting the text from the exemplar into the ruled parchment as best they could from the general guidelines about length and size. This occasional freedom to fit text may explain some of the variations that exist in copies of the same basic text. For example, versions of the *Canterbury Tales*, composed between 1387 and 1400 by English poet Geoffrey Chaucer (c. 1342–1400), are arranged in different orders, and some omit two of the tales (*The Cook's Tale* and *The Squire's Tale*) altogether, or insert another work (one that is probably not by Chaucer) to fill the space that those two tales would have taken.

Manuscript copying was exacting—and exhausting—work. Depending on their skill, the size and complexity of the text being copied, and the season of the year, scribes could produce from one to ten leaves per day, or between two and twenty pages. (The ink on the first side of the leaf would have to be allowed to dry thoroughly before the leaf could be turned and the second side begun.) If the corrector discovered any errors in the transcription, the scribe would need to scrape off the ink in that portion of the parchment with a knife or piece of pumice, smooth the parchment surface again, and then rewrite the passage. Chaucer was well aware of the consequences of a scribe's inattention. In a short poem addressed to "Adam, His Owne Scriveyn" (*scrivener*, or copier), he lamented:

> So ofte adaye I mot thy werk renewe,
> It to correcte and eke to rubbe and scrape,
> And al is thorough thy negligence and rape.

For their part, various scribes through the ages commented on the difficulties of their work and its toll on their eyes and bodies. In *colophons*, the end notes in some manuscript books that document when and where the copy was made (and sometimes by whom), or even in the margins of books, scribes commented on their working conditions:

> Margaretha von Schonbergk has written this with her left hand.

> Thin ink, bad vellum, difficult text.

> Thank God, it will soon be dark.

> Have patience with the errors. Written in my 73rd year with great labour in the Wienhausen convent during the expulsion from our monastery.

> Now I've written the whole thing: for Christ's sake give me a drink.

THE RENAISSANCE

Over the second millennium of the Common Era, Europe slowly began to recover from the decline that had followed the end of the Roman Empire. Improvements in agriculture, trade, and political systems, as well as the unifying power of the Church, helped to stabilize and improve living conditions for many. There was enough of an economic base to support a higher degree of leisure among some of the nobility and clerical classes. As a result, individuals began to turn again to the pursuit of knowledge, and by the fourteenth century, a renewed knowledge and appreciation of classical literature and culture had taken root in Italy. Over the next 300 years, this interest in classical culture and its accompanying flourishing of scholarship gradually spread throughout Europe. The movement came to be known as the *Renaissance*—the rebirth of book culture.

Initially, the revived interest in classical studies was furthered by scribal culture. Manuscripts of Greek and Roman texts were copied and circulated, sought after and loaned. Many works long forgotten were brought back into circulation from libraries and collections in the east, where Muslim scholars had kept them alive and added to them. Others were rediscovered in the vaults of monastic libraries, where they had languished for centuries. Under the auspices of thinkers like Giovanni Boccaccio (1313–75), classical mythology and works by Greek authors such as Euripides and Aristotle were again discussed and debated. Boccaccio's friend, the poet Petrarch (1304–74), helped reacquaint contemporary readers with the texts of the Roman authors Cicero, Virgil, and Seneca. Latin had remained a living language in the centuries after Rome because of its use in the Church, so classical texts in Latin were still accessible to those who could read at all; and since most of the standard Greek works had long ago been translated into Latin editions, those were available to modern readers, too. As new scholarship discussing and extending the classical Latin texts was produced, it was also written in Latin, which would remain the lingua franca of scholarship well into the seventeenth century.

However, along with Latin texts, many new works of this period were also written and circulated in the *vernacular*, or local, languages. While there were well-established oral traditions of literature (songs, ballads, histories, and so on) in the different vernaculars, written texts in these languages had tended to be limited to the mundane or practical, such as correspondence or local contracts. By the thirteenth century, however, this began to change, and works of greater purpose and aesthetic beauty began to be composed in the local tongues. One of the earliest notable authors to write in the vernacular was Dante Alighieri (1265–1321), whose great work *The Divine Comedy* (1308–21) was composed in the local Florentine dialect of Italian—even though its subject matter, a journey through the regions of Hell, Purgatory, and Paradise, certainly lent itself to the language of the Church. Chaucer wrote his *Canterbury Tales* in English, even though as an educated and well-traveled man his command of Latin was exceptional. Besides demonstrating that the vernacular could be used for more elevated purposes, these works and their authors also laid the groundwork for what would become distinctive national literary traditions.

Universities

To further support the expansion of knowledge and literacy in the Renaissance, new institutions of higher learning were created. The earliest European universities had been founded before the Renaissance, first in Bologna (1088) and Oxford (1096), followed by others over the next 100 years, including those in Paris and in Salamanca, Spain. The Renaissance accelerated and refined these educational ventures. Originally intended to train men for the new professions of law, civil service, and medicine, the early universities turned to classical models of what educated persons required. The result was a curriculum based in the seven liberal arts: arithmetic, music, geometry, and astronomy, which made up the *quadrivium*, and grammar, rhetoric, and logic, which comprised the *trivium*. The texts for study were drawn primarily from the rediscovered Greek and Roman classics, such as Aristotle and Virgil, with a dash of Arab knowledge, such as algebra and astronomy, thrown in for good measure. Because instruction was in Latin, the primary entrance requirement for the early universities was sufficiently good Latin to follow the lectures and take notes.

The course of study was centered on lectures, during which professors read from the classic works or from their own commentaries on them, and students read along and took notes. So far this probably sounds familiar, but the whole enterprise was made more challenging by the difficulty of securing books. Contemporary illustrations of university lectures depict groups of students huddled around a single copy of a book, attempting to follow along as the professor reads. Students who needed (or simply desired) their own copies of the texts had to borrow and copy them. Although the exercise of copying probably helped the students absorb the books' content, it was a major undertaking, and some students were known to begin the copying process a full year before they intended to enroll in university courses.

To help supply the demand for books, scriveners' offices opened in many university towns. These secular book-copying workshops paralleled the sacred book production in the monastic scriptoria. They would provide copies of required texts, based on exemplars provided by the master teachers, or they would copy other works as commissioned. As with the books copied in medieval scriptoria, the exemplars would be divided into gatherings. These were comprised of a folded sheet of eight pages, called *peciae*, and each *pecia* could be loaned out individually for copying. (A typical page in a *pecia* was divided into two 62-line columns of text.)

Universities also began to create libraries to provide access to books, but these were initially very limited affairs. A large library of any kind in the Middle Ages might contain only a few hundred books, and it took a long time for universities and other institutions to build larger collections, which they generally achieved through bequests from former faculty and wealthy patrons. For example, the library at Merton College, Oxford, had only forty books in 1375 and only 375 by 1500, while that at King's College, Cambridge, had only

175 in 1452. Trinity College, Cambridge, had only 250 books in its library as late as 1600. Probably the most extraordinary university library of the age was the one at the Sorbonne in Paris. Founded with an initial bequest of 300 books from the theologian Gérard d'Abbeville (c. 1225–72), the Sorbonne amassed thousands of volumes, enabling it to rival the Vatican Library, which is still one of the largest libraries in the world.

Even if a university had a library, however, access to the books was not guaranteed. Many early libraries allowed their faculty, or fellows, to borrow books for up to a year, depending on seniority. This practice was very convenient for those privileged individuals, who did not need to purchase their own copies or go to the trouble of copying them, but taking the works out of circulation for such a long period of time was not particularly helpful for others with less senior rank, especially students. Other libraries only allowed readers to consult the books on the premises, in some instances locking the readers with their volumes into cages, or securing the books to the bookcase with chains. Books are known to have been chained to the desks and lecterns in the Merton College library as early as 1338, and the practice was fairly widespread by the 1500s.

The renewed emphasis on learning that grew throughout the early centuries of the second millennium and blossomed into the Renaissance generated an ever-growing demand for books—but that demand was thwarted by the challenges of securing them. As Elizabeth Eisenstein has noted, even the shift from parchment to paper during this era could not facilitate a great increase in the production of books for circulation. Copying manuscripts was both difficult and time-consuming, professionally copied volumes were expensive, the quantities remained fairly limited, and even if one was fortunate enough to have access to a library, accessing a particular book was not assured. Hence, the time was ripe for any developments that would increase the ease, speed, and quantity of books produced, while helping to contain the costs. The innovations that would make this dream a reality and take Europe from what Eisenstein calls "several limited and transient renascences" to "a permanent Renaissance of unprecedented range and scope" finally coalesced in fifteenth-century Germany, in the town of Mainz.

SELECTED BIBLIOGRAPHY

Ackroyd, P.R., and C.F. Evans, eds. *The Cambridge History of the Bible. Vol. 1: From the Beginnings to Jerome.* Cambridge: Cambridge UP, 1970.

Avrin, Leila. *Scribes, Script and Books: The Book Arts from Antiquity to the Renaissance.* Chicago: American Library Association, 1991.

Banks, Doris H. *Medieval Manuscript Bookmaking: A Bibliographic Guide.* Metuchen, NJ: Scarecrow, 1989.

Bosch, Gulnar, John Carswell, and Guy Petherbridge. *Islamic Bindings and Bookmaking: A Catalogue of an Exhibition*. Chicago: Oriental Institute Museum, University of Chicago, 1981.

Bowman, Alan K. *Life and Letters on the Roman Frontier: Vindolanda and Its People*. 2nd ed. London: British Museum, 2003.

Bowman, Alan K. *The Roman Writing Tablets from Vindolanda*. London: Trustees of the British Museum, 1983.

Clair, Colin. *A History of European Printing*. London: Academic, 1976.

Cyrus, Cynthia J. *The Scribes for Women's Convents in Late Medieval Germany*. Toronto: U of Toronto P, 2009.

Eisenstein, Elizabeth L. *The Printing Revolution in Early Modern Europe*. Cambridge: Cambridge UP, 1983.

Fischer, Steven Roger. *A History of Reading*. London: Reaktion, 2003.

Golden Haggadah. Online Gallery: Sacred Texts. British Library. http://www.bl.uk/onlinegallery/sacredtexts/golden.html.

Hellinga, Lotte, and J.B. Trapp, eds. *The Cambridge History of the Book in Britain*. Vol. 3, *1400–1557*. Cambridge: Cambridge UP, 1999.

Hornblower, Simon, and Antony Spawforth, eds. *The Oxford Companion to Classical Civilization*. Oxford: Oxford UP, 1998.

Kilgour, Frederick G. *The Evolution of the Book*. New York: Oxford UP, 1998.

Krätli, Graziano, and Ghislaine Lydon, eds. *The Trans-Saharan Book Trade: Manuscript Culture, Arabic Literacy and Intellectual History in Muslim Africa*. Leiden: Brill, 2011.

Loyn, H.R. *The Middle Ages: A Concise Encyclopaedia*. New York: Thames and Hudson, 1989.

Madan, Falconer. *Books in Manuscript: A Short Introduction to Their Study and Use*. Trans. Peter Gulewich. London: Kegan Paul, Trench, Trubner, 1920.

Mir, Mustansir. "The Qur'an as Literature." *Religion and Literature* 20.1 (1988): 49–64.

Modarressi, Hossein. "Early Debates on the Integrity of the Qur'an: A Brief Survey." *Studia Islamica* 77 (1993): 5–39.

Partridge, Stephen. "Minding the Gaps: Interpreting the Manuscript Evidence of the *Cook's Tale* and the *Squire's Tale*." In *The English Medieval Book: Studies in Memory of Jeremy Griffiths*. Ed. A.S.G. Edwards, Vincent Gillespie, and Ralph Hanna. London: British Library, 2000. 51–85.

Vindolanda Tablets Online. http://vindolanda.csad.ox.ac.uk/index.shtml.

THE PRINTING REVOLUTION

They get really right into it

Like writing, printing was invented in more than one place and time. At its most basic, *printing* is the process of producing an image by inking a raised, or *relief*, surface and by stamping or impressing it on an absorbent surface. In this sense, some of the earliest printed texts were created in ancient Mesopotamia with the use of *cylinder seals*, engraved cylinders made from stone, glass, or ceramics that were rolled along damp clay to leave an impression. Such seals were probably used for administrative purposes, as a kind of official signature. Cylinder seals were also used in Mesoamerica before the Common Era, probably to print patterns on cloth.

However, a different kind of printing, one involving the printing of texts on paper, emerged in Asia in the eighth century, and that is the form of printing most significant to the history of the book. This kind of printing is the process of making an impression of an image from inked blocks, types, plates, or cylinders. This form of printing was originally invented in China, from where it quickly spread across Asia. Printing and papermaking centers developed in China and Japan, and artisans in Korea developed an early form of movable type made of wood or ceramics.

But it was in fifteenth-century Europe that the real "printing revolution" took place, through the ingenuity of Johannes Gutenberg. Gutenberg developed three key inventions that enabled an explosion of book production in Europe. The first invention was interchangeable pieces of metal type that could be reused and recycled almost indefinitely. Unlike the earlier technology of block printing from wood, printing from movable metal type was both more flexible and more durable. Even blocks carved from the hardest woods inevitably wore down with repeated use. Metal types eventually wore down too, but they could be melted down and recast as brand-new pieces of type. Gutenberg's second brilliant invention was a "sticky" ink that would adhere to the metal surfaces of his typefaces and transfer images cleanly to paper.

But the third invention is the one to which Gutenberg's own name has adhered. The *Gutenberg press*—or more properly, the *common press*—was the basic technology used for printing from Gutenberg's day to the nineteenth century, and it continues as the underlying technology employed in most craft or *letterpress* printing today. (The term *common press* is used because no presses, or even drawings of them, have survived from Gutenberg's own printing business, so historians are unable to determine definitively what Gutenberg's own invention looked like. However, the general similarity of surviving illustrations and presses from the sixteenth century on suggests a common original model.) At the heart of Gutenberg's last invention was the ancient technology of the screw-press, which had been used for centuries to release juice and oil from fruits and olives, as well as to flatten cloth. Gutenberg realized that the screw-press could be employed to exert firm, even pressure on an inked surface, thus ensuring that the resulting printed item would be equally legible at

Workers in a print shop, 16th century. Woodcut by Jost Amman, 1568.

all points on the page. Gutenberg devised a method to ensure that the printing surface (the *form* or *forme*) was always exactly centered under the block of wood (the *platen*) that applied pressure to the printing surface, and also a mechanism (the *tympan* and *frisket*) to ensure that the paper or parchment was always lined up precisely with the printing surface. The basic components were then in place. Over the next five centuries, artisans and engineers would adjust and refine the mechanisms and the materials out of which they were constructed, but the basic working of the press would remain the same.

Gutenberg's inventions not only increased the ease, speed, and accuracy of the book production process, but they also reduced the cost of printing and circulating books. An entire infrastructure dedicated to print culture arose. First across Europe, and then in the Americas as well, the new printing and bookselling trades helped put millions of texts into the hands of eager readers, whose ranks increased as the improved availability of books helped lift literacy rates. While some printers dedicated their craft to the production of expensive, specialist works for scholars and wealthy patrons, many more generated inexpensive publications, such as broadsheets, pamphlets, and chapbooks, that were well within the means of ordinary people. And Gutenberg's inventions also proved exceptionally timely. As religious and political forces gave rise to the Renaissance, the Protestant Reformation, and then to the Enlightenment, many people found that they not only wanted but *needed* to read and own books. Gutenberg's press made that possible.

EARLY PRINTING IN ASIA

The earliest examples of Chinese woodblock printing, or *xylography*, are from about the eighth century, during the Tang dynasty (618–907). Printing from woodblocks continued in China until the twentieth century, through the Qing dynasty (1644–1912). Chinese woodblocks were typically made of pear, jujube, or catalpa wood. The craft of woodblock carving reached its peak during the Song dynasty (960–1279), a period that witnessed a general flowering of the book crafts, including also calligraphy and manuscript illumination. From China, printing technology spread throughout Asia, with particularly important innovations in Japan and Korea.

Printing in China

Chinese woodblock printing involved four processes. First, the text had to be transcribed from the original and fitted to the block. A scribe would write out the text on paper, which would then be pasted face down on the block, to reverse the image so that it read correctly when printed. Next, a cutter would carve away the wood around each of the characters, so that the text to be printed would stand in relief. The next step was the printing itself. A printer would ink the surface of the block and lay a sheet of paper over it. To transfer the image, the paper would be rubbed with a long brush or special burnishing tool. Because Chinese paper had a relatively low opacity, it was usually only printed on one side so that the images would be clearly legible. After the image was transferred, the paper would be carefully peeled off the block and hung to dry. Finally, a binder would gather the sheets together and turn them into a book.

Early Chinese books could be bound in a variety of ways. One of the earliest bookbinding formats was the *pothi*, a style borrowed from India and frequently used for binding copies of Buddhist scriptures. (The Chinese names for the pothi binding, *fanjia zhuang* and *beiye jing*, point to the binding's origins, meaning "sandwiched Sanskrit binding" and "palm leaf sutra," respectively.) The earliest pothi-bound books were formed of thin rectangular palm leaves (in India) or slats of bamboo or other wood (in China). Each leaf or slat contained one column of text, reading from top to bottom. The leaves or slats were then tied together with string, usually at two points, each about one-third of the way from the top or bottom of the columns. Indian pothi books were usually rolled up, while Chinese ones were usually simply stacked in zigzag format. Later pothi-bound books were made of thin sheets of paper, which were either punched at one end and strung together, or sometimes simply stacked in the correct order.

Another common early binding used especially for Chinese *codices*, or paged books, was the *butterfly binding*. In butterfly bindings, printed sheets are folded with the printing to the inside and stacked, then pasted together at the folded edge of the sheet. The small amount of glued surface means that butterfly bindings can be very unstable: not only do the sheets easily pull apart, but the pastes traditionally used to glue the books together are very attractive to insects. Therefore, other binding methods were soon experimented with. Some early Chinese codices added stitching at the tops and bottoms of the butterfly bindings for added stability, and others dispensed with the paste altogether and were simply stitched together on the folds.

Another binding innovation was the *wrapped back binding*. Books that were butterfly bound had the inconvenience of many visible blank pages, as the non-printed sides of the paper were always in evidence. The wrapped back binding eliminated that problem by reversing the way the sheets were folded so that the printing was to the outside, essentially creating a two-page leaf with the crease to the outside (turning) edge. The leaves would then be bound together at the open (spine) edge with paper screws, and a protective cover would be glued to the spine. This remained the primary bookbinding format for Chinese codices until the modern age.

However, some Chinese books were also bound to evoke earlier scroll forms. One common binding was the *concertina*, or zigzag style, where pages were glued together at the edges in a continuous long text, and then folded back-and-forth. This binding created a book that looked and functioned like a codex, but that was really a kind of pleated scroll. The concertina binding was also called a *sutra* or *scripture binding*, because of its association with Buddhist scrolls.

A more unusual form of Chinese binding was the *whirlwind*. In a whirlwind book, a stack of pages of gradually increasing length are pasted together at one edge, with the longest sheet at the bottom, and the shortest on top. A thin bamboo rod is then split and slipped on to the glued edge (much like a contemporary plastic report binding might be slid on to a sheaf of papers) and stitched on. The book can then be rolled around the bamboo rod, combining both codex and scroll elements in one format.

The Chinese printing industry was well established by the time of the Song dynasty, but a number of innovations were introduced in subsequent eras. For example, multicolor printing, incorporating up to three colors, was introduced during the Ming period (1368–1644). Usually, the different colors were inked on to the printing surface at the same time, so that all of the colors printed with the same impression, but there are also examples of colors being added one or two at a time, requiring multiple impressions that demanded careful attention to the proper alignment of the sheet.

The Koreans and Gutenberg are usually credited with inventing *movable type*, or type that could be assembled, disassembled, and reassembled in a frame to print different documents. However, it appears to have been in use in China even earlier. During the Song dynasty, an artisan named Bi Shēng (990–1051) developed a system for movable type made of porcelain. The characters were formed of clay and fired, and then affixed in the desired order to an iron plate with a sticky base of wax and resin. The wax and resin congealed when cold, holding the type fast, but would soften when heated, so that the pieces of type could be removed and reused. An eleventh-century account of Bi Shēng's system notes that he sorted his type by their sounds, keeping rhyming groups together in wooden cases.

The Chinese continued to experiment with movable type in different media—wood, porcelain, metals—for centuries. Historian T.H. Barrett suggests that the Tanguts, a people living in northwestern China before the tenth century whose script was quite similar to Chinese, were working with movable wooden type as early as the twelfth century. Their word for movable type translates to "broken-up characters." Barrett also claims that the Uighur people in northern China and Mongolia had movable metal type somewhat later. The question of why movable type did not become widespread in China has long been debated. Some scholars have argued that Chinese characters were too complex and too numerous to make movable type a practicality, and that this is why most Chinese printing was from large blocks of text, carved to purpose. However, Barrett notes that in early xylography, it was common practice to fix errors in large printing blocks by removing mistakes and inserting plugs with the corrected characters. He points out that it would have been a fairly easy step from error-fixing plugs to interchangeable ones.

Despite innovations with technologies and forms, printing did not become a primary means for disseminating texts in China. China's long-established and successful scribal culture, involving writing with brushes on leaves or paper, worked perfectly well for the culture's needs. According to Barrett, a determined Chinese scholar was capable of copying up to fifty sheets of 200 characters per day, so it was possible even for individuals to amass large collections of texts in a reasonably short period of time through their own efforts. An organized book trade, entailing professional copyists who were producing multiple copies of a given text, wasn't really needed.

One significant exception to this general rule was the production of Buddhist spells and calendars, which were printed in large quantities between the eighth and tenth centuries. One of the earliest mass printings in history, thousands of copies of a Buddhist "great spell," was ordered by the Chinese Empress Wǔ Zétiān (624–705). The spells were to ensure the empress's well-being in the afterlife. Copies were probably printed with the use of ceramic seals, like those used in ancient Mesopotamia and in Mesoamerica, which were inked and then rolled along paper strips. The total number of spells printed is not known, but Barrett reports that copies were still showing up in Korea many years later, which indicates that they must have been in fairly wide circulation across Asia. This suggests that the original print run must have been quite substantial. Barrett further speculates that efforts by her successors to suppress Empress Wǔ's achievements and downplay her role in Chinese history may have contributed to the temporary abandonment of printing in China soon after her death.

Another important exception to the preference for handwritten texts in Chinese culture was the printing of the *Diamond Sutra*. The *Diamond Sutra* is not only the earliest surviving printed book in China, but it is also the earliest printed book anywhere whose precise date we know: the year 868. The book is a scroll, printed from woodblocks on seven sheets of paper that were dyed yellow. The text, one of the central stories of Buddhism, is arranged in columns to one side and accompanied by large and lavish illustrations. The colophon explains that it was printed as an act of devotion by a son for his parents.

THE DIAMOND SUTRA

Detail of the Frontispiece, Diamond Sutra from Cave 17, Dunhuang, ink on paper British Library Or.8210/ P.2 (the oldest, dated printed book, 868 CE).

Believed to be the oldest printed book that includes the date of its publication, the copy of the *Diamond Sutra* owned by the British Library is a short work of Buddhist teaching (a *sutra*), written in Chinese. The text itself is from the Mahayana Buddhist sutras, a tradition in Buddhist thought that stressed ways in which ordinary people could reach enlightenment without devoting themselves to the monastic lives and long periods of meditation required by the earlier Theravada Buddhism. The text takes its name from the story told in the sutra itself. The Buddha tells the seeker that the sutra should be called "The Diamond of Transcendent Wisdom," because its teaching will cut like a diamond through worldly illusion to illuminate the real and eternal.

The *Diamond Sutra* is a relatively short Buddhist text that could be readily memorized and repeated to help the believer move forward on the road to enlightenment. The text itself also mentions that good sons and daughters should perform charitable acts and memorize and teach Buddhist texts to others. This may explain why this particular text was printed and preserved. The colophon at the end reads "Reverently made for universal distribution by Wang Jie on behalf of his two parents," and it is dated with the Chinese characters for May 11, 868.

The *Diamond Sutra* consists of seven sections or panels of paper, each printed in black from an individual woodblock. The panels have been pasted together into a scroll over 5.5 yards (about 5 meters) in length. Hidden in a network of caves in northwest China around the year 1000, the *Diamond Sutra* remained out of sight until it was rediscovered 900 years later. Approximately 40,000 other scrolls and books have also been found in the complex of caves and grottoes, which appear to have been used for religious practices from about the fourth century.

Printing in Japan and Korea

Just as the Chinese writing system was adapted for use with other Asian languages, so too were Chinese printing and paper technologies. Woodblock printing was being practiced in Japan at least by the 760s, during the Nara period. This is also when the second—and better-documented—large-scale printing project in the world was undertaken. Curiously, this second great printing effort was also instigated by a woman. Following a period of great political turmoil, the Japanese Empress Shōtoku (718–70) commissioned the printing of a million paper prayers (*dhārani*), possibly as an act of penance. She instructed that the prayers should be inserted into small, specially built wooden pagodas and distributed throughout the kingdom. No documentary evidence survives to describe how the prayers were printed, but careful examination of some of the few remaining copies suggests that, unlike the earlier spells printed by the Chinese Empress Wŭ, they were printed with discrete blocks made of wood, ceramic, or even metal. The massive undertaking took a total of six years, and it was finally completed in 770, the year of the Empress's death.

Other large-scale printing of religious texts continued in Japan through the eleventh century. According to historian Steven Fischer, it was common in Kyoto to produce up to a thousand copies of prayers for the dead or for rain, and in Nara during the latter part of this period, some Buddhist texts were being printed for the religious instruction of monks. Beginning in the late ninth century, Japan began to create a specifically Japanese national culture, one that was distinctively different from that of China. Among other things, Japanese book culture during this period began to diverge from the Chinese. However, a distinct tradition of Japanese printing did not really begin until the Edo period (1603–1867). The Japanese experimented with movable wooden type at that time, but for the most part they reverted to the earlier woodblock practices for text printing.

Where movable type did catch on fairly early in Asia was in Korea. Fischer reports that Korean printers were already experimenting with movable type in the thirteenth century. But it was in the early fifteenth century, during the reign of Sejong the Great (1397–1450), that Korea made significant strides in printing technology. According to historian Peter Watson, Sejong believed that in order to achieve an enlightened society, it was necessary to increase the production and circulation of books. Recognizing the limitations of xylography—block carving was time-consuming, and wood as a medium for either blocks or type was subject to wear—Sejong urged that type be devised from metal, making it durable enough for many impressions. He also undertook to underwrite the cost of producing the type. As a result, 100,000 *sorts*, or specific, individual characters, were cast in 1403, with at least ten more *fonts*—complete sets of type, including all characters—created over the next thirty years. These developments, combined with the Hangul writing system reform also launched by Sejong, helped spur a print-driven literary flowering in Korea at about the same time that the Renaissance was beginning in Europe.

EARLY PRINTING IN EUROPE

In the late fifteenth century, Europe began making the slow transition from *scribal culture*, one based on handwritten documents, to *print culture*. The common press was arguably the most important technological development that drove that transition, but in the early decades of the print era, an even simpler technology was responsible for putting printed matter in the hands of ordinary people. Images and simple texts carved together on a single block of wood were used to print many popular devotional items, including illustrations of Bible stories, pictures of saints, and calendars of auspicious dates. Many of these items were relatively short—often a single page—and because they were intended for illiterate and semi-literate readers, they relied more on the power and allusiveness of their illustrations than on the nuances of text.

However, a number of popular longer documents were produced by xylography as well. The most frequently printed devotional block-books were the *Biblia Pauperum*, or "Poor Man's Bible"; the *Canticum Canticorum* (Canticles, or "Song of Songs"); the *Ars Moriendi*, or "Art of Dying"; and the *Mirabilia Romae*, or "Marvels of Rome." Among secular books, by far the most popular was a Latin grammar by Aelius Donatus (c. mid-fourth century), whose relatively short length and unchanging text meant it was easy to produce with wood blocks. Donatus's grammar was one of the most widely used textbooks in European history, selling for over a thousand years in manuscript, woodblock, and typeset and printed forms. Its sales only began to dwindle in the Renaissance, when it was finally replaced by more in-depth and up-to-date alternatives.

Despite having names like "Poor Man's Bible," the longer block-books were probably still very expensive, and historians believe they were initially most likely purchased by members of the clergy for use in educating their congregations and students. The *Ars Moriendi*, versions of which first appear in the Netherlands in the 1460s, provide guidance on how to pass successfully from this world to the next. Typical illustrations show angels helping a dying man to resist temptation.

Gutenberg

Born in Mainz, Johannes Gutenberg (c. 1390–1468) was trained as a metalsmith. After a number of years working in this trade in Mainz and in Strasbourg, in the 1440s he began working on the three interrelated technologies that would launch the printing revolution in Europe.

Gutenberg's first invention, movable metal type, grew directly out of his training as a metalsmith. As a jewelry and tool maker, he had acquired the necessary skills of metallurgy to craft very fine objects, and this meant that the detail and small scale required to create metal type was well within his range of ability. Gutenberg worked out that an alloy of lead, tin, and antimony would provide the necessary hardness to enable the type to stand up to the harshness of multiple impressions, while still being relatively easy to melt down and reuse.

THE BIBLIA PAUPERUM

The *Biblia Pauperum*, or "Poor Man's Bible," offered medieval readers a simple, illustrated text of Christian instruction. Pages featured large illustrations, often in a kind of grid system, with minimal text, so that some of them look like forerunners of the modern comic book. (This effect is enhanced by the fact that some of the characters in the illustrations are depicted with unfurled scrolls coming from their mouths—some of the first caption bubbles.) The pages in the *Biblia Pauperum* showed how Old Testament events prefigured those in the New Testament. For example, an illustration of Jonah in the whale would be compared to Christ's entombment, or an illustration of the prophet Elijah ascending into heaven would be compared to Christ's ascension.

The *Biblia Pauperum* first appeared in southern Germany towards the end of the thirteenth century, and by the end of the next century, versions could be found throughout Western Europe. Although the best-known copies were produced with woodblock printing, the genre actually predates the age of print. For example, one of the earliest existing manuscript copies of the *Biblia Pauperum* was made near Vienna and dates from about 1325. The nine extant folios in this manuscript book contain seventeen drawings, some of which are colored. The earliest block-printed version still in existence dates from about 1455, and its woodblock illustrations closely resemble the earlier hand-drawn ones.

Although the title given them suggests that the *Biblia Pauperum* were intended for poor (or at least middle-income) people, scholars think they were more likely produced for clerics, who could use them to teach their parishioners. And at least some versions of the *Biblia Pauperum* were clearly made for very wealthy patrons. A copy in the British Library, dating from the beginning of the fifteenth century, features lavish illuminations in color and gold leaf. Believed to have been made in the Netherlands for Margaret of Cleves (c. 1375–1411), a noblewoman married to the Duke of Bavaria, this copy includes ninety-three miniatures, arranged in an unusual manner on pages folded in three and bound on the fold between the first and second (central) miniature on each page. Besides blocks of text that explain the illustrations, text in unfurled scrolls that wreathe around the illustrations provide either additional commentary or the words of the characters depicted in the miniatures.

To make the type itself, Gutenberg cut each letter on the end of a steel punch, then drove the punch into a bar of soft copper, creating a recessed image of the letter. Each copper-recessed image, or *matrix*, could then be secured at the bottom of a two-part steel box, or *mold*, that fitted together with space remaining for a column of metal leading to the recessed letter. Molten metal would be poured into the mold, which was then immediately given a firm shake to ensure that the metal filled every space evenly. When the metal cooled (which it did almost instantly), the mold would be opened and the individual piece of type ejected. This process had to

Portrait of Johannes Gutenberg.

be repeated for each letter in the alphabet, as well as for all the numerals and punctuation marks and for certain frequent letter combinations or *ligatures*, such as *fi* or *st*. The crucial aspect of Gutenberg's type-molds was that each finished letter or mark was of exactly the same height as all the others. This consistent *height-to-paper* ensured a uniform surface from which to print.

A complete set of type of one uniform size constitutes a *font*, and it would be sorted into specially constructed storage cases. Conventionally, type cases were arranged with all the *majuscules* or capital letters in the top section—the *upper case*—and the *minuscules* or small letters in the lower section—the *lower case*. A typical font would include just over seventy pieces of type, or *sorts*, in each individual compartment of the type case, with letters more commonly required (such as the *e*) generally stocked in greater quantities. Early printers used dozens of ligatures, which created much larger fonts than were common in later centuries.

To prepare a text for printing, the *typesetter* or *compositor* would select the required pieces of type from the case and place them in a *composing stick*, a small wooden (later metal) shelf that fit in the hand and could hold several rows of arranged type, depending on the size of the font being set. Because printing generates a mirror image of the object to be printed, in order to have the lines of text read top to bottom and from left to right, the typesetter would need to arrange, or *set*, the letters upside-down—in other words, the first word of the printed text would be set first into the bottom, left-most corner of the composing stick. Thin pieces of metal shorter than the type height would be inserted to create spaces between words. When the line neared its maximum length, the typesetter would decide where to hyphenate the last word, if necessary, and then insert additional spaces to *justify* the line, or align it evenly on both ends with the other lines of type. Finally, the compositor would insert a *lead*, a long, narrow piece of metal that leaves space between the lines and improves legibility, before continuing with the next line of type.

When the composing stick filled up, the compositor would *tie up* the finished lines of type with string and carefully transfer them to a tray called a *galley*. When all the text intended for one side of one sheet of paper had been set, the type would then be arranged or *imposed*, so that after the printed sheet was folded down in a planned sequence of folds, the pages would appear in proper order; combined with any illustrations; and "locked up" together firmly with wooden wedges in a frame called a *chase*. When the chase was transferred to the bed of the printing press, the resulting form was ready for printing.

As this description suggests, the work of setting type was every bit as onerous as that of manuscript copying. Both kinds of text creation entailed a high degree of fine motor coordination and intense and sustained concentration. Unless working from a particularly clear exemplar, both typesetters and scribes faced the challenge of deciphering unfamiliar handwriting. And if working in a language not familiar to them, both had to rely on careful,

"Imprimerie de Lettres (Printing of Letters)." From Denis Diderot and Jean le Rond d'Alembert's *Encyclopédie*.

letter-by-letter re-creation of the original. Additionally, the process of setting type by hand was not appreciably faster than copying by hand. A skilled compositor could set as many as 1,200 characters per hour, or about three pages per day, which compared to the low end of the scribe's rate of two to twenty finished pages per day. Unlike scribes, however, who could quickly clear away their materials when a project was completed, compositors also had to allot time for *distributing* their type, or sorting the pieces back into the correct compartments of the case. Finally, because of the fineness of the work, composing rooms, like scriptoria and scriveners' workshops, required ample natural light, and the workday could be curtailed by season or weather.

However, typesetting offered two major advantages over manuscript copying. First, mistakes in reproducing the exemplar were somewhat easier to correct, and because they could be caught at a preliminary stage, they did not entail damage to the materials of the final book. When a typeset form was complete, a *proof* page would be printed and checked by a *proofreader*. If errors or damaged letters were detected in the proof, the chase would be carefully loosened (a sometimes harrowing experience) and the text revised as required. Once corrected, any errors in the text remained corrected, so

TYPE DESIGN

The development of distinct, attractive, and legible type forms was a necessary complement to the development of printing technology. Just as calligraphy had developed over the centuries to suit the uses to which manuscripts were being put, type design also evolved with the expansion of printing and different readerships.

The first typefaces in Europe mimicked the handwritten scripts that were popularly used for particular kinds of books in the regions in which printing took hold. So, for example, the type that Gutenberg designed for his Bible was a *black letter*, or *Gothic*, form that imitated the *textura* script common in northern Europe from the twelfth century on. Black letter fonts are characterized by their angularity and height: the letters are formed by sharp straight lines, and the *ascenders*, the parts of the letters that rise above the *e*-height of the text, are usually quite vertical and the stroke endings are typically sharply marked. Partly because Gutenberg had used this style of font, black letter remained the preferred type style in Germany until the twentieth century. Because of its strong early association with Protestant texts, it was also regularly used in other Protestant countries, such as parts of the Netherlands, and in England until the seventeenth century.

New forms of type developed in Italy in the 1460s. Italian printers, who early concentrated on printing the secular texts that were fueling the Renaissance, wanted to distinguish their work from that being produced in the north. Since they were re-printing the works of Greek and Latin authors, they looked for models to the classical world. The new typefaces, based on the inscriptions in Roman monuments, came to be known as *roman*. The French engraver Nicholas Jenson (1420–80) is generally credited with developing the first popular roman type, and the works printed with his typefaces in Venice were greatly admired. Jenson's roman type featured distinctive and harmoniously arranged *serifs*, short lines extending from the upper and lower ends of the letters that enhanced their forms and improved legibility. (Typefaces that were designed without these lines are known as *sans serif*.) During the same period, the great Venetian printer and type designer Aldus Manutius (1449–1515) devised one of the first *italic* types. Based on a cursive script popular in manuscript copying, Manutius's italic font curved gently to the right. Condensed, space-efficient, but still highly legible, italics proved attractive and useful for printing scholarly humanist texts in a compact form. Manutius's Aldine Press became renowned for its beautiful editions, which combined elegant roman and italic types with sculptural and sym-metrical text blocks and illustrations noteworthy for their new Renaissance features of perspective and secular ornamentation.

Further innovation in type design occurred in the sixteenth century. Renaissance printers valued balance and proportion in the arrangement of the printed page, and types were designed with those principles in mind. Claude Garamond (c. 1480–1567) is credited with creating what became the preferred typefaces for both French and English secular printing, a roman letterform that was

Aa	Aa	𝕬𝖆	Aa	Aa	Aa
Aa	*Aa*	Aa	Aa	Aa	Aa

Font table.

particularly clean and legible, even in small sizes. A type punch cutter who managed to work independently from the printers who secured his services, Garamond was among the first to combine roman and italic fonts, convincing printers that the forms could work harmoniously together. His type design became the official font of the French Royal Printing Office, and in 1541 he was commissioned by François I (1494–1597) to design a Greek typeface, which became known as *grecs du roi*, the "king's Greek." After his death, his punches became the property of the Plantin printing concern in Antwerp, which helped to further disseminate and popularize his type designs.

Another notable type designer was the English engraver William Caslon (1692–1766). His roman typefaces were inspired by Dutch Baroque models, which were popular in England up to his time, and featured short ascenders and descenders and very rounded letter forms. His typefaces were quickly adopted by printers on the Continent and in the American colonies, and among the many important texts printed with a Caslon font was the printed version of the Declaration of Independence. Building on his success as a type designer, Caslon established what became one of the largest type foundries in England, which remained in business and mostly still in family hands until the twentieth century.

Among Caslon's admirers was his countryman John Baskerville (1706–75). A printer based in Birmingham, Baskerville was responsible for a number of important innovations in paper and ink, as well as type design. His serifed Baskerville font provides a transition between the older style fonts like Caslon and the new fonts of the dawning industrial age, such as those created by the Italian designer Giambattista Bodoni (1740–1831). Baskerville's fonts, like Bodoni's, featured thinner and finer strokes than some of the earlier type styles, and they marked the final departure from type inspired by pen-formed letters. Baskerville's fonts instead emphasized a machine-made precision and a vertical axis. Baskerville was also noted for adding additional *leading* (space) between lines and for increasing the margins, which created a whiter, more inviting book page. Baskerville's typefaces were widely used, including by fellow printer Benjamin Franklin (1706–90), who selected them to print the papers of the new US federal government.

careful proofreading could ensure that finished books contained minimal errors. Second, and most important, a completed form could be used to print hundreds, even thousands, of copies of a given page, whereas the scribe's work generated only one unique copy.

Movable, reusable metal type was a brilliant innovation, but it presented one major problem. Traditional inks, which were water-based, did not adhere to metal: instead, they beaded up and ran down the sides of the typefaces. Gutenberg's second key invention, then, had to be a form of ink that would work with his new technological advance. The solution was fairly straightforward: by using oil as the base, rather than water, Gutenberg was able to create a thick, tarlike "sticky" ink similar in makeup to the oil-based paints used in fifteenth-century Flemish painting. The oil-based ink adhered to the typefaces and transferred cleanly to parchment or paper.

But there was a further complication. The traditional method for applying water-based ink to print surfaces was to paint it on with a brush, but the thick, sticky ink defied this technique. To solve the application problem, Gutenberg devised wooden-handled leather balls filled with wool. The balls would first be rocked or pounded on an *ink-stone* (an impermeable surface, typically stone, spread with ink like a palette) until the ink was evenly spread across the leather surface. Then the balls were rocked or pounded in a rotating pattern onto the printing surface, until the ink had transferred evenly to the form. When the form was brought into contact with a slightly dampened sheet of paper, the result was a clean, even, dark impression—easy to read, and also enduring.

The Common Press

Gutenberg's press almost seems anticlimactic after the brilliance of his other inventions, but he combined existing technologies in such a way as to make it possible to print much more quickly and reliably than ever before. The key to the common press is the screw. Screw-presses had been employed to press juices, oils, and fabrics for hundreds of years. They allowed broad, heavy forces to be brought to bear on the items being squeezed, getting more liquid (or air) out of the item than wringing or squeezing by hand would allow.

Gutenberg knew the traditional method of block printing for either paper or cloth: the material to be printed was laid by hand on the inked surface and carefully rubbed, often with some kind of tool, to transfer the image. The printed item was then carefully lifted off the surface, and the process began again. If the printer was very skilled, the resulting impression was clean and clear. But even the most skilled printers would vary the pressure they applied to different areas of the printing surface. A screw-press would ensure that even and controlled pressure—enough to drive the printing surface slightly into the paper, but not enough to flatten the relatively soft lead type—was applied across a large surface in one steady action, so that the resulting impression would be reliably clean and clear, time after time.

With that basic principle in mind, everything else falls into place. The screw-press is the heart of the common press. A lever attached to the screw enables the press operator to stand to the side of the press and bring the large, heavy pressing surface (the *platen*) down to make the impression. To make it easier to position the form under the platen and bring it back again, Gutenberg devised a sliding mechanism to move the printing bed. To ensure that the paper or parchment to be printed was always positioned in exactly the same spot, Gutenberg devised the *tympan*, a parchment-covered frame connected by a hinge to the front of the bed. Small pins in the tympan hold the paper in the proper position. Another parchment-covered hinged frame, the *frisket*, then folds over the tympan. The frisket has windows cut out to expose the paper only to the inked areas to be printed, protecting the margins from stray ink.

Printing on a common press involved a neatly choreographed set of steps, performed by a press operator and ideally two assistants or apprentices. (Apprentices were sometimes referred to as *printer's devils*.) Once the form was in place on the press, one assistant would position a dampened sheet of paper on the tympan, while the pressman applied the ink to the form. The second assistant, standing on the far side of the press from the operator, would fold the frisket down over the tympan, lower the tympan onto the form, and slide the assembly under the platen, while the operator pulled the lever back to bring the platen down to meet it. After making the impression, the operator would push the lever forward, raising the platen, and the second assistant would slide the bed back to the end of the press and lift the frisket. The first assistant would remove the printed sheet and insert a blank one, and then would hang the printed sheet to dry while the process began again. An experienced team could pull as many as 240 impressions per hour.

Although there would be many refinements over the next four centuries, Gutenberg's design remained the basis for printing technology until the nineteenth century. Succeeding generations of printers tweaked the mechanisms in some important ways, all of which increased the ease of use and efficiency of operation of the basic common press. For example, a spring was added to the pressing mechanism, so that the press operator didn't have to both raise and lower the platen: after pulling the lever, the operator could simply release it, and the spring would reverse the screw to lift the platen. This device significantly reduced the strain on the operator, as pulling with gravity is much easier than pushing against it. Another key innovation was to lengthen the printing bed so that it extended to both sides of the platen. By adding a second form and tympan assembly at the far end, the press could work twice as fast: assistants would replace the paper and re-ink the form at one end of the press while an impression was being pulled in the middle, then the bed would slide to the far end so that the process could be repeated there while the next impression was pulled.

In addition to refinements in the mechanisms, new materials were also integrated into the press. New methods using rollers were also developed to ink the forms more efficiently, and in the late eighteenth to early nineteenth

Gutenberg Bible (detail). Bridwell Library Special Collections, Perkins School of Theology, Southern Methodist University.

centuries, cast iron gradually replaced many of the wood fittings on the press, as iron was stronger and more enduring. With stronger materials, even more impressions could be made per hour.

Many people who know little about Gutenberg's inventions have at least heard of his greatest publication, the *Gutenberg Bible*. The Gutenberg Bible was the first complete printed book from a Gutenberg press, and it was an enormous achievement. The Gutenberg Bible was carefully designed to look like a traditionally produced manuscript copy of the Bible, with the size and arrangement of the pages, type, and ornamentation all echoing familiar formats. Some of the earliest copies were even printed on vellum, rather than on paper. The careful attention to design and to the other book arts of typesetting, printing, and binding helped to ensure that printed books would be as sought after as their handwritten predecessors.

Another important production from Gutenberg's own print shop was a 1457 Latin Psalter, which was the first printed book to include a colophon with information about the printer, place, and date of publication. The Psalter was notable not only as a Gutenberg publication, but also because it was printed in two colors (black and red). The *register*, or alignment, between the two colors on the page is so good that scholars have concluded it almost certainly could not have been made from running the forms through the press in two separate passes. Instead, they believe that the Psalter was printed from two-piece engraved plates. The two pieces were inked separately, then fitted together and run through the press to make a single, two-color impression.

THE GUTENBERG BIBLE

The first complete letterpressed book, the *Gutenberg Bible* is also among the most impressive. Also known as the *Mazarin Bible*—after Cardinal Jules Mazarin (1602–61), the great book collector and owner of a particularly splendid copy of the Gutenberg Bible—or the *forty-two-line Bible* (for its forty-two lines of text per page), the Gutenberg Bible was an edition of the Vulgate. Begun in about 1450, the Bible was finally printed in early 1456 in two volumes.

Gutenberg paid close attention to the material qualities of his Bible. The forty-two-line Bible was designed to look like a traditionally produced manuscript copy of the Bible, with the size and arrangement of the pages, the type, and the ornamentation all echoing familiar formats. On one level, this made perfect sense: to Gutenberg's contemporaries, this is what a Bible looked like. But on another level, the careful attention to design can also be seen as a savvy strategic move. Gutenberg did not want his wares to be deemed "cheap" and thus inferior to manuscript books.

Initially, Gutenberg experimented with printing the Bibles in two colors (black and red), which required two passes through the press for each page. However, later copies were printed in black only, with space left on the pages for hand rubrication. (Some surviving copies are missing some or all of their rubrics.) The text was arranged in two columns with generous margins, on sheets of paper that were folded once in half to make two-leaf, four-page folios. Typically, each gathering or signature contained five of these folded sheets nested together.

Producing the Gutenberg Bible involved a tremendous amount of capital and labor. Historian Stephen Füssel has estimated that it must have taken at least six months simply to cast the over 100,000 pieces of type required for typesetting, and another two years for the typesetting itself. Initially, four compositors were working on the project; later as many as six were engaged. At the height of production, up to twelve printers and six presses were in use. The total print run—thought to be about 180 copies—of 1,282 pages each would have involved over 230,000 passes through the press, requiring at least 330 working days. However, as Füssel observes, a scribe would have worked up to three whole years on a single copy of the Bible. Gutenberg's press produced 180 copies in less than that amount of time.

Although printing made the Gutenberg Bible less expensive than a manuscript version of comparable size and splendor, it was still extremely expensive. Thus, only one copy is thought to have been privately owned in the fifteenth century. The other copies were purchased by churches, monastic communities, and universities.

About twenty complete copies of the Gutenberg Bible are still extant, and partial versions of as many as fifty. Most of the Bibles are in Germany, the United States, and the United Kingdom. There are also many fragments and stray leaves from Gutenberg Bibles in collections around the world.

The usefulness of Gutenberg's inventions was recognized immediately. Within just a few years of Gutenberg's launching his own business, printing shops opened across northern Europe. By the early 1470s, there were printers in virtually every country in Europe, with important printing centers established in Venice, Augsburg, Nuremberg, Basel, and Antwerp. During the first fifty to sixty years of printing, up to the year 1500, more than 30,000 books were published that are still traceable today, and we can assume there were others that have disappeared. These *incunabula*—the name given to the first generations of printed books—vary dramatically in size, length, and content. Nearly 80 per cent are in Latin, reflecting both the ongoing influence of the Roman Catholic Church and the adoption of Latin as the lingua franca of humanistic scholarship during the Renaissance. Among the remaining 20 per cent is a wide range of textbooks and of popular books, including many examples of *romances* or *historia*, tales that creatively combined elements of fact and fancy in page-turning ways. In addition to these book-length publications, there were also thousands of pieces of *ephemera*, items such as posters, news-sheets or broadsides, and certificates, that were produced for commercial, social, or religious purposes. Intended for one-time or short-term use, most of these were soon discarded, but the surviving examples give a clear idea of the inventiveness to which the new printing technology was put.

The many new books being printed in this era shared some basic characteristics of construction, even though there were important regional and local distinctions among them that have sometimes helped scholars to identify precisely when and where a book was printed, even if the title page does not provide that information. One of the most important commonalities was size or format, which was determined by the size of the sheets of paper the printer used. Although some printing projects—like broadsides—took up an entire side of a sheet of paper, books were made of sheets that were folded in predictable ways, with a larger number of folds yielding an increasingly smaller eventual page size. A sheet folded only once, to create two leaves, resulted in a *folio* size book. (This book size is also sometimes referred to as a *bifolium*.) A sheet folded twice, to create four leaves, resulted in a *quarto*. A sheet folded three times, to create eight leaves, resulted in an *octavo*. These descriptions of format—folio, quarto, and octavo—have remained constant, even though the actual dimensions of the pages they reflect have changed significantly over the centuries.

In order to construct a book, printers would stack a number of printed and folded sheets into *gatherings* or *quires*. A folio size book might contain as many as five sheets in a gathering; quartos generally would have only one or two; and octavos might have only one. To ensure that the finished book would be assembled in the right order, printers used a number of techniques. First, they would carefully determine the *imposition* of the pages, which involved planning how each sheet would be printed so that when it was folded the pages would appear in the right order. Next, they would assign a letter to each quire and a number to each sheet in the quire, so that it would be clear to the bookbinder how they were to be assembled. Some books would also employ *catchwords*, words typeset at the bottom of the last page in a quire indicating the first word in the next quire. This would provide another aid to ensure that the book was assembled correctly.

In one of the great ironies of history, Gutenberg was thought not to have profited from his own innovations. In 1455, his business partner Johann Fust sued him for nonpayment of loans, and Gutenberg's subsequent declaration of bankruptcy was long thought to be the end of his printing career. However, more recent examinations of the court documents show that Gutenberg was ultimately able to pay Fust and to regain possession of the printing equipment that Fust had held as surety on the loans. It is thought that after he dissolved his business with Fust, Gutenberg established a new printing business with Berthold Ruppel and Heinrich Kefer, who continued printing in Mainz after Gutenberg's death.

THE PRESS AND THE REFORMATION

At about the same time that Gutenberg was experimenting with type and his press, voices within the Roman Catholic Church were urging reform of some practices that both clergy and the laity found difficult to support. Critics complained that the Church paid more attention to an outward show of moral behavior than to inward belief and morality. Practices such as *indulgences*, documents that were said to reduce the time that a soul would spend in Purgatory after death, and which could be earned by performing such tasks as going on pilgrimages or be purchased outright, caused some critics to suspect that the Church hierarchy was more interested in accumulating wealth than in leading the faithful.

Although such criticisms had been directed from time to time at both the institution of the Church and particular clerics, matters came to a head in Wittenberg in 1517, when priest and professor of theology Martin Luther (1483–1546) composed a list of ninety-five theses, or propositions for debate, aimed at the practice of selling indulgences and Church positions. In later writings, Luther urged that religious practice must be grounded in individual faith, which could lead to a recognition of God's love and forgiveness and to salvation through God's grace. Faith, not pious deeds such as going on pilgrimages, was the only route to salvation. Printed and disseminated by the new printing industry, Luther's arguments for reform and ideas about the refocusing of Christian practice spread throughout Europe, sparking debate and ultimately the formation of a new branch of Christianity, Protestantism.

Luther's ideas would become central to the formation of the Lutheran church in northern Germany and in the Scandinavian countries. In southern Germany and Switzerland, as well as in France, Protestantism was largely shaped by the teachings of John Calvin (1509–64), a former priest. Calvin took

Luther's ideas one step forward: if humans could not earn salvation through their own efforts, for example, through good deeds, then they also could never be certain of salvation. Only God knew who was among the *elect*, or those chosen for salvation, and that status was foreordained, or *predestined*. Although individuals could not know whether they were among the elect, it was incumbent upon them to live as though they were, shaping their daily lives through prayer and strict adherence to the authority of what Calvin's followers called the *Reformed church*.

Yet another group of reformers, the Anabaptists, also broke from the established Church. Less centralized than some of the other emerging strands of Protestantism, what unified the Anabaptists, or "re-baptizers," was their dissent from the practice of infant baptism. The Anabaptists believed that only adults who freely chose to follow Christ's teachings could be baptized into the community of believers. The Anabaptists also sought to simplify their religious life and practice, taking their guidelines primarily from the Sermon on the Mount, the teachings of Jesus recorded in the Gospel of Matthew. Because of their particular view of baptism and other practices, Anabaptists were suspected and persecuted by both the Roman Catholic Church and other Protestant sects.

Finally, yet another form of Protestantism was launched in Britain. The English king Henry VIII (1491–1547), distressed by the failure of his wife, Catherine of Aragon (1485–1536), to provide him with a male heir—the couple's only surviving child was a girl, later Mary I—sought to have their marriage annulled, so that he could marry again. When then-reigning Pope Clement VII (1478–1534) refused to declare the marriage invalid, Henry resolved to take matters into his own hands. Between 1529 and 1536 the English Parliament passed a number of acts that separated the Church of England from that of Rome. The king was established as the head of the Anglican church, his marriage to Catherine was dissolved, and his subsequent marriage to Anne Boleyn (c. 1501–36) was authorized. (Ironically, Anne's sole surviving child was also a girl, later Elizabeth I.)

The Reformation—and the subsequent Counter-Reformation, the internal reforms undertaken by the Catholic Church—fueled an enormous increase in printing in the sixteenth century. Not only did the debates over proper religious practice generate furious rounds of broadsides, pamphlets, and books, but as the new churches became established they required new liturgical and devotional materials. And because of Protestantism's emphasis on individual knowledge of the Scriptures, it also generated a dramatic increase in Bible translation into the European vernacular languages.

Printing and the Protestant Churches

The Protestant Reformation not only had a major impact on religious beliefs and practices and on the European political map, but it also had a significant effect on book history. In her classic work on the printing revolution, Elizabeth

Eisenstein notes that Protestantism was the first movement to exploit printing's potential as a mass medium, using it to excoriate Rome and to support its own points of view. While many of the religious and political publications of the age could be viciously biased and hyperbolic, Protestants also saw the elevating potential of the printing press. Luther described printing as an important sign of God's grace, enabling the spread of the gospel.

The Protestant reformers insisted that individual believers had to come to their own understanding of and relationship to God, without the mediating influence of the priesthood. In order to achieve this, the faithful needed to be able to read the Scriptures for themselves. This meant that individuals not only required ready access to Bibles, but that those Bibles needed to be in the vernacular languages, so that they were easier to read and understand. Across Europe, printers began the enormous task of producing the required quantities of vernacular Bibles. Gutenberg's edition of the Vulgate had set a high standard for printed Bible design and production, and many of the vernacular editions would imitate it by echoing earlier manuscript precedents.

The first major achievement in vernacular Bible printing was Martin Luther's translation, which was begun in 1522 and published as a complete text by Hans Lufft in Wittenberg in 1534. Although there were at least eighteen German-language Bibles in circulation before Luther's, most of these contained inferior, awkward translations from the Latin. Luther's was one of the first complete translations directly from the original Hebrew and Greek into the vernacular, and it served as a model for translations into other languages. It was almost instantaneously popular. More than 300 editions of Luther's translation, amounting to half a million copies, were published between 1522 and 1546. Indeed, Luther may very well have been the first bestselling print author: when other theological writings are factored in, scholars have estimated that as many as a third of all books produced in German in the first half of the sixteenth century were works by Luther.

The care taken with the printing of the vernacular Bible in Germany was repeated with other languages in printshops across Europe. A partial translation of the Bible into English had been made in the fourteenth century by John Wycliffe (c. 1330–84). However, the first important and widely read English translations were by William Tyndale (c. 1494–1536). Portions of his translations were printed in the 1520s and 1530s, but they were produced in Germany and in the Netherlands rather than in England. After the deaths of the Protestant kings Henry VIII and his son Edward VI, Edward's sister Mary I (1516–58) had reestablished Roman Catholicism as the official religion of England. This meant that printing and circulating a vernacular Bible was deemed to be an act of heresy, punishable by death. Although Tyndale himself was eventually tried and executed as a heretic, others continued the work of translating and disseminating the Bible in English. When Elizabeth I (1533–1603) reestablished and regularized the Church of England in 1559, these efforts were renewed. By the end of the sixteenth century, at least three separate English translations of the Bible were in general circulation, some based on translations from the original Hebrew and Greek, others based on translations from the Latin, and still others based on translations from Luther's German edition.

The ascension of King James I (1566–1625) in 1603 prompted calls for a new, official translation of the Bible into English. James organized a network of scholars and theologians who worked in small groups at the universities in Oxford and Cambridge and in the religious and civil center of Westminster in London. As drafts of different sections were submitted by the working groups, they were reviewed and reconciled by a central committee. The complete edition of the *King James Bible*, or *Authorized Version*, was issued in 1611. To maintain control of the text and its publication, only specially licensed printers were allowed to produce copies. The first copies were printed by Robert Barker, the King's Printer, and later editions were issued by the London printers Bonham Norton and John Bill. However, by 1629 the universities at Oxford and Cambridge had successfully wrested control of the license to print the Authorized Version, a privilege they maintain to the present day. The Authorized Version has remained in continual use since, with only minor updates. Because of the reach and influence of the British Empire in the intervening centuries, it lays claim to being one of the most widely circulated and influential books in history.

Printing and the Catholic Church

Although the links between the Reformation and the press are often made, printing also became an important concern of the Roman Catholic Church. In those regions of Europe that remained tied to the Catholic Church, printers were licensed to produce works for official Church use. These works ranged from book-length texts such as Bibles, missals, and theological studies, to a variety of ephemera, from baptismal and pilgrimage certificates to indulgences and attendance registers. (Gutenberg's own press printed many of these kinds of ephemera.) Especially in large parishes or at popular pilgrimage sites, preprinted forms and registers represented a significant savings of time and labor for overworked clerics. But they also represented a meaningful form of testimonial—or even just a souvenir—for the faithful to keep and display.

But in addition to licensing printers to produce official texts, the Church also moved to prevent printers from producing and circulating certain texts, especially those deemed *heretical*, or contrary to Church doctrine. Until authorized translations were prepared for circulation, vernacular versions of the Bible were among those works that found their way on to the official list of banned books, the *Index Librorum Prohibitorum*. The Church allowed vernacular versions of the Scriptures to be read by clergy and laypeople who were deemed sufficiently pious and learned to interpret them along orthodox lines, but the question of who might be included in that category of authorized readers was not fully resolved until the nineteenth century. However, Pope Benedict XIV (1675–1758) did specify that versions of the vernacular read by members of the laity should be approved by the Holy See (or at least enhanced with notes by learned Catholic scholars) before circulation, and this helped to increase the publication and circulation of vernacular Bibles in Catholic communities in the early eighteenth century.

However, in the sixteenth century printers in Catholic regions were not only forbidden to print and circulate these books, but they were also required to prominently display the list of prohibited books to warn all would-be readers. A copy of the *Index* of 1569 can still be seen on the wall next to the entry door of the Plantin-Moretus printing house in Antwerp—although a history of the firm suggests that many of the forbidden titles were in fact available for discreet sale to discerning customers. The *Inquisition*, the office of the Church charged with detecting and eliminating heresy, could order the withholding and destruction of dangerous books, as it notoriously did in 1616 in the case of the astronomer Galileo Galilei (1564–1642). Galileo's claim that the earth revolved around the sun was counter to official Church teaching. The Inquisition was also responsible for Bishop de Landa's decision to burn all the Mayan codices in 1562 (see Chapter 1).

In order to better control what could be safely printed and circulated, the Church relied on the *Congregation of the Index*, a department of official censors who were responsible for reviewing all works submitted for possible publication. If the censors approved the work, the printer was presented with a special certificate that licensed it for distribution; if rejected, the work either had to be revised in accordance with Church guidelines or withheld. The lists of permitted and prohibited books were regularly updated and enforced, at least to some extent, until 1966.

Although the Catholic Church played an important role in the early censorship of printed books, the Church was certainly not the only institution to see the potential dangers of easily produced and circulated materials. Many other authorities, both religious and civil, also enacted regulations and empowered censors to try to contain the potentially revolutionary force of the printing press. Indeed, because of its ongoing, critical importance in the history of the book, the role of censorship is discussed in greater detail in Chapter 6.

THE EXPANSION OF PRINT CULTURE

Despite efforts to slow it, print proved an unstoppable force. Having spread across Europe in only a few decades, printing presses also found their way to the Americas shortly after permanent colonies were established. Juan Pablos (c. 1500–60), a native Italian, began printing in Mexico in 1539. In the centuries between the invention of the common press and the major changes that occurred in the wake of the industrial revolution, the history of print culture was primarily one of an expansion and sophistication of books and readerships.

Among the notable developments were efforts to catalogue the world's knowledge, through reference works such as encyclopedias and dictionaries, and the general increase in pleasure reading. Also important was the rise of the *periodical*, a category of print that includes newspapers and other kinds of regularly published items, including magazines or *miscellanies*, that keep readers abreast of events and of currents of thought and taste. Along the way, the production and dissemination of books became increasingly specialized, not just in terms of the kinds of works that were produced by individual printing firms, but also in terms of what different individuals and institutions did.

THE OFFICINA PLANTINIANA

One of the most successful early printers was Christopher Plantin (c. 1520–89), whose Golden Compasses in Antwerp was one of the largest and most influential printing houses in the sixteenth and seventeenth centuries. Born in Tours, France, and originally trained as a bookbinder, Plantin moved to Antwerp in about 1550 and established a print shop, the Officina Plantiniana, in 1555. By 1563, he had built a reputation as an industrious, ambitious printer and had gained the support of a collection of wealthy financiers. He expanded his operations, purchasing a number of additional presses, and within a few years was printing as many as 260 publications, ranging from editions of Greek and Latin classics to Hebrew Bibles and liturgical works to scientific treatises.

Much of Plantin's success can be attributed to his successful navigation of the dangerous waters of sixteenth-century religious controversies. Although Belgium was under Spanish—Catholic—rule, there were quite a few Calvinists in Antwerp, and some of Plantin's backers seem to have been Protestants. To reassure the Catholic Church of his loyalty, Plantin conceived a grand scheme that he was sure would appeal to the Spanish king Philip II (1527–98): a massive scholarly edition of the Bible in five languages. The *Antwerp Polyglot* (also known as the *Biblia Regia*, or "King's Bible") was published between 1568 and 1573 in eight volumes. Supervised by the Spanish theologian Benito Arias Montano (1527–98), the first six volumes displayed the Scriptures mostly in side-by-side translations, including Hebrew, Latin, Greek, Aramaic, and Syriac texts (requiring typesetters to work in different alphabets). The last two volumes included dictionaries, grammars, and other resources necessary to Bible scholars.

Even before the edition was finished, its undertaking earned Plantin the honorary title of *architypographus*, or arch-typographer to the king of Spain. In 1571 this translated to a more practical reward: a virtual printing monopoly on all mass-produced religious books in Spain, including missals and breviaries. Plantin expanded his printing house again, employing twenty compositors, thirty-two

Where early printers such as Gutenberg also commissioned works and sold the resulting products to their customers, over the ensuing centuries the processes of commissioning or securing works, printing, and selling them became separate. By the middle of the nineteenth century, the elements of the modern publishing world were in place.

Printing and the Enlightenment

The Enlightenment, unlike many eras in history, is said to have begun with a particular, specific event: the publication of a book. The *Principia Mathematica*, or *Mathematical Principles of Natural Philosophy*, by the English scientist Isaac

printers, three proofreaders, and other sales and administrative staff in a facility with at least sixteen and possibly as many as twenty-two printing presses. According to historian Francine de Nave, the firm's production record would not be broken until the industrialization of printing in the nineteenth century.

Plantin was a pragmatist: when political upheaval brought Antwerp briefly under Protestant governance, he quietly continued his support for the Catholic Church, even while printing anti-Spanish pamphlets and books. He even became the official printer to the Protestant States General in 1578 and to the Calvinist town council in 1579. In 1582, when Plantin realized that if the Spanish reasserted control over Antwerp he might lose his business, he cannily set up a second printing house in the university town of Leiden, to which he briefly relocated. His Leiden business specialized in scientific publishing and bookselling.

The printing house established by Christopher Plantin continued for nearly 300 years, run by his daughters and their descendents. Plantin's son-in-law Jan Moretus (1543–1610) became one of the most important printers of the Counter-Reformation, specializing in liturgical and devotional works, and Jan and Martina's son Balthasar (1574–1641) expanded and redecorated the firm's buildings to their present Baroque grandeur.

The Officina maintained its reputation for producing high-quality, lavishly illustrated books for both the Church and secular scholars until 1764, when king Carlos III (1716–88) withdrew the royal privileges of all non-Spanish printers. The loss of such a significant source of revenue placed the firm on a precarious footing from which it never recovered. When industrialization changed both the pace of publication and the public's tastes in print, the Officina Plantiniana could no longer compete, and it printed its last book in 1866. Ten years later, the last owner, Edward Moretus (1804–80), sold the entire estate to the city of Antwerp and the state of Belgium, and it became the Plantin-Moretus Museum. It is now a UNESCO World Heritage site and recognized as one of the premier sources of information on European printing history.

Newton (1642–1727), details the basic laws of physics. The book was deemed so important by the astronomer Edmond Halley (1656–1742), a friend of Newton's and a fellow member of the Royal Society, that Halley determined to have it printed for the Society at his own expense. The publication of the *Principia* in 1687 was a watershed in human understanding of the way the universe was ordered. As Newton's contemporary, the poet Alexander Pope (1688–1744), put it:

> Nature and nature's laws
> Lay hid in night.
> God said, "Let Newton be,"
> And all was light.

Newton's great book was the first of many major scholarly texts published during the seventeenth and eighteenth centuries. What distinguished the works of this era was not only their erudition, but the relative rapidity with which they circulated. Where previous generations had to wait for months, years, or even decades to gain access to manuscript copies of important works, the age of print meant that books and important periodicals such as the Royal Society's *Philosophical Transactions* could be circulated to networks of interested readers simultaneously, who could then read, digest, and comment on them while they were still fresh. This inevitably spurred debate, revision, and further innovation while the insights were still new and helped to drive an intensification of inquiry, discovery, and application. Some historians jokingly attribute the blossoming of scientific and philosophical inquiry during the Enlightenment to the stimulus of caffeine, since coffee, tea, and chocolate were all introduced into Europe at this period. Caffeine perhaps played a role—but the printing press was a much more important stimulant.

Encylopedists and Lexicographers

As both the number of books and literacy rates continued to increase, readers and writers began to seek more systematic approaches to the burgeoning amount of words that surrounded them. Among the many important books published during the Enlightenment were those that sought to systematize knowledge. One of the grandest and most influential projects was the French *Encyclopédie*, published in twenty-eight volumes between 1750 and 1780. The *Encylopédie* began as a translation of an earlier, and much more modest, English book. By the time it was completed, it had become a repository of Enlightenment ideas and information, reflecting much of what was known and thought in the eighteenth century.

If the *Encyclopédie* looked at knowledge and the world through a wide-angled lens, dictionaries brought the focus in tight, to the basic elements of language. The eighteenth century saw the publication of a number of important dictionaries, works that were made both necessary and possible by print

L'ENCYLOPÉDIE

L'Encyclopédie, ou dictionnaire raisonné des sciences, des arts et des métiers—in English, "The Encyclopedia, or a Systematic Dictionary of the Sciences, Arts and Crafts"—was published in twenty-eight volumes between 1750 and 1780. Edited by French scholars Denis Diderot (1713–84) and Jean le Rond d'Alembert (1717–83), the *Encyclopédie* sought to encapsulate all of the knowledge of the Enlightenment and to present it in a clear and organized fashion to readers. Encyclopedias of one form or another had been in existence for centuries, with one of the earliest, Pliny the Elder's *Naturalis historia*, or *Natural History*, dating from about CE 77. Pliny's text included thirty-seven books, covering mathematics, natural sciences, and many kinds of arts and crafts.

Title page from Denis Diderot and Jean le Rond d'Alembert's *Encyclopédie.*

The *Encyclopédie* sought to update the genre for the modern age, and the editors commissioned experts to write signed articles on particular subjects. Contributors included some of the most renowned scholars of their time, including Voltaire, Rousseau, and Montesquieu, and the carefully crafted texts were accompanied by over 3,000 illustrations. (The illustrated plates themselves accounted for eleven volumes.) A later, expanded edition, issued by the publisher Charles-Joseph Panckoucke (1736–98) between 1782 and 1832 under the title *Encyclopédie méthodique*, was even more monumental, involving more than 2,000 contributors and requiring over a thousand workers to produce the 166 volumes.

In his preface to the earlier version, d'Alembert explained that what the *Encyclopédie* hoped to encompass was a complete "genealogical tree of the arts and sciences," or a "*Mappe-monde*." The *Système figuré des connaissances humaines*, or "Figurative System of Human Knowledge," was depicted with three main branches: memory (history), reason (philosophy), and imagination (poetry, or the arts more generally). Readers of the *Encyclopédie* would not only learn about the particular topics they looked up, but they would also learn to see them in a vast schema of human knowledge and achievements.

Critics of the *Encyclopédie* included the Catholic Church, which disapproved of the avowed secularism of some of the entries and the stated support for Protestant ideas in others, and political conservatives, who later blamed the reference book for helping foment the French Revolution. That it had the potential to be widely influential is certain: in a world in which the predominant language of politics and diplomacy was French, the *Encyclopédie* was also one of the largest printing projects of the age, with an extraordinary print run of over 4,000 copies.

culture. In the first century or so of print, spelling and usage were relatively free-form with regard to the vernacular languages, as they had been in scribal culture. Writers did their best to use standard (or at least comprehensible) *orthography*, or spelling, but variants were many and generally well tolerated. (Latin, with a longer and more established literature and grammar, remained fixed.) Especially in writings that were circulated in manuscript among groups of friends or family, it was relatively easy to work out a particular writer's style of expression. However, when texts began to circulate in print, among wider networks of readers, ambiguities were less well tolerated. Individual printing houses began to impose some order on the orthography and punctuation of the texts they set and printed. They regularized spellings, abbreviations, and punctuation usage, and they devised rules to govern when and where it was acceptable to break words across columns or pages. Both within and across texts, they hoped to provide a predictable regularity that would at the very

JOHNSON'S DICTIONARY

Samuel Johnson (1709–84) had already made a name for himself as a writer when the opportunity to compile the first comprehensive English dictionary was put before him. Although other English dictionaries were in print, recent foreign language dictionaries—most notably those produced in French and Italian—put the existing English ones to shame. A group of printers and booksellers banded together to underwrite what they knew would be the substantial costs of producing an English language dictionary that could stand up to the foreign competition.

Johnson had turned down an earlier opportunity to write a dictionary, but after struggling with his finances for years, he must have found the sum of 1,500 guineas offered to him in 1746 too good to refuse. He estimated it would take him three years to complete. In the end it took him three times as long—but still significantly less time, working

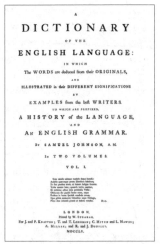

Title page from the second edition of *A Dictionary of the English Language* by Samuel Johnson, 1755.

largely on his own, than it had taken forty members of the *Académie Française* to compile its monumental dictionary, which had first appeared in 1694. In his Preface to the *Dictionary*, Johnson notes that he had looked forward with some relish to "the hours which I should revel away in feasts of literature" and to the "obscure recesses of northern learning which I should enter and ransack." He set up operation in the top of his house at 17 Gough Street in London, hired a few assistants whom he paid ten shillings a week, and started work.

least not distract readers from the matters at hand, and at best please them because of the careful cleanness of the prose.

The regularization of printed texts in turn began to exert a pressure on writers to conform to the best practices. One of the earliest movements to establish governing principles for vernacular languages was the *Académie Française*, established in 1635 by Cardinal Richelieu (1585–1642) for the express purpose of regulating the French language, a role it continues to exercise today. In England, an early consequence of the overall concern about correctness was a reconsideration of the rules of English grammar and spelling. Seventeenth- and early eighteenth-century grammarians looked closely at the structure of classical Latin—considered the most elegant and developed European language—and decided that English was debased. To bring English more into line with Latin grammar, and to call more attention to the noble Latin and Greek roots of many English words, they advocated changes that continue

According to historian Alvin Kernan, Johnson devised a production method to streamline the process of entry-writing. He would read books for examples of words and usage, underline the words to be included in the *Dictionary*, and mark the passages to be used for context and definitions. He would then write the first letter of the entry in the margin. His assistants would copy out the passages, sort them, and paste them together in the proper order when the entry was complete. In an effort to keep their costs down, Johnson and his assistants for a while tried to generate the copy text on both sides of the sheets of paper, only to be forced to recopy those pages when the compositor refused to work from double-sided text. The publishers also tried to reduce their costs, by eliminating some of Johnson's illustrative quotations and even entire entries from his manuscript.

When it was finally done, the *Dictionary* contained about 40,000 entries and 114,000 illustrative quotations, comprising more than 2,500 pages of double-column text in two volumes. Besides the main body of the text, there was also Johnson's Preface, a history of the English language, and an essay on English grammar. The initial print run was 2,000 copies, and its author was soon renowned as "Dictionary Johnson."

As might be expected of a reference work compiled by one individual, Johnson's *Dictionary* was sometimes idiosyncratic, but often charmingly so. His famous definition of a *lexicographer* as "a writer of dictionaries; a harmless drudge that busies himself in tracing the original, and detailing the signification of words" gives a taste of his sense of humor, as does his definition of *oats*, "A grain, which in England is generally given to horses, but in Scotland appears to support the people"—a wry dig at his friend and biographer, the Scot James Boswell (1740–95). Johnson's *Dictionary* definitely filled a need, remaining in print and constantly popular until the early twentieth century, when it was finally supplanted by the magisterial multivolume *Oxford English Dictionary*.

to haunt would-be careful practitioners of English. Latin sentences did not end with prepositions; therefore, English sentences should not do so either. Latin did not employ double negatives; English should not do so either. These decrees were not only contrary to age-old practice in English, including in the works of some of the most highly regarded authors, such as Shakespeare and Milton, but they occasionally led to painfully twisted syntax of the kind satirized in a quotation attributed to Winston Churchill: "This is the kind of pedantic nonsense up with which I will not put."

The self-consciousness imposed by the combination of these rather arbitrary rules and the ones being unsystematically codified by numerous printers meant that the time was ripe for a guidebook that would lay out the rules and best practices. Basic dictionaries, essentially mere word lists, had existed since the earliest times, and in English since the early sixteenth century. However, a work that provided not only correct spelling and word division but also definitions and demonstrations of correct usage was a much more ambitious undertaking. In England, the project was taken on by respected author and moralist Samuel Johnson. Convinced that he could complete the project on his own in just three years (despite the fact that it had taken a committee of the *Académie Française* forty years to compile a similar work in French), and dazzled by the sum promised him by the publisher William Strahan (1715–85) and associates, Johnson began work on his *Dictionary of the English Language* in 1747. In the end, it took him eight years, the book finally appearing in 1755.

PRINTING IN THE INDUSTRIAL AGE

The industrial revolution exploited new power sources and created new materials and products that fundamentally changed the face of the planet. Its impact on the history of the book was also profound. Not only did it prompt the first major technological advances in printing, paper-making, and typesetting technology since the age of Gutenberg, but the resulting explosion of cheap printed materials helped create and sustain new mass readerships. The industrial age also helped foster the first truly global market for published materials, by vastly improving networks of communication and transportation around the world. By the close of the nineteenth century, readers in cities as widely dispersed as London and Vancouver, Berlin and Lucknow, or Lyons and Rio de Janeiro could have ready access to the same news items, and often even the same publications, in a matter of hours or days—not months or years, as had been the case in all previous eras.

Along with the industrial revolution, the period between the end of the eighteenth century and the first decades of the twentieth century saw numerous sociopolitical developments around the globe that also affected the role of the book in society. Political revolutions, the abolition of slavery, and the mass migration of populations from the countryside to urban centers all gradually shifted power from the traditional elites, first to the industrial middle class, and then to the working classes. These changes also drove a need for widespread educational initiatives. The changing trade and political relations between Europe, Asia, Africa, and the Americas brought unfamiliar cultural ideas and technologies into relation with one another.

Developments in the Printing Trades

The most profound change that occurred in the printing trades in the nineteenth century was the shift from human-powered to steam-powered production. First printing, then binding, paper-making, and typesetting came to be run by machines that could produce thousands more copies per hour than artisans in the trades had ever been able to do. The traditional book-making arts gradually moved to the margins of the publishing world, used either for small-run, locally produced ephemera or for very high-end, collector-quality limited editions.

The industrial revolution first changed the nature of the printing press itself, and eventually the very method by which most printing was done. By the late eighteenth century, presses had been introduced in which both the bed and platen were made of iron. These were in many respects souped-up common presses, as all of the original components were there in basically the same positions. However, the stronger materials added durability and stability. The first completely iron press was designed in 1800 by Charles Stanhope (1753–1816), an English lord. The Stanhope press doubled the size of the printing area while simultaneously reducing the amount of force required to create an impression by up to 90 per cent. As a result, pressmen operating an iron Stanhope press could generate nearly 500 impressions per hour, more than twice that of a wooden common press. The Stanhope press was immediately adopted for printing newspapers, which remained the primary driver of press innovations well into the twentieth century.

The first steam-powered printing presses were introduced in the 1790s, although it took another twenty to thirty years for the technology to be refined and made reliable enough for commercial viability. A key innovation was the shift from flat platens to curved cylinders. Cylinder presses enabled impressions to be made more quickly and evenly. Gradually, almost all of the individual processes required by traditional printing methods were automated and coordinated. Inking, feeding in the paper, and moving the form into position could all be run by steam power much more quickly than by hand, and without fatigue. Although human operators were still required to supply and adjust the machines, and to check the quality of the resulting sheets, printing quickly moved from a hand-craft to a branch of engineering.

Binding technology also changed in the nineteenth century. While books in earlier eras were often issued as gatherings or as *signatures* (gatherings that have been stitched together but not bound) that purchasers would have bound to suit their needs (and to match their libraries), by the mid-nineteenth century most books were issued with covers already affixed, and binders continually experimented with different materials that were less expensive and easier to produce than the traditional wood-and-leather hand-tooled covers. *Card* (or *cardboard*) came to replace actual wood boards as the stiffener for covers, and lower-grade leathers were mechanically thinned and chemically treated to imitate the look and feel of more expensive hand-tooled leathers. Unfortunately, the chemicals used to speed up the tanning process for the less expensive leather covers proved to be highly acidic, which meant that the covers not only deteriorated more rapidly than the better-quality, traditionally treated leathers, but they also chemically interacted with the paper over time, causing a brownish discoloration.

By the latter decades of the nineteenth century, new techniques were also devised to stamp patterns and text into cloth-covered boards. Initially, the cloth was often impressed or *tooled* to evoke the look of leather, but as cloth covers became more familiar, cover designs increasingly began to exploit the advantages of the material, resulting in brighter colors and even more elaborately illustrated paper glued on to cloth, especially for fiction and children's literature.

Besides the covers themselves, new machines were developed to stitch together the signatures. Stitching remained a hand operation much longer than many processes in the printing trades (partly because binders relied on female labor, which was considerably cheaper than male), with the result that the final steps of producing a book for the public were becoming the slowest ones. Rather than running threads individually through each signature's fold and then over cords laid across the back of the stacked signatures, binding them securely together, the new binding machines produced a kind of webbed ribbon that could be affixed to the edges of all the signatures with glue. This new method of binding produced a smooth spine, rather than the ribbed spine produced by the cords of traditionally bound books. But to preserve the traditional look and feel of a book spine, the leatherette or cloth covers that were affixed to the finished book could be padded or simply tooled to add the feel—or just the look—of ribbing.

Wood-Pulp Paper

Changes in printing technology also prompted changes in paper-making. Since its migration west from China, paper had most often been produced with some form of fabric fibers—occasionally silk, but more generally flax in the Arab world and linen in Europe—as its basis. In European countries, paper-makers had relied on a steady supply of worn-out linen shirts and undergarments as their primary source of paper fiber, participating in a well-established recycling effort that was mutually beneficial. However, by the middle of the nineteenth century, the growing demand for paper meant that the traditional stocks of linen were becoming depleted, and manufacturers needed to look for new sources of fiber and for new technologies for producing paper.

In his comic 1869 travelogue *The Innocents Abroad,* American author Mark Twain (1835–1910) joked that in the absence of other local fuel sources, Egyptian railroad operators were using mummies to fuel trains—an off-handed comment that may have prompted other wags to suggest mummy winding cloths as a possible linen source for paper manufacturers. The notion of "mummy paper" certainly captured the imaginations of subsequent generations of readers and writers—it gets a mention from publishing historian Nicholson Baker and has prompted at least one presentation at the Society for the History of Authorship, Reading, and Publishing's annual conference—but there is no evidence whatsoever that paper was ever actually produced from Egyptian mummy wrappings. The real new source for paper-making was wood pulp, particularly wood logged from the pine forests of North America.

Plant-based paper, produced from leaves and bark, had existed since the earliest days of book production, but when made by traditional craft methods, it was in some respects inferior to cloth-based paper. First, most plant-based paper was coarser than cloth-based papers, because it was difficult to break down the woody fibers sufficiently by hand-pounding. This rendered plant-based papers difficult to use for either manuscript or printed documents, because the surface was uneven. (This was also a problem with parchment, which quickly fell out of use for most mechanically printed documents.) Second, even when using traditional whitening agents such as lime or chalk, most plant-based papers still turned out darker in color than silk-, flax-, or linen-based papers. It was therefore difficult to assure sufficient contrast between the writing surface and the ink.

Steam power and nineteenth-century developments in chemistry changed the figures in the equation. First, steam power made it possible to pound the wood with much greater force and for longer durations than ever before, so it was possible to break down the fibers to a greater extent at the very beginning of the paper-making process. Second, and more important, chemicals added to the slurry stage of the process further broke down the wood fibers and also rendered the resulting paper surface whiter and smoother than ever before. In the 1850s, Hugh Burgess (1825–92) and Charles Watt developed the "soda process," which involved boiling wood in caustic alkali at high temperatures to break down the fibers. Shortly thereafter, Benjamin C. Tilghman (1821–1901) developed the "sulfite process," which involved dissolving the wood fibers in sulfurous acid at high temperatures and high levels of pressure. Because the process rendered the resulting fibers reddish in color, they needed to be subjected to a second process of bleaching with sulfite of lime.

Finally, steam-powered machines made it possible to make paper in continuous long rolls or *webs,* rather than in individual sheets. This was a major advantage for use with cylinder presses, as the continuous web of paper could be fed directly into the press for longer and faster press runs. What became known as the *Fourdrinier machine,* after the London printers who successfully used it, was actually invented by a Frenchman, Nicholas-Louis Robert (1761–1828) at the turn of the nineteenth century. Robert's invention used a vacuum mechanism to scoop paper pulp out of a vat and deposit it on a rotating (and thus continuous) wire cloth bed, where the pulp was shaken in a side-to-side motion to remove the water, which drained into a vat beneath. As the wire cloth bed advanced through the machine, it eventually ran under a felt-covered roller, which grabbed the now-damp piece of paper and enabled it to be removed for drying. Mechanical dryers were later added, heated by wood, charcoal, or steam, as were various cutting devices.

Thanks to all of these advances, by the 1870s nearly all ordinary printed materials in the West, but especially periodicals and inexpensive editions of books, were printed on chemically treated wood-pulp paper. The natural resources of the almost unimaginably vast forests in western North America, combined with chemical engineering savvy, had ensured the industrial age of a continuous, reliable source of cheap paper to feed the voracious appetites of presses and readers. The downside of this achievement in publishing history would only become apparent many decades later, when the northern forests proved, after all, not to be an inexhaustible resource, and when the chemicals used to process the wood-pulp paper proved to have rendered that paper highly acidic and therefore liable to browning and brittleness. The recent legacy of disintegrating books would drive later technological developments (for good and ill), as discussed in the next chapter. (The efforts to preserve those books and others are also discussed in Chapter 9.)

Mechanized Typesetting

Finally, typesetting technology underwent some fundamental changes in the nineteenth century. A number of early inventions extended the number of impressions that could be generated from letter-set, the most important of these being *stereotyping.* A stereotype was a full-size metal duplicate of a typeset form. A plaster cast was first made of the original, typeset form, and then the plaster cast was used to create a single-piece metal copy.

Stereotyping offered some real advantages to printers. First, the stereotype, as a solid piece of metal, was more stable and thus easier to print from than a locked-up form, which always presented the danger that individual pieces of type would work themselves loose (or that the whole would come unlocked and collapse into chaos). A stereotype could also be stored relatively easily, allowing a printer to quickly produce extra editions of a popular text. In the meantime, the type in the original form could be distributed and made immediately available for use in another project. This reduced the total number of fonts that a printer needed to keep on hand, which helped to contain both capital expenditure and storage costs.

Sextuple stereotype perfecting printing press, 1899.

One consequence of stereotyping was that both publishers and authors became much more concerned, much earlier, about the accuracy of the text being produced. Up until the age of stereotyping, both printers and authors could console themselves with the knowledge that errors could be mended the next time the text was printed, either by going in and resetting lines with mistakes or other problems, or by resetting from scratch (which would invariably introduce other errors—but probably not the precise errors present in the earlier version). However, printing from a stereotype meant that future impressions would be identical to the first one. (Mending stereotyped plates was possible, but because it involved cutting into the plate or affixing a patch, it was a difficult and usually aesthetically unsatisfactory process.) This meant that before the plaster cast and resulting stereotype were made from the original, it was particularly incumbent upon all involved to make sure that the version was as perfect as possible. As discussed in Chapter 5, this was just one factor that shaped notions of "authorship" in the modern age.

The first commercially successful typewriting machine was launched in the 1860s, making it possible for the first time for an individual writer to produce a *typescript* rather than a manuscript. Typewriters harnessed the basic technology of printing: raised type—in this instance, fixed to a lever that was operated by a key on a keyboard—made an impression by striking an inked ribbon and pressing it and the paper against a platen. Despite the fiddly nature of the early mechanisms, they offered a key advantage over handwriting by vastly improving the immediate legibility of individually produced documents. As the mechanisms were refined, typing also proved to be quicker than writing or transcribing by hand—so much so, that the keyboards had to be redesigned several times in the early years to assure the mechanism wouldn't jam when typists struck the keys more quickly than the type levers could withstand. The ubiquitous *QWERTY* keyboard (named for the top line of letters on the keyboard) features an intentionally inefficient layout, one that places the most commonly used letters like *e, i, a, o,* and *s* and the critical punctuation marks away from the stronger and more agile index fingers. Generations of keyboard operators have come to rue the fact that this keyboard layout has persisted well into the electronic age: the awkward hand movements required by the *QWERTY* keyboard no longer confer an advantage by avoiding jams, and instead simply increase the risk of developing painful repetitive-stress injuries.

Linotype machine, 1889.

The success of the keyboard-driven typewriter for everyday text generation inspired a number of experiments in keyboard-driven typesetting. The goal was to combine the speed and efficiency of a keyboard mechanism with the quality of impression that could be produced with traditional movable type. Early experimenters played with the idea of keyboards that prompted a mechanism to drop type down chutes from font storage bins into a composing stick, but besides being cumbersome, it was hard to ensure that the type arrived in the correct position and without being damaged. In addition, the very labor-intensive job of sorting the type at the end of the printing job remained part of the process.

The mechanization of typesetting was finally achieved when inventors took the matter of type storage and sorting out of the equation. Instead of storing fonts of precast type, the new machines combined typecasting and typesetting in what came to be known as *hot metal* composing. When the key for a particular letter or punctuation mark was struck, the machine would cast a new piece of type to order and place it in the composing stick, so that every piece of type was brand-new for every project, ensuring the best-quality impressions. When the project was finished, the type would be poured into a hopper and melted down for reuse, rather than redistributed, thus eliminating the time-consuming work of sorting.

The first commercially successful typesetting machine was the *Linotype*, invented in 1886 by Ottmar Mergenthaler (1854–99). Resembling an organ console more than a typewriter, the Linotype composed lines of type in *slugs*, solid blocks that included all the letters and spaces in relief along one edge. The machine's keyboard released a brass matrix corresponding to the character required, and sent it to an assembler box. After each word, a space-band of two opposing wedges was released. When a sufficient number of type matrices had been released to make up a complete line, the wedges could be forced up until the line was spaced to measure—thus eliminating the difficulty of justifying the line by hand. Molten metal was then pumped into the matrix to form the

CHAPTER THREE *The Printing Revolution* | 111

slug, which was automatically trimmed and ejected to a receiving galley while the matrices returned to their place in the machine's storage magazine. Like individual pieces of metal type, the slugs could be melted down and reused after the form was printed, but unlike individual types, they did not need to be sorted and distributed by hand.

Another important typesetting machine was the *Monotype*, first patented in 1885 by its American inventor Tolbert Lanston (1844–1913), but not launched until 1897. Lanston adapted the punch-card system used in many cloth factories to typesetting. The Monotype keyboard punched perforations into a ribbon. The ribbon would then be passed over air vents, and the punched perforations would cause pins to rise in sequence. Each pin would stop a matrix case corresponding to the desired letter or punctuation mark at the required position over a type mold. The desired character would then be instantly cast from molten metal and ejected into its proper place, while the matrix would return to its original position.

Although the font styles and sizes offered by these mechanical typesetting machines were much more limited than the options available with hand-set type, the new machines effectively spelled the end of hand-setting for large-run publications like newspapers and some books. The readily distinguishable look of books and other publications produced by different printshops over the ages were increasingly subsumed by a couple of generic, uniform layouts that conformed to the demands of the new machinery. By rendering texts cheaper and quicker to produce, they certainly helped drive down costs and put ever-more publications in the hands of ever-more readers, but at the definite cost of aesthetics and creativity.

The Book Arts Revival

Not everyone was happy with the industrialization of the arts, and at the turn of the twentieth century a number of artists and designers sought to reinvigorate many of the traditional craft trades, including the book arts. Inspired by writers like the art historian and critic John Ruskin (1819–1900), and led by artists such as William Morris (1834–96), the Arts and Crafts movement looked to earlier traditions for inspiration to revive the decorative arts and provide a distinctly human touch in an increasingly mechanized world.

Megan Benton notes that book arts revivalists rejected much of Victorian book design as "no design at all," driven merely by mechanization and commercial concerns. They urged a return to preindustrial, craft-based production, and to design principles modeled on the best examples of the medieval and Renaissance periods. For example, the engraver and printer Emery Walker (1851–1933) urged that printed pages should evidence unity, balance, and symmetry. This meant, among other things, that page spreads should be treated as a single element, with due attention to the contrasts between dark and light, type and other images.

One of the most important influences on the revival of the traditional book arts was Morris, an artist, poet, and socialist thinker who established his Kelmscott Press in 1891. Morris hired a retired master printer to help him, and he purchased a secondhand iron Albion hand-press and some other equipment to get started. According to biographer Fiona MacCarthy, Morris later explained that he began printing with the hope of producing books that, while beautiful, "should be easy to read and should not dazzle the eye, or trouble the intellect of the reader by eccentricity of form in the letters." He set about studying the history of printing and papermaking, determined that the Kelmscott Press would make use of the best of past practices. Besides finding models of ideal, linen-based papers (he particularly admired a fifteenth-century paper made in Bologna), Morris also tracked down a supplier for vellum, which he insisted be made white by traditional methods and not by cheating with lead. He had to specially commission a linseed oil ink from German manufacturers. After studying the history of typography, he also decided to design his own types.

With its emphasis on traditional hand crafts and materials, the Kelmscott Press had no intention, nor capability, of mass-producing books. Its publications were limited in number and quantity. Aside from producing editions of Morris's own works and those of a few nineteenth-century authors, the Kelmscott Press published new (but old-looking) editions of classic medieval texts. Among the best-known and most glorious was the *Kelmscott Chaucer*, begun in 1892 and finally published in 1896. Featuring eighty-seven illustrations by Morris's lifelong friend and fellow artist Edward Burne-Jones (1833–98), the *Works of Geoffrey Chaucer* was Morris's last great project. He designed a new typeface for it, and Burne-Jones worked assiduously every weekend to transfer his designs to woodblocks for cutting. The resulting book was a triumph of handwork. Morris printed 425 copies on paper, for £20 each, and an additional thirteen copies on vellum—for the very substantial sum of 120 guineas apiece.

Morris's Kelmscott Press inspired a number of imitators, who also began to create beautiful, handcrafted books in limited editions. For example, in the United States in 1895, Elbert Hubbard (1856–1915) founded the Roycroft Press in an artists' community established in East Aurora, New York. Named after the seventeenth-century London printers Thomas and Samuel Roycroft, the Roycroft Press published a monthly magazine entitled *The Philistine* and a number of small books by Hubbard and others. The books were printed in limited editions on handmade paper and bound with a distinctive soft suede leather cover. Many of the books, including Hubbard's lovely 1899 tribute to Morris, part of his *Little Journeys to the Homes of English Authors* series, also featured hand-colored illuminations. By 1901, his printing business was so successful that Hubbard had 300 employees and had to expand his facilities, but the Press rapidly declined after Hubbard and his wife went down with the *Lusitania* in 1915.

Another important figure associated with the book arts revival was the English artist and type designer Eric Gill (1882–1940). A student of Edward Johnston (1872–1944), who revived the art of calligraphy, Gill transferred his love for letterforms to the art of typography, creating some of the most attractive and enduring typefaces of the early twentieth century, including Gill Sans, Perpetua, and Joanna. He would also help to add elegance and style to one of the most significant developments in book culture in the first part of the new century: the mass-market paperback.

At the close of the nineteenth century, all the factors were in place for what would prove to be a golden age of print. Both global populations and global literacy levels were increasing, so that the planet not only supported the largest number of people ever, but a record percentage of those people could read. Educational initiatives were driving up the numbers of individuals who had access to schooling and putting books and other publications into their grasp. In addition to technological advances, developments such as the rise of advertising helped to drastically lower the costs of various kinds of publications, especially newspapers and other periodicals. As a result, publishers around the world launched increasingly specialized publications, carefully targeted to particular groups of readers. Gender, class, age, political orientation, religious belief, leisure interests, work requirements, educational aspirations—all of these characteristics were identified, analyzed, and catered to by the publishing world. For a time, the book and other kinds of texts were not only a part *of* society, they would become very central *to* it.

SELECTED BIBLIOGRAPHY

Barrett, T.H. *The Woman Who Discovered Printing*. New Haven: Yale UP, 2008.

Benton, Megan L. *Beauty and the Book: Fine Editions and Cultural Distinction in America*. New Haven: Yale UP, 2000.

Benton, Megan L. "The Book as Art." *A Companion to the History of the Book*. Ed. Simon Eliot and Jonathan Rose. Chichester: John Wiley, 2009. 493–507.

Charles, Doug. "Bed and Platen Printing Machines." Letterpress Printing in the 1960s. 2012. http://letterpressprinting.com.au.

Chen Hongyan. "A Joy to the Eye and the Mind: Books Transcribed by Celebrated Artists." *The Art of the Book in China*. Ed. Ming Wilson and Stacey Pierson. London: Percival David Foundation, 2006. 29–42.

Chinnery, Colin. "Bookbinding." International Dunhuang Project. 2011. http://idp.bl.uk/downloads/Bookbinding.pdf.

Dane, Joseph A. *What Is a Book? The Study of Early Printed Books*. Notre Dame: U of Notre Dame P, 2012.

de Nave, Francine. *The Plantin-Moretus Museum: Printing and Publishing Before 1800*. Antwerp: Musea Antwerpen, 2004.

Diamond Sutra. Online Gallery: Sacred Texts. British Library. http://www.bl.uk/onlinegallery/sacredtexts/diamondsutra.html.

Eisenstein, Elizabeth L. *The Printing Revolution in Early Modern Europe*. Cambridge: Cambridge UP, 1983.

Fischer, Steven Roger. *A History of Reading*. London: Reaktion, 2003.

—. *A History of Writing*. [London]: Reaktion, 2001.

Füssel, Stephan. *Gutenberg and the Impact of Printing*. Trans. Douglas Martin. Aldershot: Ashgate, 2005.

Gaskell, Philip. *A New Introduction to Bibliography*. New Castle, DE: Oak Knoll, 1995.

Glaister, Geoffrey Ashall. *Encyclopedia of the Book*. 2nd ed. New Castle, DE: Oak Knoll, 1996.

Hellinga, Lotte, and J.B. Trapp, eds. *The Cambridge History of the Book in Britain. Vol. 3, 1400–1557*. Cambridge: Cambridge UP, 1999.

Hunter, Dard. *Papermaking: The History and Technique of an Ancient Craft*. 2nd ed. London: Cresset, 1957.

Kamei-Dyche, Andrew T. "The History of Books and Print Culture in Japan." *Book History* 14 (2011): 270–304.

Kernan, Alvin. *Samuel Johnson and the Impact of Print*. Princeton: Princeton UP, 1987.

Maravelas, Paul. *Letterpress Printing: A Manual for Modern Fine Press Printers*. New Castle, DE: Oak Knoll, 2005.

Reed, Christopher A. *Gutenberg in Shanghai: Chinese Print Capitalism, 1876–1937*. Vancouver: U of British Columbia P, 2004.

Soeng, Mu. *The Diamond Sutra: Transforming the Way We Perceive the World*. Boston: Wisdom Publications, 2000.

Watson, Peter. *Ideas: A History of Thought and Invention, from Fire to Freud*. New York: HarperCollins, 2005.

CHAPTER FOUR

MODERN TIMES: FROM PAPERBACKS TO E-BOOKS

The first half of the twentieth century was arguably the age of the book. The period saw a huge increase in the kinds and quantities of published materials and the concurrent rise of a truly mass reading audience. An inexpensive but reasonably durable new format, the *paperback*, put books within economic reach of nearly anyone who wanted them. And as the oceans of printed material rose, new actors emerged to help readers navigate them. Critics and university academics stepped forward to offer advice about what—and how—to read. Public libraries and new distributional networks brought steady supplies of books even to small towns and local neighborhoods, while mail-order book clubs sifted through the multitudes of new publications and delivered their recommendations straight to readers' homes. The new entertainment media of film, radio, and even early television all offered tie-in products that helped to publicize and sustain the demand for books.

But the last medium, television, also began to effect changes in leisure patterns that would begin to tarnish this golden age of the book, and developments in the second half of the twentieth century would further complicate the picture. While small independent booksellers had served many communities of readers well, by the 1970s the overall demand for books suggested that there was real money to be made by larger competitors who could consolidate their ordering and distribution networks and offer even more books at lower prices. The so-called *big-box stores* emerged: Barnes & Noble, Borders, Chapters, Waterstone's. Able to support book stocks that dwarfed those of the smaller independents, the big-box outlets inexorably drove many of the smaller stores out of business.

But the most important development was the coming of the digital age. As computers dominated the workplace and migrated into homes, assumptions about what and how to read and write changed yet again. Visionaries early on imagined vast libraries of free and instantly accessible digitized books; the first of these, aptly named *Project Gutenberg*, was launched even before the infrastructure existed to get the digital books to readers.

Computers not only changed what was available, but how it was made available. Electronic typesetting, design, layout, and printing technologies developed rapidly, and increasingly sophisticated software reversed the trend towards specialization in the books arts. By the turn of the twenty-first century, a single individual at a screen could write, set, lay out, edit, and publish a book, either in a *hard copy*, printed out and bound, or in a virtual or *e-book* edition. While the first generation of devices for reading e-books failed to capture readers' hearts and wallets, the wave of new devices introduced in the early twenty-first century finally took hold. Online booksellers, which had already begun to send the big-box stores down the same route as the independent booksellers they had replaced, quickly added e-books to their more traditional offerings. By early 2011, the Association of American Publishers was reporting that e-book sales had overtaken traditional trade book sales (hardcover, paperback, and mass market books) for both adults and children.

This chapter will examine in greater detail some of the important factors surrounding the book in society during the twentieth and early twenty-first century, beginning with the growth of readerships at the turn of the twentieth century and taking in both the "paperback revolution" of the 1920s and the "digital revolution" of today. While many of the recent developments in book culture have been positive ones, they have been accompanied by a steady drumbeat of warnings about the debasement of literacy and culture. Particularly now that e-readers have been embraced by ordinary readers, naysayers have launched jeremiads about the "death of the book." The current uncertainty about what the future holds has been a contributing factor to the emergence of publishing studies, or *history of the book*, as a serious scholarly enterprise. What happens from here will depend very much on you, the readers of this book, and others like you.

EDUCATION, LITERACY, AND MASS READERSHIPS

As previous chapters have made clear, books and readers exist in a dynamic synergy. An increased demand for books helps drive the supply of reading materials, and an increased supply of interesting or potentially useful materials helps motivate individuals to secure and read them. Crucial to all of this is *literacy*, or the ability to read. And one of the significant developments near the end of the nineteenth century was a series of major educational initiatives that dramatically increased access to education and helped to build and sustain a mass reading audience.

Educational reforms were adopted in the West at different times, in response to local needs and pressures. In general, however, the effect was to provide ordinary residents of each country or region with a better quality of education, and for a longer, more sustained period of time. This ensured that students not only absorbed basic literacy skills—the ability to decode texts and to generate simple ones—but that they had a longer exposure to more demanding and sophisticated kinds of texts. Students who had had access to improved schooling were better equipped to continue reading in their private lives if they wished to, whether for self-improvement or simply for pleasure.

Among the first Western countries to institute a system of public education was Scotland, which had various public education schemes in place as early as the seventeenth century. Another early reformer was Prussia, which introduced the eight-year *Volksschule* (people's school) in the eighteenth century. This model served as the basis for later educational systems in the united Germany. Although Thomas Jefferson (1743–1826) recommended public schooling for children in the United States as early as 1779, it wasn't until the 1860s, after the American Civil War, that most states offered public education to nearly all students, regardless of race or religion. In the early 1900s, US education became increasingly better organized and more widely available, resulting in a significant increase in students' attending and graduating from high school.

In Great Britain, the key reform was the 1870 Elementary Education Act, which ensured all children in England and Wales a publicly funded education; in 1872, Scotland restructured its systems to parallel those in England. Education throughout the British Empire varied greatly by region. In Canada, the 1867 British North America Act established the separate Protestant and Catholic systems in what was then Upper (Ontario) and Lower (Quebec) Canada. In France, the general framework for a public educational system was instituted in the early nineteenth century under Napoleon, but the modern system was largely put in place in the 1880s.

These various educational reforms were augmented by important contemporary social developments, including the public library movement. Until the nineteenth century, most libraries were private: owned outright by individuals or institutions, or open only by invitation or subscription through membership. In the mid-nineteenth century, both governments and individual philanthropic associations began to urge the creation of public libraries that would make books available to all. However, it wasn't until the end of the century that such libraries actually began to be built and to open their doors. (The history and development of libraries is discussed in more detail in Chapter 9.) Often elegantly designed, these public palaces of knowledge allowed the newly educated access to a wide variety of books. The stocks of the best ones, such as the main Public Library on Fifth Avenue in New York City, which opened in 1877, were extraordinary. In addition to schoolchildren seeking picture books and office workers looking for reading matter for their journeys home, the new public libraries' reading rooms were filled with immigrants seeking to prepare themselves for life in a new culture, scholars conducting research, and future prize-winning authors developing ideas. Libraries helped develop and sustain a reading habit that would accompany many individuals throughout their lives.

Periodicals

But readers did not just read books at the turn of the twentieth century—in fact, bound volumes of fiction or nonfiction were probably the lesser part of their reading material. Far more important, because virtually ubiquitous, were the numerous *periodicals* of the day—newspapers, weekly and monthly magazines, quarterly journals, and the whole range of shorter and longer, bigger and smaller publications that appeared at intervals and catered to the interests and concerns of any identifiable readership. First important in the eighteenth century, periodicals had become the dominant print medium in the nineteenth, used to circulate everything from news and fashion to scientific developments, entertainment, and recipes. Poetry and fiction

Cover of *The Illustrated London News*, 1876.

were serialized in periodicals, but so were important works of science, history, and philosophy. Because they were unbound and (mostly) of limited length, periodicals were relatively inexpensive to produce and to purchase. Wealthy and middle-class readers could purchase or subscribe to a range of different periodicals that catered to their work or leisure needs, but even readers of limited means could afford the occasional penny paper or perhaps pool together for a favored subscription. Periodicals could also be read or borrowed from libraries and other educational, work-related, or even social institutions.

Towards the end of the nineteenth century, the overall rise in literacy meant that new groups of potential readers were being identified, and publishers rushed to create periodicals to cater to them. Women, children, and working-class readers were the most important new audiences, but many subgroups were carved out as well. For example, women could choose magazines that catered to their religious affiliations, their class identification, or their views on whether women should get the vote. Special-interest magazines might offer features and fiction about the late-century craze for bicycling or mountain-climbing or fossil-collecting. Both old (medicine, law) and new (nursing, typewriting) professions had journals and papers targeted to their members, offering the latest developments and news about employment opportunities. Even daily newspapers wrote for very specific readerships, offering assessments of the day's events that were targeted to political affiliation, class, or ethnic heritage, and often appearing in multiple editions throughout the day, so that readers would be constantly updated about breaking news.

Both technological advances and large readerships helped keep the per-copy costs of these periodicals down, but the explosion of print at the turn of the twentieth century was also significantly underwritten by another major social development: the rise of the modern advertising industry. The book trade had used advertisements since the early days of manuscript copying to publicize its own wares, and the growth of the periodical press in the eighteenth

THE SATURDAY EVENING POST

Magazines have their origins in a form of periodical that emerged in the eighteenth century, the *miscellany*. Miscellanies offered up a variety of kinds of articles, including news and entertainment, letters and jokes. They were considered safe reading for all members of the family, and as leisure time spent in the domestic sphere became a more important element of nineteenth-century life, weekly miscellanies and magazines became increasingly popular.

One of the most popular and long-lived magazines in the United States is the *Saturday Evening Post*, which began as a newspaper published by Benjamin Franklin in 1728 as the *Pennsylvania Gazette*. It was renamed in 1821, and in the late 1830s shifted from mainly covering politics to addressing a wider range of topics. By mid-century, it was selling about 90,000 copies a year, a very good figure in the United States at the time.

However, it was in the glory days of the late nineteenth and early twentieth centuries that the *Saturday Evening Post* achieved its greatest successes. Magazine publisher Cyrus H.K. Curtis (1850–1933) purchased it in 1897 and soon put it under the editorship of George Horace Lorimer (1867–1937). Under his guidance, the *Post* became among the first to reach a circulation of a million copies. Contributors included such notable authors as F. Scott Fitzgerald, Sinclair Lewis, and Ring Lardner. Among Lorimer's many innovations was his realization that covers could help establish a magazine's identity and sell issues. He hired a number of distinguished artists and illustrators to create cover art, the most famous of whom was Norman Rockwell (1894–1978). Rockwell's covers often reflected the content of the issues, but they also held a mirror up to the world. Some of the best-known images of mid-twentieth-century American popular culture are Rockwell covers. (He later painted covers for *Look* magazine.)

Like many other periodicals, the *Saturday Evening Post*'s circulations fell after mid-century. After briefly ceasing publication from 1969 to 1971, it was relaunched under new ownership and continues today as a bimonthly.

century had seen an increase in advertising for other kinds of goods as well. But it was in the nineteenth century that advertising became an essential part of most publishers' business models. The technologies that improved the appearance and brought down the costs of printing larger publications also improved the look and cost-effectiveness of ephemera such as circulars and posters. Cities and towns could be blanketed with posters overnight, and contemporary paintings and photographs show how every bit of available space could be covered with signs vying for the attention of passersby. The volume of advertising ephemera even changed the look of some cities in defining ways. For example, in Berlin, distinctive kiosks were erected to provide a designated place for poster-hangers, so that they would refrain from pasting their signs on other surfaces. Although now less ubiquitous, these kiosks are still part of the city's identity.

By the turn of the twentieth century, periodical publishers were well aware that paid advertising could provide a predictable, steady income that would underwrite regular costs and cushion the publication against the temporary fluctuations of circulation figures. The significant change was that the producers of various goods and services began to appreciate that specialized publications could provide much more targeted audiences for their wares. Instead of sticking up posters in public places or handing out flyers to random persons on the street, businesses could send their messages directly into their potential customers' homes. Children's boots, men's hats, women's corsets, the latest medical device, the most promising new brand of soap—whatever the product, there was a magazine or newspaper whose readers would be the likeliest purchasers, and putting an advertisement in that publication's pages could provide just the required edge. Special departments and eventually independent firms sprang up to write and design the advertising copy, and this mutually beneficial business model became the prevailing one for much of the twentieth century.

THE PAPERBACK REVOLUTION

Periodicals provided a steady supply of diverting and informational material, and with advertising keeping the costs down, they were within the means of virtually all readers. But some works were better suited for publication in volumes, and some readers simply preferred the more substantial feel and longer format of a book. How could the price of books be managed so that they, too, could sell to a mass audience?

This became a particular problem for British publishers at the beginning of the twentieth century, because the systems for publishing and circulating books that had long been in place finally broke down. For over a generation, most new books in Britain had been purchased by subscription-based *circulating libraries*, rather than by individual readers. Much like the later video and DVD rental shops, circulating libraries purchased multiple copies of best-sellers and checked them out for a fee to readers. Since most books were issued in two or three volumes, and borrowers were charged by volume, this was potentially a very lucrative business. The largest circulating library, Mudie's Select Library, was renowned both for its elegant flagship store on New Oxford Street in London and for the global reach of its lending facilities.

The circulating library system worked reasonably well for authors and publishers, as it created a mostly closed market in which initial sales were guaranteed and the cost of new books was kept up. (Perhaps not surprisingly, many publishers had an investment interest in the circulating libraries, so that they made money not only through sales *to* the libraries, but also through customers' rentals *from* them.) The down side was that because purchasing decisions were effectively concentrated in the hands of one person (usually the circulating library's proprietor), there were inevitably some restrictions on what was published—or even considered for publication. In addition, the arrangement with the circulating libraries also created a large secondary market for used books. When the demand for particular titles began to fall off, the libraries sold the excess copies—and they, not the authors and publishers, pocketed the profit. If the used copies happened to go on sale at the same time that the publisher issued a "cheap" reprint edition of the book in question, authors saw a further reduction of their royalties and publishers of their profits. In the end, it was authors who forced a change in the system, pressing publishers to issue affordable, one-volume editions of their books direct to the public. When readers proved that they would just as happily purchase books as borrow them, the circulating library system quickly collapsed.

As general readers gradually acquired the book-buying habit, their access to books was both enhanced and impeded by the two world wars and the Great Depression. During the wars, service members at the front and families at home turned to books for education, solace, and escape, and governments tried to encourage the reading habit. However, the wars also created shortages of book-producing materials, and the overall economic circumstances meant that there was a real impetus to find less expensive means of producing and distributing books. The answer was the paperback.

Penguins and Pockets

Paperbound books had been around since the early decades of the nineteenth century, but paper covers were generally thought to be temporary wrappers, intended for eventual replacement with case bindings customized to the book buyers' libraries. One exception to this general rule were the inexpensive reprints of English language titles issued from the 1840s to the 1940s by the Leipzig publisher Bernhard Tauchnitz (1816–95). Tauchnitz editions were aimed squarely at the nineteenth-century British and American tourist industry, providing travelers on the Continent with reliable, lightweight, and inexpensive reading material. The firm also published a line of bilingual dictionaries that furthered the cause of cross-cultural communication.

In the 1930s, the paperbound book model was updated for domestic consumption. In 1932, Albatross Books in Hamburg launched a new series of attractive paperbound books, color-coded by genre. The British publisher Allen Lane seems to have borrowed the Albatross Books model for his own line of paperbound books. Lane launched Penguin Books in 1935, offering readers contemporary fiction in a simple, attractive format—also color-coded by genre—and at a very low price: just sixpence, the same as a packet of cigarettes. Penguin expanded to the United States in 1939, and at about the same time Robert F. de Graff (1895–1981) joined forces with publisher Simon and Schuster to start a similar, homegrown American paperback imprint, Pocket Books. Pocket Books initially sold for just twenty-five cents apiece—about one-tenth the cost of a new hardcover book.

The informality of the new ventures is marked by their tongue-in-cheek names and logos. Albatrosses, penguins, and, in the case of Pocket Books, a cheerfully reading kangaroo with a spare book tucked into her pocket, signaled a fundamental lack of stuffiness. Unlike traditional hardcover books, which continued to be sold mainly through bookstores, the new paperback imprints were offered in a wider range of venues, from rail stations to drugstores and grocery stores. Relatively inexpensive to ship, and often issued in series, paperbacks quickly took their place on the store shelves besides magazines. In fact, they often were not only handled by the same wholesale distributors who handled magazines, but they were even published and printed by the same firms.

The success of Penguin and Pocket Books soon spurred other new paperback start-ups, including Avon Books (1941), Bantam Books (1945), New American Library (1948), and Pyramid (1949). The war years presented some challenges to the earliest paperback publishers, as paper for book publishing was strictly rationed to pre-war quotas. However, the American branch of Penguin entered into an alliance with the US military, publishing paperback editions of service manuals and other works, as well as continuing to offer leisure reading. The Council on Books in Wartime, created in 1942 to use books as "weapons in the war of ideas," helped ensure that books remained available to both troops and the home front throughout the Second World War.

After the war, there was a boom in paperback book production and sales. The American G.I. Bill, which funded college education for returning veterans, helped to spur the continued market for books, as did Britain's 1944 Education Act, which reorganized all levels of public education in the United Kingdom. To serve the burgeoning educational market, Penguin initiated its Penguin Classics line in 1946 with an edition of Homer's *Odyssey*, and New American Library (NAL) also launched a line of inexpensive classics and scholarly works, boasting that it offered "Good Reading for the Millions" and "Rich Reading at Low Prices." However, that didn't mean that NAL had gone exclusively highbrow: it also published its share of lowbrow fiction, including the notorious genre of "hard-boiled" crime novels. The overall popularity of paperback books can be seen by the climbing print runs, which regularly began to top 100,000 copies. By the mid-1950s, paperback editions of works such as Dale Carnegie's *How to Win Friends and Influence People* (1936) had gone on to become million-copy bestsellers.

Although other countries, including Germany, France, Switzerland, and Japan, developed substantial paperback publishing industries over the second half of the twentieth century, they have remained dwarfed by the scale of the industry in the United States, which regularly has print runs in the millions.

PENGUIN BOOKS

Penguin Books, the first major paperback imprint, was launched in 1935 by British publisher Allen Lane (1902–70). Frustrated when he was unable to find something good to read while traveling by train, he started the firm with the goal of offering readers contemporary fiction in a simple, attractive format and at a very low price. According to the company's website, the penguin was chosen as a logo because Lane wanted something "dignified but flippant" to represent his new line of books. An employee was sent off to the London Zoo to make appropriate sketches.

Among the earliest authors featured in the Penguin line were Ernest Hemingway (1899–1961) and Agatha Christie (1890–1976), popular writers whose books were eagerly snapped up by readers. Within just one year, the publisher had sold three million books. The firm expanded rapidly. With war looming, it issued a line of Penguin Specials dealing with topics such as how to identify enemy planes and launched an Armed Forces Book Club. In 1939, Ian (1916–95) and Betty (b. 1919) Ballantine brought the Penguin name to the United States.

Although the first Penguins were by modern authors, after the war the firm branched out. Penguin Classics were begun in 1946, and the line now includes over 1,200 titles. Favored by students and other thoughtful readers, Penguin Classics have built a reputation for well-edited but affordable volumes. Keeping with its seabird theme, Penguin Books also created a children's imprint, Puffin Books, in 1940, and also a more academically minded imprint, Pelican Books. The latter series was discontinued in the 1980s.

Penguins' distinctive colors made the books easy to spot in any library or bookstore, whether arranged spine-out or face-out. The colors (in spectrum order) were red for drama, orange for fiction, green for crime fiction, yellow for miscellaneous, dark blue for autobiography, purple for essays, cerise for travel and adventure, and—however pessimistically—gray for current affairs.

Popular Genres

The low cost and ubiquity of paperbacks helped support the growth of a number of popular genres from the 1920s to the 1940s, including detective fiction, science fiction, westerns, and romances. Detective fiction took off in the wake of Sherlock Holmes, the brilliant invention of Scottish author and physician Arthur Conan Doyle (1859–1930). By the 1920s, Agatha Christie was already on the way to establishing herself as one of the bestselling authors of all time, with two well-beloved detectives, Hercule Poirot and Miss Marple. Christie's novels became the model of *whodunits*, mysteries that posed a puzzle to be solved by the detective and by readers. While detective fiction in the UK tended to follow along the classic lines of Doyle and Christie, a leaner and meaner *hard-boiled* version developed in the United States, featuring tough-talking "private eyes" who were less interested in solving puzzles than in dispensing rough street justice. In the hands of writers such as Dashiell Hammett (1894–1961) and Raymond Chandler (1888–1959), these novels were closely associated with the cheap, pulp-paper magazines in which they were frequently serialized— hence the expression *pulp fiction*. (Magazines printed on better-quality paper were known as *slicks*.)

Among the factors contributing to detective fiction's popularity during this period was the growth of the movie industry and the expansion of radio programs, both of which featured crime and detective stories. Many popular authors also wrote screenplays and radio plays, and their work thus became familiar to audiences through a variety of venues. This synergy also helped to promote science fiction, which got an additional boost through the pulp magazine *Amazing Stories*, launched in 1926 by Hugo Gernsback (1884–1967). Westerns also had a growing readership throughout the first half of the twentieth century, peaking in the 1950s and 1960s thanks to television.

Romance novels also began to draw large readerships in the 1930s and 1940s, thanks in large part to British publisher Mills & Boon. However, most romances were hardbound and sold to libraries until the 1950s, when Mills & Boon and other publishers, including Harlequin in Canada, decided to shift to the more inexpensive paperback format, at least for reprints. It wasn't until the early 1970s that romance publishers began issuing first editions of novels in paperback—and romance sales exploded. Within twenty years, romance had become the largest category of mass-market paperbacks, constituting about half of all paperback books sold in the United States. (Genre fiction will be discussed in more detail in Chapter 10.)

Mass Market versus Quality

Paperbacks have long been sold in two primary formats: *mass-market* and *trade*. The mass-market format has a smaller trim size, usually about 4 x 7 inches (110 x 178 mm). Because they can be printed in quantity on large presses and quickly bound, they are the least expensive format to produce. The trade format is always larger than this, although the final dimensions are more flexible. Many trade paperbacks are the same size as the hardcover editions, and they are often printed from the same plates and simply glue-bound with a less expensive cardboard cover.

In the 1980s, some publishers decided to make a virtue of the fact that trade paperbacks featured the same size text but at a lower price than hardcover books, and they began to market these books as "quality" paperbacks. The Book-of-the-Month Club even launched a special subunit to sell these editions to readers. More recent iterations of the quality paperback have featured slightly heavier cover stock and folded ends that give the impression of a casebound book's dust jacket.

THE DIGITAL REVOLUTION

When asked how the digital revolution has affected the history of the book, most people will probably think first of the fairly recent emergence of the *e-book* and the *e-reader*. However, the electronic age made itself felt much earlier in the printing and typesetting trades. Developments in *xerography* or *photoreproduction* technology, more commonly known as *photocopying*, paved the way first for inexpensive, small-scale printshops, and then for home use. As photocopiers became faster and more powerful, they began to replace mechanical presses for many kinds of printing jobs, eventually even including longer-run and longer-format publications such as books. In the 1980s and 1990s, computers—first dedicated word-processing and typesetting systems, but eventually ordinary PCs running a variety of increasingly sophisticated software—replaced both typewriters and hot metal typesetting.

Printers for home and business use began as glorified typewriters: they used inked ribbons that were struck in response to keyboard commands to make an impression on paper. Many early printers required paper that was specially punched on the edges, so that the cogged wheels at the edges of the *platen* could pull the paper through while the impressions were being made. But *ink-jet printers*, which spray the paper with electrically charged droplets of ink, and *laser printers*, which fuse dry ink particles to paper through heat, eventually provided better-quality images and also allowed a wider range of applications. Text and images could be easily combined and printed by the home or office user, so that with the right paper and a modicum of care, nearly anyone could produce a finished product that emulated those created by printing professionals. And once the fixed-cost *prepress* work (typesetting, design, and page layout) was done, projects could be printed in whatever quantity was immediately required. Instead of printing a large number of copies while the presses were up and running and then warehousing the books until they were ordered and sold, publishers could use the new photoreproduction presses to economically print and bind single copies. *Print on demand* had arrived.

But, of course, at the very time that individuals were gaining the power to generate hard copies of texts that rivaled professional productions, other developments were raising questions about the very need for—or desirability of—hard copies. The massive increase in the number of periodicals at and after the turn of the twentieth century had a major impact on libraries and archives, which found themselves running out of space to store printed and other materials. In the early decades of the twentieth century, photographic technology came to the rescue. *Microfilming* enabled technicians to make a reduced photographic record of printed materials. The resulting rolls (*microfilm*) or sheets (*microfiche*) of photographic copies could be stored in a much smaller space than was required by daily broadside newspapers and long runs of weekly magazines. Beginning in the 1940s, literally millions of pages of periodicals, especially newspapers, were microfilmed, and, as Nicholson Baker documents in his book *Double Fold*, the originals were, for the most part, discarded—not only by those producing the microfilm, but also by hundreds of libraries that chose to replace their paper copies with film. (The full impact of these measures are discussed in more detail in Chapter 9.)

Although microfilm and microfiche require less storage space than paper copies of documents, they still take up a substantial amount of space, besides requiring the purchase and maintenance of special equipment (itself quite bulky) to read the encoded texts. The PC age introduced new, even more space-efficient text storage possibilities. Succeeding waves of ever-smaller and supposedly more stable media were heralded as the new best way to preserve and access documents. However, the first to really have an effect on the world of books were *CD-ROMs*, compact discs with "read-only memory," meaning they could be programmed with content that readers could not alter. Because CD-ROMs could hold vast quantities of data, publishers quickly realized that they might be very useful for producing reference works like dictionaries and encyclopedias.

The *Oxford English Dictionary* released a CD-ROM version of its first edition in 1988, and updated versions have been available since, although the online version, launched in 2000, has probably overtaken the CD version in popularity. The first truly multimedia encyclopedia was *Compton's Multimedia*, released in 1989. However, the best known CD-ROM encyclopedia is probably Microsoft's *Encarta*, which was launched in 1993. Because it was bundled with Microsoft-based computer operating systems for a number of years, thousands of computer users came to know and rely on *Encarta* until it was discontinued in 2009. Even the venerable *Encyclopedia Britannica*, first published in 1768, has been available in a digital format since 1994.

The key advantage of CD-ROMs (and their online successors) for these kinds of large, multivolume reference works is that they eliminate the need for readers to leaf through multiple individual volumes in search of particular pieces of information. Simply by entering a few key words into the search

Wikipedia landing page. The Puzzle Globe is a registered trademark of the Wikimedia Foundation and is used with the permission of the Wikimedia Foundation. This book is not endorsed by or affiliated with the Wikimedia Foundation.

feature, a reader can turn up all relevant passages, which can then be accessed immediately by clicking on the highlighted links. As a result of digital editions' convenience and relatively low cost, some publishers have chosen to phase out their paper editions of such works altogether. For example, the *Encyclopedia Britannica* announced in 2012 that it was discontinuing its print edition, ending a nearly 250-year tradition. (Perhaps ironically, the announcement immediately spurred demand for the remaining print copies.) Like other published encyclopedias, *Encyclopedia Britannica* also found it was facing significant competition from the more recent phenomenon of *wiki*, or crowd-sourced, collaborative reference works, such as Wikipedia.

However, whatever the format's advantages for reference works, neither publishers nor readers initially found the CD-ROM (or other portable media) especially attractive for other kinds of books. As physical objects, CD-ROMs still needed to be purchased or borrowed and carried and stored. They also could only be read on a computer, which in the early years usually still entailed a bulky central processing unit (CPU) and a screen whose *resolution* (sharpness of focus) was not particularly good. At least some of those factors had to change before an electronic book format could really gain a following among the general reading public.

Gutenberg and the Internet

Although we now take it for granted, the linked network of computers providing instantaneous access to information, entertainment, and a myriad of communication and other services was a revolutionary notion in the early days of computing. The immediate predecessor of today's system, the *Arpanet* (for Advanced Research Projects Agency Network), was created in the 1970s to link computer centers in the US Department of Defense with those of some of the major university research centers. In the late 1980s and early 1990s, the *internet* emerged, a global network of linked computers. (The computers communicate on the basis of a common set of rules or guidelines, the *Transmission Control Protocol*, or *TCP*, and *Internet Protocol*, or *IP*. Most ordinary computer users encounter these only when something goes wrong with their modems or wireless devices.)

WIKIPEDIA

The *wiki* concept, based on a Hawaiian word for "quick," was first launched in the early 1990s by Ward Cunningham (b. 1949). Wikis are websites that encourage creative collaboration: contributors may add, edit, or delete text. By far the best-known wiki is *Wikipedia*, a collaborative encyclopedia that was first brought online in 2001 by Jimmy Wales (b. 1966) and Lawrence Sanger (b. 1968). Its predecessor, *Nupedia*, had been created with the goal of having expert contributors upload scholarly, peer-reviewed pieces on a variety of topics. However, in the same time that it took to create the first couple dozen articles for Nupedia, Wikipedia—originally intended as a complement to Nupedia, where the public would be allowed to suggest and vet articles that could then be upgraded to Nupedia standards—had generated over 20,000.

Wales and Sanger decided to reconsider their plans. Although Wales was comfortable with the anyone-can-write concept, Sanger was less so and decided to leave the company; he has since become a critic of the project. The initial model for maintaining quality control—in other words, accuracy—was charmingly utopian: just as the greater internet community would upload content, the greater community would also check and revise that content. However, problems with intentional vandalism by some contributors, who not only sabotaged entries of persons and movements they disagreed with, but also sometimes added nonsense and unrelated links to pages, plus some fundamental disagreements about what should be included on the site, led to a rethink. In addition to software that monitors and can reverse possible vandalism, a cadre of higher-level volunteers and employees with administrator privileges now also review and revise text. Additionally, some entries with a high number of sabotage incidents are effectively locked out to certain categories of contributors.

Although initially there was a great deal of skepticism about Wikipedia's accuracy and authority, the encyclopedia's reputation has improved with time, just as its most optimistic early supporters had predicted. Some credit the site's success to its hewing pretty closely to its espoused "Five Pillars," or fundamental principles. The Five Pillars state that Wikipedia is an encyclopedia; that its entries should exhibit a neutral point of view; that anyone is free to use or edit its content; that editors should interact with one another respectfully; and, ironically, that there are no firm rules—everything is, at least in theory, up for renegotiation.

For many users, the internet initially served mainly as a novelty communication network, with various service providers hosting e-mail accounts as well as *listservs* (subscriber-based group e-mail systems). One of the first such providers was CompuServe, which was launched in 1989 and remained one of the industry leaders through the 1990s. Among the early *content-driven* internet providers was America Online (later AOL), which began in the early 1980s as an online gaming site. The company changed its name and broadened its focus in 1989. The revamped AOL offered its subscribers online games as well as communication options, access to news and entertainment, and one of the first interactive fiction series.

For those who knew where (and how) to look, however, the internet offered other options for education and leisure as well. One of the pioneers was *Project Gutenberg*, dedicated to the provision of electronic copies of non-copyrighted texts, free of charge and universally accessible. The oldest digital library, Project Gutenberg was created in 1971 by Michael Hart (1947–2011), who at the time was a university student with only occasional access to the Arpanet. Project Gutenberg's first 300 or so documents were entered and uploaded by Hart himself, the earliest ones laboriously typed on punched computer tape. After transcribing the Declaration of Independence and other American civic documents, Hart gradually moved on to the King James Bible and other works. By the mid-1990s, when more and more users were discovering the internet, Hart was able to harness the power of *crowd-sourcing*. Volunteers helped type and upload documents, dramatically increasing the number of texts available. Thanks to *optical character readers*, or *OCRs*, scanning eventually replaced typing, and the volunteers shifted to proofreading the resulting texts and correcting coding errors. By 2011, the main archive had amassed an online library of over 38,000 texts, mostly literature in English, but also some non-English items; over 100,000 free books are available through Project Gutenberg's many partners and affiliates, which include undertakings in other European languages and literatures. There are also a number of non-text files available.

Project Gutenberg was only the first of many book and periodical digitization projects. As the internet became more wide-reaching, more reliably accessible, and faster, a number of digitization initiatives took hold. Some initiatives tried to tackle the problems of microfilm and microfiche, which over several decades of collecting were becoming increasingly cumbersome for some libraries and archives. For example, *JSTOR* (for *Journal Storage*) was launched under the auspices of the Andrew W. Mellon Foundation in 1995, primarily as an off-site archiving resource for academic libraries. In return for allowing JSTOR to scan the microfilmed and hard-copy versions of journals in their collections, libraries were offered ongoing access to the resulting digitized editions. JSTOR originally began with only seven member libraries and a handful of journals, but it now includes over 7,000 participating libraries and more than 1,000 journals. Other scholarly and commercial presses have followed JSTOR's example, offering either their own titles in digital editions or collecting a range of periodicals and offering them as digital research packages.

Government-supported institutions became involved as well, with initiatives like *PubMed*, an international online database of health science journals and literature maintained in the United States by the National Library of Medicine, in the United Kingdom by the British Library, and in Canada by the Canadian Institutes of Health Research and the Canadian National Science Library. Smaller, independently run projects have generated other digital archives of works by particular authors, of particular eras, or even by genre. Reading the literature of another time and place no longer requires travel to a particular library or collection.

Other initiatives have specialized in creating high-quality digital editions of extremely rare and valuable books, helping not only to bring these works into the reach of ordinary readers and scholars, but also to protect the originals, or *leaf masters*, from overuse. Some of the most famous books in the world, like the Dead Sea Scrolls, the *Book of Kells*, and the Chinese *Diamond Sutra*, are now digitized, allowing them to be read, searched, and examined in extremely close detail. While many of these digitized editions are only available for purchase, others are fully available online. Thus, readers anywhere in the world who wish to compare the differences between, say, papyrus texts of the Egyptian *Book of the Dead*, illuminated Books of Hours, or copies of Gutenberg's Bible, can do so via the net.

Undoubtedly the largest and most ambitious of the digitization projects is *Google Books*. Launched in 2004 as "Google Print" by the popular internet search giant, Google Books' grand scheme is to make a digital copy of every book ever published. To achieve this, it entered into partnership arrangements with major publishers, as well as with some of the world's largest and most respected research libraries, including those at Oxford, Harvard, Michigan, and Stanford, as well as the New York Public Library. Google's logic was that these institutions had the largest and most comprehensive collections of texts for scanning, an estimated 15 million-plus volumes. Google also entered into agreements with the Library of Congress and with a number of European countries. More publishers and universities have since joined the venture, including Keio University in Japan and the University of Mysore in India.

In return for libraries' allowing Google to scan their collections, Google promised to provide the libraries with access to the resulting digital copies. At the outset, some librarians expressed concern that their original copies would suffer the kinds of indignities and outright destruction that occurred with earlier format migration projects, such as microfilming. To prevent such problems, Google designed special cameras and cradles that would hold the books open and turn their pages gently. Google Books now boasts somewhere upwards of 12 million scanned books, of which at least one million are in the public domain and thus available for complete access and download.

Although Google's informal corporate motto is "Don't be evil," some skeptics have viewed Google Books as legally and ethically dubious, and the project has been subject to numerous legal challenges and restrictions. Most of the challenges have hinged on Google's intention to digitize *every* book in the participating libraries, regardless of copyright status. The fear among copyright holders was that these books would be made available for free, thereby undercutting their authors' and publishers' profits. A series of lawsuits assured that copyright holders would retain control of their works, even to the extent of removing them from Google Books, and restrictions on full searches and on downloading or printing even excerpts of copyrighted books have blunted (if not eliminated) some critics' fears.

Another category of book that caused dissension is so-called *orphan books*, those whose copyright status cannot be readily determined because their authors have died, their literary estates are unclear, or their publishers have gone out of business. In response to challenges, Google conceded that any orphan books still determined to be in copyright would be properly protected. Finally, some have been concerned about Google's commercial control of the books it has digitized. For example, public librarians have been worried that even though Google has promised that public libraries will have access to the digitized books, there are potential restrictions on the number of copies that any particular library system could view, due to limitations on the number of computer terminals that would be licensed to access those books.

The public libraries' concern about providing computer access leads to another important aspect of the book in the digital age: devices capable of reading e-books. Although the brief history related here shows that e-books have existed for about 50 years, it is only recently that they have begun to reshape the publishing world. The key development has been the rise of more affordable and easy-to-use e-readers.

e-Readers

In the late 1990s, headlines blared that the age of the electronic book had arrived. The long-promised paperless society was upon us, journalists declared. Traditional paper books would go the way of the buggy whip: while some would persist in preferring the old codex format, most readers would embrace the new. Promoters touted the advantages of carrying only one device that contained dozens—even hundreds—of volumes. With manufacturing and warehousing costs taken out of the equation, books would become ever-cheaper to produce and distribute, so readers could afford to buy more of them. Publishers entered into agreements about formats to ensure that e-books could be read across a range of devices and platforms, resulting in the *Open eBook (OeB)* format in 1999. (OeB was later replaced by the *ePub* format, which was compatible with the then nearly universal PDF format.) Large and small publishers established divisions that would specialize in e-books, and authors began to experiment with the new medium. Horror and suspense writer Stephen King's decision to issue his 2000 novel *Riding the Bullet* exclusively in e-format was hailed as a landmark. If a bestselling author like King was embracing electronic books, they were bound to take hold.

Only they didn't. After the initial excitement, most of the newly launched digital imprints were quietly shut down again within just a few years by the publishing houses. Except for genre fiction—science fiction, but especially romance—e-books did not catch on with readers. The problem was not so much with e-books themselves as with the devices first marketed to read them. Even those genre fiction readers who did embrace e-books tended to read them on computer screens, rather than on dedicated e-readers.

The first generations of e-readers, with names like *Rocket Ebook* and *Softbook*, faced some serious technological challenges and also some unanticipated competition. In the first place, e-reader designers had to meet or beat the ease of use and portability of traditional books, especially the popular and inexpensive paperback. Ideally, this meant designing an e-reader that was no larger—or heavier—than an average book, but that still had a battery capable of holding its charge for long periods of time, a memory capable of storing multiple volumes of text (and illustration), and a frame that was neither flimsy nor unwieldy. Furthermore, the e-reader's screen needed to provide maximum legibility: sharp characters with very little pixelation, high contrast between the type and the background, quick loading of screen images and no ghosting when turning pages, and no glare. Backlighting, so the device could be easily read in dim light, would be an advantage, as would a means of increasing the font size. The mechanisms for moving around within the e-book—in other words, for reading it—would also need to be intuitive to use and easy to manipulate. The e-reader should enable readers to do everything with e-books that they did with regular books: flip pages back and forth, check notes and indexes, bookmark both where they were in the text at any given moment and any significant passages, and add annotations. The device should feel comfortable in the hands but also be easy to prop up on a desk or table.

The first generation of e-readers met some of these challenges and failed miserably at others. Where the early devices largely succeeded was in creating an electronic screen that mimicked the high-contrast look of a traditional white page printed with black ink and that loaded sufficiently quickly to allow readers to turn their pages. Where they largely failed was in usability and convenience. The early e-readers proved fiddly: buttons for turning pages were too small or poorly located, and the bookmarking functions and the means of shifting between main text and notes or between different books were difficult to use. Some of the devices froze up too easily—a fatal flaw sadly on display in a special exhibit of e-readers in the main lobby of the British Library in about 2004, where thousands on their way to the reading rooms probably had their very first encounters with e-book technology. The devices were also unwieldy: they usually required direct links to a computer in order to download the books, the batteries ran down sooner than expected, leaving users unable to access their reading material, and they were relatively heavy. Last but not least, they were also expensive. As single-feature devices, they offered very little advantage over laptops, which, ironically, were growing smaller, lighter, and more efficient. Readers who wanted mobile access to e-books might as well stick with their multipurpose devices.

By the time the second wave of e-readers came on the market a few years later, several crucial things had changed. First, improvements in wireless technology meant that far more telephone and computer data could be transmitted without cable connections, and wi-fi hotspots allowed quick and often free access to the web. Second, developments in mobile phone computing and battery technology meant that hand-held devices could now perform higher-powered functions and for longer periods of time before they needed to be recharged. Additionally, portable music players, particularly the Apple iPod, had demonstrated that large volumes of data could be stored in tiny, attractive devices—and that users would pay for them. The release of the first Apple iPhones in 2007 combined many of these features in a compelling package, with touch-screen technology that was easy to use and felt intuitive. The iPhone and other smart phones further accustomed users to the expectation that vast amounts of data should be instantly available, literally at one's fingertips, and to the idea of paying to download the material they wanted. The ground was prepared for a new generation of e-book readers.

The release of the Sony Reader in 2006, the Amazon Kindle in 2007, Barnes & Noble's Nook in 2009, and Apple's iPad in 2010 were all met with a much different response than the first generation of e-readers. Mostly smaller, lighter, faster, more mobile, and also more attractive than their predecessors, these devices promised users a book-reading experience that met or exceeded their interactions with traditional books. In addition to reducing or eliminating the disadvantages of the previous generation of readers, the new e-readers also improved the contrast and responsiveness of the screens, so that the image resolution was even better. Since three of the major players in the field—Amazon, Barnes & Noble, and Apple—also had well-established online retail presences, purchasers of the new readers could quickly find a wealth of materials to read and download them through existing accounts.

Publishers of both books and periodicals came on board fairly quickly, and since changes in printing technology meant that virtually all new works were prepared in an electronic format prior to paper printing, it was relatively easy to make those versions available for sale. This meant that in addition to the myriad free books already available through Project Gutenberg, Google Books, and other sources, there was also a large and growing store of new titles available for sale. After some experimentation with pricing, the costs of both e-books and e-readers came down into ranges that readers were willing to pay, and the e-book finally established a solid foothold. In 2010, Amazon. com reported that sales of e-books for its Kindle reader outstripped sales of all hardcover books for the first time, and by 2011, e-books were beginning to overtake other traditional book categories as well.

THE FUTURE OF THE BOOK

What are the implications of digitization for the future of print culture, and especially for the future of traditional books? These two interconnected questions have been plaguing book historians for decades already, and they are of deep concern to all who are interested in the role of the book in society. A look back at other periods of transition in the history of the book should provide hope for those who fear that the new era spells the death of the book. New formats and technologies have, on balance, tended to increase the number of readers and thus the demand for text. Furthermore, there is clear evidence of traditions and formats from previous ages long coexisting with new traditions and formats. The curtain didn't come down on scribal culture when the age of print culture began in the fifteenth century. Serious hardcover works didn't stop being published when the paperback format gained ground. Despite the gloomy (or gleeful) prognostications, it is highly unlikely that the curtain will fall on print culture now that the digital age is here to stay.

What does seem likely is that certain kinds of works and readers will migrate to particular formats. Light reading of every genre is probably more likely to appear in electronic formats in the future, just as it has tended to be published in paperback until now. On the other hand, serious works of moral philosophy, say, may be more likely to continue in limited, hardcover editions—not least because readers of such works tend to be scholarly and more conservative in their relationship to the material book.

Anyone who has formed an attachment to a particular copy of a physical book knows that there are pleasures to be found in handling and reading that very copy. Since the publishing and bookselling industries are full of these kinds of people, it seems pretty certain that the opportunities for owning and loving traditional books will not disappear any time soon—the writers, publishers, and sellers will make sure that copies continue to be produced and circulated among those who desire them. Additionally, just as the mechanization of the printing trades in the nineteenth century sparked a reappreciation of the crafts and aesthetics of the traditional book arts, it appears that the digitization of the printing trades at the turn of this century is encouraging a reappreciation of physical books and their production. All of these developments suggest that while the relationship between the book and society is changing dramatically, the relationship itself will continue to endure, probably far into the future.

In order to help readers of this book better understand and analyze the ways in which that relationship is likely to develop, Part Two of *The Book in Society* shifts from a chronological approach to focus on the many actors who shape the relationship. The second section is structured loosely on what book historian Robert Darnton described as a book publishing "communication circuit," in which different aspects of the book world interact to shape what kinds of books are produced and what their impact is on and in the broader society. In addition to looking at what authors, publishers, and readers contribute to the world of the book, Part Two will also look at some of the other forces that come into play, including governments and other entities that explicitly censor or promote particular books and ideas, and booksellers and libraries, which are responsible for getting those works into the hands of would-be readers.

SELECTED BIBLIOGRAPHY

Altick, Richard D. *The English Common Reader: A Social History of the Mass Reading Public, 1800–1900*. 2nd ed. Columbus: Ohio State UP, 1957.

Baker, Nicholson. *Double Fold: Libraries and the Assault on Paper*. New York: Random House, 2001.

Ballantine, Betty. "The Paperback Conquest of America." In *The Book in the United States Today*. Ed. Gordon Graham and Richard Abel. New Brunswick, NJ: Transaction, 1996. 101–12.

Fletcher, Dan. "A Brief History of Wikipedia." *Time*, 18 August 2009.

Google Books. http://books.google.com/intl/en/googlebooks/history.html.

Greco, Albert N. *The Book Publishing Industry*. Boston: Allyn and Bacon, 1997.

JSTOR. http://about.jstor.org/about-us/our-history.

Lebert, Marie. *A Short History of Ebooks*. NEF, U of Toronto P, 2009. http://www.gutenberg.org/catalog/world/readfile?fk_files=1308553.

Mayfield, Kendra. "e-Books King: Stephen the First." *Wired*, 14 March 2000. http://www.wired.com/culture/lifestyle/news/2000/03/34940?currentPage=all.

Miller, Claire Cain. "e-Books Top Hardcovers at Amazon." *New York Times*, 20 July 2010.

Penguin Company History. http://www.penguin.co.uk/static/cs/uk/0/aboutus/history.html.

Petersen, Clarence. *The Bantam Story: Thirty Years of Paperback Publishing*. New York: Bantam, 1970.

Project Gutenberg. http://www.gutenberg.org/wiki/Main_Page.

Schudson, Michael, and Katherine Fink. "Happy Birthday, Wikipedia!" *Columbia Journalism Review* 50.3 (2011): 63.

Sporkin, Andi. "Popularity of Books in Digital Platforms Continues to Grow, According to AAP Publishers February 2011 Sales Report." *Association of American Publishers*, 14 April 2011. http://www.publishers.org/press/30/.

Wikipedia: About. http://en.wikipedia.org/wiki/Wikipedia:About.

ACTIVITIES

The Material Book

One of the best ways to learn about the history of the book is to experience it by closely examining different kinds of books, produced in different places and times. To expand your knowledge of different bookmaking materials and techniques, arrange a visit to a library, archive, or museum whose collection contains a range of diverse texts. Larger libraries may have a special collections department or rare books room that will include items that are older and more rare, and they may also include *artist's books*, artworks whose structure and design evoke the book form but which are not necessarily intended for reading in a conventional sense. However, even relatively small libraries and archives can contain a surprising range of examples of papers, printing methods, and binding techniques.

Examine the books carefully to compare the materials from which they are made, the copying, printing, and illustrating techniques used in them, and the bindings. Note the differences in texture and color between, say, papyrus and parchment, or linen and wood-pulp papers. Look for indications on the pages or bindings of the books' producers or previous owners.

The Digital Book

Many digitization projects are primarily concerned with making only the content of the books more accessible to readers. However, some projects seek to recreate the whole experience of a given book. Frequently, the items selected for digitization by such initiatives are especially valuable: they are rare (even unique) examples of a given text, or they contain especially beautiful examples of book design, illustration, and binding. In the past, access to such books was restricted to specialist scholars, who had to travel to the archive to view the book. However, sophisticated software now allows interested readers anywhere in the world to examine these works from their own homes and offices.

Visit one of the digital book sites listed immediately below, or any other sites you can discover that have high-quality digital images of rare books. (Some digitized items are also available on CD-ROM and may be available through your library.) Select one of the digital books on display, and page through it carefully. What details about the book's production and history are clearly visible? What does the digitized version allow you to see that you would not be able to see if you were only allowed to view the work in a glass museum cabinet? How does the experience of reading such a book digitally enhance or detract from your appreciation and understanding of it?

British Library Online Gallery: Turning the Pages. http://www.bl.uk/onlinegallery/ttp/ ttpbooks.html.

Catalogue of Digitized Medieval Manuscripts. UCLA. http://manuscripts.cmrs. ucla.edu/index.php. Global index with direct links to digitized books in library collections.

Digitized Materials from the Rare Book and Special Collections Division. Library of Congress. http://www.loc.gov/rr/rarebook/digitalcoll.html.

English Emblem Book Project. http://emblem.libraries.psu.edu/.

World Digital Library. UNESCO. http://www.wdl.org/en/. Global index with direct links to different kinds of text around the world; not all linked texts are digitized in full, but reproduction quality of available pages is good.

The Age of Periodicals

The nineteenth and early twentieth centuries saw the proliferation of periodicals, works published serially that enabled readers to keep abreast of news, currents of thought, and the latest fashions in everything from clothing and home décor to travel routes. Originally printed on acidic and thus brittle paper, many of these periodicals have now been converted to digital forms, which has not only preserved them for future generations but has also made them much more easily accessible and searchable.

Newspapers and weekly and monthly magazines can function as time capsules for readers curious about events and attitudes in other times and places. Because periodicals were directed to particular reading audiences, comparing several periodicals published in the same timeframe can help provide perspective on events and issues.

Access one or more of the digital periodicals archives listed immediately below, and determine some search criteria for browsing the archive. For example, you might choose a date range, a geographical region, a type of reader (such as women, children, university students, or members of a particular profession), or a topic. Then compare the articles that come up in your search and the publications in which they appear. If the archive allows you to view both individual article texts and the whole pages on which they originally appeared, toggle between these views. What do you learn about the time period or the intended readers by comparing how a topic is treated in different publications? How does viewing a given article in its original context—surrounded by other articles, illustrations, and advertisements—differ from viewing it as a standalone, autonomous piece of text? How do the periodicals of earlier eras compare to and differ from periodicals today?

A number of periodicals archives are freely accessible online:

Chronicling America: Historic American Newspapers. Library of Congress. http://chroniclingamerica.loc.gov/.
Dickens Journals Online. http://www.djo.org.uk/.
Nineteenth Century Serials Edition (NCSE). http://www.ncse.ac.uk/index.html.

In addition, a number of individual periodicals, including popular magazines such as the *Saturday Evening Post*, *Time Magazine*, and *Harper's* have made their archives available for free. Others are subscription-only but readily available through libraries, including the historical archives of *The Times* of London and the *New York Times*. Research universities and larger metropolitan and national libraries also usually subscribe to a number of the commercially managed periodicals archives, including Chadwyck-Healey's *British Periodicals* and Cengage's collections of eighteenth- and nineteenth-century British and US newspapers.

The Book Arts: From Gutenberg to POD

Another way to learn about the history of the book is to see and experience the traditional book arts—papermaking, typesetting, printing, and binding—in action. Universities sometimes have book arts facilities that are open for tours and exhibits, and independent letterpress artists will sometimes allow visitors to their studios or offer classes. In addition, local printers and booksellers will sometimes host a *wayzgoose*, or printing celebration. Commercial printers may also host visits, and their shops can sometimes contain everything from nineteenth-century printing and bookbinding equipment that is still used for special projects to the latest print-on-demand or POD machines.

Arrange a visit to a working printshop. How do the materials and processes being employed compare to those used in Gutenberg's time? In what ways have the materials and processes changed so much as to be virtually unrecognizable? If you are allowed to experiment with or operate any of the tools used by the printer or book artist, what does the physical experience of making them add to your understanding of the end products?

History of the Book Wiki Project

A *wiki* is a collaborative website, whose content can be created or edited by anyone in a given community. To develop and build your knowledge of the history of the book, create a dedicated wiki. The wiki will allow you to explore and conduct preliminary research in a variety of topics in the history of the book, most of which will likely supplement and extend the reading that you are doing in your course. The wiki might be designed to be open just to your class, to the wider university community, or to the public. Alternatively, you might contribute to one of the many existing wiki projects that cover material related to the history of the book, including Wikipedia.

Start by developing a list of possible topic stubs. You might organize these under broad headings, such as historic periods or geographic regions, materials used to make books, or important books or authors. Then start inputting and revising the content, being sure to document sources appropriately. Entries might include links to other websites that provide additional information on the topic.

Bibliographic Description: The History of the Book Through One Book

A *descriptive bibliographer* views books as physical objects and examines them the way geologists, botanists, or forensic scientists examine the primary data in their fields. In their *Introduction to Bibliographical and Textual Studies*, W.P. Williams and C.S. Abbott explain that bibliographers are interested in determining such facts as the book's date and method of composition, the source and nature of the compositors' copy, the kind and quantity of type or the kind of machine used in composition, and how the book was released to the public (sold or given away, how many copies, what sources, when). They are not really concerned with what the book has to say, but in how it came to be.

Select one particular book and write a bibliographic description of it. Although you may choose a brand-new book, you will probably find that a book that has a little more "lived experience" behind it will prove more satisfying to work with. In your description, you should include basic information about the text (author and publisher, date and place of publication, physical description of the book), as well as any additional information you can deduce either through your physical examination of the item or through bibliographic research. On the basis of your examination and research, you should try to deduce who were the intended readers of your book, and explain the reasoning behind your conclusions.

You can determine a great deal of information about a book from a careful investigation of its material form and a quick look over its contents. For example, by examining the front and back pages, you can usually learn something about the author, publisher, printer, typographers, illustrators, when and where the book was published, and (sometimes) who sold it (and for how much), who bought it, and why. (The information provided in the front and back pages of most modern books is usually unproblematic, but older books may not be entirely reliable. For example, many older works of fiction claim to be "true" or "edited" rather than "written" by their authors, and details about their supposed printers and date of publication may be fabrications.) You can also determine quite a lot about the real or perceived value of the book (either as an object or as a set of ideas between covers) from the style and expense of its paper and binding, the simplicity or elaboration of the design, and the condition it is in.

Furthermore, by looking up the book (or its author, publisher, or any identified readers) in various catalogues and databases, you can learn even more about it. For example, a library catalogue may tell you when the book was acquired and who paid for it; WorldCat can tell you how many copies of a particular book are held in libraries around the world, where those libraries are, and whether the book is available for general circulation; Books in Print or Amazon can tell you if the book is still available for sale in some format; and other reference sources and databases can tell you information about other books written or published by the book's producers.

RESOURCES IN BOOK HISTORY

The following organizations have collections and programs related to the history of the book. Most also provide links to other organizations and collections that may be of interest.

International

Society for the History of Authorship, Reading, and Publishing (SHARP). http://www.sharpweb.org/.

Australia and New Zealand

Centre for Books, Writing and Ideas, Wheeler Centre, State Library of Victoria, Melbourne. http://wheelercentre.com/.
Centre for the Book, Monash University, Victoria. http://arts.monash.edu.au/the-book/about/.
National Library of Australia, Canberra. http://www.nla.gov.au/.
National Library of New Zealand, Wellington. http://www.natlib.govt.nz/.

Canada

Bibliothèque et Archives Nationales du Québec, Montreal. http://www.banq.qc.ca/accueil/.
Canadian Children's Book Centre, Toronto. http://www.bookcentre.ca/.
Libraries and Archives Canada, Ottawa. http://www.collectionscanada.gc.ca/index-e.html.
Toronto Centre for the Book, University of Toronto. http://bookhistory.ischool.utoronto.ca/TCB.html.

United Kingdom

British Library, London. http://www.bl.uk/.
Centre for the History of the Book, School of Literatures, Languages and Cultures, University of Edinburgh. http://www.hss.ed.ac.uk/chb/.
Centre for the Study of the Book, Bodleian Libraries, Oxford. http://www.bodley.ox.ac.uk/csb/.
St. Bride Library, London. http://www.stbride.org/.

United States

Bibliographical Society of America, Lenox Hill Station, NY. http://www.bibsocamer.org/.
Center for the Book, Library of Congress, Washington, DC. http://www.read.gov/cfb/.
Center for the History of Print and Digital Culture, School of Library and Information Studies, University of Wisconsin, Madison, WI. http://www.slis.wisc.edu/chpchome.htm.
Minnesota Center for Book Arts, Minneapolis, MN. http://www.mnbookarts.org/.
Penn State Center for the History of the Book, University Park, PA. http://www.pabook.libraries.psu.edu/histofbook/.
Rare Book School, University of Virginia, Charlottesville, VA. http://www.rarebookschool.org/.
San Francisco Center for the Book, San Francisco, CA. http://sfcb.org/.
Yiddish Book Center, Amherst, MA. http://www.yiddishbookcenter.org/.

PART TWO

THE BOOK CIRCUIT: AUTHORS, AUTHORITIES, PUBLISHERS, READERS

CHAPTER FIVE

AUTHORS

In a 1982 article entitled "What Is the History of Books?" historian Robert Darnton (b.1939) argues that in order to properly understand how books come into the world and shape it, we should start by asking some key questions about the nature of authorship. "At what point did writers free themselves from the patronage of wealthy noblemen and the state in order to live by their pens?" he asks. "What was the nature of a literary career, and how was it pursued? How did writers deal with publishers, printers, booksellers, reviewers, and one another?"

As Darnton's questions make clear, the notion of an author as an autonomous genius who generates great texts and bestows them on a grateful world is an inadequate one. Authors may sometimes live in garrets and sometimes in more splendid retreats, but they don't live in vacuums—their words are shaped by the worlds around them. Both reading and unfolding events inform their minds and furnish their imaginations, and the economic and intellectual climates in which they find themselves shape both what they can say and how they say it. Finally, there has to be some means of transmitting their words from the authors' own heads and desks to the heads and desks of their readers, and those means of transmission—traditionally publishers and booksellers, now perhaps the more direct means of the web—also exert an influence over the authors' works.

There have been authors since the dawn of writing, but notions of authorship have changed significantly over the past three to four centuries. We now commonly think of an "author" as someone whose connection to a particular text or texts must be acknowledged. However, French literary critic Michel Foucault (1926–84) has suggested that this notion of authorship is fairly recent, and that it only arose when there began to be negative consequences for making certain kinds of statements: until an individual could be punished for saying or writing things that were deemed to be irreligious or unlawful, there was no particular need to establish who wrote what. Once this principle of authorship (what Foucault calls the "author-function") had been generally accepted, it was quickly reinforced by conventions and laws that not only punished authors for saying the wrong things, but also protected their claims to their work.

As currently understood, an *author* is someone who originates or creates with words, who adds something new to the store of ideas, knowledge, imagination. That "something new" may be simply a new twist or fresh perspective on old ideas, or it may be something revelatory, earthshaking, paradigm shifting.

But perhaps as importantly, an author is usually someone who also sees him- or herself as a writer—as someone who has something to say in written form. So in addition to the action or occupation, there is also an element of identity and intention. Depending on the time and the place, authors might claim their works by putting their names on them, or they might be content to see their works circulate anonymously, or as "by the author of." Alternatively, they might adopt *pseudonyms* or *pen names* to hide their identities, or they might collaborate in ways that subordinate their individual identities to the larger identity of a given project (as, for example, in the *wiki* model of collaborative text generation).

However, in addition to involving both the act of writing and the practice of identifying oneself as a writer, authorship as popularly understood also entails the notion of *transmission*. An author is usually thought to be someone who writes for an audience. That audience may be large or small, contemporary or in the future, but generally there must be a real or imagined reader out there somewhere.

This chapter will look at the rise of the modern author: someone who writes as either occupation or vocation, whose identity is at least somewhat bound up in the act of writing, and whose works are intended for some kind of public dissemination to readers. It will examine how authorship as a profession emerged in the seventeenth and eighteenth centuries and developed subsequently, with particular attention to the economic conditions that made it possible for writers to live by their pens and to the degrees of prestige (or opprobrium) accorded to different kinds of authorship over the centuries. The chapter will also look at literary agents and other institutions that emerged to help authors negotiate the terms of publication. The chapter will conclude with a consideration of what happens when authors' works are modified and adapted for other audiences, through such means as translation, stage or screen adaptation, or reformatting for audio or electronic distribution.

THE RISE OF THE MODERN AUTHOR

While there have been named, identifiable authors throughout history, most scholars agree that in the late seventeenth century something significant began to change in Western society's notion of what *authorship* meant. In many respects, this change was shaped by the growing emphasis in the West on the importance of the individual. The Reformation and the Enlightenment had stressed that individuals were moral agents who were responsible for both their own self-development and the betterment of the world in which they found themselves. By putting their ideas into circulation, authors actively participated in that culture of improvement. If they failed to make an impact, so be it—but if they had an effect, whether negative or positive, they were increasingly expected to be punished or rewarded for that influence.

a very linear perspective

This general shift to personal accountability began to change the circumstances in which authors wrote and distributed their works. Prior to this period, authors and other creative individuals, like artists and musicians, generally relied on *patronage*, financial sponsorship from individuals or from institutions such as the state or the church. Patrons would provide authors with an allowance and other practical support, sometimes including room and board, and in return the authors would produce their works and, as thanks, dedicate them to their patrons. The author was thus relieved from the pressure to earn a living through some other means, and the patron could hope for public acclaim and even a kind of immortality through having nurtured and supported creative endeavor.

The patronage system, in use in the West until the nineteenth century, had some obvious drawbacks. Not unreasonably, some patrons assumed they ought to have a say in what an author did or didn't write. An author might be expected to adopt a particular tone or point of view or to avoid particular topics or modes of expression. If their patrons' opinions or taste were not in line with their own, authors might easily feel cramped and thwarted by the mutual obligations of patronage. However, if an author attempted to break out of the mold in some way that the patron disagreed with, the patron might feel betrayed—and exact retribution.

Patronage could work in direct and indirect ways. For example, the Anglo-Irish writer Jonathan Swift (1667–1745) was materially helped in his early writing career by his patron Sir William Temple (1628–99), a retired diplomat. Temple hired Swift as a secretary in 1689, and over the next ten years, Swift helped Temple organize and revise his essays for publication. This work constituted a valuable literary apprenticeship for Swift: not only did he internalize useful habits of scholarship and application, but he also practiced and refined various modes of rhetorical expression. In recognition of Swift's conscientious and valuable assistance, Temple granted his protégé the right to publish the remainder of his writings after his death, providing him with a very useful entrée into the London publishing world. Critics trace at least some of the powerful rhetorical impact of Swift's later political and satirical writings, among the best-known of which are *Gulliver's Travels* (1726) and "A Modest Proposal" (1729), to the earlier practice of working on Temple's writings.

The French Enlightenment author Voltaire (pen name of François-Marie Arouet, 1694–1778), continuously forced into exile (or prison) for his anti-state and anti-church writings, found a particularly generous patron in Frederick II of Prussia (1712–86)—at least for awhile. In 1750, Frederick the Great invited Voltaire, whose work he greatly admired, to the palace of Sanssouci in Potsdam, near Berlin. (This was a courtesy not extended to Frederick's wife, who was banned from Sanssouci.) Voltaire was granted his own set of chambers in one wing of the palace, as well as a generous salary of 20,000 francs per year. Frederick's patronage initially gave Voltaire immense freedom, and he composed one of his more curious and creative works, an early science-fiction story "Micromégas" (1752), while in Potsdam. However, after Voltaire fell out with the president of the Berlin Academy of Science and subsequently published a satire on the president's ideas, the king, no longer enchanted with his resident genius, ordered the publication destroyed and Voltaire arrested. The author eventually escaped to Switzerland, where he remained until a final journey home to Paris in 1778.

Patronage also was extended to some women writers, but less frequently, and most often by other women. Literary historian Dustin Griffin notes that this was at least in part because of the dangers to women writers' reputations of being under the "protection" of male patrons: outsiders might infer that the relationship was sexual, rather than literary and professional. Margaret Clifford (1560–1616), Countess of Cumberland and a maid of honor to Elizabeth I, appears to have been a fairly generous literary patron. Among her protégées was the poet Emilia Lanier (1569–1645), believed to be the first English woman to have had her poetry published. Lanier's 1611 volume also includes the first country-house poem in English, "The Description of Cooke-ham," which praises a manor-house owned by the Clifford family and, not incidentally, the home's owner as well. The English novelist Charlotte Lennox (1720–1804) seems to have had mixed success with patrons. She secured much financial and publishing assistance through the help of Samuel Johnson (1709–84), who introduced her to a number of peers who were interested in her work and allowed her to dedicate it to them. Her most important novel, *The Female Quixote* (1752), included a dedication (written by Johnson) to Lionel Sackville (1688–1765), then Earl of Middlesex and later the first Duke of Dorset; another important patron of Lennox's was Thomas Pelham-Holles (1693–1768), the Duke of Newcastle.

The efforts of authors to court potential patrons or to thank previous benefactors could sometimes backfire. Literary historian Jean Brink notes that in the 1590 three-book edition of Edmund Spenser's (c. 1552–99) great allegorical poem *The Faerie Queene*, there are twenty-five dedicatory poems included at the end of the text, in addition to the opening—and most important—dedication of the work to Queen Elizabeth I (1533–1603). Arranged in two groups, the poems overlap and repeat in some ways, and the effect is to suggest that some dedicatees in the first group were later dropped, and that others were hastily added at a later stage in the production of the book. The embarrassing (and potentially offensive) assemblage of dedicatory poems at the back of the edition appears to have been the work of Spenser's printer, who seems to have haphazardly rounded up the dedications from a number of presentation copies of the manuscript version of the poem. It is unclear whether the gaffe cost Spenser the support of his high-ranking patrons, but it did earn him a satiric lash from his contemporary Thomas Nashe (1567–c. 1601). In any event, Spenser took pains to oversee the publication of the 1596 expanded edition of *The Faerie Queene*—which omitted the troublesome dedicatory sonnets.

Of course, authors who had independent means could write to suit themselves, as they always had—and in eras when literacy and education were more restricted, writers usually arose almost exclusively from among the higher levels of society. However, as authors who supported themselves by their pens began to emerge from among the lower ranks, upper-class writers sought ways of distancing themselves from the new arrivals. If they circulated their writing, they might do so privately, only to select friends and acquaintances. They might also avoid the commercial taint of having their works printed, and instead circulate them only in manuscript form. Or they might adopt strategies for concealing their identities, by publishing anonymously or pseudonymously.

Anonymous and Pseudonymous Publishing

Until well into the nineteenth century, many authors of all social classes chose to conceal their identities when venturing into print. In some cases, this was prudent: authors whose works were critical of the authorities, for example, might choose some form of subterfuge to avoid arrest and other sanctions. The classic work of political philosophy, *Two Treatises of Government* by John Locke (1632–1704), was published anonymously in 1689. Written in the years immediately preceding the Glorious Revolution, when the Catholic James II of England (1633–1701) was replaced on the throne by the Protestant William of Orange (1650–1702), the *Two Treatises* was too politically incendiary to have been owned by Locke, and although he subsequently revised the text and oversaw its republication, he never did acknowledge its authorship. In other cases, disguise was a matter of reputation. Members of the aristocracy, well-connected individuals, or women might fear that their social positions would be undermined if their names appeared in print. In her 1929 essay about female authorship, *A Room of One's Own*, Virginia Woolf (1882–1941) ventured that "Anon [Anonymous], who wrote so many poems without signing them, was often a woman."

Anonymous or pseudonymous publication could also be used to provide a blanket identity that would help direct readers' attention away from individual contributions towards the work as a whole. This was the case for most periodical publishing from the earliest days until the beginning of the twentieth century. Publishers sought to give their periodicals a unified feeling, and identifying the various contributors was thought to undermine that unity. Therefore, not only were most contributions unsigned, but the identity of the editor was also often concealed. However, editors' and contributors' identities were often open secrets, and guessing who might be behind a particular essay, poem, or piece of fiction was a perennial form of entertainment for those involved in the world of letters. One important benefit of the practice of anonymous and pseudonymous publishing was that it provided opportunities for many individuals who might otherwise have been kept out of the ranks of authorship, especially women and others who were denied access to formal education. A number of individuals who went on to establish successful literary careers in their own names got their start with anonymous contributions to local or regional newspapers or to small special-interest magazines.

In at least some instances, the motivation for concealing or revealing identity had to do with the prestige of the genre being circulated. To cite one of the most famous examples, William Shakespeare does not seem to have been particularly concerned about the publication (or non-publication) of his plays. This led to the rather vexing outcome that even those plays published during his

WILLIAM SHAKESPEARE

One of the best-loved and best-known authors in world literature, William Shakespeare (1564–1616) began his theatre career sometime in the 1580s. The first mention of him in print occurred in 1592, when a pamphlet attacked him for supposing he was "as well able to bombast out a blanke verse as the best of you" and for being "in his owne conceit the only Shake-scene in a countrey." By 1594 he was a leading player and writer for the Lord Chamberlain's Men, who became the King's Men upon James I's ascension in 1603.

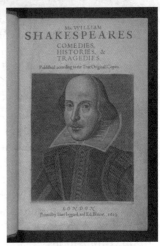

Frontispiece of the First Folio collection of William Shakespeare's plays, 1623.

The only works published under his name, and presumably with his approval, during his lifetime were the narrative poems *Venus and Adonis* (1593) and *The Rape of Lucrece* (1594). His sonnets were published in 1609 by Thomas Thorpe, but it is not clear if Shakespeare was involved with their publication. He certainly took no particular interest in the publication of his plays, about half of which were published during his lifetime in inexpensive *quarto* editions. According to Shakespeare scholar Eric Rasmussen, such quarto editions were very popular reading in the seventeenth century: in fact, a contemporary of Shakespeare's complained that so many quarto-size plays were being printed, it would take more than two years to read them all. From the variants that exist between the early quarto editions and the later and larger Folio editions of Shakespeare's plays, scholars have assumed that most of the play texts were reconstructed from actors' playbooks.

The first collected edition of Shakespeare's plays, the *First Folio*, was published in 1623 at the instigation of two former colleagues of Shakespeare's from the King's Men, John Heminges (1556–1630) and Henry Condell (d. 1627). More than 900 pages long, the volume divided the plays into the three categories familiar to all subsequent readers and playgoers—Comedies, Histories, and Tragedies—and arranged lifetime seem to have had very little authorial attention paid to them, and those published only after his death, in the 1623 *First Folio* edition, contain frustrating errors and opacities that have plagued scholars ever since—and contributed to the silly but enduring theory that Shakespeare was not the author of his own works. However, although he was lackadaisical about the publication of his plays, Shakespeare took personal pains with the publication of his poetry. The first work of his to appear in print, and under his name, was the long poem *Venus*

them to ensure that plays not previously published began and ended each section. The edition was 750 copies, which were advertised for sale at about one pound each by the London printers William and Isaac Jaggard.

Scholars who have carefully examined the surviving 230 or so copies of the First Folio have determined that five compositors worked on the project over the two years it was in production. The compositors' work can be identified by idiosyncrasies of spelling and of line and page completion, and at least in one case—that of "Compositor E"—because of the relative carelessness with which some of the lines were set. Three more editions (the Second, Third, and Fourth Folios) were published between 1632 and 1685, providing evidence of the plays' continuing popularity. The various errors and inconsistencies within each of the Folios and between them have provided work for generations of Shakespeare scholars, who have struggled to get back to an "original" rendition of Shakespeare's texts. Lacking either the author's manuscript copies or even the versions from which the Folio editions were set, that remains a difficult task, but modern editions provide clear rationales for why particular arrangements and interpretations of the play texts have come to be preferred.

The absence of original manuscripts has been one factor in the long-running debate among some readers and actors over the identity of the "author of Shakespeare's works." Some have claimed that the "man from Stratford" lacked the rank and education necessary to write the poetry and plays attributed to him. These so-called anti-Stratfordians argue that the language and knowledge embodied in the texts point to someone of much higher class status and educational attainments, and over the years they have variously championed such candidates as the philosopher Francis Bacon (1561–1626), the courtier Edward de Vere, seventeenth Earl of Oxford (1550–1604), and even Elizabeth I. The controversy, such as it is, appears to have arisen in the nineteenth century, when the lack of both manuscripts and details about Shakespeare's life began to gnaw at some readers' imaginations. Romantic notions of authorship prevalent at the time didn't sit well with what *was* known about Shakespeare: that he was a successful commercial theatre actor and manager. So some began to look for other candidates whose backgrounds and supposed aesthetics accorded better with their notions of authorship. While the speculation has generated some amusing counterfactual histories and a movie or two, academics are mostly unshaken in their belief that the Bard of Avon was, in fact, William Shakespeare.

and Adonis, in 1593. (Both *Venus and Adonis* and the later *Rape of Lucrece* were dedicated to the Henry Wriothesley [1573–1624], the Earl of Southampton, who was also probably the addressee in some of Shakespeare's sonnets.) As Stephen Greenblatt explains in his 2004 book *Will in the World*, the care Shakespeare took with the poem and its printing made it seem as if Shakespeare "had decided to start afresh in a new profession": "He was attempting to establish himself now not as a popular playwright but as a cultivated poet, someone who could gracefully conjure up the mythological world to which his university-educated rival poets claimed virtually exclusive access."

Similarly, like popular plays before them, novels had a reputation as a rather low-brow form of literature until the mid-nineteenth century, and writers who wanted to be taken seriously did not wish to be associated with them. Literary prestige explains the actions of Scottish poet and novelist Walter Scott (1771–1832), who hid behind the label "Author of *Waverley*" after 1814. Scott's name had appeared prominently on the title pages of his many volumes of poetry, beginning with *The Lay of the Last Minstrel* in 1805, but he did not want to acknowledge that he was a novel-writer. Poetry was the work of a gentleman—fiction was not. His very first novel, *Waverley, or 'Tis Sixty Years Since*, was published with no author's name on the title page, only the title, an epigraph, and the publisher's details. After the first novel's phenomenal success, however, Scott and his publisher Archibald Constable (1774–1827) realized that it would be wise to signal that any succeeding titles were by the same author. The subsequent twenty-five novels, published from 1815 to 1831, were thus advertised as being "By the Author of *Waverley*." Even after Scott's identity as the author was well known, he still did not wish to have his name on the novels' title pages: as a lawyer and the Laird of Abbotsford, he worried that being seen as a mere novelist would compromise his "solemnity of walk and conduct." Scott's near-contemporary, the English novelist Fanny Burney (1752–1840), also published her novels anonymously (later novels were advertised as "By the Author of *Evelina*"). However, she willingly placed her (married) name on her edited version of her father's *Memoirs* when she published them in 1832: nonfiction was a safer, more prestigious literary form.

For Scott, Burney, and many others, "By the Author of" became, in effect, a pen name. Pen names had been used by authors going at least as far back as Roman times. For example, the Roman comic playwright Titus Maccius Plautus (c. 254–184 BCE) probably was working under a pseudonym: while "Titus" was a common enough name, "Maccius" seems suspiciously close to the stock character "Maccus," or clown, and "Plautus" means "flat," as in the ears of a hound or the flat feet of a barefoot actor. As may have been the case with Plautus, authors through the ages have sometimes adopted pen names that would signal the kinds of writers they saw themselves to be, or how they hoped their works would be received. American writer Samuel Langhorne Clemens (1835–1910) adopted the pseudonym Mark Twain, a nod both to his days as a riverboat pilot and to the lighthearted nature of much of his important work.

Similarly, Lemony Snicket, the pen name of contemporary American author Daniel Handler (b. 1970), derives from the narrator in his popular *Series of Unfortunate Events* books, and more clearly signals the dark and witty nature of the books than the more prosaic "Daniel Handler" might do.

Political reporter and *Newsweek* magazine columnist Joe Klein (b. 1946) originally intended to use a pen name when, after a quarter-century of writing journalism, he decided to try his hand at fiction. According to an Afterword he wrote for the tenth-anniversary edition of his novel *Primary Colors* (originally published in 1996), Klein had chosen the pen name "Nicholas Badnaille" as an indirect reference to Niccolò Machiavelli (1469–1527), whose *The Prince* (1532) is one of the classics of political thought. However, the manuscript was submitted to Random House by Klein's agent as "Untitled Novel by Anonymous Author," and although the publisher did choose a title, it also chose to publish the novel by "Anonymous," rather than using Klein's suggested pen name. (As it happens, the book was copyrighted as being by "Machiavelliana, Inc.") Klein saw that there were at least three good reasons for publishing anonymously: he was trying something new and wanted it to stand (or fall) on its own merits, rather than on his own reputation; he was wary of fellow journalists' responses; and he thought it would be a good marketing ploy and also "a hoot." It certainly was a good marketing ploy: the efforts to penetrate the identity of "Anonymous" kept the book steadily in the public's eye. After the eventual discovery that Klein was the author—a claim made first by a fellow journalist and by a university academic and "forensic linguist" (later confirmed by the *Washington Post*) who compared the handwriting in one of Klein's journalism notebooks with that on an early manuscript draft of the novel—the novel continued to sell.

Besides using anonymity or pen names to conceal their identities, authors also have adopted pen names simply to create a writerly persona distinct from their everyday selves. This seems to have been the motivation of authors as different as Bashō, pen name of Japanese poet Matsuo Kinsaku (1644–94); Stendhal, pen name of French writer Marie-Henri Beyle (1783–1842); Lewis Carroll, pen name of English novelist and mathematician Charles Dodgson (1832–98); and George Orwell, pen name of English author Eric Blair (1903–50). Furthermore, established authors have sometimes adopted secondary pen names when they wish to publish in a genre or style that their readers may not be familiar with. For example, the popular romance novelist Nora Roberts (b. 1950) also writes police procedurals under the pen name J.D. Robb.

Pen names can sometimes be a double-edged sword. For example, in 1984, Nobel Prize–winning writer Doris Lessing (b. 1919), exasperated that name recognition was such an important factor in gaining publishing contracts, attempted to publish two works under the unknown pseudonym Jane Somers. She proved her point when her own publisher failed to recognize the quality of her writing without the umbrella of her real name and refused the manuscripts. And pen names can also be used to conceal the fact that there is no single, identifiable author behind the name. Carolyn Keene, the ostensive author of the popular *Nancy Drew* girls' books, is actually a pen name that masks a whole host of writers hired for contract by the Stratemeyer Syndicate in the 1930s. Stratemeyer also invented the persona Franklin W. Dixon as the author of the *Hardy Boys* series, again masking a number of for-hire writers.

Besides allowing authors to shield their everyday selves, pen names are sometimes adopted by authors who hope that their work will be judged more neutrally under a false name than it might otherwise be. The latter rationale has been used by a significant number of women authors over the past several centuries, many of whom have adopted gender-neutral or overtly masculine pseudonyms to try to ensure that their work would not be read (at least initially) as supposedly inferior "women's writing." The Brontë sisters adopted this approach rather uncomfortably when they submitted their first volumes of poetry and fiction for publication, deciding that the neutral pseudonyms Ellis, Acton, and Currer Bell would better protect both their own reputations and the reception of their literary offerings than issuing them under their own names of Emily (1818–48), Anne (1820–49), and Charlotte (1816–55). The French writer Amandine Lucille Aurore Dupin, later baronne Dudevant (1804–76), collaborated with her lover Jules Sandeau (1811–83) on a novel in 1831, and they adopted the pen name "Jules Sand" for their joint effort. The following year she chose a similar pseudonym, "George Sand," for her first independent venture in fiction-writing, the novel *Indiana*.

George Sand's success may have inspired English writer Mary Anne (or Marian) Evans (1819–80) when she sought both a professional writing name and a break from her previous life. Following her elopement with fellow author and critic George Henry Lewes (1817–78), she chose the pen name George Eliot. Her first novel, *Scenes of Clerical Life* (1857), met with almost instantaneous success, as did most of her later writings, particularly *Middlemarch* (1872). Most contemporary readers were willing to look past the unconventionalities of her personal life and focus on the authorial persona that George Eliot represented. This was also the case with Michael Field, the pen name adopted by the poets Katherine Harris Bradley (1846–1914) and Edith Emma Cooper (1862–1913) for their many volumes of collaborative writing.

However, the practice of women writers adopting a masculine or gender-neutral pen name was not merely a quaint, eighteenth- and nineteenth-century practice. Perhaps one of the most famous recent examples is that of Joanne Rowling (b. 1965), who was advised to abandon her recognizably feminine first name in favor of initials (J.K.) when publishing her first young adult novel in 1997, on the grounds that the boys who were presumably a significant portion of the target readership for a book about a schoolboy wizard would not want to read a work written by a "girl." The phenomenal success of the *Harry Potter* books suggests that readers of whatever sex or age were not especially put off by their knowledge of the author's gender.

AUTHOR BY PROFESSION

In the late seventeenth and early eighteenth centuries, authors began gradually to disentangle themselves from the patronage system. This was possible in part because of contemporary economic and social changes. As the West gradually embraced a capitalistic, mercantile economic system, a growing middle class emerged who could make their own choices about both didactic and leisure reading. When they began to demand new reading material, authors and booksellers hurried to supply it. The public, rather than the patron, became the primary audience and main support of the book trades.

In the early centuries of print, booksellers performed the work now done mainly by publishing houses: they secured, published, and distributed books. And prior to the eighteenth century, it was primarily the booksellers' interests that were protected by local law and convention, not the author's. Authors were sometimes paid for new work, either in money or in printed copies, but once a text was in the bookseller's hands, the book became the property of the bookseller. Authors who hoped to make more money from the same work might sell different versions to different booksellers, or even put a different title on an existing work in the hope of passing it off as new. However, booksellers carefully policed the local trade to make sure that texts billed by authors and other booksellers as "new" really were, and that unauthorized or pirated versions were not released in their regions. Their livelihoods depended on maintaining control over the particular titles in their lists. If they uncovered irregularities, they could appeal to the local authorities or take action to drive the offending individuals out of business. Authors had virtually no concern in the matter. (The role of the state in protecting—or interfering with—booksellers' interests is covered in greater detail in Chapter 6.)

By the turn of the eighteenth century, this finally began to change. The rise of the modern author depended very much on the concurrent rise of the concept of *copyright*, the legal right to produce and distribute someone else's creative work. As authorship became a profession, authors not only wanted due credit for successful and influential books, but they also wanted to benefit financially from their books' sales. The *copy* part of *copyright* is critical, as it is the copying and circulation of texts that gives those texts life, influence, and economic value. Novelist and lawyer Scott Turow (b. 1949), in an essay coauthored with Paul Aiken and James Shapiro of the Authors Guild, has called copyright "one of history's great public policy successes." Copyright affirmed authors' interests in their own writing even after the writing had left their hands, by allowing them to sell their works outright or for a specified period of time. By purchasing the "right to copy" from an author, a bookseller or publisher would acquire the exclusive license to print and distribute copies of the author's text. Thus, copyright laws not only protected authors' interests, but they also protected the publishing world's interests, just as the local arrangements in previous centuries had done. (Copyright is discussed in greater detail in Chapter 6.)

Copyright was a real benefit to writers and a key factor in the transformation of authorship from vocation to profession. However, as more individuals attempted to support themselves by writing, the economic uncertainty inherent in the writing life began to affect more individuals. Some authors who initially met with success later found themselves in dire financial straits. With

THE ROYAL LITERARY FUND

The Literary Fund (later Royal Literary Fund) was created in 1790 by the Welsh philosopher David Williams (1738–1816), a friend and correspondent of many scholars and writers in England, America, and Germany. Although he had proposed the idea of a fund to help support indigent writers some years earlier, Williams was particularly dismayed by the death in debtors' prison of Floyer Sydenham (1710–87), a Fellow of Wadham College, Oxford, and a translator of Plato. Within a few years, Williams had gathered together a list of members and subscribers, including the Prince Regent, later George IV (1762–1830). In its first decade or so, the Fund distributed over £1,700 to more than 100 individuals, including such worthies as the poet and critic Samuel Taylor Coleridge (1772–1834) and the French writer and politician François-René de Chateaubriand (1768–1848), who was at that time in exile in Britain and scraping out a living by translating texts and giving French lessons. As the grant to Chateaubriand suggests, the Fund's benevolence was not restricted to nationality; neither did it take into account religion, politics, or gender.

Over the years the Literary Fund has supported not only luminaries but also many virtually unknown writers and their families. In most cases, the need is brought to the attention of the Fund through the efforts of another writer. After various details are gathered from the applicant, a committee convenes to consider the case. One important factor is literary merit: committee members and others provide testimony about the quality of the author's work and the trajectory of his or her career. The archives of the Fund, on deposit in the British Library, tell many sad stories of the rise and fall of writers' fortunes.

The Royal Literary Fund remains an important source of support for authors and their families. Many successful authors have left their estates or significant bequests to the Fund, including the World War I poet Rupert Brooke (1887–1915) and the children's writers Arthur Ransome (1884–1967) and A.A. Milne (1882–1956). In recent years, about 200 writers and dependents per year have received grants and pensions from the Fund. Since 1999, the Royal Literary Fund has also supported a fellowship program, which places distinguished writers in institutions of higher education throughout Great Britain.

the patronage system in decline, there was a need for other resources to help writers through hard times. This led to the development of other kinds of support networks for authors, such as the Literary Fund, established in London in 1790. Devised in the wake of the death in debtors' prison of a distinguished translator of Plato, the Fund sought to relieve the financial difficulties of authors and their families, by providing either temporary assistance or pensions. Its efforts were supported by grants and subscriptions, and thanks to continued support from the crown, it became the Royal Literary Fund in 1842.

Over the past two centuries, many countries have created various grants and pensions to support writers, some government-supported and others private. For example, the Authors League Fund, established in 1917 and based in New York, offers assistance to professional writers and dramatists who have extraordinary medical needs or are suffering from other misfortunes. Similarly, the American Society of Journalists and Authors (ASJA) administers a Writers Emergency Assistance Fund, which helps freelance writers who are unable to work due to illness, disability, or professional crises. Another source of emergency aid for US freelance authors (and other creative artists) is the Haven Foundation, which was begun in 2006 by author Stephen King (b. 1947). King was grievously injured when he was struck by an automobile in 1999, and his experience of being incapacitated for nearly a year made him wish to do something for authors who lacked the financial cushion his own success had provided him. The Haven Foundation can provide grants for up to five years to established writers and artists.

As the demand for books continued to grow and authors insisted on greater control over their intellectual productions, booksellers discovered that they needed to make new arrangements with authors in order to guarantee a steady supply of text. A number of payment arrangements developed that sought to more fairly compensate authors for their work and to help booksellers cover their risks and expenses.

Subscription Publication

One publishing strategy devised to help both authors and publishers was the *subscription* system, a direct descendant of the patronage system. Under the subscription system, authors or booksellers would appeal to potential readers to pledge funds. When enough funds were pledged or collected (for obvious reasons, cash in hand was preferred), the project would proceed. Assuming the author actually completed the promised work—which didn't always happen—the bookseller would arrange to have the text printed, usually in quantities at or just slightly in excess of the numbers spoken for. When the copies were ready, they would be distributed to the sponsors, who might be listed in a prominent acknowledgments page. A few extra copies might also be circulated to persons of influence, in hopes that they might increase demand for the book beyond the circle of subscribers. In most cases, that would be the end of the matter, and if the author wished to produce another book, he or she would make the rounds again, seeking subscribers for the new one. However, if demand warranted, the bookseller might produce another edition, and authors who proved thus marketable might well find booksellers willing to pay them for future works, rather than requiring them to collect subscriptions.

One of the earliest subscription publications in England is thought to have been a multilingual dictionary, *Ductor in Linguas, The Guide into Tongues*, compiled by John Minsheu (1560–1627) and published in 1617 by John Brown of London. Minsheu apparently tired of wheedling the support of a fickle patron and turned to a subscription scheme instead to get the job done. Once the dictionary was published, Minsheu used his initial subscription list to entice further purchasers and patrons, and the complete list of subscribers eventually comprised more than 400 individuals and libraries.

Subscription publication was fairly commonplace in the eighteenth century and was used by both known and unknown authors. Dr. Johnson turned to the subscription system in 1756 to support his proposed edition of Shakespeare's works. Although he rounded up a large list of subscribers and apparently collected a fair amount of money from them, the edition was delayed until 1765, prompting his contemporary, the satiric poet Charles Churchill (1732–64) to write accusingly:

> He for subscribers baits his hook
> And takes your cash; but where's the book?
> No matter where; wise fear, you know,
> Forbids the robbing of a foe;
> But what, to serve our private ends
> Forbids the cheating of our friends?

Although Johnson's experience shows the potential downside of subscription publishing, the system could prove very beneficial to authors. Fanny Burney published her first novels, *Evelina* (1778) and *Cecilia* (1782), by selling her copyright outright. However, in order to reap a better financial reward, she turned to subscription publishing for her 1796 novel, *Camilla*. The subscriber list ran to thirty-eight pages and contained 300 names. The first edition of 4,000 copies sold quickly. Between the subscriptions and the later outright sale of her copyright, Burney cleared over £2,000 for the novel, and she and her husband were able to build a house—"Camilla Cottage"—from the proceeds.

Subscription publication was also employed in North America in the eighteenth and early nineteenth centuries. In both the United States and Canada, prospective publications were often advertised in newspapers, along with information about how interested parties could join the subscription. Canadian publishers sometimes appealed to their readers' patriotism, urging them to subscribe to "home productions." In the United States, subscriptions were sometimes collected door-to-door, with sales representatives displaying special *canvassing books*, usually partial prototypes of what the finished books would look like, to potential subscribers. This method was used to sell everything from cookbooks to Bible study guides to the complete works of Benjamin Franklin.

From Profit Sharing to Royalties

Another publishing scheme that developed during this period was the *shared profits* system, sometimes also known as the *half-profits* system. Rather than accepting a one-time, upfront payment for their work, authors would agree to receive a share of the profit (up to 50 per cent) on any copies that sold beyond the number needed to recoup the total printing expenses. In some cases, this scheme could be fairer to authors than the one-time payment, because it meant the author would continue to gain from a book that sold well. However, the scheme depended very much on the honor and accounting skills of the bookseller in question. Unscrupulous booksellers might either inflate their reported costs or minimize their sales records to avoid paying authors their due, claiming that sales hadn't covered the printing and distribution costs. And many booksellers demanded that authors contribute substantially towards production costs as well, on the grounds that the authors should share in the risk as well as the potential profit.

The profit-sharing scheme pointed the way to what would become, by the middle of the nineteenth century, the normal practice for modern publishing agreements. Rather than agreeing to share half-profits after all production costs were recovered, authors began to sign contracts in which the bookseller—now usually a publisher in the modern sense of the term—agreed to incur all the risks associated with the production of the book, and the author agreed to receive a *royalty* payment, or a fixed share of the sale of each copy. Royalty rates are generally far below 50 per cent—they have tended to range from 5 to 20 per cent over the past century and a half, depending on the time, place, and the kind of book being produced—but because they are based on each copy sold, they have generally been regarded as more fairly reflecting the authors' and publishers' contributions to the enterprise of publishing a book.

For example, the American poet and short-story writer Edgar Allan Poe (1809–49) received 10 per cent royalties from G.P. Putnam in 1848, for his poem *Eureka*, and just two years later, fellow poet Henry Wadsworth Longfellow (1807–82) was offered a 20 per cent royalty from Ticknor and Fields for *Evangeline*. The higher rate may have been due to Longfellow's popularity at the time, or it may have been because he was helping underwrite the cost of the stereotype plates for the poem.

Demonstrated popularity certainly colored Blackwood's royalty payments to novelist George Eliot: in 1861 she received an offer of what amounted to a 33 per cent royalty for the publication of her novel *Silas Marner*. The following year she was offered the then-stupendous amount of £10,000 by publisher George Smith for the serialization and volume publication rights to her historical novel *Romola*; in the end, Smith paid only £7,000, which was still the highest amount paid to that date for a novel. Royalties could also be *graduated*, or ramped up with increasing numbers of copies sold. For example, the Canadian feminist and social activist Nellie McClung (1873–1951) was offered a graduated royalty for her 1910 novel *The Second Chance* by publisher William Briggs (1836–1922), who offered to pay her 15 per cent on the first 10,000 copies, and 20 per cent thereafter.

Although some publishers continue to pay royalties only on copies actually sold, especially for books with uncertain sales potential, the custom now for books with strong projected sales or for authors whose appeal is already established is to offer an *advance* against royalties. An advance is usually issued at the time of the signing of a publishing contract, or when the completed manuscript has been submitted. (Advances can also be divided into two or more payments, ordinarily with about half paid on signing, and the remainder on the satisfactory completion of the manuscript.) The rationale for issuing an advance is that it provides the author with a guaranteed income while finishing the manuscript, which helps protect the publisher's investment in the proposed book.

Typically, advances for first books are relatively modest, while those for famous authors can be immense. Novelist Dan Brown (b. 1964) was originally paid about $400,000 by Doubleday for *The Da Vinci Code* and one other book, but after *The Da Vinci Code* proved one of the bestselling books of all time, the contract was significantly renegotiated—adding about $500,000 more in advances, in addition to the previously paid royalties. More strikingly, J.K. Rowling received only about £1,500 as an advance for *Harry Potter and the Philosopher's Stone*, but later books reportedly received advances of six and even seven figures. However, occasionally even a first-time author will be offered an extraordinary sum. In 2011, Irish writer Kathleen MacMahon was offered £600,000 by Little, Brown for the manuscript of her novel *So This Is How It Ends*.

Copyright and Contracts

Copyright underlies the basic set of agreements in any contract negotiated between an author and a publisher. In general, a publishing contract defines the commitments of both author and publisher and sets out the financial terms that will govern their interactions.

From the publisher's point of view, perhaps the most important sections of any publishing contract are the author's warranty and the grant of rights. The *warranty* is the author's guarantee that the manuscript is the author's own, original work, and publishers will usually try to insist that authors indemnify them against any lawsuits that might arise about the originality of their work, or about any content that might be deemed libelous. The *grant of rights* is the assignment by the author to the publisher of the right to publish, sell, or license the work.

Contracts may specify a geographical territory in which the publisher will have exclusive rights to produce and circulate the work—such as "North American" rights, which cover Canada and the United States—but "world" rights are sometimes granted as well. Initial contracts often cover only the *primary rights* of print and electronic publication. Other *subsidiary rights*, such as serialization, audiobook, translation, or film or television adaptation, are usually negotiated separately. In most cases, copyright in the text is retained by the author and simply licensed—in effect, rented—to the publisher for a specified time and place. However, if the copyright is to be sold outright, that is specified.

From the author's perspective, the most important sections of the contract are probably the agreement to publish, the royalties arrangements, and the termination clause. The *agreement to publish* is the publisher's undertaking to actually bring the work out by a particular date, assuming that the manuscript was submitted on time and in good order. *Royalties* are a percentage of the sale of each copy of the published book. Although royalty rates can vary depending on the time, place, and kind of book, as well as on the number of authors involved, they generally fall in the range of 5 and 20 per cent of the net price of the book, with 10 per cent a fairly common base arrangement. (The *net price* is the cost of the book to bookstores and other distributors, which includes the publisher's costs and profit; the slightly higher *list price* is what those distributors in turn charge their customers, as it includes the distributor's costs and profit.) Again, depending on the kind of book being contracted for, the royalties arrangements may also specify that the author will receive an advance. If so, the advance ordinarily will be deducted from the royalties until it is earned out, at which point the author will be eligible to receive additional payments, usually quarterly. Finally, the *termination clause* spells out the publisher's obligation to try to keep the book in print, and it specifies what will happen if the publisher decides to allow it to go out of print. Usually, if a book goes out of print, all rights revert to the author, who is then free to try to license the book to another publisher.

When an author licenses copyright to a publisher, there is sometimes potential for additional income beyond simple royalties. For example, a portion of a copyrighted work might be reproduced in another book, such as an anthology or textbook. In order to legally reprint the section of the original copyrighted material, the editor or publisher of the new work would approach the first publisher and request *permission to republish that material*. Based on the kind and quantity of copies to be made, the first publisher would grant permission, in return for a formal *acknowledgment* of where the copyrighted material was originally published and an appropriate fee. An agreed-upon percentage of any such fees would be added to the author's royalty payments.

LITERARY AGENTS AND PROFESSIONAL SOCIETIES

As the previous sections suggest, securing a publishing contract and protecting one's copyright can be challenging tasks. However, since the nineteenth century, authors have had assistance in navigating the waters of the publishing world.

As publishing contracts based on royalties became the norm, authors began to rely on advisors to protect their interests when the contracts were being drawn up. What began informally—more experienced authors advising the less experienced, or sometimes lawyers or business advisors reviewing the proposed arrangements with publishers—gradually became more formalized, with authors increasingly turning for advice to professional associations or to a new breed of publishing professional, the *literary agent*.

Literary agents serve as artistic and business representatives for authors, advising them on everything from how their work might best be revised to meet current literary tastes, which firms to pitch the work to, and what financial terms to expect. In return, agents are paid a percentage of an author's earnings, typically between 10 and 20 per cent. Agents are expected to keep abreast of trends and developments in publishing, so that they can steer both new and established talent to the right places. Some agents and literary agencies specialize in particular areas of publishing—say, fiction or self-help or cookbooks—while others take on clients across the board. Traditionally, agents were mainly responsible for financial negotiations on behalf of their clients. However, in recent decades many agents have taken on a greater role in vetting unsolicited manuscripts and helping to develop manuscripts from rough drafts to publishable ones, roles that were once performed by in-house editorial staffs at publishing firms. In addition, as industry analyst Giles Clark notes, agents can provide a useful service for authors simply by providing "a degree of continuity in the face of changing publishers and editors." Many authors remain loyal to their agents throughout their writing careers, and also entrust their agents with managing their literary estates after their deaths.

The first important literary agent was A.P. Watt (1834–1914), who initially worked in London as an advertising agent for a number of major periodicals and seems to have begun representing authors in contract negotiations by the mid-1870s. Watt described the literary agent's role as encompassing "all business arrangements of every kind for Authors," including placing the manuscript, selling or licensing copyright, collecting royalty payments from publishers, and seeking reviews. By the 1890s he was a force to be reckoned with, negotiating terms for authors not only with publishing houses, but also with *syndicators*, companies that sold serialized fiction and other work to newspapers. (Today, syndicators frequently handle columnists and cartoon strips.) Thanks to his efforts, many authors saw their advances and royalty rates increase significantly, and at least one of his clients, the poet and fiction writer Rudyard Kipling (1865–1936), credited Watt with doubling his income. (Watt also testified on Kipling's behalf against American piracy of Kipling's works.)

Watt's personal client list included many of the important and popular British novelists of the turn of the twentieth century, and his agency continues to represent many major contemporary authors today.

Having pointed the way, Watt was fairly generous in helping others to establish literary agencies. Among his more important protégés was James Brand Pinker (1863–1923), who established his agency in 1896 and whose clients included the science fiction writer H.G. Wells (1866–1946) and novelist Joseph

EUDORA WELTY AND DIARMUID RUSSELL: AN AUTHOR AND HER AGENT

Many agents have been extremely important to their authors. Thanks to literary scholar Michael Kreyling, the relationship between one writer and agent—that of American novelist and short story writer Eudora Welty (1909–2001) and her agent Diarmuid Russell (1902–73)—is now well chronicled. From their first exchange of letters in 1940 to his death in 1973, Russell was a friend, literary confidant, and business manager for Welty, serving as her first reader, offering thoughtful criticism about her work in progress, and seeking venues for publication.

Russell's self-introduction to Welty had a comic edge: he acknowledged that agents were parasitic on author's earnings, but he pointed out that an agent was "rather a benevolent parasite, because authors as a rule make more when they have an agent than they do without one." Welty was ready for someone to help her break out of regional publication and into a wider readership, and she wrote back almost immediately, sealing the deal. Over the next years, Russell sought to place Welty's works in better paying and widely read publications, beginning with *The Atlantic*, and he also gently encouraged her to move beyond what was for her a comfortable niche of shorter fiction to the more popular (and more lucrative) form of the novel.

Russell negotiated well for his client, even though he was suspicious of new players in the field like Ballantine, who was publishing paperback originals. (Russell didn't believe the paperback format was suitable for anything other than reprints.) By 1953 he had been so successful in placing Welty's work, especially her forthcoming novella *The Ponder Heart* (1954), that he warned her she might need to defer some of her income for tax purposes. The book sold nearly 11,000 copies, far beyond any previous sales Welty had seen. By 1969, Russell had helped build up Welty's literary stature such that he was able to secure about $100,000 from Random House and Book-of-the-Month Club for her novel *Losing Battles* (1970).

Welty paid tribute to Russell in an interview after his death. "I just can't tell you what it meant to me to have him there," she told Peggy Prenshaw. "His integrity, his understanding, his instincts—everything was something I trusted."

Conrad (1857–1924). The latter commended Pinker for his patience in treating "not only my moods but even my fancies with the greatest consideration." Another important early literary agency that remains a major player in the publishing world was Curtis Brown, founded in London in 1906 by American-born Albert Curtis Brown (1866–1945) and carried on by his son, Spencer Curtis Brown (1906–80). The firm's New York office opened in 1914. Over the past century, Curtis Brown has represented a range of popular authors on both sides of the Atlantic, including A.A. Milne, creator of the beloved Winnie the Pooh, and novelists Daphne du Maurier (1907–89), John Steinbeck (1902–68), William Faulkner (1897–1962), David Lodge (b. 1935), and Robertson Davies (1913–95). Indeed, as Spencer Curtis Brown's entry in the *Dictionary of National Biography* points out, "there were few writers of importance who were not Curtis Brown clients at some point in their careers."

Literary agents are bigger players in the Anglo-American publishing world than elsewhere, mainly because of the predominance of English-language publishing. In the United Kingdom, many agents are members of the Association of Authors' Agents (AAA); in North America, many are members of the Association of Authors' Representatives (AAR). Both of these organizations provide sounding boards for their members, keeping them apprised of developments in the publishing world, and they also subscribe to a professional code of conduct, helping to assure that authors are dealt with honorably. The AAR also maintains a database to help authors find an agent who might be appropriate for them.

Authors' Associations

In addition to literary agents, authors have also turned for advice and support to various professional associations, such as the Society of Authors, the Authors Guild, and PEN International. Many of these associations arose at roughly the same time as the literary agent, and for much the same reason: to help authors protect their financial interests as the publishing industry grew.

One of the oldest authors' associations, the Society of Authors, was founded in London in 1884, largely through the efforts of Walter Besant (1836–1901). Besant wanted to improve the status and financial conditions of the profession of writing, and among the Society of Authors' early projects was the reform and defense of copyright law. Besant originally envisioned an organization that would be something of a cross between the Académie Française and a professional body, one that would have a major impact on both the status of English letters and the status of authors. In 1890, he founded the society's journal, *The Author*, which helped to increase the organization's visibility and influence. The Society of Authors currently has over 9,000 members in all branches of professional writing. In addition to offering writers assistance with contracts and other professional negotiations, the Society also awards a number of literary prizes and administers the Authors' Foundation, which is charged with making grants to working authors.

The success of the Society of Authors in advocating for British authors prompted many other countries to form their own authors' associations. For example, the Authors Guild was founded in 1912 as the Authors League of America. Like the Society of Authors, it provides resources to help writers protect copyright and negotiate contracts, and it also offers a range of educational opportunities, from seminars to web resources. In recent years, the Authors Guild has been deeply involved with asserting and protecting the rights of authors in relation to the Google Books project.

The Canadian Authors Association (CAA) was founded in Montreal in 1921, primarily to improve copyright protections for Canadian writers. It was instrumental in moving key legislation in 1924, and it established the Canadian Writers' Foundation in 1932 to help support indigent authors and their families. It was also the originator of the most important Canadian literary prize, the Governor General's Award. Its active membership program includes writing seminars, publications, and various literacy projects across Canada. The Fellowship of Australian Writers, founded in 1928, provides similar resources for authors in the Antipodes.

In addition to these national authors' associations, there are also many genre-focused associations, such as the Romance Writers of America (RWA), Sisters in Crime (a mystery writers' group), and the Horror Writers Association. Although these organizations offer resources related to copyright and other professional issues, they tend to concentrate more on providing resources and information about their particular portion of the publishing industry. For example, the RWA is a particularly useful source of statistical information about the prevalence and popularity of romance fiction.

Finally, a very important transnational writers' organization is PEN International. Founded in 1921, its name was originally an acronym for "Poets, Essayists, and Novelists." As the organization grew, especially in the post-war years, PEN increasingly embraced writers in all genres and languages, and it now has members in more than 100 countries around the world. PEN International has long been involved in advocacy for freedom of the press and freedom of expression, beginning in the 1930s, when it expressed extreme concern about the treatment of writers under the fascist regimes in Spain and Germany. In 1949, PEN was officially recognized by the United Nations as a "representative of the writers of the world." Among its many outreach and advocacy efforts, it includes an Emergency Fund that helps provide financial and legal support to persecuted writers.

PEN INTERNATIONAL

One of the first nongovernmental organizations in the world, PEN International was founded in London in 1921, primarily as a social club for authors. By 1939, there were PEN Centres across Europe, as well as in North and South America and Asia. The Centres assured that traveling writers would have a place to meet fellow authors.

PEN International President John Ralston Saul and the Editorial Board of *La Prensa*, 2013. Photograph by Alain Pescador; reprinted with the permission of PEN International.

However, the political changes and tensions in the 1920s and 1930s that eventually led to the outbreak of war helped redefine the mission of PEN. As early as 1926, German writers including Bertolt Brecht (1898–1956) were warning that politics were deforming the culture of literature in Germany, and that the members of the German PEN Centre were not representative of the culture as a whole. When the German PEN failed to protest against Nazi book burning and the persecution of Jewish writers, its membership in the international organization was withdrawn. After the war, PEN realized that it needed to reorganize in response to the treatment of authors by political authorities, and it established an Executive Committee to help ensure that members could meet and contact one another regularly. By 1960, it had also established a Writers in Prison Committee, to monitor the situation of writers who had been imprisoned, tortured, threatened, made to disappear, or even killed for their work. It continues to publish a biannual "Case List," which documents the status of endangered writers.

As an activist for freedom of expression, PEN has been involved in the defense of many prominent writers over the years. For example, as early as 1937, PEN was instrumental in securing the release of the Hungarian-born author Arthur Koestler (1905–83), who was working as a journalist in Spain when he was taken prisoner by the Nationalists and sentenced to death. (Koestler wrote about the experience in his 1942 memoir *Dialogue with Death*.) In the 1960s, PEN came to the aid of Nigerian playwright Wole Soyinka (b. 1934), who was under sentence of execution for his activities during the country's civil war. On receipt of a letter from then-PEN president, the American dramatist Arthur Miller (1915–2005), the military leader, General Yakubu Gowon, released Soyinka. (Gowon was apparently impressed that Miller had married actress Marilyn Monroe.) Soyinka would go on to win the Nobel Prize for literature in 1986. PEN was also critically involved on behalf of Indian-born British writer Salman Rushdie (b. 1947). Rushdie's 1988 novel *The Satanic Verses* provoked major controversy and protests for its supposed insults to Islam and the Prophet Muhammad. In 1989, the Ayatollah Ruhollah Khomeini (1902–89), Iran's spiritual leader, issued a *fatwa*, or religious edict, denouncing the book and calling for the author's death. Rushdie was forced into hiding for many years afterwards, while PEN undertook a global campaign to have the fatwa lifted, and to protect publishers and sellers of his book worldwide. Rushdie has remained an active member of PEN.

Unfortunately, PEN's efforts to protect writers have not all ended so successfully. The Nigerian novelist and human rights activist Ken Saro-Wiwa (1941–95) was arrested for his alleged role in a protest on behalf of the Ogoni people of the Niger Delta against multinational petroleum interests. Despite a protest campaign by PEN, he was executed. Anna Politkovskaya (1958–2006), a Russian journalist who persistently reported on the war in Chechnya despite receiving death threats, was found murdered. Although it had been unable to prevent her death, PEN International continues to support efforts to hold her murderers to account. Similarly, after the Turkish-Armenian editor Hrant Dink (1954–2007) came under pressure from the Turkish government for writings challenging the government's denial of the 1915 Armenian genocide, PEN endeavored to step up its support for him. After Dink was assassinated, PEN supported his family and pressed for the apprehension and trial of his assailant.

In addition to these prominent figures, many other less well-known writers have found champions in the ranks of PEN International. The organization continues to advocate for freedom of expression and international friendship among writers and nations alike.

TRANSLATION, ADAPTATION, AND OTHER TRANSFORMATIONS

e-Books are just the latest of a number of possible transformations that an author's work might undergo. Other common transformations of an author's text, also protected by copyright and generally negotiated by agents and publishers as part of the initial contractual arrangements, are translations, adaptations for stage or screen, and reproduction in special formats such as audiobooks or Braille editions. Each of these transformations might involve the author to some degree.

Translation is one of the most common but also most challenging of adaptations or transformations. Most translators would probably agree with the tenets laid down by John Dryden (1631–1700) in his 1685 Preface to *Sylvae* that "Translation is a kind of drawing after the life; where every one will acknowledge there is a double sort of likeness, a good one and a bad. 'Tis one thing to draw the outlines true, the features like, the proportions exact, the colouring itself perhaps tolerable; and another thing to make all these graceful, by the posture, the shadowings, and, chiefly, by the spirit which animates the whole." But as French philosopher Jacques Derrida (1930–2004) noted, achieving Dryden's ideal of translation entails a "redoubtable, irreducible difficulty," a difficulty compounded not only in the move from one language to another, but from one *discourse*, or mode of thinking, to another. Novelist Michael Cunningham (b. 1952) suggests the whole process is even more complicated than that, as any book is itself a kind of translation, "a translation from the images in the author's mind to that which he is able to put down on paper."

Because relatively few authors have equal facility in multiple languages (and those who do might lack the time or inclination to translate their own work), most depend on others to generate translations of their work for foreign language markets. In some cases, translators might specialize in particular authors' works, gradually internalizing the author's attitudes and turns of phrase and becoming able to render them more consistently from one book to the next. For example, in recent years the translators Richard Pevear (b. 1943) and Larissa Volokhonsky have concentrated on translating Leo Tolstoy (1828–1910) into English from the original Russian. Their 2004 translation of *Anna Karenina* (1873–77) and their 2007 translation of *War and Peace* (1863–69) have been critically acclaimed, supplanting the earlier Constance Garnett (1861–1946) translations. Their translations have also been popular successes—thanks, in part, to *Anna Karenina* being an Oprah's Book Club selection in 2004, which resulted in the sale of upwards of 90,000 copies.

The translation of prose works might be thought to be relatively straightforward, but as Tiina Nunnally (b. 1952) notes in her recent translation of *Kristin Lavransdatter* (1920–22), the epic trilogy by Norwegian novelist and Nobel Prize winner Sigrid Undset (1882–1949), it can be difficult to get this right, and there is also the problem of changing tastes. The first translations of Undset's novels into English adopted what Nunnally describes as "an artificially archaic style," one that "completely misrepresented Undset's beautifully clear prose." The effect of these choices was to twist the syntax and make the dialogue seem stilted. This may have suited readers' tastes in the 1920s, perhaps because readers were assumed to expect a more archaic style for novels set in the Middle Ages, but Nunnally observes that contemporary notions of translation are different: "Accuracy and faithfulness to the original tone and style are both expected and required."

Poetry poses special challenges for translation, as it is not just tone and style that must be recreated or evoked, but also—often—imagery, rhythm, and rhyme. In their Introduction to a 2004 translation of the works of Nicaraguan poet Rubén Darío (1867–1916), Will Derusha and Alberto Acereda suggest that Darío's ingenuity as a poet is what makes his work so difficult to translate. "The musicality of his rhyme and rhythm becomes extravagantly singsong when followed too tightly and sounds curiously flat when not followed closely enough," they explain, adding that "much of the original charm of his verse depends on a craftsmanship that has gone out of style in the United States and elsewhere and may sound like affectation to the contemporary ear." In part to get around those difficulties, the translators chose to produce a bilingual, side-by-side edition of Darío's verse, thus enabling readers to move easily back and forth between the original and translated texts.

Because of these challenges, literary translation is frequently considered an art in itself, and some translators have received numerous awards for their careful and sensitive work in rendering works from one language into another. For example, the Canadian Governor General's Awards include a category in translation, and Sheila Fischman (b. 1937), who specializes in the translation of Quebec literature from French to English, has been regularly honored, with fourteen nominations and one award, the latter for her 1988 translation of Michel Tremblay's (b. 1942) *Les vues animées*. (In English, the novel was titled *Bambi and Me*.)

In addition to translation, adaptations for stage or screen are also quite common. Some authors prefer to write their own adaptations, while others are content to let someone else with a particular facility for stage- or screenplay writing undertake the work. For example, contemporary British writer David Nicholls (b. 1966) has written both novels and screenplays, and he wrote the screen adaptations of his novels *Starter for Ten* (2003) and *One Day* (2009). However, Pacific Northwest author Garth Stein (b. 1964), although he is both a novelist and a playwright, preferred to allow Myra Platt, one of the artistic directors of Book-It Repertory Company in Seattle, to write the stage adaptation of his bestselling novel *The Art of Racing in the Rain* (2008). (One of the challenges of bringing this work to stage was that it is a first-person narrative by a dog, Enzo.) Book-It specializes in bringing adaptations of books to the stage, having adapted over sixty full-length novels over the past twenty years, many by living authors.

Finally, editions in special formats, such as audio or Braille, might be licensed by authors. Until fairly recently, both audiobooks (books on tape) and Braille books were produced almost exclusively by agencies established to improve access to books for visually impaired readers. For example, since 1931, the Library of Congress has had a division dedicated to producing aural and Braille editions, the National Library Service for the Blind and Physically Handicapped (NLS). The Canadian National Institute for the Blind (CNIB), a private charity founded in 1918, provides similar services in both French and English in Canada. Thanks to recent technological advances, audiobooks for the visually impaired no longer need to be individually and laboriously read on to tape: software programs can now voice almost any text that can be accessed onscreen.

With the advent of personal music players in the 1980s, publishers began to realize that there was a broader commercial market for books on tape and CD. As a result, authors and professional actors were increasingly recruited to record audio versions of popular books, often in abridged versions. These audiobooks were sometimes packaged to resemble paperbacks, and some titles sold as well as them. More recently, downloadable audiobooks in MP3 format have become popular. According to the Audio Publishers' Association's (APA) most recent industry survey in 2011, the combined (all formats) audiobooks industry in the United States is worth about $1 billion, with downloads now amounting to about one-third of all revenues. The additional exposure—and royalty revenue—generated by audiobooks has mostly been welcomed by authors. A number of bestselling authors, including Judy Blume (b. 1938), Nicholas Sparks (b. 1965), Janet Evanovich (b. 1943), and David Baldacci (b. 1960), have been enlisted by the APA to help promote their annual "June is Audiobook Month" campaign.

SELF-PUBLISHING

Although most of this chapter has looked at authors in relationship to publishers, authors have always had the option of copying and distributing their works on their own. Private publishing or *self-publishing* has had its ups and downs. Especially after booksellers and publishing firms began to assume a significant portion of the financial risk of bringing books to market, self-publishing was often derided as "vanity" publishing, on the assumption that only inferior authors who couldn't find a publisher willing to underwrite their work would bring it out at their own expense.

However, not all authors who have resorted to self-publishing have done so because of the quality of the work. What has driven many authors to seek alternative means of getting their writing before the public is the content. Certain kinds of political, religious, and sexual material have always been problematic, and authors have sometimes chosen (or been forced) to publish more controversial works on their own, rather than risk embroiling others in the consequences of their actions. For example, after being blacklisted by the House Committee on Un-American Activities for his membership in the Communist Party, writer Howard Fast (1914–2003) was unable to find a publisher for his novel *Spartacus*, so he self-published it in 1951. It went on to sell 48,000 copies and was later reissued by Crown Books in 1958. (For a more in-depth discussion of the causes and effects of censorship, see Chapter 6.)

Other authors have chosen to self-publish because their writings were experimental. This was the case with a number of Modernist writers in the early twentieth century, including Virginia Woolf: even if an established publisher might have accepted their work, these writers doubted that they would be allowed to shape the final form of their writing according to their own ideals, or whether mainstream publishers would be able to position their works properly for their potential readers. Virginia and husband Leonard Woolf (1880–1969) formed their own publishing firm, the Hogarth Press, in 1917, to publish their own more experimental works, and they also published the works of other members of the avant-garde Bloomsbury Group. In order to establish themselves as self-publishers at the beginning of the twentieth century, the Woolfs needed not only to learn the mechanics of typesetting, printing, binding, and distribution (and to hire experienced workers to oversee each of these operations), but they also needed to invest a fair bit of capital in the necessary equipment.

By the end of the twentieth century, technological changes made it much easier for an author to set up a self-publishing operation, first through the use of high-speed photocopiers, and then through *desktop publishing*, using personal computers and good-quality inkjet or laser printers for hard copies or the internet for electronic ones. Professional-grade typesetting and layout software, now readily available for home use, has also made it relatively easy for authors to design and lay out their own books with good results.

Furthermore, the growing interest among authors in self-publishing has sparked a network of à la carte support services to help with all stages of the publication process, from manuscript assessment and editing to design to printing and distribution. Companies such as XLibris provide editing, layout, marketing, and distribution services to self-published authors. The increasing popularity of e-books and e-readers has also led industry giants Amazon and Barnes & Noble to launch their own self-publishing subdivisions for authors. Amazon's Kindle Direct Publishing (KDP) encourages authors to publish in Amazon's proprietary format, but authors can also opt to make their works available through the Amazon Advantage program or through CreateSpace. Barnes & Noble's PubIt! venture encourages authors to publish in the company's proprietary Nook format. In both cases, Amazon and Barnes & Noble retain a percentage of the list price of the e-books in return for allowing authors to use their large and well-organized distribution systems.

Some authors turn to self-publishing because certain kinds of books have such a limited readership that a publishing house is unlikely to take them on. Family histories and cookbooks, as well as specialist hobby books, may fall into this category. Self-publishing enables authors of such works the satisfaction of seeing their words in print, and of offering copies to selected readers, some of whom may have contributed to the costs of production, just as eighteenth-century book subscribers did. Other authors choose to self-publish because they wish to maintain total control over their projects, intellectually, aesthetically, and economically.

BAPSI SIDHWA AND THE SELF-PUBLISHING SPRINGBOARD

After failing to find a publisher in either England or America for her first two novels (despite the efforts of an agent at Curtis Brown), Pakistani-born author Bapsi Sidhwa (b. 1938) turned to self-publishing. After some practical difficulties—not the least of which was that the typesetters in Lahore didn't read English—she finally published *The Crow Eaters*, a comic but sympathetic account of the minority Parsee (Zoroastrian) community, in 1978. She then became her own sales force as well, peddling copies from store to store. A copy of the self-published novel eventually found its way from Pakistan to England, where it was soon picked up by publisher Jonathan Cape and reissued under their imprint in 1980. *The Crow Eaters* promptly won the

Portrait of Bapsi Sidhwa reprinted with the permission of Milkweed Editions.

David Higham Award for first books, and thanks to its success, Jonathan Cape also published Sidhwa's first-written novel, *The Bride*, in 1982.

After emigrating to the United States, Sidhwa went on to publish her most successful novel, the critically acclaimed semi-autobiographical *Cracking India* (originally titled *Ice-Candy-Man*), with Heinemann in 1988. *Cracking India* is a heartbreaking account of the 1947 Partition of British India and the creation of the independent nations of India and Pakistan, told through the eyes of a young girl, Lenny, whose birthday (like Sidhwa's) corresponds with the birth of the new nations. In addition to garnering literary prizes, *Cracking India* also provided Sidhwa with an entrée into cinema. *Earth*, the 1999 film adaptation of the novel by the Indian-born Canadian director Deepa Mehta (b. 1950), was also a critical success, and Sidhwa returned the favor by later adapting Mehta's 2005 film *Water* into a novelization by the same title in 2006. She has also adapted her own novel *An American Brat* (1994) for the stage, both under its original title in 2007 and as *Sock 'em with Honey* in 2003.

Still others use self-publishing as a possible avenue to a standard publishing contract. For example, Irma Rombauer (1877–1962) self-published a cookbook in St. Louis, Missouri, in 1931. Five years later, the book was picked up by Bobbs-Merrill and became an American kitchen staple and perennial bestseller, *The Joy of Cooking*. In the literature arena, one of the more impressive success stories is that of Bapsi Sidhwa, who self-published her first novel *The Crow Eaters* (1978) after efforts to obtain a conventional publishing arrangement fell through. She, too, was soon picked up by a publishing house on the strength of the self-published volume, and went on to become a successful and award-winning novelist.

e-Books have greatly increased the opportunities for self-published authors to build a successful—and sometimes lucrative—career. One such success story is that of Amanda Hocking (b. 1984), a writer of paranormal young adult novels who began self-publishing in 2010. By 2011, she had sold over one million copies of her nine e-books and earned over $2 million in sales, from downloads that retailed at just 99 cents to $2.99. Her Trylle Trilogy (*Switched*, *Torn*, and *Ascend*) has since been picked up by St. Martin's Press and issued in traditional formats.

The success of Hocking and other self-publishing authors suggests that the publishing models that have been in place for the past several centuries will continue to undergo significant changes in the digital age. However, as in previous eras, the expansion or contraction of this particular form of publishing will depend in large part on the actions taken by states and other institutions to support or impede the new developments in the book trade. The importance of such institutions to the production and dissemination of books is the subject of the next chapter.

SELECTED BIBLIOGRAPHY

"Agents Wanted": Subscription Publishing in America. Penn Libraries, University of Pennsylvania. http://www.library.upenn.edu/exhibits/rbm/agents/introduction.html.

Amazon.com. Self-Publish with Us. http://www.amazon.com/gp/seller-account/mm-summary-page.html?ie=UTF8&ld=AZFooterSelfPublish&topic=200260520.

American Society of Journalists and Authors. http://www.asja.org.

Ashton, Rosemary. *George Eliot: A Life*. London: Penguin, 1996.

Association of Authors' Agents (AAA). http://www.agentsassoc.co.uk/index.php.

Association of Authors' Representatives (AAR). http://aaronline.org.

Authors Guild. http://www.authorsguild.org.

Authors League Fund. http://www.authorsleaguefund.org.

Bapsi Sidhwa: Author, Essayist, Playwright. http://www.bapsisidhwa.com/index.html.

Brink, Jean R. "Materialist History of the Publication of Spenser's *Faerie Queene*." *Review of English Studies* 54 (2003): 1–26.

Canadian Authors Association. http://www.canauthors.org.

Casper, Scott E., Jeffrey D. Groves, Stephen W. Nissenbaum, and Michael Winship, eds. *A History of the Book in America. Volume Three: The Industrial Book, 1840–1880*. Chapel Hill: U of North Carolina P, 2007.

Clark, Giles. *Inside Book Publishing*. 3rd ed. New York: Routledge, 2001.

Cunningham, Michael. "Found in Translation." *New York Times*, 3 October 2010.

Darnton, Robert. "What Is the History of Books?" 1982. *The Case for Books: Past, Present, and Future*. New York: PublicAffairs, 2009. 175–206.

Darnton, Robert. "'What Is the History of Books?' Revisited." *Modern Intellectual History* 4.3 (2007): 495–508.

Derrida, Jacques. "Plato's Pharmacy." Trans. Barbara Johnson. In *The Norton Anthology of Theory and Criticism*. Ed. Vincent B. Leitch. New York: Norton, 2001. 1830–76.

Derusha, Will, and Alberta Acereda. Introduction to Rubén Darío's *Songs of Life and Hope/Cantos de vida y esperanza*. Durham: Duke UP, 2004. 1–46.

Fellowship of Australian Writers. http://www.writers.asn.au.

Fleming, Patricia Lockhart, Gilles Gallichan, and Yvan Lamonde, eds. *History of the Book in Canada. Volume One: Beginnings to 1840*. Toronto: U of Toronto P, 2004.

Foucault, Michel. "What Is an Author?" Trans. Donald F. Bouchard and Sherry Simon. *Language, Counter-Memory, Practice*. Ed. Donald F. Bouchard. Ithaca: Cornell UP, 1977. 124–27. Available from Athenaeum Library of Philosophy. http://evans-experientialism.freewebspace.com/foucault3.htm.

Greenblatt, Stephen. *Will in the World: How Shakespeare Became Shakespeare*. New York: Norton, 2004.

Griffin, Dustin. *Literary Patronage in England, 1650–1800*. Cambridge: Cambridge UP, 1996.

Gross, Robert A., and Mary Kelley, eds. *A History of the Book in America. Volume Two: An Extensive Republic: Print, Culture, and Society in the New Nation, 1790–1840*. Chapel Hill: U of North Carolina P, 2010.

Haven Foundation. http://www.thehavenfdn.org/index.html.

Hepburn, James. *The Author's Empty Purse and the Rise of the Literary Agent*. Oxford: Oxford UP, 1968.

Kelly, Caitlin. "It's Not Billions, But It Can Help Rescue an Artist." *New York Times*, 3 June 2012.

Lewalski, Barbara K. "Re-Writing Patriarchy and Patronage: Margaret Clifford, Anne Clifford, and Aemilia Lanyer." *Yearbook of English Studies* 21 (1991): 87–106.

Millgate, Jane. *Walter Scott: The Making of the Novelist*. Toronto: U of Toronto P, 1984.

Nunnally, Tiina. "A Note on the Translation." In Sigrid Undset, *Kristin Lavransdatter*. New York: Penguin, 1997, 1999, 2005. xix–xx.

PEN International. http://www.pen-international.org.

PubIt! by Barnes & Noble. http://pubit.barnesandnoble.com/pubit_app/bn?t=pi_reg_home.

Rasmussen, Eric. *The Shakespeare Thefts: In Search of the First Folios*. New York: Palgrave Macmillan, 2011.

Satran, Richard. "'War and Peace' Translations Duel for Tolstoy Fans." Reuters.com, 21 October 2007. http://www.reuters.com/article/2007/10/21/us-warandpeace-idUSN1928920320071021.

Smith, Janet Adam. "The Royal Literary Fund: A Short History." Royal Literary Fund. http://www.rlf.org.uk/documents/RLFshorthistory_000.pdf.

Society of Authors. http://www.societyofauthors.org.

Turow, Scott, Paul Aiken, and James Shapiro. "Would the Bard Have Survived the Web?" *New York Times*, 15 February 2011.

Wilson, A.N. *The Laird of Abbotsford: A View of Sir Walter Scott*. Oxford: Oxford UP, 1989.

Xlibris. http://www2.xlibris.com.

CHAPTER SIX

STATES AND CENSORS

Political and religious entities, such as rulers, states, or churches, have always had a powerful influence over the history of the book. Through their ability to encourage or discourage certain kinds of content, to elevate or punish authors and publishers, and to support or inhibit the book trades, governments and other official entities have fundamentally shaped reading and writing habits. As the historical chapters of this book have illustrated, sometimes this influence has been very much for the good. Measures to improve scripts and raise literacy levels, for example, have helped to increase both the number of available texts and the number of readers who can interact with them. At other times, the power exerted by rulers has been incontrovertibly bad. Certain acts of official censorship have been known to destroy not only works, but also lives.

Since the rise of the print age, states and censors have been increasingly important in shaping the relationship between the book and society. Some of these impacts have been indirect. For example, political support behind such measures as building and maintaining transportation and communication networks have materially helped authors and distributors of books by making it easier for them to obtain and circulate reading materials. The efforts of civil and religious authorities to provide and enhance educational opportunities have also shaped book culture by helping to build and support the demand for books. Various taxes, tariffs, fines, and other penalties imposed and enforced by civil authorities have had both positive and negative effects, in some instances helping to protect local printing trades, and in others creating too high a burden for the trades to survive. Other impacts have been very direct. Prohibitions against various kinds of reading materials, for example, have driven certain forms of expression underground or away altogether. On the other hand, laws that protect freedom of expression or that provide for the establishment and maintenance of libraries have helped ensure that book culture becomes deeply rooted in the communities covered by those legislative acts.

This chapter will look at some of the ways in which civil and religious authorities have contributed to the shaping of print culture by regulating, censoring, protecting, or even employing writers and publishers. In particular, the chapter will explore the effects of regulation on the sale and distribution of books; the effects of state and religious censorship; the official promotion and protection of books through the creation of intellectual property laws; and efforts to harness the press for official purposes, or propaganda.

REGULATING PRINT

The rapid spread of the printing press across Europe in the fifteenth and early sixteenth centuries was met by some with great consternation. Both civil and church authorities recognized that the speed and relative ease with which texts could be printed and disseminated meant that it would become increasingly difficult to monitor what was being published—and to weed out anything that might be dangerous to either state or soul. Very early on, new regulations were enacted to control what was being printed and to restrict where certain texts could be circulated and who was allowed to distribute them. But governments and religious authorities were not the only entities that were worried about the rise of the print industry. Workers in the manuscript book trades, particularly copyists and illuminators, were also alarmed. Historian Colin Clair notes that as early as 1465—only about ten years after Gutenberg printed his famous Bible—manuscript book workers in Paris managed to confiscate a shipment of printed books brought in from Germany by Gutenberg's partner Johann Fust (fl. 1450–66). In at least this one instance, the manuscript trades' efforts to hold back the tide of change were successful: Fust was forced to return to Germany without selling a single printed book.

What emerged over the next couple of centuries was a patchwork of civil, church, and trade regulations that attempted to control the printing and circulation of books. Many of these regulations were very local in nature. They might govern the production and sale of paper, the licensing of presses, or the printing or sale of specific texts. Local authorities also might levy special fees or taxes on the book trades, or impose tariffs on imported or exported books or book-making materials. In response to these controls, if it became too expensive or simply too difficult to print or bind in one city or region, the book trades might shift their work to partners or subsidiaries elsewhere. They even might decide to simply shut down and start again when the business climate improved. The history of the book abounds with examples of authors, printers, publishers, and booksellers following the paths of least resistance, by shifting residences or arranging to have texts printed in regions where they were not prohibited and then importing them for sale where they were wanted.

Many of the restrictions affecting the book trades were due to religious and political strife. As Europe divided first along Roman Catholic and Protestant lines and later along authoritative or democratic political lines, both religious and civil authorities sought to control what kinds of books were produced and by whom. For example, in the early sixteenth century, civil authorities and printers in England began to worry about foreign influences on the English book trades. In response, Parliament passed a number of acts

Allegory of Louis XIV, Protector of Arts and Sciences, Jean Garnier, 1672.

that restricted foreigners' participation in the English trades. By 1534, it was illegal to buy a book that had been bound abroad or to buy one sold in England by foreigners. At about the same time, Parliament also imposed some of the first print censorship laws. In 1530, it decreed that local bishops had to pre-approve any theological books before publication. By 1538, the requirement for prepublication review had been expanded and secularized, so that for the next century and a half, no book of any kind could be printed in England without the prior approval of a royal licenser.

These kinds of prepublication laws quickly became the norm in Europe, and some of the strictest regulations were enacted in France. From 1612 on, only royal authority could grant the *lettres de permission* required for printing, and in 1635 the law was strengthened so that anyone who dared to print or sell written material without royal permission would do so under penalty of death. After his ascension, King Louis XIV (1638–1715) tightened restrictions on the book trades. In 1649, he decreed that all apprentices to the book trades had to be of French birth and Roman Catholic faith. And in 1686 he clamped down even harder, restricting the number of printing offices in Paris to just thirty-six, and transferring the authority for their oversight from the University of Paris to the government. Aware that the ability to both print and sell books could give certain tradespeople significant power over the intellectual life of the nation, the French crown also enacted regulations to restrict any individual tradesman's share of the business. Booksellers were prohibited from applying for printing office licenses, and printers were allowed to sell printed texts directly only from shops located in the university quarter of Paris.

In addition to regulations and general trade tariffs, authorities could also impose specific taxes on the book trades, with the express purpose of raising the cost of printed materials sufficiently to inhibit their circulation. This was the intention behind the various *taxes on knowledge* imposed by the British Parliament in the late eighteenth and early nineteenth centuries. Levied on certain kinds of publications, especially newspapers, on advertisements, and on paper itself, the effect of these taxes was to raise the cost of newspapers so high that their circulation was suppressed.

All copies of a newspaper—including those that remained unsold and uncirculated—had to display stamps showing that the appropriate taxes had been paid by the proprietor. "Unstamped" copies were subject to confiscation, and their producers to fines and imprisonment. Printers, booksellers, and would-be readers all protested against the imposition of these taxes, and resistance to them could prove fierce. For example, the specific tax imposed on colonial newspapers under the 1765 Stamp Act was one of the factors that caused the American colonists to revolt against the British government.

In 1815, the stamp duties on domestic newspapers in Britain were increased to fourpence per copy, effectively putting the cost of the *taxes alone* beyond the reach of working-class readers—never mind the newspapers themselves. As publishing historian Richard Altick notes, this was no mistake. In the context of the 1819 redefinition of the kinds of publications subject to the newspaper tax, it was clear that the point of these taxes was not merely to raise revenues for a government still reeling from the costs of the Napoleonic wars, but to eliminate dissent: the tax was not really on "news," but on "views." It was only in the wake of the 1832 Reform Act, which significantly redefined rights and representation in the United Kingdom, that the taxes on knowledge began to be repealed. As they were, the quantity and variety of affordable publications exploded.

Trade Associations

Although civil and religious authorities exerted a significant impact on the book trades, they were not the only agents of regulation. Local guilds and trade associations also played an important role, and this role became more important as the printing trades expanded throughout Europe and into the New World. Initially, almost anyone with enough capital to set up a press could try to run one, subject to local trade restrictions. But as the printing trade matured, so did the number of printers and booksellers who had an interest in maintaining their share of the local markets. Many printers and booksellers entered into formal and informal confederations to protect their own businesses and ward off new competitors. Some of the resulting organizations remained major players nationally and internationally for many years. One particularly influential early trade association was the Stationers' Company of London. Stationers' guilds had been operating in England since at least the thirteenth century in Oxford and Cambridge, where they were connected to the booksellers who served the universities. *Stationer* initially meant just bookseller, but the term gradually came to include the four crafts engaged in the creation of manuscript books, including parchment makers, scriveners, illustrators, and bookbinders. After William Caxton (c. 1415–92) introduced printing to England in the 1470s, small producers and traders were gradually squeezed out by larger, better capitalized printers. And those printers wanted to ensure that their business wouldn't be undercut by newer, foreign traders.

The printers and other craftsmen who formed the Stationers' Company incorporated in 1557 with the royal approval of Mary I (1516–58) and her husband, Philip II of Spain (1527–98). The Stationers' Charter granted its members a virtual monopoly on printing in England (nonmembers could print only if granted royal permission). Crucially, the Charter also gave the Stationers key powers to enforce their monopoly. The Stationers' Company had the right to search houses and businesses anywhere in England for printed materials, and to confiscate anything printed contrary to the Charter. The Stationers also had the right to imprison anyone who was found to have been printing illegally— or even anyone who resisted search.

Having won an overall monopoly on printing for the Company as a whole, the next critical step was to ensure that individual members did not encroach on one another's publications. The problem of poaching others' printed publications was almost as old as printing technology itself. The first grants or *patents* authorizing particular individuals as the sole legitimate printers of specific works had been granted as early as 1469 in Venice, and the practice quickly became widespread on the Continent. The practice eventually reached England, where the first grants were issued in 1518.

The question of what authority would issue those grants and enforce them was of keen interest to the Stationers. After actively lobbying to become the official administrator of those rights, in 1637 the Stationers' Company became an official arm of the government, charged with keeping the records of which works were licensed for printing and with collecting copies of approved manuscripts. As part of the official decree, the total number of master printers was also restricted, as was the number of presses that could be owned and operated by each master printer. Printers were required to post bonds to guarantee against printing unauthorized books, and offending printers not only risked losing their bonds but were also subject to being whipped in the pillory. Besides overseeing the domestic printing trade, the Stationers' Company also became the de facto customs agents for all printed material imported from abroad. Books had to be landed in London, and a representative of the Stationers' Company had to be present when the containers were opened. Most of these restrictions remained in force until 1693.

CENSORSHIP

In addition to restrictions, tariffs, and trade practices, the last and most direct way to regulate print culture is through censorship. *Censorship* is the process

BOOK BANS AND CHALLENGES

When most people think of *censorship*, they think of the official acts of governments and other powerful entities to limit or deny access to certain kinds of materials. However, many acts of censorship and attempted censorship are undertaken by unofficial entities. A common form of censorship in the West, especially in the United States, is the *book challenge*. In a book challenge, an individual or group tries to make the case that a particular book is inappropriate for a given library or school curriculum. Frequently, such challenges are based on content—including such elements as language, characters, and situations—or on the perceived messages or impact of the books in question. If the challenger succeeds in having the book pulled from the library, classroom, or reading list, the book is considered to be *banned*.

In an effort to call public attention to the practice of book challenges and bans, the American Library Association (ALA) sponsors an annual Banned Books Week. The ALA's Office for Intellectual Freedom also collects data on challenged and banned books and issues regular reports. Although contemporary literature, especially by minority authors, makes up a significant portion of the books challenged and banned in the United States in recent years, the ALA notes that classic works of literature are far from exempt. Indeed, nearly half of the books identified as the Best 100 Novels of the Twentieth Century by the Radcliffe Publishing Course in association with the Modern Library editorial board have been challenged. In fact, all but one of the top twelve novels have been challenged or banned, including F. Scott Fitzgerald's *The Great Gatsby*, J.D. Salinger's *The Catcher in the Rye*, John Steinbeck's *The Grapes of Wrath* and *Of Mice and Men*, Harper Lee's *To Kill a Mockingbird*, Alice Walker's *The Color Purple*, James Joyce's *Ulysses*, Toni Morrison's *Beloved*, William Golding's *The Lord of the Flies*, Vladimir Nabokov's *Lolita*, and, ironically in light of its anti-censorship messages, George Orwell's *1984*. The only novel in the top twelve not known to have been challenged is William Faulkner's *The Sound and the Fury*.

Individuals and groups who challenge books usually make the case that content, language, or themes are inappropriate for the age or maturity level of the readers into whose hands they may fall. The most common challenges are for sexually explicit content, offensive language, unsuitability for age groups, and violence. American novelist Alice Walker's (b. 1944) 1982 novel *The Color Purple*, for example, has been challenged for employing racist and misogynistic language and situations, as well as for its frank treatment of sexuality. That it is a historical novel set in the Deep South and Africa in the era before the civil rights movement has not always been accepted as mitigating evidence, nor has the book's having been awarded both a Pulitzer Prize for Fiction and a National Book Award in 1983. According to the ALA, book challenges are most commonly launched by parents who are unhappy with a book's inclusion in a school classroom or library, although public libraries also receive a significant amount of challenges from those who identify themselves as parents or patrons.

of preventing particular texts or images from being read, either by altering or deleting them or by denying access to them. Usually enforced by civil and religious authorities, censorship can be enacted either before or after publication. Authors, titles, or categories of texts might be banned and kept from the marketplace of ideas; portions of texts or images might be deleted or obscured before circulation; or published works might be confiscated or destroyed.

Although most forms of censorship over the ages have been fairly local and particularized, there have also been some very far-reaching efforts. Until the twentieth century, the most notable and wide-reaching of these were the restrictions on print culture enacted by the Roman Catholic Church. Through the office of the *General Inquisition*, the body charged with suppressing non-orthodox thought, the Church sought to protect its members by strictly controlling the trade in works that might be deemed *heretical*, or dissenting in any way from official Church doctrine.

Censorship and the Inquisition

One of the first truly international attempts to regulate the printing trades came from the Roman Catholic Church in 1515, when Pope Leo X (1475–1521) promulgated the bull *Inter sollicitudines*. This directive on the censorship of books began by affirming that printing technology was, for many, a blessing. It acknowledged that printing enabled individuals to possess and read numerous books, and that the discipline of regular reading helped to foster scholars who could instruct others in the true faith. But—and this was a big *but*—printing also made it possible to disseminate books containing "errors opposed to the faith" and "pernicious views" contrary to Christian religion.

Thus, in order to protect both the faith and the faithful, Leo X announced that from that moment on

> no one may dare to print or have printed any book or other writing of whatever kind in Rome or in any other cities or dioceses, without the book or writings having first been closely examined, at Rome by our vicar and the master of the sacred palace, in other cities and dioceses by the bishop or some other person who knows about the printing of books and writings of this kind and who has been delegated to this office by the bishop in question, and also by the inquisitor of heresy for the city or diocese where the said printing is to take place.

Effective immediately, printers would have to present a signed warrant attesting that this preapproval had been granted for each text. And lest they not take the edict seriously, offenders were threatened with not just a significant fine and a one-year suspension from all printing activities, but also excommunication and the confiscation and burning of the unlicensed books.

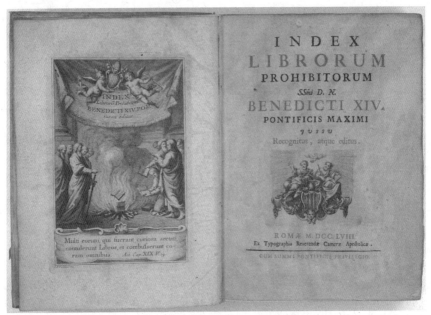

Index Librorum Prohibitorum (detail). Bridwell Library Special Collections, Perkins School of Theology, Southern Methodist University.

The Church further codified its restrictions on the printing trades under Pope Paul IV (1476–1559), who introduced an official list of prohibited books, the *Index Librorum Prohibitorum*. Local lists of prohibited books had been generated from the 1520s on in the Netherlands, Venice, and Paris, all of which had become important printing centers. For the most part, the works on the local lists were those that expressed support for Protestant, and therefore heretical, ideas. But the compliance with these local lists was mixed. In Venice, for example, where an *Index* was drawn up in 1549, printers and political leaders succeeded in getting the local list suppressed, on the grounds that it was asking Venetian authorities to take stronger steps against heresy than the Pope was taking in Rome.

The first official, international list of prohibited books was finally issued from Rome in 1559, and it became the basis for 400 years of press policing and censorship by the Church. According to Church teaching, works on the *Index* could only be read by religious scholars who were deemed wise and sophisticated enough to peruse them without peril to their soul. Other would-be readers were threatened with excommunication and, under the power of the Inquisition, even death. Offending books were gathered and burned, and printers and booksellers who dealt in them risked excommunication and seizure of their businesses. Although the rules governing which books were prohibited were revised numerous times over the succeeding centuries, the *Index* continued in force until the mid-twentieth century and was only finally discontinued in 1966. Though the *Index* is no longer published, the Catholic

Church still maintains strictures against authors and publications that it considers a threat to the faith.

The edicts behind the *Index* were enforced to different degrees over the intervening centuries. For example, despite the strength of the Church in French Canada, ecclesiastical censorship really wasn't a significant force there until after 1840, when the Diocese of Montreal finally consolidated enough personnel and power to effectively control book culture in Quebec. Curiously, although Spain was among the fiercest proponents of the Inquisition in the early years, it significantly relaxed its restrictions on the printing trades in the eighteenth century under the reign of Carlos III (1716–88). Carlos III not only expelled the Jesuits and thereby reduced the power of the Inquisition, but he actively supported the Spanish book trades. He appointed Joaquín Ibarra (1725–85) as *Impresor de Cámara del Rey*, or royal printer, and he urged Ibarra and others to experiment with new printing techniques. Among the many beautiful books produced under Ibarra's guidance was a renowned 1780 edition of Miguel de Cervantes' (1547–1616) novel *Don Quixote* (published in two volumes in 1605 and 1615) for the Royal Academy. In addition, Carlos III exempted printers and type-makers from military service, and he reduced tariffs on the printing industry and brought down the cost of type metal. Critically, he also ended the monopoly on religious texts that had been granted to the Plantin printing house in Antwerp. This enabled printers in Madrid to produce these texts, assuring them of a steady income stream. In return for this show of royal favor, the Spanish printers promised to use only Spanish supplies and artisans, thereby further strengthening the local trades.

Librarian and archivist Pearce Carefoote notes that the *Index* serves as a useful guide to some of the most important currents of thought during the eras in which it was enforced. By telling its followers what *not* to read, the Church ironically left a permanent record of what was culturally significant. And in non-Catholic regions, such as England, the *Index* could even be used as a buyers' guide for bibliophiles. The first librarian working for Thomas Bodley (1545–1613), whose books formed the basis for one of the finest libraries in the world, Oxford's Bodleian, used to regularly consult the *Index* to determine precisely which editions he should purchase for his patron's collection.

State Censorship

Like religious censorship, state censorship is also concerned with dissent. In the modern era, censorship by civil authorities largely kept pace with the perceived threats of a rapidly expanding print culture. From the sixteenth century on, many European nations sought to suppress the printing of texts that challenged or defamed the ruling authorities. Of particular concern were texts that might be considered *seditious*, urging resistance or rebellion against the authorities, or *treasonous*, urging the actual overthrow of the government or threatening the person of the sovereign.

For example, in England under Elizabeth I (1533–1601), the Act Against Seditious Words and Rumours included a clause forbidding anyone to "devise and write, print or set forth any manner of book" deemed seditious or slanderous to the crown, on penalty of death. In France, censorship efforts initially focused on heresy, sedition, and libel, but from the early seventeenth century the crown's concerns gradually expanded, eventually taking in immorality and indecency as well. Sedition legislation was still being enacted in the early twentieth century, when, for example, the United States banned all "disloyal, profane, scurrilous, or abusive language" against the government during times of war and also forbade the US Postal Service from delivering mail that contained such messages. The Sedition Act of 1918 was repealed two years later, and court decisions in the intervening decades have deemed that in the United States such laws are largely unconstitutional. However, in the wake of international terrorist attacks at the turn of the twenty-first century, sedition legislation has been renewed in other nations, including in Australia.

OBSCENITY LEGISLATION AND LADY CHATTERLEY'S LOVER

Legislation to prevent the publication and circulation of obscenity exists in most contemporary nations. What constitutes "obscene" material is notoriously difficult to pin down, and legal authorities in most instances have had to rely on definitions that take into consideration underlying community values in a given place and time. For example, *pornography*, material that depicts erotic behavior with the goal of stimulating sexual excitement, has frequently come under the auspices of anti-obscenity legislation. There is currently a strong international consensus against pornography depicting children, but there are few other agreed-upon guidelines. US Supreme Court Justice Potter Stewart (1915–85), in a 1964 court decision, famously stated that although he couldn't define pornography, "I know it when I see it." Most thoughtful people are likely to be unsatisfied with such a vague definition, but they are also likely to acknowledge that values and levels of tolerance are constantly changing. Therefore, works that are deemed obscene (or not) in one place and time may fall on the other side of the fence in another place and time.

While most people can understand how material that is obviously and expressly pornographic may galvanize censorship efforts in certain nations and communities, at least to the extent of controlling juveniles' access to such material, efforts to censor material that is less unambiguously pornographic or obscene in intent have created greater controversy. In particular, national and local efforts to grapple with the censorship or protection of material with literary or artistic intentions have been fraught with difficulty. One of the most contested works that ultimately redefined obscenity legislation in the Anglophone world was the 1928 novel by English writer D.H. Lawrence (1885–1930), *Lady Chatterley's Lover*.

State-sponsored censorship can also target ideas and practices that are considered inimical to the current regime. Under the Protectorate of Oliver Cromwell (1599–1658), for example, the Puritan Parliament banned all publications that supported Anglican worship practices. As the French Revolution descended into the Terror, the National Convention began to issue decrees that effectively negated the press freedoms guaranteed in the Declaration of the Rights of Man. The 1793 Law of Suspects set up surveillance committees around the country who were empowered to arrest anyone who by behavior, contacts, words, or writings appeared to be "enemies of liberty." As many as 40,000 may have been executed as a direct result of denunciation and arrest under the decree.

In British and French North America, many of the colonies and settlements enacted censorship regulations to prevent certain kinds of books (often of a religious nature) from circulating within their borders. Even after the Constitution of the United States enshrined press freedom, localities

Having run into censorship problems with some of his earlier works, Lawrence knew he would have difficulty publishing *Lady Chatterley's Lover* in the United Kingdom, because of the book's sexual content (the main character has a frankly described affair with her gamekeeper) and use of language which, in the words of a 1962 Afterword to the unexpurgated New American Library edition, included "words not usually permitted to appear in print in Anglo-Saxon countries." The novel was therefore first printed in Italy, by a printer who didn't know English and thus introduced myriad typographical errors. Despite being banned, the Italian printing was smuggled into both the United States and the United Kingdom, and over the next twenty years a number of pirated editions were also produced on both sides of the Atlantic.

Finally, Grove Press in New York issued the first complete edition of *Lady Chatterley's Lover* in 1959, and the following year Penguin Books issued a complete edition in the United Kingdom. The Postmaster General of the United States banned the Grove edition from circulation in the US mails, citing contemporary obscenity legislation, and in Britain Penguin was prosecuted under the 1959 Obscene Publications Act. The publishers fought back, and the bans were struck down. US District Court Judge Frederick van Pelt ruled in July 1959 that the novel was a work of art and not obscene, and an English jury cleared the book in November 1960 on similar grounds. A Canadian judge in Montreal, T.A. Fontaine, rejected testimony from American witnesses and ruled the American edition of *Lady Chatterley* obscene in June 1960, which effectively banned it from circulation in Quebec. However, the Supreme Court of Canada overruled the Fontaine judgment in March 1962. Ironically, the main effect of what Lawrence sardonically referred to as the "censor morons" was to drive up demand, and thence sales, of the book.

were granted a certain amount of latitude to prohibit certain kinds of publications—a situation that contributed to the phenomenon of books being "banned in Boston" by the Catholic-influenced civic authorities. National censorship in both Canada and the United States was mostly reserved for works that were deemed obscene, rather than religiously or politically suspect. *Obscenity*—material that is regarded as abhorrent or taboo, usually because of sexual or violent content—was banned from Canada by the 1847 Customs Act, which governed the importation of "immoral or indecent" books or drawings; similar laws were enacted in the 1930s and enforced until the late 1960s. In the United States, the 1873 Comstock Act forbade the use of the postal system to send "obscene, lewd, and/or lascivious" materials. Originally aimed at suppressing the circulation of contraceptives and information about birth control, the federal law and numerous state law imitators were gradually cited as authority to censor a much broader range of materials, including literary works such as the 1928 novel *Lady Chatterley's Lover* by D.H. Lawrence. Obscenity laws in both Canada and the United States were eventually curbed by court challenges brought by publishers, distributors, and bookstores.

Although most of the examples provided so far are of civil or religious censorship, there have also been significant instances of self-censorship among different sectors of the book trades. In most cases, self-censorship has been enacted in the face of a threat of stronger action from the government. One well-known and long-lasting example of self-censorship within print culture was the Comics Code Authority (CCA). Created in 1954 by the Comic Magazine Association of America, the CCA was an industry-sponsored attempt to curb criticism levied at comic books in the wake of Fredric Wertham's (1895–1981) diatribe *Seduction of the Innocent*, which was published the same year. Wertham charged that the violent and gruesome content of some comic books corrupted the minds of the children who were a major part of comics' readership, and his book prompted a congressional investigation. The CCA promised to police its own ranks, and comics published under its oversight displayed a special seal prominently on their covers; many distributors refused to carry comics that did not display the seal. The CCA's influence over the comic book industry endured for more than half a century, with the last publishers only dropping out of the system in 2011.

Censorship and the Third Reich

Among the more iconic images of state-sponsored censorship in the modern era are films and stills of the elaborate book-burning rituals staged in Germany in May 1933. Under the rule of Adolf Hitler (1889–1945) and the National Socialist German Workers' Party, or Nazis, dissent and difference of all kinds in Germany were ruthlessly suppressed. While Jews were the largest and most relentlessly persecuted population under the domination of the Third Reich, others whose backgrounds or ideas were contrary to official Nazi policies

Book burning in Opera Square, Berlin, 10 May 1933. Image courtesy of the US Holocaust Memorial Museum/NARA.

were also targeted. Authors of all kinds were censored and harassed, including novelists Erich Maria Remarque (1898–1970) and Thomas Mann (1875–1955). Authors' works would be pulled from bookstore shelves and the authors' homes and families attacked.

Although the harassment and de facto censorship began earlier, some of the earliest official censorship laws were enacted in February 1933, under the Law for the Protection of the German People. Passed the morning after the German assembly building in Berlin, the Reichstag, was burned, the Law severely restricted freedom of assembly, of the press, and of expression. A few months later, Joseph Goebbels (1897–1945), the Minister of the Reich for Enlightening the People and for Propaganda, saw the passage of the Law Relative to State Government, which granted him oversight over all aspects of education. He promptly launched a campaign of censorship, enforced by both civil and military authorities, aimed at wiping out all ideas not approved by the Nazi regime. The intimidation campaign was so effective that many people voluntarily surrendered or burned their own books, and publishers and book dealers collaborated in drawing up blacklists of suspect authors. Libraries and publishers' warehouses were systematically stripped of their contents, both by the authorities and by frenzied students. In addition to book burnings, there were also displays of "books of shame": in Münster, for example, prohibited books were tied to a tree outside the cathedral.

Among the particular targets of Nazi censorship were books about Jewish culture, communism, or sexual matters. After the May book bonfires, the psychoanalyst Sigmund Freud (1856–1939) drily told a journalist that this actually represented an advance in human behavior: "In the Middle Ages, they would have burned me. Now they're happy burning my books." The poet and playwright Bertolt Brecht (1898–1956), whose works were also destroyed in the fires, composed an ironic poem in response, *"Die Bücherverbrennung"* or "The Book-Burning." The speaker of the poem, whose works have not been destroyed, takes exception to the oversight and demands that they, too, be confiscated and burned.

Nazi censorship went beyond book-burning. By 1945, more than 500 authors had been officially banned. The libraries and other cultural repositories of subject nations were systematically looted and destroyed, with major archives in the Netherlands, Belgium, and France particularly hard hit. And, of course, the personal libraries of those Jews who were deported and murdered in the Holocaust were also subject to Nazi predation. In the Netherlands alone, between 1942 and 1944, more than one million volumes belonging to 29,000 Jews were destroyed—and this is just a small portion of the millions of persons caught up by the Holocaust. According to historian Fernando Báez, the Commission for Jewish-European Cultural Reconstruction calculated that in 1933 before the rise of the Nazi regime, there were more than 3.3 million Jewish books in various locales around Europe. At the end of the war, less than one-quarter of those books remained.

Censorship in the Modern Era

After World War II, many in the West hoped that the most extreme censorship tactics would end with the regimes that had practiced them. The foundation of the United Nations, and the proclamation of the Universal Declaration of Human Rights, provided a brake on the systematic destruction of the human record. However, some of these practices did indeed continue, especially in Stalinist Russia and in some of the newly arising dictatorships in Latin America, where authors' works were not only banned and destroyed, but the authors themselves could simply "disappear" into a gulag or unmarked grave.

In the United States, a postwar wave of anti-communist paranoia fueled the establishment of the House Committee on Un-American Activities, charged with investigating espionage, subversion, and propaganda against the American government. One of the more notorious investigations was that of the Hollywood movie industry, which was suspected of exerting a pro-communist influence in its films. The result of the hearings was that a number of artists associated with the film industry were *blacklisted*, or unofficially restricted from work. Among the more than 300 individuals boycotted by the movie studios were many screenwriters, many of whom also wrote in other genres. Some of these were forced to write under pseudonyms or simply abandon their careers. The Committee was increasingly discredited through the late 1950s and into the 1960s, and finally abolished in 1975.

At about the same time that the "red scare" in the United States was burning out, censorship from the opposite end of the political spectrum was ramping up in the People's Republic of China. The Cultural Revolution (1966–76) sought to transform Chinese education, literature, and the arts in accordance with Chairman Mao Zedong's (1893–1976) beliefs about the importance of political orthodoxy over other values. In the first year of the Cultural Revolution, more than four million copies of textbooks, primarily in the humanities, politics, and foreign languages, were denounced as "poisonous weeds" and pulled from shelves. Led by a paramilitary student movement called the Red Guards, over the next two years students systematically sacked libraries and consigned their contents to bonfires, seeking to root out the "Four Olds": old ideas, old culture, old customs, and old habits. All libraries in China are believed to have been closed for at least some period of time during the Cultural Revolution, to ensure that they could not serve as "the paradise of the capitalist class," and some remained closed for the entire decade. Educators, writers, and other artists were denounced and subject to torture, imprisonment, or forced labor.

Whatever the pernicious effects of the red scare in the West, the Cultural Revolution, and other efforts to censor and suppress book culture in the middle decades of the twentieth century, many onlookers consoled themselves with the knowledge that these attempts at state censorship ultimately collapsed under the weight of their internal illogicality or their incompatibility with increasingly widely held support for basic human rights. When the Cold War ended, many Western thinkers assumed that a more democratic tide would gradually lift global tolerance for freedom of expression. The philosopher and political theorist Francis Fukuyama (b. 1952) even predicted that the world was achieving the "end of history": the triumph of democratic liberalism and market capitalism over other forms of governmental and economic arrangements. The reemergence of various forms of totalitarianism in the 1990s was thus, for many, a terrible shock.

The end of the Cold War not only lifted sociopolitical and economic restrictions in many regions, it also lifted the barriers that had helped keep ethnic tensions in check. One consequence of this was the reemergence of ultranationalist forces that actively sought the elimination of their rivals and a consequent new resurgence of genocide. *Ethnic cleansing* in the former Yugoslavia and elsewhere involved the systematic elimination of rival cultural groups, through mass deportation, rape, and execution. Not only were the people targeted, however: so were their books and other cultural artifacts. For example, in August 1992, Serbian nationalist forces outside Sarajevo shelled the National and University Library of Bosnia and Herzegovina. In a matter of minutes, the building was on fire. The fire burned for three days, destroying an estimated 1.5 million volumes. Miraculously, library workers managed to save nearly 100,000 volumes, despite sniper fire, by passing them along a human chain. Bibliophile Nicholas Basbanes interviewed the chief librarian, Kemal Bakaršic, about the night of the fire. Bakaršic described the surreal experience of watching the burning pages of books disintegrating before him:

> because there was no wind, the leaves of the books were floating very slowly. And really, you can capture a leaf in your hand, and you can *read* it before it disintegrates.... there is a moment where you have a final chance to make out a line or two, a word or two, and you realize you are the last person on earth who is able to do this. Then you see it crumble and disintegrate in your hands.... I tried to catch as many pages as I could, but what could I do except collect the ashes, because when you catch it, it just melts.

Censorship through destruction also reemerged in the wake of the Soviet departure from Afghanistan in 1989. Fairly stringent press censorship had been practiced in Afghanistan during the 1970s under the communist regime of the People's Democratic Party of Afghanistan, in response to the rising power of the Islamist Mujahedeen, and the violent destruction of books intensified through the period of civil war that followed the Soviet exit. When the Taliban finally wrested control of the country in the mid-1990s, their interpretation of Islamic law, or *Shari'a*, included a strict adherence to traditional interdictions against the visual depiction of living things.

The effect of these interdictions on booksellers and readers in Afghanistan were devastating, and the wider world was made aware of them through *The Bookseller of Kabul* (2002), Norwegian journalist Åsne Seierstad's (b. 1970) moving account of the travails of Shah Muhammad Rais. Rais, a book dealer in Kabul (whom Seierstad calls Sultan Khan), had rescued books looted from the National Library of Afghanistan and had also witnessed the Taliban's destruction of the National Museum. In late 1999, his own bookshop was raided by the religious police, who burned everything containing the banned images. In an effort to prevent further raids and conflagrations, Rais began to "censor" the remaining books in his shop himself, first by blacking out any images of living things, and later by pasting business cards over them.

PROMOTING PRINT

As the discussion of regulations, taxes, and censorship suggests, the question of who is allowed to produce and distribute copies of particular texts has long been an important one for both the authorities and the printing trades. By the beginning of the eighteenth century, it was also becoming a significant concern for authors. The time was thus ripe for two important developments in the history of the book: the rise of support for the concept of free expression, and particularly a free press, and the emergence of the legal concept of copyright. In subsequent centuries, the principles underpinning freedom of the press and the notion of a moral and legal right to creative works would come to inform many of the national and international laws developed to protect free expression and an individual's claim to his or her own intellectual property.

Freedom of the Press

Among the more radical and far-reaching notions arising out of the Enlightenment was the idea of freedom of the press. The notion was a logical consequence of ongoing arguments about the desirability of more democratic forms of government. Defenders of press freedom insisted that a healthy and moral state was impossible without an educated or informed populace. Therefore, it was necessary in a democracy (or even in a reformed constitutional monarchy) that a wide variety of ideas be circulated and debated, and the best way to do this was through the press. The English poet John Milton (1608–74) was an ardent early defender of freedom of the press. His 1644 *Areopagitica* was an impassioned argument against the English practice of licensing—which, he pointed out, was nothing less than prepublication censorship. Yet despite his and others' pleas, it would be another half-century before the English print licensing laws were allowed to expire, and nearly two centuries before the kind of freedom of expression Milton envisioned would be protected in the United Kingdom.

However, press freedom was established by law in other countries in the mid-eighteenth century. The Scandinavian countries were among the first to abolish censorship and guarantee press freedom, in the 1760s and 1770s. The United States did so in 1787, in the First Amendment to the Constitution, which specifies that "Congress shall make no law respecting an establishment of religion, or prohibiting the free exercise thereof; or abridging the freedom of speech, or of the press; or the right of the people peaceably to assemble, and to petition the government for a redress of grievances." The First Amendment would serve as a model for laws enacted in many subsequently formed democratic nations, beginning with France. In 1789, France affirmed that freedom of thought and opinion was one of the most precious of natural rights. These ideas are also echoed in Article 19 of the United Nations' Universal Declaration of Human Rights, passed in 1948, which states that "Everyone has the right to freedom of opinion and expression; this right includes freedom to hold opinions without interference and to seek, receive and impart information and ideas through any media and regardless of frontiers."

Hard-fought and frequently subject to erosion from authorities across the political spectrum, who continue to worry that genuine freedom of expression will almost certainly lead to criticism, dissent, and even rebellion, press freedom remains one of the beacons of Enlightenment thought. According

THE DANISH CARTOONS CONTROVERSY

Censorship and attempted censorship are not always enacted by official censors, or even within national or regional boundaries. In 2005, the Danish newspaper *Jyllands-Posten* solicited illustrations for a forthcoming article on self-censorship. The article had been prompted by reports that a children's author writing a book about the Prophet Muhammad had used an anonymous illustrator, out of fears that Islamic prohibitions against depicting the Prophet could create repercussions against any named illustrator. Acting on a naïve and rather misguided impulse to defend press freedom, the editors of *Jyllands-Posten* subsequently printed twelve cartoon depictions of the Prophet, one of which depicted him with a turban shaped like a bomb.

There were immediate protests from observant Muslims in Denmark, and the protests spread out more widely in early 2006. Danish diplomats were called in for official consultation in Iran and Iraq; Sudan, Saudi Arabia, and other countries began a boycott of Danish products; and protesters took to the streets in Gaza, Tunisia, and elsewhere. When a Norwegian magazine reprinted the cartoons, Norway also became a target of diplomatic and popular protest—which in turn persuaded more publications and news outlets in more countries to reprint the contested images in order to project solidarity on the issue of press freedom. Like many other world leaders, the Secretary General of the United Nations, Kofi Annan, found himself in a delicate balancing act, reassuring Muslim nations that he too found the images offensive but also urging the importance of press freedom.

By February, the protests had grown violent: the Danish and Norwegian embassies in Damascus and Beirut were torched, other European cultural and business premises in various countries were attacked, rioters in Nigeria turned on one another and at least 100 died, flags were burned, and the overall sense of anger and indignation approached fever pitch. In subsequent months, death threats were also issued against the editors and cartoonists who had produced the images. Although *Jyllands-Posten* issued an apology for offending Muslims (but not for printing the cartoons in the first place) and the Danish government organized an interfaith conference to try to resolve the conflict (and end the boycott), the problem continued. As late as 2008, Denmark and other Western nations were still wary about reopening the issue, and when Yale University Press decided in 2009 to publish a book on the controversy, they firmly declined to reprint the offending images.

What has continued to fuel controversy over the Danish cartoons is that their publication pitted two protected human rights and recognized goods against one another: the right of religious freedom and the right of freedom of expression. The most indignant defenders of both sides have claimed moral superiority, but it is clear to more temperate commentators that neither right can exist in a vacuum, particularly in an increasingly connected world.

to the international organization Reporters Without Borders, the countries in 2011–12 who scored highest on the "Press Freedom Index" included some of those with the longest history of guaranteeing such freedoms, with Finland and Norway at the top of the table. Canada, at tenth place, also scored very high. The United Kingdom and Australia are at twenty-eight and thirty, respectively, and the nations who enshrined press freedom in their founding documents, France and the United States, are ranked at thirty-eight and forty-seven, respectively. The very bottom ranks, perhaps unsurprisingly, are filled by countries whose records on human rights have long been notoriously weak: North Korea and Eritrea.

The History of Copyright

Prior to the eighteenth century, manuscript ateliers, printers, and booksellers largely looked after their own interests, by arranging with one another about who would produce and distribute particular texts. These arrangements were usually only locally recognized and enforced, so that they were always subject to erosion by books printed outside a given area, but they did provide some protection for the book producers' investments. Surprisingly, however, the *author's* interests in his or her own work were rarely considered. A particular bookseller might pay an author for a new work, but once the original transaction was completed, that was usually it: authors often saw no further financial gain from their work, only (perhaps) fame—or infamy. Growing concerns about who should profit from the publication and distribution of a work, as well as who should be held accountable for it if there were any problems, gradually gave rise to the first intellectual property laws.

The first law governing copyright was enacted in England in 1710. Although it formally established authors' rights in their works for the first time, the law largely derived from English printers' and booksellers' desire to protect their commercial interests in the texts they published and sold. The prepublication licensing system that had been overseen by the Stationers' Company came to an end in the mid-1690s, and new competitors sprang up almost immediately. When the booksellers failed to convince Parliament to renew the 1662 Printing Act that had protected their monopolies, they asked instead for a new law that would protect their future right to make copies of texts.

The resulting Copyright Act provided protection for both printers and authors. In particular, it guaranteed an author's rights in his or her work for twenty-eight years from the time of creation (an initial fourteen years, plus an optional extension of an additional fourteen years). By granting authors a time-delimited monopoly over the sales of their work, copyright ensured that authors would have a prospect of earning a living from their writing. During the term of copyright, only the author could sell or license the right to copy the work, and the licensee was the only one who could make and circulate copies of it. Anyone else who tried to produce copies of the work would be subject to fines and other penalties. After twenty-eight years, the author's rights in the work would expire, and it would enter into the *public domain*. The concept of the public domain ensured that, eventually, all creative works would be free to circulate among all members of society.

The 1710 Act provided the basic framework and rationale for nearly all subsequent copyright laws and conventions, not only in England, but elsewhere. The original Act was amended and refined many times over the next century or so, as authors, printers, and booksellers struggled to work out the best ways to keep profits up and costs down. One of the more significant changes came in 1842, when copyright protection was extended throughout the British Empire (especially if the author arranged to have an edition published in London). At the same time, copyright protection was also affirmed to continue after the author's death. This notion had important ramifications for family and heirs of authors, and it laid the groundwork for the notion of a *literary estate* that could be passed on. By 1911, copyright protection in the United Kingdom and its possessions and territories had been extended to a full fifty years after the author's death.

British copyright law was particularly influential not only because it was first, but also because of Britain's broad reach around the globe. British imperial laws were enforced in its many colonies and possessions, and they also influenced the laws of territories that broke away from the empire. For example, the first US copyright law closely followed the English model that had been in force prior to the American Revolution. The US Constitution granted Congress the right to create copyright legislation, despite the reservations of some of the Founding Fathers. Thomas Jefferson (1743–1826), for example, worried that allowing authors extensive exclusive rights in their own works might restrict the free flow of ideas. The resulting 1790 Copyright Act enshrined authors' rights in their work and guaranteed the extension of copyright beyond the author's death. However, the 1790 Act also applied only to works published in the United States. Foreign authors and publishers weren't protected, an omission that proved very lucrative for American publishers over the next hundred-plus years.

Ironically, the 1842 extension of British copyright law throughout the Empire, coupled with the United States' intransigence about recognizing the copyright of those in other nations, left Canadian authors and publishers in a uniquely disadvantaged position. Canadian authors were protected by British copyright, but only if their works were published in London. At the same time, printers in Canada and elsewhere in the empire were forbidden to reprint texts originally published in London without obtaining permission. Canadian printers who might want to produce editions of local authors thus had to pay extra for the privilege, and even if they did so, they were likely to see their efforts undercut by cheaper reprints brought in across the border from the States. Throughout the second half of the nineteenth century, the Canadian Parliament tried repeatedly to achieve copyright reforms that would protect

The Storming of the Bastille, 1789. Museum of the History of France.

Canadian authors and help to stimulate the local printing and publishing trades, but these efforts were unavailing. As a result, many Canadian authors, printers, and would-be publishers relocated south of the border, establishing Canadian literary enclaves in New York City and elsewhere.

Copyright law in France developed along somewhat different lines than the law in the Anglophone world. Rather than focusing on how the *right to copy* could be designated and protected—a right that keeps the printer or publisher plainly in the frame—French law instead focused on the *droit d'auteur*, or the "right of the creator." The notion that an author had a moral claim to his or her works had been established in French common law as early as the sixteenth century, although in practice editors or publishers had more control over published books than authors did until well into the eighteenth century. However, the French Revolution (1789–99) swept away the notion that the right to print was in the gift of the king or any other sovereign authority. Instead, the government declared that that authors' rights were *natural*, and that they inhered directly from the act of creation. The 1793 Chénier Act affirmed that authors had *droits patrimoniaux*, or rights to the economic benefits deriving from their works. However, the Revolution also intensified debates over authors' responsibilities for their writing, so an additional goal of the 1793 Act was to hold authors legally accountable for what they wrote.

Under the Chénier Act, an author's control over the publication of his or her texts was protected for a stated period of time, and amendments to the law in the nineteenth and twentieth centuries eventually extended that period, first to fifty years after the author's death and then to seventy years (with a bonus thirty years' protection added for authors who died in active military service). The Act formed the basis for current French law. Passed in 1957, the *Code de la propriété intellectuelle*, or Intellectual Property Code (IPC), affirms authors' rights to be acknowledged as the creators of their works, to determine their publication or nonpublication, to withdraw or modify a work made public, and to preserve their work from alteration or even from excessive criticism. According to French law, these moral rights of the author cannot be renounced or assigned in any way, as they are attached to the creator of a work, not to the work itself.

International Copyright Protections

As the example of Canada suggests, although individual countries could enact legislation to guarantee their own authors' and booksellers' rights, these laws did not necessarily provide protection beyond their national borders. Especially as technological advances drove an explosion of print in the nineteenth century, the lack of effective international agreements about copyright proved problematic. Britain entered into a series of treaties with other European countries that provided mutual copyright protection, but it could exercise no influence at all over the second-largest publishing power. Throughout most of the nineteenth century, American publishers wantonly produced copies of any and all British works they could get their hands on, without regard for the original copyright holders or their licensees. This understandably infuriated popular English authors such as Charles Dickens (1812–70), who saw what should have been extremely lucrative book sales seriously eroded by American piracy.

The first major breakthrough in managing copyright protections internationally was the 1887 Berne Convention. Formally known as the *Berne Union for the Protection of Literary and Artistic Property*, and now administered by the World Intellectual Property Organization (WIPO) in Geneva, the Berne Convention was joined early on by most of the European countries, as well as by Japan. The Berne Convention guaranteed copyright protection to all authors who were resident in the signatory countries: while the extent and terms of copyright protection might vary between the signatory nations, each agreed to enforce its own copyright laws with respect to authors of other countries. This guaranteed that authors would have at least a minimum of protection virtually everywhere in Europe and Japan, and also that authors or their agents could confidently enter into arrangements with foreign publishers to produce licensed editions or translations of their works.

The United States was invited to the meeting in Berne but did not sign the treaty then—in fact, it only officially joined the Convention in 1989, more than a century later. And it took several years after the initial Berne Convention for the United States to extend even a modicum of copyright protection to foreign authors. However, it finally did so, very reluctantly, with the 1891 Chace Act. The primary motivation behind the Chace Act was that successful American authors were beginning to worry about their own literary heritage: without the protection of international copyright, their works were as subject to piracy by publishers in other nations as foreign authors' works had been in the United States. For example, Mark Twain (1835–1910) had been furious that a Canadian edition of *Tom Sawyer* was issued in 1876 before the American edition came out, and in 1881 he went so far as to establish residency in Toronto, in order to protect his copyright in *The Prince and the Pauper*. To soften the potential blow to American printers, who would hereafter have to respect the rights of foreign nationals, the Chace Act specified that in order for foreign authors' rights to be protected, their books would have to be typeset in the United States, a catch that came to be known as the "manufacturing clause."

The first truly international copyright protection was finally enacted in the middle of the twentieth century. The Universal Copyright Convention (UCC), administered by UNESCO, was enacted in 1952 and signed over the next few years by most countries around the globe. (One important holdout was China, who only joined in 1992.) It was revised again in 1971. The UCC derives its basic principles from the Berne Convention. In essence, it states that individual nations' copyright laws shall not be in conflict with the Berne Convention, and that those laws will be enforced on behalf of authors resident in any of the signatory nations. The UCC also states that to ensure that copyright is protected, it must be formally asserted in a published text, by the use of either the word *copyright* or the universal copyright symbol ©, the year, and the name of the copyright holder.

Although national copyright laws continue to vary in important details, the UCC as most recently revised means that a number of statements about copyright hold true in most cases. Generally speaking, copyright in a given work is accepted to extend for the life of the author, plus seventy years. This means that as of 2012, virtually all works published before 1923 are deemed to be in the public domain, and they now can be reproduced and circulated without restriction. (The status of works that were produced before 1923 but not published depends on national copyright laws and can vary significantly.)

According to some experts, the UCC has been superseded by the Agreement on Trade-Related Aspects of Intellectual Property Rights (TRIPS), which was negotiated in 1994. Administered by the World Trade Organization (WTO), TRIPS governs the dealings of WTO members and would-be members on all matters related to intellectual property rights, including respect for copyright and patents.

Limits on Copyright: Fair Use

The fact that a work is protected by copyright does not mean that only the licensee who has paid for the privilege may reproduce and circulate it. Copyright law also allows for the reproduction of a portion of most copyrighted works for free under the principle of *fair use*. Whether or not a use is fair rests on four key considerations: the intended nature or purpose of the use; the nature of the original work; how much, or what proportion, of the original will be used; and the effect the potential use is likely to have on the original work.

While the rules are not hard and fast, the following kinds of reproduction of copyrighted works usually have been deemed to be fair use: quotation in a review or in a critical, scholarly, or technical work; summary or incidental use in a relevant news report or broadcast; reproduction in a legislative or court proceeding; and library reproduction to replace part of a damaged work. All of these kinds of reproduction tend to respect the claim and status of the original copyrighted item, by entailing only a small proportion of the original and by doing so for primarily noncommercial purposes. Authors may not always like what critics have to say about their texts, but they acknowledge that it would be very difficult for a reviewer to make any kind of case without putting some of the author's words in front of readers for their consideration.

Also generally accepted as fair use is the reproduction of a portion of a work for use in an educational setting. However, this kind of activity has come under increasing scrutiny in recent decades, and a number of copyright holders and their licensees have successfully claimed that some educational uses have been far from fair. The battles over educational fair use began in the late 1980s and early 1990s, when the first efficient high-speed photocopiers came on to the market. Suddenly it was possible to make high-quality photocopies of works for relatively little cost, and some educators and institutions cheerfully began to produce substantial packets of course materials with little regard for the rights of copyright holders. After a number of successful lawsuits against both photocopying companies and educational institutions, the course-pack market either went legitimate or went underground. Those who wished to properly secure permission to reproduce material could apply through *copyright clearinghouses*, which helped handle the details of securing licenses. The general shift to digitizing course materials and making them available to students through electronic bulletin boards has added another layer of complexity to the question of fair use in educational settings, and it has also incited another round of court challenges on behalf of copyright holders. Many institutions have subsequently launched initiatives aimed at educating teachers and students about copyright law.

Humor is another arena in which fair use has been regularly contested. Many authors have been understandably sensitive about satires or parodies, which, by definition, depend on a close identification with the original work in order to succeed. Although most satires or parodies of copyrighted works have been ruled by courts to fall under fair use, this has not inhibited authors and publishers from charging that such works infringe upon their copyrights. For example, in one particularly high-profile case in 2001, the executors for the literary estate of American novelist Margaret Mitchell (1900–49) filed an injunction to prevent the publication of a new novel by Alice Randall, entitled *The Wind Done Gone*. The Mitchell estate alleged that the new novel infringed the copyright of *Gone with the Wind* (1936). Randall and her publisher, Houghton Mifflin, protested that the new novel's relationship to the original blockbuster was parodic, and thus that it was protected by fair use. After Randall and Houghton Mifflin won one round in court, the case was finally settled.

Copyright Law Today

Most authors working today can assume a fair degree of protection of their creative efforts. In principle, copyright protects original works from the moment they are set into a fixed form (printed or saved), even if authors do not formally file to assert their copyright. This means, for example, that if an author sends his or her work out for review, hoping that it will be accepted for publication, the organization that receives it cannot simply seize all or part of the work and use it without permission, acknowledgment, and appropriate compensation. This inherent power of copyright protection has, perhaps ironically, led some publishers and publications to refuse to read unsolicited manuscripts. For example, organizations like the *New Yorker* magazine and a number of film studios have felt that they needed to shield themselves from any possible allegations of misuse of authors' unpublished materials.

While inherent copyright protection is sufficient for most purposes, authors who wish a little extra protection when circulating their work should officially assert their copyright. This may be done by printing *copyright*, the date, and the author's name on the work, either on the title (or first) page, in the running heads or running feet of every page, or as an electronic watermark in a PDF version of the manuscript. If authors desire absolutely unambiguous copyright protection, they may also register their work with their national copyright registry office. (If a work is accepted for publication, registering copyright is ordinarily one of the responsibilities undertaken by the publisher.) In most countries, the copyright office is associated with the national library, which is also usually a *copyright depository*, meaning that it is entitled to a free copy of every work published within that country. For example, in the United States, the copyright office is a department of the Library of Congress, and in the United Kingdom, it is associated with the British Library.

To register copyright, an author or publisher needs to complete the appropriate forms, pay the required fee, and submit a copy of the work. In many countries, this can now be done electronically, which generally reduces both the costs and the amount of time required to issue the registration license. Official registration of copyright assures that, in the unlikely event that someone either *plagiarizes* an author's work (by passing all or a portion of it off as their own) or *pirates* that work (by producing unauthorized copies), the primacy of the author's claim to the work will already be established. If it becomes necessary to pursue legal action to redress plagiarism or piracy, registered copyright provides a stronger starting position for the claimant.

The digital age has presented some definite challenges when it comes to enforcing copyright protection. The music industry was the first to feel the negative effects of easy electronic file sharing in the late 1990s. Sites like Napster, established in 1999, and Grokster, established in 2001, encouraged users to pool their music libraries through peer-to-peer file sharing, thereby opening up a vast collection of downloadable songs, apparently for free. Musical artists, music publishers, and film studios quickly cried foul, and the Record Industry Association of America (RIAA) and various movie companies launched a series of lawsuits based on the sites' copyright infringements, mostly targeting the sites and their owners, but in some cases also the internet service providers (ISPs) and individual users. As a result of these lawsuits, Napster shut down in 2001 and Grokster in 2005.

Although many of the early file-sharing sites were forced into bankruptcy (or into the more shadowy corners of the web), some successful models for legitimate, copyright-respecting, music- and video-sharing networks did emerge. Apple was among the first to resolve the copyright issues of file sharing. In 2003, it began charging a small fee for each download from its iTunes Store, a percentage of which goes back to the copyright holder. The fee-paying model has since been imitated by a number of music, video, and e-book providers.

Another challenge to copyright has involved works that were copyrighted before the electronic age. Over the past twenty or so years, publishers have been scrambling to secure digital rights for works previously published in more traditional formats. While some authors have granted their print publishers the right to produce electronic versions of their texts, others have turned to new specialty publishers to design and launch the e-versions of their works. This has occasionally led to some confusion over who precisely has the right to authorize an electronic edition. One book whose digital copyright was temporarily unclear was George Orwell's classic dystopian novel, *1984*. In 2009, the digital publisher MobileReference began offering e-book versions on Amazon of two of Orwell's novels, *1984* and *Animal Farm*. The rights for digital versions of these novels were actually controlled by Orwell's publisher, Houghton Mifflin Harcourt, and Houghton issued a complaint. Amazon accordingly recalled the books, causing them to mysteriously vanish from the e-readers of all customers who had purchased them—a startling instance of Big Brother-like monitoring of readers' theoretically private worlds.

Copyright and Copyleft

Some creative artists have responded to the complications of copyright in the electronic age by instead embracing a culture of *open access*. Under the principles of open access, works are made available to readers for free, and they can be further modified and added to, with the resulting hybrid products also offered for free. Unlike works in the public domain, however, the authors' moral rights in open-access materials are still asserted—basically, all that is surrendered is the right to profit from the work or from any derivations. Some adherents of open access refer to the movement as *copyleft*, and to underscore the movement's contrary attitude to restricting and profiting from creative work, they have devised a logo that is a reversed version of the universal copyright symbol. Authors, musicians, software creators, and others who are part of the open-access movement generally post their works on the internet.

Copyleft logo.

To help protect and promote open-access creators, a number of nonprofit organizations have arisen that offer advice on open-access licensing. For example, the Creative Commons is headquartered at Harvard University, which has been instrumental in promoting open-access publication of scholarly journals. Another open-access support network, the GNU Project, has its origins in a free computer operating system self-reflexively dubbed "GNU's Not Unix." The GNU Project's silly name was chosen in part because it was fun to say, and like the copyleft symbol, the very name of the organization underscores how the open-access community thumbs its nose at the usual ways of doing business.

Open access is not just limited to individual authors and artists, either. For example, the National Institutes of Health (NIH) sponsors a number of online, peer-reviewed scientific journals, collectively known as the *Public Library of Science (PLoS)*. Unlike standard peer-reviewed journals, which are available to readers only through paid subscription, *PLoS* journals are free to all on the net. The editors of *PLoS* count on the rigor of their manuscript reviewing process to maintain the academic standard of their journals, so that they will draw the best contributors and thus compete for readers with the best commercial journals in their fields. Governments and other organizations that fund scholarly research have begun to press for more access to the work they have underwritten, and this is likely to result in further mandates that such material be published in open-access forums.

Also characteristic of the open-access movement are collaborative, or *wiki-based*, publications, the best-known and most successful of which is probably Wikipedia. Typically, authors who contribute to wikis do so anonymously, but some may receive credit for their contributions. For example, the collaborative online publications Scholarpedia and Citizendium both provide signed, peer-reviewed articles on scientific and other topics. *Fanzines*, the increasingly web-based publications written by fans of any cultural phenomenon, from music groups to Harry Potter, are also often collaborative, with contributors adding to and amending the various offerings. In all of these instances, the overarching goal is to provide quality information and entertainment, free at the point of demand, to all interested parties. Individual contributors' motivations for participating can vary significantly. For example, studies of so-called *Wikipedians*, those who contribute text and editing to Wikipedia, have suggested that they mostly participate out of pleasure and a desire to feel useful. This seems to parallel the motivations of volunteers who become engaged in online "citizen science" projects, such as Oxford University's Zooniverse.

While free access to entertainment and information is certainly appealing to readers, the implications for authors are still unclear. Some individual authors and musical artists have developed loyal followings for their work on the internet, through blogs, personal websites, or collaborative forums. And because they have been able to demonstrate that there is an established audience for it, making their work available through open access has sometimes led to traditional publishing contracts. However, these instances are still rare enough to be noteworthy. In many respects, being able to sell one's copyright is what made authorship as a profession possible. The economics of writing in an online, payment-optional medium are still being worked out, and it is likely that a number of models will have to be experimented with and discarded before a fully sustainable system falls into place.

HARNESSING PRINT

In addition to regulating or promoting print, governments and other official bodies can also employ print to further their own ends. *Propaganda* is the employment of arguments and impressions to achieve specific aims, especially when undertaken by institutions of authority. Although the word *propaganda* is of fairly recent usage, deriving from the Catholic Church's *Congregatio de propaganda fide*, or Congregation for the Propagation of the Church, established in 1622 by Pope Gregory XV (1554–1623), written propaganda has existed throughout human history. Both the volume of propaganda and its effectiveness increased in the age of print, especially in the twentieth century, when authorities began to exploit the possibilities of the mass media of newspapers, radio, film, television, and eventually the internet. Although in popular usage the word *propaganda* is often taken as pejorative, propaganda is not necessarily a bad thing. It can be used to urge public-spirited, positive actions and responses, as in the case of public health drives to increase immunization levels or seatbelt use or to reduce smoking.

Print as a medium for propaganda began to be important in the sixteenth and seventeenth centuries, during the European religious wars. Believers of all stripes printed broadsides and pamphlets supporting their positions and excoriating their opponents. Often reproduced cheaply, on poor paper, and sometimes featuring blood-curdling woodcut illustrations, these publications could be easily circulated, concealed, or destroyed. Many of the more stringent censorship laws enacted against printers across Europe during this era were in an effort to suppress the trade in pamphlets.

As religious rebellions gradually gave way to political ones in the eighteenth century, and new forms of government came to be debated, pamphlets and broadsides remained the medium of choice. Some of the foundational texts of modern democratic thought originated as pamphlets and broadsides. For example, Thomas Paine's (1737–1809) influential attack on the monarchy, *Common Sense*, was issued as an anonymous pamphlet in 1776. The pamphlet helped clarify the thoughts of the American colonists and contributed to their decision to declare their independence from British rule. Similarly, Emmanuel Joseph Sièyes (1748–1836) issued his ringing defense of the Third Estate—those members of the French Estates General who were neither aristocrats nor clergy—as a pamphlet in 1789. *What Is the Third Estate? (Qu'est-ce que le tiers-état?)*, Sièyes asked rhetorically, answering: *Everything (Tout)*.

Thomas Paine. Engraving by William Sharp, 1783.

But while propaganda could be used by forces below to foment revolution, it could also be used by those in power to consolidate their control. The twentieth century saw some of the most pervasive and influential political propaganda in history, particularly during the First and Second World Wars and in the subsequent Cold War era.

Propaganda and War

The Greek tragedian Aeschylus (c. 525–456 BCE) may have been the first to observe that one of the first casualties of war is truth, but he was probably merely stating succinctly what had long been understood. Even those who are generally skeptical about the use of propaganda will often acknowledge that there may be a need for it during wartime, when a state's need to marshal its resources and support on behalf of its very survival are paramount. Thus it is not surprising that the use of official propaganda has tended to expand during periods of armed conflict.

One of the most significant, sustained, and widespread uses of propaganda was during World War I (1914–18). Governments on both sides of the conflict deployed posters and pamphlets and controlled the newspapers. Initially, propaganda efforts focused on bolstering recruitment and building civilian support; later, as the war ground on, the efforts shifted to maintaining morale and suppressing dissent. Exaggerations of reported war atrocities and depictions of the enemy as subhuman were common and frequently very heavy-fisted: for example, soldiers might be drawn casting shadows shaped like apes or wolves. However, war propaganda could also be much more subtle. For example, a 1915 British recruiting poster designed by Savile Lumley shows a young girl reading a picture book on her father's lap while her brother plays with toy soldiers at their feet. The little girl asks, "Daddy, what did *YOU* do in the Great War?" The man, dressed in an ordinary civilian suit, gazes out at the viewer with furrowed brow; the implication is that he may not have a satisfactory answer.

The success of propaganda during World War I drew the attention of a number of thinkers. For example, the American political commentator Walter Lippmann (1889–1974) observed that a significant portion of the public tended to believe what was put in front of them, regardless of whether it was true. In his newspaper columns and in books such as *Public Opinion* (1922), he suggested that if the populace were generally both too ignorant and too lazy to inform themselves about issues and events in the world, then a governing class would have to take responsibility for running civic life. Intellectual elites could shape public opinion by putting in front of the people the images that the elites wanted believed and reinforced, a process Lippmann called "the manufacture of consent." Since such a shaping of ideas was going to happen anyway, it would be better if a well-intended power controlled the public's beliefs for good purposes, rather than leaving their imaginations prey to random or nefarious forces. In 1988, linguist and political analyst Noam Chomsky (b. 1928) used Lippmann's phrase in the title of his biting analysis of the American media, *Manufacturing Consent: The Political Economy of the Mass Media*. Chomsky claimed that by the final decades of the twentieth century, the system Lippmann had suggested for positive propaganda was firmly in place.

Most nations established official propaganda departments during this period. For example, Britain created the Ministry of Information (MOI), which was disbanded after the war and then reinstated during World War II, and the United States created the Committee on Public Information (CPI), which was disbanded in 1919 and replaced in 1940 by the National Defense Research Committee. Both of these organizations enlisted prominent and established journalists to write for and otherwise further their efforts, including Alfred Harmsworth, the first Lord Northcliffe (1865–1922), publisher of the London *Times*; the Canadian-born William Maxwell Aitken, Lord Beaverbrook (1879–1964), publisher of the *Daily Express*; and George Creel (1876–1953), editor of the *Denver Post* and *Rocky Mountain News*. In addition to supervising the publication of materials supportive of the war efforts at home and abroad, these organizations were also responsible for wartime censorship and often disinformation.

The most infamous propaganda machine of the era, however, was that established by the Nazi Party in Germany. Adolf Hitler had begun his propaganda campaign for the conquest of Europe with the publication in 1925 of *Mein Kampf* (*My Struggle*). In 1933 he appointed Joseph Goebbels as Minister of Public Enlightenment and Propaganda. Goebbels thought that people could be convinced to believe anything if they were told it in the "proper way," and he evolved a vast and alarmingly effective network for presenting the Nazi point of view as the only one. In addition to building support for the Nazi Party and manufacturing justifications for Germany's invasion of other countries, Goebbels also oversaw the creation and dissemination of the virulently anti-Semitic literature that underpinned the Nazis' "final solution" for the Jews of Europe and helped make the Holocaust possible.

Although the end of the Second World War also brought about the end of the wartime propaganda departments, it did not eliminate various governments' perceived needs to maintain propaganda campaigns. The subsequent multi-decade struggle for global domination between the United States, the Union of Soviet Socialist Republics (USSR), and China led to a significant redeployment of propaganda efforts. In each case, the governments were concerned to build support for their own *ideology*, or system of beliefs, and for their programs at home and abroad. Departments like the state-run Telegraph Agency of the Soviet Union (TASS) and China's General Administration of Press and Publication (GAPP) exerted a strong control on domestic newsgathering and dissemination and also filtered the news to and from abroad, especially in those regions and countries directly or indirectly under Soviet or Chinese control. In the United States, where domestic press freedom is constitutionally guaranteed, the government's propaganda efforts were more generally directed abroad, through the services of organizations like the US Information Agency (USIA), whose mission is to positively represent American interests and values in other countries. During the Cold War era (c. 1945–91), TASS and the USIA sought to shape international support for or against communism, countering each other's efforts around the globe. With the end of the Cold War, both organizations have been largely redirected into educational and informational activities, but pro-national propaganda remains central to their (and GAPP's) missions.

As this chapter has suggested through a few representative instances, states and other authorities have immense power to shape book culture by promoting or preventing the publication and circulation of texts. The challenge for authors and publishers is to work with (or sometimes around) the regulations in order to put books into readers' hands. The next chapter will examine how modern publishers go about the business of acquiring and publishing texts.

SELECTED BIBLIOGRAPHY

Altick, Richard D. *The English Common Reader: A Social History of the Mass Reading Public, 1800–1900*. 2nd ed. Columbus: Ohio State UP, 1998.

American Library Association. Banned and Challenged Books. http://www.ala.org/advocacy/banned.

Baéz, Fernando. *A Universal History of the Destruction of Books: From Ancient Sumer to Modern Iraq*. Trans. Alfred MacAdam. New York: Atlas, 2008.

Basbanes, Nicholas A. *A Splendor of Letters: The Permanence of Books in an Impermanent World*. New York: HarperCollins, 2003.

Blagden, Cyprian. *The Stationers' Company: A History, 1403–1959*. London: Allen & Unwin, 1960.

Carefoote, Pearce J. *Forbidden Fruit: Banned, Censored, and Challenged Books from Dante to Harry Potter*. Toronto: Lester, Mason & Begg, 2007.

Clair, Colin. *A History of European Printing*. London: Academic, 1976.

Cole, Robert, ed. *The Encyclopedia of Propaganda*. 3 vols. Armonk, NY: Sharpe Reference, 1998.

Copyright Law of the United States of America and Related Laws Contained in Title 17 of the United States Code, Circular 92. Washington, DC: US Copyright Office, 2011. http://www.copyright.gov/title17/circ92.pdf.

Feather, John. "Copyright and the Creation of Literary Property." *A Companion to the History of the Book*. Ed. Simon Eliot and Jonathan Rose. Chichester: Wiley-Blackwell, 2009. 520–30.

Fife, Graeme. *The Terror: The Shadow of the Guillotine: France 1792–1794*. New York: St. Martin's, 2004.

Fine, Richard. "American Authorship and the Ghost of Moral Rights." *Book History* 13 (2010): 218–50.

Fleming, Patricia Lockhart, Gilles Gallichan, and Yvan Lamonde, eds. *History of the Book in Canada. Volume 1: Beginnings to 1840*. Toronto: U of Toronto P, 2004.

Gadd, Ian, ed. *The History of the Book in the West. Volume 2: 1455–1700*. Burlington, VT: Ashgate, 2010.

Knuth, Rebecca. *Libricide: The Regime-Sponsored Destruction of Books and Libraries in the Twentieth Century*. Westport, CT: Praeger, 2003.

Lamonde, Yvan, Patricia Lockart Fleming, and Fiona A. Black. *History of the Book in Canada. Volume 2: 1840–1918*. Toronto: U of Toronto P, 2005.

MacLaren, Eli. *Dominion and Agency: Copyright and the Structuring of the Canadian Book Trade, 1867–1918*. Toronto: U of Toronto P, 2011.

Moore, Harry T. "*Lady Chatterley's Lover*: The Novel as Ritual." Afterword to *Lady Chatterley's Lover* by D.H. Lawrence. New York: New American Library, 1962.

Reporters without Borders. Press Freedom Index 2011/2012. http://en.rsf.org/press-freedom-index-2011-2012,1043.html.

Seierstad, Åsne. *The Bookseller of Kabul*. Trans. Ingrid Christophersen. London: Virago, 2004.

Stone, Brad. "Amazon Erased Orwell Books from Kindle." *New York Times*, 18 July 2009.

"Tous ces livres sont à toi!" De l'Oeuvre des bons livres à la Grande Bibliothèque (1844–
2005). Montreal: Bibliothèque Nationale du Québec et Les Presses de l'Université
Laval, 2005.

United Nations. The Universal Declaration of Human Rights. http://www.un.org/en/
documents/udhr/index.shtml.

Wikipedians. Wikipedia. http://en.wikipedia.org/wiki/Wikipedians.

CHAPTER SEVEN

PUBLISHERS

The nineteenth and twentieth centuries saw the transformation of publishing from a set of interconnected, largely crafts-based trades to a professionally run major industry. The technological advances in printing and paper-making described in Chapters 3 and 4, combined with the abolition of paper and newspaper taxes and the rise of the advertising industry, greatly reduced the cost of producing books and periodicals. Improved transportation systems, especially the development of railroads, and the expansion of telegraph and other modes of transmission made it possible to develop increasingly complex and far-reaching distribution networks for all kinds of printed materials. Simultaneously, rising literacy rates continued to drive a demand for reading materials. Previous ages had frequently combined the commissioning, production, and selling of books, but in the nineteenth century these activities began to separate out, and the first *publishing houses* in the modern sense of the term emerged. While these firms often retained ties to printing and bookselling ventures, they now began to focus on the securing, development, and promotion of texts.

This chapter will examine the emergence and functions of the modern publishing firm. As with many other industries, as the publishing industry grew it developed a need for specialized workers. In particular, as firms grew from small, often family-owned printing and bookselling concerns into larger publishing concerns, they needed individuals who were skilled in finding and nurturing authors and in editing and shaping their texts to meet the evolving demands of the literary marketplace. This new workforce of skilled intellectual laborers, the men and women of letters, gradually became the large and diverse cadre of writers, editors, designers, illustrators, marketers, and others who produce most of today's print and electronic publications.

In addition to specializing in the production of texts rather than in the printing and selling of them, many publishers also began to specialize in particular kinds of texts. Although there had always been sectors of the printing trades that concentrated on, say, publications for religious uses, in the modern era publishers increasingly carved out market niches. Major sectors of the publishing business began to concentrate on certain types of publications, such as daily newspapers, women's magazines, ethnic literature, comic books, literary fiction, or textbooks. To give a sense of how this kind of specialization has affected the workings of the industry, this chapter will look at one particularly large and important sector of the modern industry, educational publishing.

Finally, the chapter will provide an overview of the publishing process from acquisitions to print or digital publication. This last section will cover the special tasks performed by various players in the modern industry and introduce some of the tools and terminology used by publishing professionals.

THE PROFESSIONALIZATION OF PUBLISHING

Although text correctors, designers, and illustrators of one sort or another have been around since the earliest eras of literate culture, the more immediate origins of today's publishing professionals can be found in the nineteenth century. For example, the predecessor of the modern editorial force, from acquisitions editors to developmental editors to sub- or copyeditors, was the *manuscript reader* or *publisher's reader*. Book publishers began employing manuscript advisors as early as 1799, and by the 1830s, when the rate and volume of book publication began to pick up pace, they were a well-established force in the industry. Initially, publisher's readers were responsible simply for reading manuscripts that had been submitted by authors and selecting those that were appropriate for the firm's lists. Gradually, however, readers also began suggesting revisions that might make the works more saleable, and by the end of the nineteenth century, readers had taken on most of the roles of the modern editor, including recommending and acquiring manuscripts, working with authors, and preparing manuscripts for typesetting and printing.

Individuals engaged in various forms of editorial labor worked under very different conditions. Some publisher's readers were salaried and assigned offices at the firms for which they worked. One such individual was W.S. Williams (1800–75), the primary reader for the London firm of Smith, Elder, and one of the few nineteenth-century publisher's readers whom casual readers of English literature may have heard of. It was he who rejected novelist Charlotte Brontë's first manuscript so very nicely that she promptly sent Smith, Elder her second attempt—which, fortunately for the firm, turned out to be the novel *Jane Eyre* (1847), an instant success. Other notable publisher's readers included writer and critic John Morley (1838–1923), who read for Macmillan from the 1860s to the 1880s; the novelist George Meredith (1828–1909), who read for Chapman and Hall from 1860 to 1894; and Edward Garnett (1868–1937), who read for a number of firms from the 1880s into the 1900s, including Unwin, Heinemann, Duckworth, John Lane, and Jonathan Cape. This group of high-profile publisher's readers acquired the responsibilities and perquisites of professional status, but other manuscript readers, including most of the women who worked in this capacity, did not. Most readers were paid piecemeal and worked from home. Perhaps the most influential of these unsalaried readers was Geraldine Jewsbury, the primary reader for the London firm of Bentley and Son from 1858 to 1880. Bentley's became one of the leading British fiction houses during this period, and since Jewsbury read most of the manuscripts that came their way, her judgments had a significant effect on the shaping and success of their business.

GERALDINE JEWSBURY: A PUBLISHER'S READER

Although nineteenth-century publishers often hired a number of readers who evaluated manuscripts in particular fields, most publishing houses had one primary fiction reader. From 1858 to 1880, Geraldine Endsor Jewsbury (1812–80) was the primary reader for Bentley and Son, a London publisher whose specialty was three-volume fiction for the circulating libraries. Her reports for the firm from the years 1860 to 1874 are in the archives of the British Library. In many respects, Jewsbury was the ideal fiction manuscript reader: she was a successful novelist herself and also served as one of the most prolific book reviewers for the prestigious literary magazine the *Athenaeum*, for whom she reviewed about 2,300 titles between 1849 and 1888. Jewsbury was thus intimately acquainted with the Victorian fiction market.

Contemporary publishers and readers believed that the primary audience for Victorian fiction was women, and Jewsbury was willing to let her sex work in her favor. Her manuscript reports repeatedly describe her own tastes as being typical: "*Take it*," she urged in 1861, "if I am any example of the general reader nobody will lay it down till they get to the *end*." However, in addition to presenting herself as a representative reader, Jewsbury also kept a keen eye on the publisher's bottom line. Her most successful recommendation was *East Lynne* (1861) by Ellen Price Wood (1814–87), an early entrant in the lists of popular "sensation" novels that lifted authors such as Wilkie Collins (1824–89) and Mary Elizabeth Braddon (1835–1915) to fame and financial independence. Jewsbury also recommended Braddon's *Lady Audley's Secret* (1862) and *Aurora Floyd* (1863), but Bentley's lost them in a bidding war, and the two novels went on to earn a fortune for publisher William Tinsley instead.

Although Jewsbury read many manuscripts that would go on to be successful books, most of what she read was pretty awful, and she was unsparing in her criticisms. Some of her reports consist of only a couple of sentences, dismissing the titles as "rubbish" or "dish washings." In an 1874 report on "Presented by Mrs Daisy," Jewbury wrote witheringly: "The author says he does not care whether he pleases his readers or not, so that it will not grieve him to learn that if his most stupid story should ever get into print ... few persons will be likely—short as it is—to read it through. If they do, they will find that it leads to nothing." Yet however biting they might occasionally be, Jewsbury's judgments were not arbitrary. "If I told you the story was not worth your having I had *good grounds* for the advice," she explained to publisher Richard Bentley (1794–1871) in 1863: "I never say a thing is 'rubbish,' unless I am full certain that further criticism wd be a waste of health—I always tell you if there are mitigating circumstances."

While some publishing firms specialized in particular kinds of texts—just books, or weekly magazines, or daily papers—many issued publications in a variety of formats. For example, proprietary, or firm-owned, magazines were considered a particularly effective means of marketing books and other publications, and many houses published them. Their manuscript advisors quickly learned to look out for longer texts that might be serialized in the magazines, thereby building demand for the books when issued as complete volumes, as well as for appealing shorter pieces that could fill out the pages. Some of these proprietary magazines continued as household names for decades, including *Blackwood's Edinburgh Magazine* (one of the longest running, from 1817 to 1980) and *Macmillan's Magazine* (1859–1907) in the United Kingdom, and *Scribner's Magazine* (1886–1939) in the United States. A few are still published today, such as *Harper's*, launched in 1850 by the American book publisher Harper & Brothers (the predecessor of HarperCollins), and *Maclean's*, launched in 1911 by the Canadian newspaper publisher John Bayne Maclean (1862–1950).

Periodicals also created opportunities for other types of publishing professionals. The high profile—and occasionally very good pay—offered by periodicals attracted many authors who primarily wrote books to the ranks of contributing writers and reviewers. Prominent authors were especially prized as *conductors* of magazines, whose names would be displayed prominently on the mastheads. Among the major British writers who served in such roles in the earlier decades were William Thackeray (1811–63), Charles Dickens (1812–70), Mary Elizabeth Braddon (1835–1915), and Oscar Wilde (1854–1900), and others, such as Margaret Oliphant (1828–97), were very keen to secure such posts because of their financial security. In the United States, noted authors Margaret Fuller (1810–50) and Ralph Waldo Emerson (1803–82) were among the founders of the *Dial*, Edgar Allan Poe (1809–49) was briefly editor of *Graham's American Monthly Magazine*, and Sarah Josepha Hale (1788–1879) conducted the number one American women's magazine, *Godey's Lady's Book*, for forty years, from 1837 to 1877.

In theory, conductors were responsible for developing coherent editorial policies and assembling the contributors and copy that would build a loyal readership. But with the exception of particularly energetic individuals such as Thackeray, Dickens, and Hale, who really did involve themselves in the fine details of putting the publication together, most conductors were primarily figureheads. For example, the Scottish novelist Annie S. Swan (1859–1943) was widely touted as the editor of *Woman at Home*, which was subtitled and advertised as "Annie S. Swan's Magazine." However, she claimed in her autobiography that she lacked the necessary organizational and administrative skills to manage the magazine: the real work of editing *Woman at Home* was done behind the scenes. This did not mean the work was performed by nonentities. Mary Anne (or Marian) Evans, the future novelist George Eliot (1819–80), worked behind the named editor John Chapman (1821–94) on the prestigious *Westminster Review* for several years before she began writing fiction. As time moved on, the role of editor became sufficiently respectable and engaging that individuals began to aspire to that kind of work, rather than doing it on the side or only pretending to do it. By the twentieth century, those who edited the most popular or influential magazines and newspapers commanded not only power and respect, but often wealth and honors.

Others working in the periodicals industry concentrated on writing content. A key development in the professionalism of publishing roles in the late nineteenth century was the emergence of the so-called *new journalism*, which placed a greater emphasis on personalities. New journalism created more opportunities for *reporters* of all kinds to literally make a name for themselves, as it was one factor that helped bring about the end of the long tradition of mostly anonymous publication in periodicals. *Columnists* also emerged as distinctive publishing professionals in this era. For example, in the early twentieth century, writers like Walter Winchell (1897–1972) and Louella Parsons (1881–1972) turned their gossipy treatments of the burgeoning American entertainment industry into must-read columns that significantly increased their papers' circulations.

An Explosion of Publishing Ventures

By the beginning of the twentieth century, the modern publishing industry had come of age. Not only were there more potential readers than ever before, but there was a wealth of available materials, catering to every possible taste and all price ranges. At one end of the scale were mass-market publishers, who specialized in inexpensive books and periodicals for very broad-based readerships. These included a myriad of cheap reprint houses, such as Grosset & Dunlap, which began in 1898 by pirating English language books printed in the United Kingdom and eventually became one of the largest legitimate reprint publishers in the United States. (It is now part of Pearson.) Mass-market publishers also included the larger newspaper publishers, such as the Hearst Corporation. Under the direction of William Randolph Hearst (1863–1951), the firm became one of the largest newspaper and magazine publishers in the United States. By the 1920s, it published daily papers in cities and towns across the country, and it is estimated that as many as one in four Americans read a daily Hearst paper. Circulations for some of the largest dailies, like Hearst's *New York Journal*, reached previously unheard-of figures, especially during the Spanish-American war (1898) and its aftermath. The sensationalistic (and often simply untrue) articles that appeared in Hearst's and others' papers during the period, including those published by Hearst's rival Joseph Pulitzer (1847–1911), came to be known as *yellow journalism*. The term derived from the title of one of the first color comic strips to appear in a newspaper, *The Yellow Kid*, which began in Pulitzer's *New York World* in 1895 and later ran in Hearst's *New York Journal*.

Counterbalancing these giant publishing endeavors were the productions of many smaller publishing houses. Some firms concentrated on

Cover of the *New York World*, 17 February 1898.

particular readerships or types of publications. For example, the combination of European imperial expansion and a worldwide increase in immigration meant that there were many isolated language communities in far-flung parts of the globe. New publishers sprang up to serve, say, the Finnish and Bohemian immigrants in northern Minnesota and southern Manitoba, the Yiddish communities of New York City, Spanish speakers in New Mexico, and native language populations in India. A distinct publishing sector arose to serve African American communities in the United States, especially those who relocated to the northern and western regions of the country during the Great Migration. For example, Johnson Publishing was founded in Chicago in 1942 by John H. Johnson (1918–2005). Its flagship magazines, *Ebony* and *Jet*, are still some of the best known and widest read magazines catering to African American readers. Although ethnic presses in North America contracted significantly in and after the two world wars, they expanded again towards the end of the twentieth century to meet the needs of many new immigrants, especially from Asia. Similarly, religious presses and publications were founded to provide materials not only for particular faith groups, but also for smaller sects and language minorities within those groups. One such long-standing firm is the Watch Tower Bible and Tract Society of Pennsylvania, originally founded in 1881 to publish religious tracts or pamphlets, and eventually becoming the publisher and distributor solely for publications of the Jehovah's Witnesses.

Other smaller publishing firms concentrated on producing books for associations and societies, for organizations, or for other readerships with special interests. Still others published particular genres or mediums, such as comic books, graphic novels, or how-to books. Reference materials have often been produced by specialty houses, which may issue only dictionaries, cookbooks, maps, or travel books. For example, London-based Lonely Planet was founded in the early 1970s by Tony and Maureen Wheeler, whose first book was a stapled-together pamphlet about their trip across Europe and Asia to Australia. Lonely Planet now publishes over 500 guide books that help intrepid travelers span the globe.

In all of the instances mentioned here, firms that began with relatively modest plans eventually grew to be large, international ones. And in Lonely Planet's case, the firm went one step further, becoming in 2007 a subsidiary of a larger, multinational media corporation, BBC Worldwide. This would be the trajectory of many publishing houses in the late twentieth century and early twenty-first centuries, with consequences that have been debated since the first large wave of mergers and acquisitions.

Multinationals

Until well into the third quarter of the twentieth century, the basic organization of publishing firms remained fairly stable. Many firms retained the names—Macmillan, Harper—of their founders, and in some cases they were still owned wholly or in part by their descendants. Although new publishing houses arose and older ones folded or merged, the general business practices and assumptions changed very little. Most publishing houses relied on in-house staffs to commission, edit, design, and market their publications, and the relationships between authors, publishers, and distributors were much as they had been for decades. Publishing—especially book publishing—was a genteel business. Healthy firms saw small but steady returns every year, thanks to established backlists, and most employees collected modest but dependable salaries. For many who worked in the industry, the primary pleasure was felt to inhere in the work itself, not in the paychecks. As long as there were interesting projects in the pipelines and enough money coming in to fund the next season's books, many publishers were content to let their businesses tick over.

However, by the 1970s and 1980s, things had begun to change. The publishing industry began to be compared to other media companies, particularly those that produced films and music, and it was thought to fall short of its economic potential. In a general climate of corporate mergers and acquisitions that affected nearly all sectors of the global economy, long-established, formerly independent publishing houses found themselves the target of takeover bids, often by conglomerates that sought to create so-called "synergies" between the media firms within their holdings. Book lists would be mined for screenplays; films would spawn movie tie-in editions or their scripts would be novelized; magazines and newspapers would sell serialized fiction or advertise spinoff television series; music lists would be used to score films and television shows and to promote them.

In a relatively short time, the number of independent publishing firms declined, with many of the older houses being folded into the corporate arms of much larger companies. Many readers (and even some authors) may have remained unaware of these changes, as the familiar *imprints*, or names under which the books were published, still appeared on the books' spines and copyright pages. However, readers who took the trouble to investigate would learn that these imprints had become subdivisions of major corporations. By the turn of the twenty-first century, a handful of major international conglomerates owned most of the publishing imprints in the West. According to *Publishers Weekly*, the ten largest publishers in 2010 were Pearson (based in the United Kingdom), Reed Elsevier (Netherlands, United Kingdom, and United States), Thomson Reuters (a division of Woodbridge, based in Canada), Wolters Kluwer (Netherlands), Bertelsmann (Germany), Hachette Livre (a division of Lagardère, based in France), McGraw-Hill (United States), Grupa Planeta (Spain), Cengage Learning (Canada and the United States), and Scholastic (United States). By far the largest in terms of total revenues are Pearson and Reed Elsevier, with approximately $8.1 billion and $7.1 billion in sales—figures far beyond those of number ten Scholastic, which saw about $1.9 billion in sales in the same period. (Only the top twenty global publishers reported sales even above $1 billion.) Pearson, with over twenty separate imprints in its commercial Penguin Group and about a dozen in its educational division, plus the newspapers in its Financial Times Group, has now held the top publishing rank for most of the current century.

This rapid concentration of the publishing industry into the hands of just a few firms has had a number of consequences. In the first place, the cost of acquiring the various businesses was significant, and the new owners had to recoup their expenses. In some cases, this led to wildly inflated assumptions about earning potentials. Although publishing houses had traditionally generated a modest but dependable income, some of their new corporate owners expected them to generate significantly higher annual revenues. Since that wasn't usually possible, the alternative was to reduce costs. One way of doing that was to eliminate as much duplication in personnel as possible. Thus, instead of maintaining the original editorial, design, and marketing divisions of each former house, many conglomerated publishing houses assigned a senior management staff to head the different lines or imprints, and then pooled the services of much smaller supporting staffs.

In some cases, departments were *outsourced*, with services that had been provided in-house now being performed by outside contractors. Design and production work were typically the first to be shifted to outside independent contractors, and a number of *production houses* sprang up in the late 1980s and early 1990s to perform this work for publishers. However, in some firms, the outsourcing eventually extended to editorial and marketing services as well, so that the "publisher" became an entity who mainly signed authors and managed rights. All of the other hands-on work that had been the publisher's purview

PEARSON

Pearson is the largest publishing firm in the world. Headquartered in London, with another major office in New York City, Pearson is the dominant player in both trade and educational book publishing, and it also wields significant influence in the arena of financial information through its Financial Times Group. Pearson's trade division, the Penguin Group, contains over twenty separate imprints, including some of the most widely recognized and respected in English-language publishing. In addition to the ubiquitous Penguin lines themselves, other notable imprints are Putnam, Viking, Dorling Kindersley, Dutton, New American Library, and Grosset & Dunlap. Pearson Education now embraces most of the best-known and previously independent English-language textbook publishers, including Longman, Scott Foresman, Prentice Hall, Addison-Wesley, and Allyn & Bacon.

Although it is now a global power with nearly $8.1 billion in sales revenues in 2010, Pearson's origins were remarkably modest. Initially founded as a building firm in northern England in 1844, in 1890 the company relocated to London and became involved in international commerce, first building docks and railroads around the world, and eventually investing in energy generation. The firm finally became involved in the media business in 1921, when it acquired a group of provincial English papers. In 1957, it also purchased the leading business-related paper in Britain, the *Financial Times*, taking pains to provide the paper with a high degree of editorial autonomy.

Pearson expanded into book publishing in 1968, with the acquisition of the venerable British publisher Longman, which had been founded in 1724. From that point on, Pearson commanded the waves of media mergers and acquisitions that characterized the late twentieth century. Penguin was acquired in 1970, Viking Press in 1975 (expanding Pearson's market in the United States), and Grosset & Dunlap, Frederick Warne, Hamish Hamilton, and Addison-Wesley in the 1980s. Pearson also acquired publishing interests in France and Spain during this period.

In the 1990s, Pearson used the *Financial Times* to capitalize on the emerging internet and to extend its reach into Europe and Asia. It acquired Putnam Berkley and HarperCollins in the middle of the decade, and in 1998 it established Pearson Education to enfold both its existing educational publishing line and its new acquisition of Simon & Schuster. Its educational division now included over 100 imprints. As the new century began, Pearson also added Dorling Kindersley, an illustrated reference publisher, and National Computer Systems, one of the leading educational testing and data management systems. It next acquired a controlling interest in Kirihara, one of Japan's major educational publishers, the Rough Guides line of travel books, and the Harcourt educational line (which had been owned by Reed Elsevier). The end of the decade saw Pearson expand into Africa and China, as well as Latin America, and in 2011 it began to invest in the virtual school market with the acquisition of Connections Education.

for centuries was farmed out to independent contractors. To a significant extent, the specialized workforce that had arisen in the nineteenth century to serve the expanding publishing industry found itself off publishing-house payrolls and instead working freelance.

In a further effort to maximize their revenues, many of the conglomerate publishers began to focus on signing "big" books: books by authors whose names alone would guarantee sales, or books that appeared to have block-buster potential. The so-called "star system," under which one or two bestselling titles could help carry the rest of the line, had been operating among some publishers since at least the 1940s. For example, the historical romance novel *Forever Amber* (1944) by Kathleen Winsor (1919–2003) reportedly accounted for a full 10 percent of Macmillan's business in one year. However, the focus on blockbusters began to intensify in the latter part of the twentieth century, and in order to secure these books, publishers offered increasingly larger advances for them. According to Michael Meyer in the *New York Times*, typical book advances offered by publishers in recent decades have tended to be in the range of $30,000, or about £20,000. (First-time authors still receive significantly lower advances, often $5,000 or less.) However, by the mid-1990s, novelist Martin Amis (b. 1949) received half a million pounds (nearly $800,000) from HarperCollins for *The Information* (1995). And at the turn of the century, Simon & Schuster offered US Senator and former First Lady Hillary Rodham Clinton (b. 1947) the nearly unprecedented amount of $8 million for her memoir *Living History* (2003). The record didn't stand for long: Alfred A. Knopf nearly doubled it by offering Clinton's husband Bill (b. 1946), the former President, a $15 million advance for his own memoir, *My Life* (2004).

Of course, such extraordinary payments to superstar authors reduce the amount available to secure other, more midlist authors, so in some cases publishing houses have had to shrink their lists. Furthermore, since seven out of ten books published never earn back their advances, such enormous outlays must be regarded as generally unsustainable over the long term. For example, when the news broke of Hillary Clinton's large book advance, newspapers direly predicted that Simon & Schuster would need to sell at least 1.5 million copies of *Living History* in the first year—and sustain that level of sales for several years—in order to recoup its investment. Fortunately for the publisher, the book sold more than a million copies in the first month alone.

Interestingly, the absorption of most of the older independent houses into subdivisions and imprints of giant multinational corporations has led to the creation of some new, smaller houses, which frequently specialize in the types of books that the conglomerates tend to neglect. Some of the new houses have emerged mushroom-like from the decaying trunks of their predecessors, as former editorial staff members have decided to launch their own publishing ventures, and others have simply been launched by book-loving entrepreneurs. For example, the New Press, founded in 1990 by André Schiffrin (b. 1935), was created when Schiffrin and his partners became disenchanted with the corporate publishing world. Schiffrin had been a long-time editorial director at Pantheon Books, which was founded in 1942, acquired by Random House in 1961, and since 1998 has been part of the immense Bertelsmann empire. As he recounts in his 2000 memoir *The Business of Books*, Schiffrin left Pantheon in 1990 because he found that the pressure to acquire highly commercial titles made it increasingly difficult for him to pursue the kinds of books he really wanted to publish. By establishing the New Press as a nonprofit with foundation underwriting, Schiffrin and his colleagues believed that they would be able to publish more challenging, important books. An example of a small, independent house created simply out of love is Copper Canyon Press in Port Townsend, Washington. Founded in 1972, originally to produce hand-printed, limited editions of poetry, in 1983 Copper Canyon began to branch out into trade editions. Since 1990, it has been a nonprofit with an impressive backlist of poets and an international reputation for good editing and quality book design and production.

Even if they are conducted as for-profit businesses, the newer, smaller publishing houses typically have lower overheads than larger companies, or even than many imprints housed within larger corporations. Many of them have found that they can produce good-quality, steady-selling books. Furthermore, recent advances in electronic publishing and the ability to tap into the distribution networks of major online booksellers has meant that the start-up costs and ongoing overhead involved in publishing ventures both continue to fall. (See Chapter 4 for a discussion of electronic publishing.) This has already resulted in a dramatic explosion in the number of what might be described as "micro-publishers," who may have only one or two titles in their lines. Although they are starting out in a very small way, odds are that some of these new publishers will one day become significant forces in the industry.

SPECIALIZED PUBLISHERS: EDUCATIONAL PRESSES

Most publishers specialize in particular kinds of books, either certain genres or topics, or books targeted to particular groups of readers. Specialization not only enables them to build expertise about the kinds of content and format that best suit a particular readership, but it also makes it easier for writers and readers to locate the right houses to publish their works or to provide them with the kind of reading material they require. Firms that publish broad categories of poetry, fiction, or nonfiction may also specialize in particular genres or subgenres, or they may have dedicated imprints for these. For example, Harlequin Enterprises publishes a vast quantity of romance fiction under a number of imprints that promise different levels of sweet tameness (the American Romance and Love Inspired lines) or steaminess (the Blaze line), as well as imprints that feature particular kinds of plots or characters, such as the multicultural Kimani Romances and paranormal Harlequin Nocturnes.

Scholastic, which specializes in children's books, has special imprints for graphic novels (Graphix) and how-to and crafts books (Klutz). The Christian publisher Tyndale House, previously known mainly for its modern-English *Living Bible*, took a chance in 1995 with a millenarian novel by Tim LaHaye (b. 1926) and Jerry B. Jenkins (b. 1949). After the runaway success of *Left Behind*, Tyndale continued to publish fiction, producing an entire series of the *Left Behind* books, as well as other novels.

However, firms may also specialize in particular categories of publishing. One of the largest categories is educational books, which includes everything from textbooks for preschool to postgraduate level as well as publications produced by university presses. Because they produce written materials used by every type of reader at every age level, textbook publishers and university presses together are one of the most important sectors of the modern publishing world.

Textbook Publishing

Textbook publishers produce teaching texts for students of any age. Unlike other categories of publishing, textbook publishing is not premised on the end result of providing individual copies of books to individual readers. Instead, it is organized on the assumption that a firm will provide multiple copies—*classroom sets*—of books to instructors, schools, or school districts. There are two primary subdivisions: primary- and secondary-school textbook publishing, also known as *K–12* or *el-hi* (for elementary and high school), and college textbook publishing (which includes all higher-education or postsecondary textbook publishing). The kinds of books and how they are produced differ significantly in these two subdivisions, primarily because of the way the books are purchased. At the el-hi level, books are usually purchased or *adopted* in four- to seven-year cycles, so first-year sales and initial print runs can be huge. Such potentially large sales justify author and reviewer teams that can run into the dozens, as well as years of development work. By contrast, at the university level, most textbooks are adopted by individual departments, or even by individual instructors. Unless a book is intended for one of the large, perennially offered courses like introduction to psychology or freshman writing—in which case enormous sales are indeed possible—sales figures are likely to be relatively modest over a short number of years or terms, until the market is saturated with used copies. It is this need to sell the books campus-by-campus and instructor-by-instructor, plus the effect of used book sales on new book sales, that accounts for much of the cover price of higher-education textbooks.

Publishing textbooks for the primary- and secondary-school market entails some particular pleasures and challenges. On the pleasure side, el-hi textbooks can be fun to develop and produce. They tend to be brightly colored and heavily illustrated, and they often involve supplemental or *ancillary* materials that can include everything from flashcards and hand puppets to computer programs. Also, because many schools and school districts prefer to purchase sequenced series of books in given subject areas, editors may find themselves working on multiple, graded volumes of a given work. Many school districts require that materials be classroom-tested before they will consider them for adoption, so editors working on el-hi textbooks may also find themselves working with real-life young readers in model classrooms and focus groups. And when it comes time to present the books for consideration to textbook adoption committees, editors may work with marketing personnel and educational consultants to prepare the necessary promotional and sample materials.

On the challenge side, elementary-school textbooks in particular are subject to some of the most stringent criteria for content and formatting of any category of modern book. In terms of content, school districts may specify very rigidly what should—and should not—appear in textbooks aimed at particular grade levels. This means that authors and editors must carefully read and follow the district's published curriculum guidelines to ensure that the textbooks fully comply with the legal standards. Between content and formatting fall *readability levels*, which are based on formulas that govern the vocabulary that can be used in books targeted to readers at a particular grade level. Readability is also impacted by legibility, so el-hi customers usually have strict rules about the fonts, size of type, and the amount of white space that are required. Generally, books produced to lower readability scores will have shorter words, a larger serif type, and slightly more space separating each word and each line of copy from the next. On the strictly physical level of formatting, most textbook adoption specifications will also be very particular about the quality of paper (weight, color, coating, acidity) and sturdiness and overall durability of the binding materials. Since the books are intended to be used by multiple groups of students over a number of years, they must be able to hold up to repeated (and often not especially gentle) use.

The college textbook adoption process is much more individualized, with many more departments and instructors making their own decisions about which books to assign for their courses. College (and other postgraduate) textbook publishing is therefore much more focused on single titles than on series. However, while an el-hi publisher may produce just one series of books tailored to, say, middle-school mathematics, and offer that series to all potentially interested schools, college textbook publishers take an almost completely opposite approach. They may produce multiple titles all designed for an introductory macroeconomics course, in the hope that each will prove popular with particular instructors. Similarly, while an el-hi publisher works on fairly widely spaced production and adoption cycles, producing or updating its series every four or more years, textbook publishers in the higher education market need to produce new titles virtually every year and to issue revised editions of the better-selling titles every two to three years.

There are two main reasons for the more hectic publication and revision schedules. First, higher-level content can quickly go out of date, especially in scientific and technological fields. For example, the announcement in November 2011 that three new elements had been added to the periodic table instantly rendered obsolete all previously published chemistry and physics textbooks that included a copy of the older table. New discoveries, new hypotheses, and new techniques all need to be reflected in the educational materials in a given discipline as quickly as possible, so that students who are

READABILITY

Readability has to do with how easily a text can be understood. Especially in books meant for educational purposes, knowing and controlling the readability level of a text can ensure that it is appropriate for the age or comprehension level of its intended readers. Although educators and scholars first became interested in readability in the late nineteenth century, it was only in the twentieth century that scientific systems for measuring and controlling the readability levels of texts began to be developed and used.

Some of the earliest means of assessing readability were vocabulary lists. Educators and psychologists noted the frequency with which certain words appeared in different works, and they attempted to match the words with the reading skills of particular students. By the 1920s vocabulary was being scrutinized to ensure that there was not too much "technical" language in texts intended for younger or less-skilled readers. Early investigators also began to examine how "interested" readers were in particular texts, and they began to establish a point system that factored a text's potential likability into its readability. Investigators also began to pay attention to sentence structure and variability as additional factors that could affect a text's readability. By the 1940s, all of these factors were combined into a variety of *readability formulas*, statistically based means of testing (and also of adjusting) the levels of texts to ensure that they were appropriate for their designated readers.

Among the most commonly used readability formulas are Flesch, Dale-Chall, and Fry, although there are many others. The Flesch formula is based on a 100-point scale, with 0 equivalent to a twelfth-grade reading level, and 100 a fourth-grade level. The Flesch Reading Ease system calculates the average sentence length and average word length in syllables. Publishers found it an accurate predictor of reading comprehension, and it became very influential in journalism, where it was used to ensure that particular magazines and newspapers were pitched at the right reading level. The Dale-Chall formula works in a similar manner, although it incorporates a refined vocabulary list (its devisers were dissatisfied with the existing vocabulary lists) and uses a roughly 10-point scale to determine whether a work is at a fourth-grade level or below (score of 4.9 or below) or at a high-school or college graduate level (9.9 or 10.0 and above, respectively). Dale-Chall is regarded by many as the most reliable readability formula and is widely used. The Fry formula plots the reading difficulty level (or grade level) by arranging sentence length on one axis of a graph preparing to practice or teach in the field have access to the most up-to-date information. Second, the large and well-organized market in used textbooks means that authors and publishers have only a limited window in which to sell "fresh" wares. Because many university courses are offered multiple times during the academic year, textbooks can move from the new to the secondary market in the space of a quarter—just three months. Although campus

and syllables per word on the other. The readability level is determined by the intersection of the sentence difficulty and word difficulty. The Fry graph is often used in health-related publications, to ensure that readers will be able to comprehend the information being presented to them.

Although readability formulas are particularly important in education, they

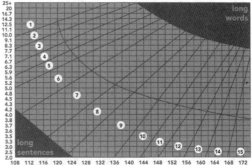

Fry graph.

are also used in assessing whether texts will be comprehensible to adult readers. Research has suggested that to reach the largest potential number of adult readers, most of whom read at about a ninth-grade level, readability in magazines and popular novels should be held at about a seventh-grade reading level. Newspapers are typically pitched at a slightly higher reading level, on the assumption that readers of daily papers tend to be slightly better educated. The typical newspaper is thus pitched at about an eleventh-grade reading level.

While hewing to a strict readability level may certainly restrict the sophistication of ideas that can be conveyed and may also compromise the potential aesthetic value of a given text, that is not always the case. One of the best-loved modern children's books, *The Cat in the Hat* (1957) by Dr. Seuss—the pen name of Theodor Seuss Geisel (1904–91)—was written specifically to demonstrate that a book with a carefully controlled vocabulary could be witty, vibrant, and engaging. A friend who was an editor for Houghton Mifflin supplied Geisel with a list of 348 words that six-year-olds should know and challenged him to write a book with no more than 225 words. *The Cat in the Hat* came in with 236 words, nearly all of which were on the approved vocabulary list, and only one of which *(another)* has more than two syllables. First published as a joint edition between Random House and Houghton Mifflin, *The Cat in the Hat* sold over a million copies in its first two years and has been a perennial bestseller ever since.

bookstores, specialty distributors, and resellers can make some money from the purchase and resale of used textbooks, the publishers themselves receive no revenues from the used books, and that means the authors receive no royalties from them, either. Practically speaking, this means that in order to ensure a continuing income stream, authors and publishers need to make significant revisions to the books on a regular basis, so that new editions supplant the used copies already in the marketplace.

All of this contributes to the fairly high cover prices of most new textbooks—and student resistance to those prices is the primary factor behind the thriving resale industry. However, technological innovations may help to keep the future costs of new upper-division textbooks in a more moderate zone. Some publishers are experimenting with textbook "leasing": instead of purchasing new textbooks outright, students arrange to, in effect, borrow them for a period of between one and six months, often at as little as half the regular purchase price. Because the rental agencies represent only one middleman between publisher and reader—instead of the usual three or four—the markup between the publisher's net price and the cover price is kept down. Publishers can also count on renewed sales to the rental agencies, who need to regularly replace lost or damaged books (or those that students ultimately decide to keep, once they have actually handled and read them). But leasing schemes not only relate to traditional, printed books, they are also available for e-books. For example, Amazon has activated a textbook leasing scheme for Kindle users.

Textbook publishers are also experimenting with bundling multimedia, internet-only materials with their traditional textbooks. Because access to the internet content requires a user code that is only available to purchasers of new books, bundled packages can suppress the secondary market for those titles. However, perhaps the most promising technological solution to the secondary market in textbooks is the creation of e-textbooks. Designed for optimal use on tablet computers, e-textbooks typically contain enhanced digital content and hyperlinked materials, such as videos, that can help make the presentation of the educational content both more engaging and more accessible. Available as either downloadable files or controlled online publications, e-textbooks are less expensive to produce and distribute, even if they are customized to meet particular instructor's requirements, and they are not susceptible to resale. This means the list prices can be significantly lower than those on traditional textbooks, while still ensuring adequate profits for publishers and acceptable royalty revenues for authors.

University Presses

Scholarly or *academic* publishing is related to educational publishing because the resulting books are often used by instructors and students in colleges and universities. However, academic publishing is usually regarded as a separate field within the book industry. Unlike most other publishers, university presses usually are established on a not-for-profit basis. At any one time, there may be only a handful of readers who are sufficiently qualified to read a truly important and paradigm-shifting book in a given field. Such books definitely need to be published in order to have their potential impact on their fields and on the world, but their greatly restricted sales potential would make most ordinary, profit-based publishers pause: the cost of actually producing the books could easily outweigh any sales revenue. As nonprofits, however, university presses have much more freedom to acquire and publish titles for their intrinsic intellectual or aesthetic value, rather than because of their potential marketability.

While every scholarly press certainly hopes to issue an intellectual bestseller, large sales are not the primary motivator when signing authors and titles. Only a few books intended for primarily academic audiences will prove to have broader, crossover appeal, and those are usually published by the major players among the university presses: Harvard, Yale, Oxford, Chicago, Princeton, and Cambridge. For example, Oxford scored a happy success with the 1976 publication of *The Selfish Gene* by ethologist and evolutionary biologist Richard Dawkins (b. 1941). Dawkins's book proved to be paradigm-changing and went on to sell over a million copies—a very significant number in academic publishing, although the sales were achieved over a thirty-year period. Similarly, Harvard was fortunate to secure *Invention by Design: How Engineers Get from Thought to Thing* (1996) by Henry Petroski (b. 1942), whose trade-published accounts of engineering successes and failures, such as *To Engineer Is Human* (1982) and *The Pencil* (1989), had sold very well. *Invention by Design* also did very well. Timeliness proved unexpectedly profitable for Yale, which published *Taliban: Militant Islam, Oil and Fundamentalism in Central Asia* by Ahmed Rashid (b. 1948) early in 2001. The attacks on New York City and Washington, DC, the following September, and the subsequent war in Afghanistan, propelled the book into the bestseller lists. In general, however, the prestige of having issued significant works, and the steady sales of certain titles on the backlist, combine to make the academic press an ongoing concern.

Of course, although they may be conducted on a not-for-profit basis, scholarly presses cannot be exclusively money-losing entities, either. Most manage their finances either through *endowments*, substantial sums of money established by patrons or trusts that underwrite the day-to-day operations, or through *subsidies*, allowances offered by sponsoring institutions (such as the university with which a given press is affiliated) or by authors or other contributors. Some university presses also operate both trade and noncommercial lines, using income from commercial sales to help underwrite their more scholarly publications. Some of the most significant bestsellers for university presses have been reference books of various kinds, such as the *Concise Oxford Dictionary*, Kate Turabian's *Manual for Writers of Research Papers, Theses, and Dissertations*, or Patrick Lynch and Sarah Horton's *Web Style Guide*. Regularly updated versions of these essential reference books have generated major sales for Oxford, Chicago, and Yale respectively, and they have helped to support the presses' other publishing ventures.

Among their many contributions to the history of the book, university presses have been particularly noted for issuing scholarly editions of classic texts and biographical materials. A *scholarly edition* is a version of a text that is considered to be the most reliable or authoritative. Arriving at that ideal, definitive version of a text involves the careful comparison of all previously existing versions, a practice that is known as *textual criticism*. The preparation of a scholarly edition can be fairly straightforward or exceptionally daunting, depending on how many different versions of the text are *extant*, or still in existence, and on what kinds of secondary evidence there is for the author's creative processes and for the production history of the text. For example, preparing a critical edition of *Beowulf*, of Christine de Pisan's (1363–1430) *Book of the City of Ladies* (c. 1405), or of T.S. Eliot's (1888–1965) *The Waste Land* (1922) all entail very different challenges, because of the different conditions under which these works were produced and what we know about the authors who created them. In all instances, the editor would need to examine all the known variants, as well as any other documents that might shed light on the composition and production processes.

Which variant text to use as the basis for a scholarly edition is the first major decision. For manuscript books, editors *collate* the different versions, examining them closely so as to determine the order in which they were copied. The age and origin of particular manuscripts can be ascertained by physical tests of the materials used to produce the manuscript; by *provenance*, or ownership records; and by internal clues, such as calligraphy or illuminations known to be characteristic of a particular time or place, or by information provided in the *marginalia* (notes in the margins) or in the *colophon*. By observing where variations in spelling, organization, and page layout appear, editors can often work out which version of the text was copied from which original or *exemplar*. Ideally, the editor will be able to work out which is the earliest version of the manuscript and thus closest to the author's original. This will usually serve as the basis for the scholarly edition.

For early printed books, or *incunabula*, original author's manuscripts are quite rare, so the process of determining the earliest and most authoritative variant is often similar to that of collating manuscript books. However, because the advent of print was accompanied by a new appreciation of the role of the author—as well as a new economics of authorship—there is typically much more extant evidence about an author's intentions and the publication processes as we draw nearer to the present day. (This is beginning to reverse in the digital age, as physical drafts and other evidence are increasingly much harder to come by.) Often editors will choose to base a scholarly edition on the first printed version of a work, on the grounds that it is the closest to the manuscript version. However, when there is evidence that the author significantly revised the text after it was in print, as in the case of the poet Alfred Tennyson's

(1809–92) works, editors may choose to base the scholarly edition on the last printed edition that shows evidence of the author's revisions.

Having decided which version of the text to use, the editor next needs to prepare the additional features that distinguish a scholarly edition from an ordinary one. Most scholarly editions include substantially more front and back matter than ordinary books do. These typically include a detailed introduction to the text itself, information about the author's life and times (sometimes as a biographical essay, and sometimes as a *chronology* or timeline), and additional contextual information (such as explanations of relevant historical events, definitions of obsolete or dialect terms, translations of foreign passages, and explications of allusions). In addition, the differences between the extant versions will usually be carefully described, either in notes or in a special section, so that readers can see the differences and understand the editor's decisions about which version to privilege. For some critical editions, this can be a very substantial part of the text as a whole. For example, there are a number of *variorum*, or comparative version, editions of Shakespeare's works, some of which are huge. Even modern literature can sometimes present significant challenges for textual critics trying to compile authoritative editions. One particularly vexed text has proven to be the novel *Ulysses* (1922) by James Joyce (1882–1941). Published in at least five editions during the author's lifetime, and numerous times since, the imperfections of the original edition and ongoing debates about what the author had intended in certain passages yielded a handful of editions from the 1960s to the 1980s that all claimed to be definitive. With the novel soon to fall out of copyright, the debate about which version is "authoritative" will likely be reopened.

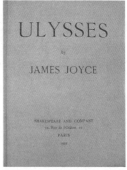

Title page of James Joyce's *Ulysses*, 1922.

THE PUBLISHING PROCESS

Since their emergence as a distinct force, modern publishing houses have concentrated on the content of books—on shaping the creative and intellectual contributions of authors into the best possible forms for their eventual readers. Publishers are also responsible for designing and marketing the physical books that result from this creative and collaborative process. In order to understand what publishers bring to the creation and publication of a book or other text, it is helpful to examine the steps in the publication process.

Books and other printed materials typically proceed through a number of departments within a publishing firm (or under the management of outsider suppliers) before they are released to the reading public. The publishing process is not strictly linear: certain steps can occur simultaneously, or a particular manuscript may circle back through parts of the system before moving forward again. However, in general a manuscript will pass through the following stages before it is ready for publication: acquisitions and development; production, which is sometimes handled by the editorial division and sometimes by a separate production department or production house; and marketing.

ACQUISITIONS AND DEVELOPMENT

In most publishing houses, the *editorial division* is responsible for bringing manuscripts and authors into the firm and for preparing the manuscripts for publication. In large firms, some editors are primarily financial and managerial personnel, concerned more with budgets and staffing than with the texts being produced, while other editors work directly with the authors and with the texts. In smaller firms, of course, one individual may perform all of these roles. Among the most important functions performed in editorial divisions are acquisitions and development.

Acquisitions

Acquisitions is, as its name suggests, the stage of acquiring, or bringing in, an author or manuscript to the publishing process. The acquisitions process typically proceeds in one of two ways. In the first instance, a publisher may decide that a particular kind of book would be a valuable addition and actively go looking for someone to write it. Such *commissioned* texts may be signed under standard royalty contracts, in which case the author retains an interest in the copyright and earns royalties from sales, or they may be secured with a *fee-for-service* arrangement, in which case the author relinquishes copyright and receives a one-time payment.

The second common way of acquiring manuscripts is to receive them from an author or the author's agent. These kinds of manuscripts may be *solicited* or *unsolicited*: sent after an initial inquiry about the publisher's potential interest in the proposed project, or sent cold, with the hope that the publisher will find the project sufficiently engaging to take it up. Because publishers tend to look more favorably on submissions that have already been vetted carefully by trusted advisors in the field, solicited manuscripts are nearly always submitted to publishers by literary agents. Not only are most literary agents more knowledgeable than authors about which publishing houses to target for particular projects, but in some cases they may work with the author before attempting to submit the work, helping to shape the author's text in a way that will make it a better fit for the targeted publisher.

By contrast, unsolicited manuscripts enter into the publisher's range of view without any particular introduction or preparation. Some publishers refuse to accept unsolicited manuscripts, either because they fear opening themselves up to later charges of having stolen an author's work, or because of the sheer volume of material that might be sent in. Publishers who do accept unsolicited manuscripts typically consign them to review by junior editorial personnel, often interns expressly hired for such work. Although over the years many good and successful books have been rescued from the anonymity of the so-called *slush pile* of unsolicited manuscripts, this is clearly not the ideal way to have one's life work appraised.

When a likely manuscript has been identified, a representative of the publisher—usually an editor—will contact the author or author's agent to express interest in the work and to ensure that it is not under active consideration elsewhere. Although in rare instances a contract might be offered right away, usually the manuscript is subjected to further review. Reviewers often recommend that a book be accepted or rejected outright, but they may recommend that an author *revise and resubmit* the manuscript, or rework it according to specific instructions and send it back for a second round of consideration. Authors who are able to revise their work in accordance with the publisher's directions will usually have their manuscripts accepted the second time around—but not always.

Especially in large publishing houses, a manuscript under active consideration may be circulated to the business and marketing divisions. Personnel in these divisions are unlikely to read the manuscript in any detail, but they will consider how it fits with pending arrangements for editorial services, paper purchases, or planned marketing campaigns. A proposed book that dovetails nicely with ongoing plans may be more likely to be picked up (or even moved ahead in the projected schedule) than one that presents unique challenges.

Once a manuscript has been accepted, a publishing contract will be offered. The contract secures the license to the author's copyright for a specified time. In return for the author's guarantee that the work in question is original and will be submitted on time and in good order, the publisher agrees to publish the work in the agreed-upon formats and time frame, to keep the work in print or to notify the author that it will be going out of print, and to pay royalties on a regular basis at the specified rates. Most publishers work from standard, preformatted contracts that are developed by their legal advisors. These standard contracts reflect past experiences and current practices, and they are fairly predictable from firm to firm. However, because they are legally binding, authors should always review them carefully and, when necessary, seek expert advice before signing. (For more details about publishing contracts from an author's perspective, see Chapter 5. Copyright is discussed in more detail in Chapter 6.)

ISBNs and CIP Data

Since 1970, most published books have had an *ISBN*, or *International Standard Book Number*. ISBNs are thirteen-digit numbers that identify a specific edition and format of a book and provide information about the language or region of publication and the publisher. Each version of a given title needs its own ISBN. ISBNs originally contained only ten digits, but in 2007 they were increased to thirteen digits in order to make them more readily compatible with the *International Article Number (EAN-13)* barcodes that are used on products around the world for inventory, ordering, and point of sale. ISBNs are also used for maps and for some electronic media, notably audiobooks and educational films and videos. Publications issued in series, like magazines or journals, have *ISSNs*, or *International Standard Serial Numbers*; printed music is issued with *ISMNs*, or *International Standard Music Numbers*. Besides being incorporated in the barcode on the back cover, ISBNs also may be printed on the copyright page.

ISBN.

Most parts of an ISBN are easy to decode. The first three digits are a prefix from the International ISBN Agency, which is based in London. Currently, these three digits are always either 978 or 979. The next one to five digits provide information about the registration group: the country, region, or language area in which the book is published. For example, 0 and 1 both represent English language; 2 represents French language; 7 represents the People's Republic of China; and 970 represents Mexico. The middle section of up to seven digits identifies the specific publisher. For example, 14 stands for Penguin Books, 19 for Oxford University Press, 439 for Scholastic, and 55 for Broadview Press. The next-to-last section of up to six digits specifies the particular book. The final single digit is a check code that mathematically validates the preceding digits.

Although the International ISBN Agency oversees the overall workings and administration of the ISBN system, the numbers themselves are issued by authorized agents in each country or region. For example, in the United States, ISBNs are issued by R.R. Bowker; in Canada, by the Library and Archives Canada (for English language publications) and by the Bibliothèque et Archives national du Québec (for French language); and in the United Kingdom and Republic of Ireland, by Nielsen Book. ISBNs are usually issued in blocks of ten, 100, or 1,000 numbers. Once a publisher has purchased a block of ISBNs, it can assign the numbers in any way it chooses. Some publishers assign ISBNs on a straight first-come, first-served basis, while others reserve certain groups of numbers for different lines or types of books, or use a particular penultimate digit to signal the version (hardcover, paperback, and so on).

A publisher may also request *Cataloguing in Publication* or *CIP data*, so that it can be printed on the copyright page of the book. CIP is a service

operated by national libraries or their authorized agents that gathers cataloguing information before books are published and disseminates that information to libraries and book distributors. CIP data represents the official
library catalogue entry for the forthcoming book. Besides the author's name,
title, and publisher information, the CIP entry also includes the subject headings under which the book can be searched and a Dewey decimal classification
number under which it can be shelved. (Books submitted for CIP data in the
United States also receive an LOC classification number.) By convention, most
national libraries now use the US Library of Congress's subject headings. (For
more discussion of cataloguing, see Chapter 9.)

Development

Editor Scott Norton describes *developmental editing* as the "significant structuring or restructuring of a manuscript's discourse," which may involve moving
content from one chapter to another, rearranging items of the text, and even
rewriting. At its simplest, developmental editing involves making certain that
the author is aware of the publisher's guidelines about length, complexity of
ideas and presentation, appropriateness of language, required formatting, and
so forth—the most general contours of the project. In its more intensive forms,
manuscript development can entail a close collaboration between author and
editor, as the specifics of content, presentation, and organization are worked
out. In such instances, multiple drafts may be exchanged for review and
comment as the overall project takes shape, and the editor may even rewrite
particular sections of the text to provide models or guidance to the author for
the final version. In some cases, such as textbook series for the elementary- and
secondary-school markets, draft versions may also be circulated among reviewers, so that the final version can incorporate outside advice and feedback.

   In addition to editorial input, the development stage of a manuscript
may also involve design, production, and marketing considerations. Even
before the manuscript is complete, a designer may be working on cover and
interior layouts, or an illustrator may be assigned to create or secure a bank of
desired images. If a book is intended primarily for electronic formats, creating
an appropriate design template and anticipating how the manuscript files
should be prepared to enable the smoothest migration to that final format is
often undertaken at this stage.

   Marketing and sales work may begin during development as well. The
details may not be filled in until the manuscript is actually received in house,
but the planning stages may get underway well in advance, as marketing
pieces and sales campaigns are often organized far ahead of publication dates.
Depending on the nature of the book and its intended audience, marketing
staff may want to contact the author about possible promotional opportunities. Especially if the author is already well known, it may be necessary to
schedule book signings and other public appearances significantly ahead of

MAX PERKINS: A LITERARY EDITOR

One of the best-known editors in the history of publishing is William Maxwell Perkins (1884–1947), who had the good fortune to work with some of the early twentieth-century's greatest literary artists. Perkins started his publishing career as a reporter for the *New York Times*, and in 1910 he began working for Scribner's, which was then one of the most distinguished US publishing houses. Although he admired Scribner's stable of established authors, which included such late nineteenth-century literary giants as Henry James (1843–1916) and Edith Wharton (1862–1937), he was keen to secure new authors for the house.

Perkins's first coup was to sign F. Scott Fitzgerald (1896–1940) in 1919, even though he was the only one in the house who liked Fitzgerald's unwieldy manuscript, then entitled "The Romantic Egoist." After working closely with Fitzgerald to dramatically reshape the piece, it was published in 1920 as *This Side of Paradise*, and it established Fitzgerald as a major new talent in American letters. Perkins also worked intensely with Fitzgerald on his masterpiece *The Great Gatsby* (1925).

Perkins also convinced Scribner's to sign Ernest Hemingway (1899–1961), even though Hemingway's first novel *The Sun Also Rises* (1926) raised concerns at the firm because of coarse language. The critical and commercial success of this book and, especially, *A Farewell to Arms* (1929), convinced his colleagues that Perkins's literary judgment was sound, and he was given a much wider berth to nurture the authors he discovered. In 1929 he succeeded in wrestling a masterpiece out of a rather hopeless looking manuscript discovered in Scribner's slush pile—a work that became a classic of another branch of American literature—*Look Homeward, Angel* by Thomas Wolfe (1900–38). Perkins was also the driving force behind what has become a much-loved young adult novel, *The Yearling* (1938) by Marjorie Kinnan Rawlings (1896–1953), which won the Pulitzer Prize for fiction and was also made into a popular movie.

While the often dramatic differences between the early drafts and the published books led some to believe that Perkins rewrote his authors' works, a close examination of the published correspondence between the editor and his many authors reveals that he mostly just provided advice, serving as a sounding-board on matters of structure, selection, and creativity. For example, Perkins wrote to Hemingway that all he really had to do was trust himself: "the utterly real thing in writing is the only thing that counts & the whole racket melts down before it." He also established the one essential in author-editor relations: trust. When his authors needed it, Perkins patted them back into shape, offered financial assistance, and made them believe they could achieve greatness. The fact that many of them did is one testament to his effectiveness as an editor, but so is the fact that many of his authors chose to dedicate their work to him. Nearly seventy titles were dedicated to Perkins, including Hemingway's *The Old Man and the Sea* (1952), published five years after the editor's death.

the projected publication date—and it may be positively desirable to promote the fact that the book is under contract and eagerly expected.

PRODUCTION

When the complete version of the final manuscript is received and accepted by the publisher, it officially enters into the production phase. *Production* includes all of the physical work that must be done to transform the work from a manuscript to a physical or electronic book. This includes copyediting, any design and illustration that has not already been undertaken, layout, typesetting, proofreading, indexing, and either printing and binding or coding for electronic release. In general, a manuscript will be assigned to a *production editor*, who will shepherd the project through to completion and keep track of the budget. In a small publishing firm, the production editor may be the same person who acquired or developed the manuscript; in a large firm, the production editor may be a freelancer or employee of an outside production house.

Copyediting

The first major undertaking for any accepted manuscript is copyediting. *Copyediting* or *subediting*, also referred to as *line editing*, is the detailed, word-by-word and letter-by-letter combing over that most manuscripts receive before typesetting. Copyeditors attend to the details of spelling, punctuation, grammar, usage, and structure. They also keep an eye on consistency of voice, style, and organization. For works that contain footnotes and other scholarly apparatus, copyeditors ensure that the numbers and content line up properly, and that information is treated consistently from page to page, section to section, and chapter to chapter.

When manuscripts were submitted as hard-copy typescripts only, copyeditors would also edit them by hand, using traditional copyediting or *proofreader's marks*, the symbols and systems of underlining that signal to typesetters how to render the edited manuscript into its final form for printing. Now that nearly all manuscripts are submitted as electronic files, copyeditors usually edit onscreen, using a text editor that shows deletions, insertions, and formatting changes. Electronic editing usually represents a significant time and labor savings: the complete manuscript only needs to be typed once, updated versions can be easily transmitted back and forth between authors, editors, typesetters, and others, and because backups are easy to create, the risk of losing or damaging the sole working copy are eliminated. Indeed, the only real disadvantage of electronic editing is that it is generally harder to proofread accurately onscreen than on paper, so there is a greater risk of errors continuing into the final copy.

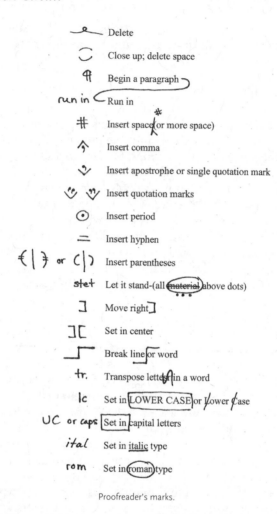

Proofreader's marks.

While copyeditors are primarily responsible for correcting linguistic and stylistic inconsistencies, they may also be responsible for *fact checking*, or verifying that information is correct and quotations are accurately rendered. Generally, this is more of an expectation for nonfiction than for other kinds of texts, especially for journalism and periodicals. For example, the *New Yorker* magazine has long been famous for its fact-checking department, which minutely scrutinizes virtually every piece of text that is slated for publication—and most illustrations as well. A recurring feature of the magazine over the years has been galleries of cartoons that were subject to fact-checking, forcing revisions (for example, a cartoon with a suit-wearing dog in a bar had to be revised, not because the dog was wearing a suit, but because the suit buttons were on the wrong side of the jacket) and occasionally deletions (sometimes a strict adherence to the facts renders a cartoon unfunny).

MISGUIDED EDITING: BOWDLERIZATION

Most authors who fear editing do so because they are afraid an editor will make them look bad or will ride roughshod over their work. The latter offense is not really editing but a form of *bowdlerization*, a kind of editing that intentionally distorts the author's text.

The verb *to bowdlerize* derives from the name of the late eighteenth- and early nineteenth-century English physician, philanthropist, and editor Thomas Bowdler (1754–1825). Bowdler is best known for *The Family Shakespeare* (1807), which he produced with his sister, Henrietta Maria Bowdler (1750–1830). The Bowdlers were concerned that although Shakespeare was one of the world's greatest authors and ought to be read by all, his works also contained content and language that were thought to be inappropriate for younger readers, and especially for young women. So, as they explained in their preface, the Bowdlers decided to remove from Shakespeare "everything that can raise a blush on the cheek of modesty"—which amounted to about 10 per cent of Shakespeare's work. Comparing *The Family Shakespeare* with another edited version of Shakespeare that appeared in the same year, *Tales from Shakespeare* by Charles (1775–1834) and Mary (1764–1847) Lamb, historian Noel Perrin observes that both books "omit not only everything that might start a blush, but everything that might provoke a yawn." However, while *Tales from Shakespeare* was a prose retelling of the stories in the plays and didn't pretend to be anything else, *The Family Shakespeare* purported to be an actual edition of Shakespeare's work. Readers were not fooled, and the book was so widely ridiculed and denounced that within a generation Bowdler's name had become synonymous with a particular kind of ham-fisted censorship or expurgation—and a form of "editing" to be reviled.

Title page of Thomas Bowdler's *The Family Shakespeare*, 1807.

Because authors are assumed to be the experts about their own subjects and prose, and to have written what they intended, experienced copyeditors generally do not simply correct presumed errors, but instead query them. *Querying*—drawing a possible error to an author's attention—is definitely an art. Less experienced copyeditors may adopt an unintentionally accusatory tone ("You didn't really mean to say *that*, did you?") or an equally fatal subservient one ("I'm really not sure about this, and I'm sure you know best, but—— "). In the first case, the author may feel attacked and defensive; in the second, the author may fail to take good or even necessary advice. By contrast, a good copyeditor will be able to point out a possible error and offer a solution in such a way that the author simply feels grateful for the assistance—and perhaps some relief at having been saved from an embarrassing exposure in print. Carol Fisher Saller, an editor at the University of Chicago Press and author of *The Subversive Copy Editor* (2009), advises that copyeditors should always "Ask first, and ask nicely," framing queries as positives rather than negatives. And veteran editor and journalist Arthur Plotnik (b. 1937) warns that there are good and bad forms of editorial compulsiveness. Dysfunctional compulsiveness drives editors to adhere to rules too rigidly and to fixate on minor matters that might just as well be left alone, while functional compulsiveness instead leads to properly following up to ensure that what is published serves both author and readers well.

Design

Design work is typically undertaken during the production stage. While text-only books of standard sizes and lengths are relatively easy to design, anything more elaborate can require a substantial amount of preparation and organization. Text designers need to choose typefaces and layouts that accommodate the expectations of the intended readers. In the case of textbooks intended for public schools, for example, the type size and spacing may be specified by state agencies, so the designer needs to know and meet those requirements. In the case of heavily illustrated or oversize books, such as atlases or coffee-table books, a designer will need to carefully plan such aspects as the proportion of text to illustration on a given page, or the scale of reduction or enlargement of images.

In order to prepare a manuscript ready for design, the production editor will typically go through the manuscript and identify each of the elements that might require special typographical or other treatment. Even books that are all text and no illustration can have a surprising number of elements that require design. In addition to the text that makes up the majority of the book's content, known as the *body text* or *basic text*, there may be chapter or section numbers and titles, various levels of headings (usually delineated by letters, from A to D), different kinds of lists (such as numbered or bulleted), and special treatment for long quotes or *extracts*. In addition, the author may have included quotations or *epigraphs* at the beginnings of chapters or sections, reading lists or bibliographies at the end, and footnotes or endnotes along the way. There are also two essential reading guides on most pages: the *running heads* or *running feet* that provide the author's name and the book or chapter title, and the page numbers or *folios*. If the book contains illustrations, there may also be *captions* or *legends* that describe what the illustration is, and *credits* that identify the source of the illustration. Finally, all books have *front matter* (at a minimum, a title page and copyright page, but also tables of contents, lists of acknowledgments or illustrations, dedications, and forewords or prefaces), and many have *back matter* (indexes, glossaries, appendixes). In a well-designed book, all of these textual elements will coordinate with each other in such a way that the design enhances the reading experience.

To give a sense of what the final book pages will look like, most text designers will prepare sample pages, or a *mock-up*. A mock-up shows all the identified textual elements in their proper fonts, sizes, and positions on the page. Crucially, it also shows how the *white space*—the blank areas of the page—will be deployed. The balance of type to white space is a very important design concern, as pages that are particularly type-heavy or gray can appear to some readers to be too daunting, and pages that are very airy can be either difficult to scan or seem to be aimed at the wrong reading level—or perhaps not a good value. Designers pay careful attention to the widths of the *margins* around the outer edges of the page, as well as to the width of the *gutter*, the space between the pages. Although illustrations may be allowed to *bleed* or run into those bands of white space, text usually never should. Anyone who has tried to read an inexpensive book whose content disappeared into the gutter or was cut off on the edges, or who has had to look more than once to find a page number on a given spread, knows how important good page layout is.

For books with illustrations, the production editor will also oversee or coordinate the *art program*. Depending on the kinds of illustration involved, the editor may commission new artwork and photography or arrange to secure the required images from individual copyright holders, independent archives, or commercial collections of stock photographs and illustrations. In the past, production editors would need to secure physical originals or copies and prepare them for reproduction, but today images are generally provided as high-resolution electronic files that can be easily *scaled* (sized) and dropped in to final page layouts.

In addition to the text, the cover also requires design. While the interior design is usually overseen and approved by the editorial department, cover design is more frequently undertaken and approved by the marketing department. The cover is probably the most important sales tool for a book, and the old adage about judging books by them has held true for centuries. A good cover will persuade potential readers to pick up the physical book or click the "look inside" option online, and the more that readers handle or browse in a book, the better the chance that the book will follow them home. By contrast, an ineffective cover can cause a book to be overlooked—not only by its ideal readers, but sometimes by everyone.

Covers only really began to be seen as marketing tools in the second half of the nineteenth century. Prior to that, both attached covers and the loose paper *dust jackets* or *wrappers* were generally functional. The covers protected the leaves of the book and kept them flat, and they were often attached by

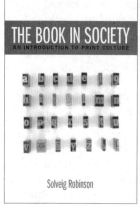 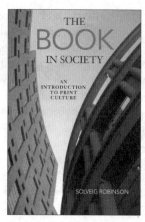 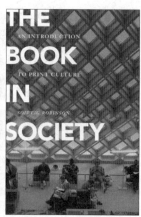

Cover design mock-ups.

special request after the contents of the book had been purchased. Readers could commission simpler or more elaborate covers, depending on what they wanted to pay, or they could arrange to have their new books bound to match the others in their personal libraries. For example, when his financial circumstances improved in the late 1660s, the English diarist Samuel Pepys (1633–1703) arranged to have all of his books rebound in fine tooled leather, so that they would better reflect his more elevated social and professional status. In the nineteenth century, Mudie's Circulating Library purchased all of its book stock as unbound, folded pages, and then had them bound in the company's distinctive bright-yellow covers. Even when the cover became an integral part of the package, books were often advertised at different prices, depending not only on the size of the volume and quality of the paper, but also on the type and quality of the bound cover.

However, by the 1880s, the idea of designing covers and dust jackets to suit and identify specific books had taken hold. Cloth bindings gradually replaced the traditional leather, and they were relatively easy to customize with printed or stamped designs. Just as the first printed books had been designed to imitate their manuscript forebears, the earliest cloth bindings were designed to imitate leather ones. They were largely typographical, with gilding and graphic design intended to resemble traditional tooling. But cloth covers soon began to incorporate illustrative elements as well, especially on books intended for children and on inexpensive reprint editions. Dust jackets became more graphically elaborate as well, and soon began to sport promotional quotes, or *blurbs*, from positive early reviews. When paperbacks began to dominate the book market in the twentieth century, cover designs underwent another transformation. High-minded publishers like Penguin initially preferred strictly typographical covers with a limited range of colors, while the many publishers of the notorious *pulps*—crime and detective fiction, Westerns, and science fiction—tended towards lurid full-color treatments, many of which are now considered classics of industrial design. The explosion of the romance fiction genre in the 1970s and 1980s produced the *bodice rippers*, with covers featuring well-endowed females swooning in the clutches of intense and dangerous-looking males. These in turn paved the way for the predictably pink *chick lit* covers of the 1990s and 2000s.

Typesetting, Printing, and Binding

The final stages of production make the book a reality for readers—a material reality in the case of printed books, and a virtual reality in the case of e-books. With the editing and design complete and approved, the production editor next releases the manuscript for typesetting and printing. As previously noted, this is now a much simpler process than in previous ages, as contemporary publishing software has significantly streamlined the process of converting typescript to pages. In most instances, either the copyeditor or the production editor will have inserted *markup* or *type codes* into the edited manuscript, indicating which copy is to be treated as basic text, heads, footnotes, and so on. The editor, designer, or typesetter then completes the necessary programming steps that enable the text to migrate from the word-processing software to the publishing software, and the first set of *page proofs*—typeset pages that show all text and illustrations in the proper fonts and places—are produced.

Copies of the page proofs are typically sent to the author for review, and they are also checked carefully by someone in the publishing house: usually by the production editor, and sometimes by professional proofreaders as well. Because all revisions from this point on entail added costs, authors are strongly discouraged from making any changes to page proofs that are not absolutely necessary. Not only do alterations need to be rekeyed and double-checked, but they can also affect page layouts, as changes in lines can force whole blocks of copy and even illustrations to shift forward or backward. This is the primary reason that most publishing contracts state that authors will be charged for emendations to page proofs that exceed about 10 per cent of the total text.

If the book will have an index, as is the case for most nonfiction texts, an extra set of final page proofs is provided for that purpose. Some authors prepare their own indexes, but publishers often arrange for a professional indexer to perform this task. An index should include all the possible terms by which a reader might try to locate information in the text, and those terms must be arranged logically, with practical cross-references. The number of entries and subentries is usually dictated by the topic and the depth and degree of difficulty with which that topic is addressed. Taking cookbooks as an example, a short book on cupcakes may have a relatively simple index that merely points readers to key ingredients and flavorings, or perhaps to themes for special occasions. However, a more comprehensive cookbook, such as *Delia's Complete How to Cook* (2009) by the bestselling British author and television personality

Delia Smith (b. 1941), requires a much more detailed index. In addition to being tailored to the complexity of the topic, an index must also be absolutely accurate, with all entries in alphabetical order and all page references correct. An index that fails to include some logical term or that sends the reader to the wrong page is a particularly irksome inconvenience.

When all of the pages, including the index, have been reviewed and corrected, the book is ready to be printed and bound or formatted for e-book release. Before electronic typesetting and page layout, this required a separate step, in which the paper copies of the pages and all of the artwork would be photographed, with the resulting film used to create *printing plates*, the negative-image sheets, originally made of metal, that would be attached to the rollers of an offset press. *One-color* printing (as in most all-text books) would require only one set of plates (which would usually print black); *full-* or *four-color* printing would require separate plates for each of the four *process colors* of ink—black, cyan, magenta, and yellow—that are combined in layers in the printing process to make the other possible colors and shades. (Modern *six-color* process printing adds two more colors, orange and green, to the original four, yielding a wider range of more vibrant color possibilities.) For the most part, the step of creating film has now been eliminated, and the plates for each color—now mostly made of plastic coated with a photosensitive emulsion—are created directly from the electronic files through the use of a digital scanner.

Printing and binding represent the largest expense category in the publishing process. It is more economical to buy paper in bulk and more efficient to print and bind many books of the same size at one time, so most mid-sized to large publishers have a special production department whose personnel are responsible for purchasing paper and scheduling press and bindery time. If a given house will have, say, ten books in a season's list that will all be printed in the same, standard 5 x 7 format, it will probably make good financial sense to print most or all of them at the same time. That way the paper can be ordered in quantity (at a bulk discount) and delivered to one printshop (at a savings in transportation costs), and the printer could do all of the *prepress* work (checking the electronic files or printing plates to make sure all the content is correctly coded and in the right place, and making the initial adjustments and calibrations of the presses to make sure that the jobs print properly) at one time. Once everything is checked and ready, all of the books can be run continuously. It may be similarly efficient to purchase all of the cover stock and print all the covers at once, as well. Again, the publisher would save on stock, transportation, and prepress and press time.

Bookbinding is another process that is sometimes handled by one supplier and sometimes by several. Modern technology has made it possible to print and bind some standard-sized paperback books on one press: the paper goes in one end, and bound and trimmed books come off the other, straight into shipping boxes. (As discussed in Chapter 4, this can also be done on a very small scale by print-on-demand machines.) However, in many cases printing and binding are separate steps, which may be completed at separate venues. Paperback or *perfect-bound* books are bound by gluing a heavier card-stock cover directly to the trimmed spine edges of gathered sets of *signatures* (folded sheets of pages). The entire book, cover in place, is then trimmed on the three remaining sides to the specified width and height. Perfect binding is significantly less expensive than other forms of binding, which is why paperback editions generally cost less than hardback editions, and they are now fairly robust. Contemporary adhesives mean that spines are more flexible and less susceptible to cracking, and special coatings can help protect covers from tears or fading. Some paperbacks now also feature cover *flaps* that can are folded inside the book and function like the flaps on dust jackets, typically being used for plot synopses and author information.

Hardback or *clothbound* books are now also usually bound with glue; however, the trimmed spine edges of the pages are glued to a sewn and flexible backing sheet. The backing sheet is in turn secured to the *front and back boards* (originally wood, but now usually heavy cardboard) of the book's *case*, while the spine section of the case (the part that shows when the book is on a shelf) floats free of the spine itself, helping to prevent damage to the book when it is opened and handled. The joins where the case meets the inner contents are then covered with glued *endpapers*, which provide another level of interior protection (and may be attractively decorated). The two parts of the endpapers that are not glued down but appear to be part of the book's contents are called *flyleaves*. The outer part of the case may be covered with actual cloth or, more commonly now, with durable heavy paper. The outer case may be printed, covered with a paper dust jacket, or frequently both.

When the books are bound and packed for distribution, or the electronic files are ready to be downloaded to e-readers, the publisher's work is done. The most important next step is to actually get those works into the hands of the readers for whom they are intended. Since the nineteenth century, this too has become a more specialized part of book culture. The next chapters will look at the two primary players who distribute books to readers in the modern world: booksellers and libraries.

SELECTED BIBLIOGRAPHY

Casper, Scott E., Jeffrey D. Groves, Stephen W. Nissenbaum, and Michael Winship, eds. *A History of the Book in America, Volume 3. The Industrial Book, 1840–1880*. Chapel Hill: U of North Carolina P, 2007.

Epstein, Jason. *Book Business: Publishing Past Present and Future*. New York: Norton, 2001.

"Global Publishing: Staying Put." *Publishers Weekly*, 1 July 2011.

Greco, Albert N., Clara E. Rodríguez, and Robert M. Wharton. *The Culture and Commerce of Publishing in the 21st Century*. Stanford: Stanford UP, 2007.

Kaestle, Carl F., and Janice A. Radway, eds. *A History of the Book in America, Volume 4. Print in Motion: The Expansion of Publishing and Reading in the United States, 1880–1940*. Chapel Hill: U of North Carolina P, 2009.

Lee, Marshall. *Bookmaking: Editing, Design, Production*. 3rd ed. New York: Norton, 2004.

Meyer, Michael. "About That Book Advance ..." *New York Times*, 10 April 2009.

Nel, Philip. *The Annotated Cat: Under the Hats of Seuss and His Cats*. New York: Random House, 2007.

Nord, David Paul, Joan Shelley Rubin, and Michael Schudson, eds. *A History of the Book in America, Volume 5. The Enduring Book: Print Culture in Postwar America*. Chapel Hill: U of North Carolina P, 2009.

Norton, Scott. *Developmental Editing: A Handbook for Freelancers, Authors, and Publishers*. Chicago: U of Chicago P, 2009.

"Pearson Leads the Pack." *Publishers Weekly*, 21 June 2010.

Perrin, Noel. *Dr. Bowdler's Legacy: A History of Expurgated Books in England and America*. New York: Atheneum, 1969.

Plotnik, Arthur. *The Elements of Editing: A Modern Guide for Editors and Journalists*. New York: Collier, 1982.

Saller, Carol Fisher. *The Subversive Copy Editor: Advice from Chicago (or, How to Negotiate Good Relationships with Your Writers, Your Colleagues, and Yourself)*. Chicago: U of Chicago P, 2009.

Schiffrin, André. *The Business of Books: How International Conglomerates Took Over Publishing and Changed the Way We Read*. London: Verso, 2000.

Swan, Annie S. *My Life: An Autobiography*. London: Nicholson & Watson, 1934.

Tanselle, G. Thomas. "Book-Jackets, Blurbs, and Bibliographers." *The Library* 26.2 (1971): 91–134.

Weedon, Alexis, ed. *The History of the Book in the West: 1914–2000*. Volume 5. Burlington, VT: Ashgate, 2010.

CHAPTER EIGHT

BOOKSELLERS

Bookselling has been in a process of continual evolution since it became a distinct branch of the book industry in the nineteenth century. While readers located near the printing and publishing centers in major cities had always been fairly well served by the book trade, readers in more remote areas represented a significant and largely untapped market. Much of the real innovation in the bookselling business over the past 200 years, therefore, has involved devising new means for getting books to people wherever they are. Whether their primary distribution systems have been built on railways, postal services, shopping centers, or the internet, the most successful booksellers have always sought to make book buying as convenient as possible for their customers.

Models of bookselling have changed significantly in the modern age. Independent bookstores, which first became significant players in the nineteenth century, continue to play a role in the book market today, although their numbers are down dramatically from their heyday of the mid-twentieth century. The independents were largely supplanted towards the end of the century, first by the smaller bookstores chains like B. Dalton and Waldenbooks, which opened outlets in suburban shopping malls, and then by the big-box superstore chains like Borders, Barnes & Noble, Chapters, and Waterstone's. But bookstore chains were not really a new idea: W.H. Smith had pioneered them a century before, when he opened his ubiquitous stalls in railway stations throughout Britain. The independents were also supplemented and ultimately challenged by mail-order booksellers. Canadian department store T. Eaton and Company began offering books in its mail-order catalogues in the 1880s, running the gamut from popular fiction to Bibles and denominational hymnbooks. After 1900, the store also made a concerted effort to promote Canadian authors, as well as children's books and periodicals. But the largest mail-order book retailer was Book-of-the-Month Club (BOMC), begun in 1929 with less than 5,000 subscribers and rapidly expanding to a customer base of over 100,000 in the 1930s and as many as 3 million in 1993. But even BOMC's best numbers look quaint when compared to those of the internet retailer Amazon.com, whose customer base in 2011 was over 137 million.

This chapter will examine the contemporary book trade. Although the focus will be on the retail book industry—books sold directly to end readers—the chapter will also examine the wholesale side of the business. Most books do not go directly from publisher to bookseller, but from publisher to distributor. The wholesale trade is also organized around a regular schedule

246 | The Book Circuit

of book trade fairs, the largest of which is held annually in Frankfurt. These fairs enable publishers to assess publishing trends, feature key authors, build excitement about forthcoming titles, and sign new distribution and subsidiary rights deals with colleagues from around the world. The decisions reached at the wholesale level have significant impacts on what books are available—and at what price—to ordinary readers down the line.

INDEPENDENT BOOKSELLERS

Independent bookstores have been at the heart of the book-buying experience for millennia. In his *History of Reading*, Steven Fischer describes how bookshops followed the spread of the Roman Empire. The poet Horace (65–8 BCE) boasted that his works were available in Spain, Gaul, and Africa, while Pliny the Younger (CE c. 61–113) was delighted to learn his works were available as far away as Lugdunum, the Roman city that became Lyon, France. Historian Elizabeth Eisenstein notes how the fifteenth-century Florentine publisher-bookseller Vespasiano da Bisticci (1421–98) worked especially hard to match particular titles with the right clients. His efforts earned him the immense gratitude of Renaissance poets and patrons and a certain amount of celebrity as the "prince of publishers." And Samuel Pepys (1633–1703) wrote frequently in his diary about the hours he spent looking over the wares in his favorite bookstalls around London's St. Paul's Cathedral in the 1660s. The booksellers he most frequently patronized pointed him towards particular books and editions and were often entrusted with procuring and rebinding works to furnish his growing library.

Perhaps one of the most affecting accounts of the personal relationship that can be established between a conscientious independent bookseller and a voracious reader is *84, Charing Cross Road* by Helene Hanff (1915–97). Published in 1970, the book consists of twenty years of correspondence between Hanff, who lived in New York City, and the staff of Marx and Co's bookstore in London. From the first letter, in which Hanff inquires whether the "antiquarian" books Marx and Co. advertises might be within her price range, to the last, in which she laments that she had never been able to meet the individuals who had supplied her with books for so many years, the memoir conveys the genuine friendships that developed as Hanff's reading needs were met by a physically distant but intellectually close cohort of dedicated booksellers.

Independents Today

Independent booksellers are a significant part of the book trade. According to the various national trade associations that represent independents, there are currently more than 1,900 independent booksellers in North America, representing all of the states and provinces, about 1,100 independents in the United

Kingdom and Ireland, and about 500 independent bookstores in Australia and 200 in New Zealand. The number of booksellers in many other developed countries is comparable. For example, there are approximately 360 independent booksellers in Sweden. It is more difficult to determine the number of independent stores in Japan, as the 6,000 members of the Japan Booksellers Federation include both major bookstore chains and convenience stores like 7-11s that sell primarily magazines and comic books. But however the figures are calculated, they represent a significant number of outlets with links to local communities of readers.

However, in recent decades the independents have faced some major challenges. Nearly everyone knows of storefronts that once featured books and are now either empty or taken over by an entirely different kind of business. The online *Toronto Review of Books* recently published an elegiac piece about the disappearance of independents around the world, particularly mourning the loss of Pages, a thirty-year destination for residents in Toronto's Queen West neighborhood. According to a 2010 study of the Japanese publishing industry, Japan is losing about 800 independent bookstores a year. Charing Cross Road, once the heart of London's book trade, is now mostly restaurants and takeout venues, and Hanff's beloved Marx and Co. is now part of a restaurant off Cambridge Circus. (Thanks to the popularity of *84, Charing Cross Road* and the 1987 film version starring Anne Bancroft and Anthony Hopkins, there is now a plaque marking where the store used to be.) The Book Row area of New York City, which once contained dozens of booksellers, is now home to only one, the Strand. Bibliophile Nicholas Basbanes (b. 1943) refers to it as one of the "splendid anachronisms" of the bookselling world. And independents' struggle to stay in the black can be fierce. As Meg Ryan's character Kathleen Kelly learned to her dismay in the 1998 film *You've Got Mail*, even a long-established and much-loved independent can find it difficult to stay in business when an enormous chain outlet moves into the neighborhood.

Those independents that have continued to thrive have done so through a combination of factors, the most important of which are knowing the local market and providing the kinds of personal touches and personal services that large chains and online vendors cannot. For example, Politics and Prose in Washington, DC, hosts not just author events, but a wide variety of classes and workshops. The store's website and blogs also provide tools for customers to order books, learn what others are reading and what they think about it, and even find a local restaurant for a pre- or post-browse meal. Like many other independents, King's Books in Tacoma, Washington, provides sponsorship and meeting space for a variety of local book clubs, as well as performance space for independent theatre and arts groups. King's Books also hosts an annual *wayzgoose*, a letterpress and book arts festival that brings together small printers from around the region. Even casual passersby have been drawn in by the sight of a steamroller being used to print oversized letterpress posters. Westminster Books in Fredericton, New Brunswick, has its own book club

248 | *The Book Circuit*

that offers members discounts on special items and future purchases. Women & Children First, as its name suggests, ties in to feminist organizations and events in the Chicago area. Like other successful independents, all of these stores make significant use of the internet and various forms of social media to alert their customers to new releases, upcoming events, and other information, and to make it easy for customers to order and purchase books locally.

These kinds of efforts to serve local readers and communities particularly well appear to be paying off for some independents. Although the recent global recession has hit many small businesses, including bookstores, very hard, the overall business climate for independent bookstores previously appeared to have stabilized, and the American Booksellers Association (ABA)

THE STRAND BOOK STORE

The Strand Book Store was opened by Benjamin Bass in 1927 on Fourth Avenue in New York City. From the 1890s until the 1960s, the stretch of Fourth Avenue between about Union Square and Astor Place was known as "Book Row." During its heyday in the late 1940s and 1950s, the area was home to nearly fifty bookstores, most offering secondhand books. But now the Strand, named after the long-established book publishing district in London, is the last survivor. Currently located just around the corner from its original location, on Broadway and Twelfth Street, the Strand started out with its founder's own books as part of the stock. It is now home to about 2.5 million new, used, and rare volumes in over 55,000 square feet of space—about 18 miles of shelf feet—making it one of the largest mixed stock bookstores in the world.

Now run by the second and third generations—Fred Bass and his daughter Nancy Bass Wyden—the Strand acquires most of its books from walk-ins, estate purchases, and personal libraries. Nancy Wyden jokes that her father "has to have everything, and he never passes up an opportunity for a bargain." As a result, the 6,000-plus customers who visit the store each day know that they will be able to find almost anything in its tightly packed floors. One long-time feature of the store is review copies, readily available in this publishing center. Another feature is the rare book department on the third floor, which contains over 50,000 volumes at any time, including such treasures as a complete edition of Mark Twain's works, signed by the author. Still another is the "Best of the Best" section, containing books that have been rated highly by the Strand's customers. The store also offers a "Books by the Foot" service, which promises to assemble any kind of book collection for patrons, either for purchase or for rental. (The Strand supplied books for the sets of the film *You've Got Mail*.)

In his description of the Strand in *Patience and Fortitude* (2001), bibliophile Nicholas Basbanes notes that the store lacks many supposed non-negotiables of and Booksellers New Zealand both reported recently that the number of new independent store locations had increased. Book sales at independents also appeared to be up somewhat, despite the economy and a concurrent general decrease in the total number of books purchased. In 2010, the *Globe and Mail* interviewed a number of Canadian independent bookstore owners from across the country. One store owner cited younger readers' "ferocious" level of reading as a sign of hope for the future, but she also noted that the real challenge confronting many smaller retailers was meeting ever-increasing rents. Another owner observed that independent bookstores continued to evolve, with some stocking a broader mix of books and other goods, and others moving towards greater specialization: "bespoke bookselling, so to speak."

The Strand Bookstore, Manhattan, 2005. Photograph © Postdlf.

modern retail, including off-street parking, central air-conditioning, or a coffee shop. Despite that, the Strand continues to thrive. The store's website, a fairly recent addition, provides a highly organized and easily accessible portal into the store's vast inventory and opens its riches to a larger marketplace of avid readers. But although the Strand has spruced up some of its public spaces in the past decade, including adding a room on the third floor for readings and other events, Fred Bass warned in 2001 that he wanted to preserve the store's distinctively vintage vibe. "I absolutely insist on keeping the same crummy look," he told Basbanes. "Every time I make the place too neat, business goes down."

Used and Antiquarian Booksellers

One important subdivision of the independent bookstore market is the used book trade. The resale market has been part of the book world since the beginning, as readers have always sought to acquire titles that are no longer in print or to pass along books that they no longer need or want. *Antiquarian* dealers—those who sell old and rare books and manuscripts—are a special subcategory of the used book trade. These dealers tend to work especially with book collectors, whether individuals or libraries, helping them to buy and sell rare editions and to assess the value of their books for insurance and other purposes.

As the total number of independent booksellers has decreased, the number of independents that sell used books or a mix of old and new, like Powell's Books in Portland, Oregon, appears to have increased. For example, in 2006 the Book Industry Study Group (BISG) reported that approximately 68 per cent of the bookstores in the United States sold at least some used books, amounting to about 8.4 per cent of total consumer spending on books. While sales of new trade books were only predicted to rise at about 1 percent annually over the next five years, used trade books were predicted to grow at 25 per cent, and to constitute 10 per cent of total book sales by 2010. (The used textbook market is even larger than the trade book market, constituting nearly 35 per cent of all used books sold, and adding up to over 73 per cent of total used book revenue.) So far, those predictions seem to have been borne out.

Independent stores that specialize exclusively in new titles cannot always compete directly on price and convenience with the other kinds of retailers now in the market (especially the superstores and internet retailers). However, independents that deal in used books have often been able to identify a market niche or specialism that enables them to hold their own. For example, a store might deal exclusively in used genre fiction—such as romances, science fiction, fantasy, detective stories, thrillers, or westerns. Since these genres tend to attract voracious readers, stores that specialize in genre fiction can usually rely on steady foot traffic and a constantly renewing supply of recycled stock. The proliferation of stores with names such as Book'em Mysteries, Grave Matters, Uncle Hugo's Science Fiction Bookstore, or Rendezvous testify to the ongoing popularity of such genre shops. Other stores might specialize in books related to children, to particular crafts or hobbies, or to local history and culture. Although their inventories may consist primarily of used titles, many such specialist stores also carry a limited number of carefully selected new titles, to help ensure that their customers' book needs are well served.

Whether they are specialist stores or deal in more general stock, many used book stores endeavor to build customer loyalty by providing trade-in allowances or discounts for bulk purchases (such as a bundle of assorted romance novels or spy thrillers for $1). Typically, used book dealers will offer to purchase books either for in-store credit or for cash—savvily offering more credit than cash, since they know that most people who have books to sell can also be enticed to buy more books. Some used book stores are extremely orderly and well laid out, with stacks organized by genre or subject, an up-to-date inventory system, and knowledgeable sales staff. Others are much more haphazard, with knocked-together shelving and an inventory system that depends mainly on the proprietor's memory and mood at the time of inquiry. Still others are positively ramshackle, with random piles of books everywhere and an asthma-inducing miasma of dust, cat fur, and mold that may deter all but the most determined bargain hunters from entering, let alone making a purchase. Depending on the size and extent of their operations, used book dealers may offer many of the features of new book retailers: coffee shops, book club sponsorship, author events, and special orders. Some, like the Strand, may also select and sell complete libraries of books to individuals or institutions, or arrange to rent books to designers who need props for a theatre set or who wish to stage a room for an open house. Not only are the used books more economical than new ones would be, but they can be selected to represent a particular historic period, match a color scheme, or suggest that the inhabitants of the room are of a particular educational level or pursue a particular kind of lifestyle. Used books help sustain these illusions because they have clearly been *read*.

Although many used book sellers are very well informed about the history of the book and the values of different titles, antiquarian book dealers specialize in this aspect of the used book trade. Many are members of the Antiquarian Booksellers' Association, founded in Britain in 1906 to help sellers cope with the flood of old books making their way into the marketplace at that time. Antiquarian dealers may trade only in books from a particular period, printer, or publisher, or only in rare first editions, or they may work almost exclusively with private collectors and institutions. Unlike ordinary used book sellers, antiquarian dealers may purchase most of their stock from private estates or auctions, and they also may accept titles from would-be sellers on consignment.

Because they are working with rare and thus intrinsically valuable artifacts (whether or not the books are antiques), antiquarian dealers and their customers are very concerned with details of *provenance*, or who previously owned the book, and with the book's physical condition. There is an entire specialist vocabulary to describe the details of a book's construction or its evidence of wear and tear. Most people are familiar with the term *dog-eared* to denote a corner of a page that has been turned over and creased. But there are many other vivid terms. The brownish spots that sometimes appear on older paper are known as *foxing*, and they can sometimes be removed by *washing*, or applying chemicals to the paper to remove any extraneous discoloration or writing. (Because washing also removes the *size*, or protective coating from the paper, washed books are also often *re-sized*.) A *shaken* or *loose* book is one in which the contents are progressively coming away from the covers. A used

POWELL'S BOOKS

A destination bookstore in the Pacific Northwest, Powell's Books in Portland, Oregon, was founded by Walter Powell in 1971 in a rundown area. Powell's son, Michael, had started a used book store near the University of Chicago the previous year, and Walter so enjoyed his visit to his son's store that he opened his own. Since 1979, Michael has also worked in the Portland location, and his daughter Emily is in the process of taking over the family business. (The Chicago store remains a Hyde Park icon, with a second branch on Chicago's North Side.) Powell's "City of Books" flagship store on Burnside is a wonder: a vast, multi-level bookstore that covers a whole city block and readily convinces visitors that they may very well be in the largest new and used bookstore in the world. Powell's City of Books alone stocks more than a million books, and there are now four other locations in the Portland area. The main store draws an average of 3,000 visitors each day to browse and buy, and the chain's revenues are in the region of $40 million per year.

One of Walter Powell's unconventional strategies was to stock new and used, hardcover and paperback books on the shelves right next to each other, so readers seeking works on a particular topic or by a specific author can see all of the available options at the same time. His son initially thought it was a crazy scheme, but it worked: combining the books in this way "had synergy way beyond what we expected. If you put all the new books in one store and all the used books in another, each wouldn't get half the total business—they drive each other." In addition to the expansive stacks of general books, Powell's also contains a rare book room, which has a large assortment of first edition and signed books. Besides selling books, Powell's is also home to a large and attractive coffee shop—a necessity in the region—that serves brew from a local coffee-roasting company. The store hosts a number of events that regularly draw in readers and other members of the community, including author signings and writing workshops.

Powell's has been a retail innovator in online book sales and print-on-demand. The store launched its first, tentative website in 1994 and expanded it rapidly over the next few years, as internet inquiries showed that there was a demand for online access to used books. By 1998, online sales at Powells.com already accounted for 3 per cent of the company's business. By 2005, Powell's had been named as one of the "Top 50 Retail Web Sites" by *Internet Retailer* magazine, and two years later it inaugurated its online buying program. Powell's has also recently launched an Espresso Book Machine (EBM) program, which enables buyers to purchase print-on-demand titles. As part of its print-on-demand program, the store also offers services to help authors print their own books.

W.H. Smith and Son railway bookstall, Manchester, 1932. Courtesy of Manchester Libraries, Information and Archives, Manchester City Council.

book can also be *honest* or *unsophisticated*, meaning that any efforts to clean it up or mend it are readily apparent, or *sophisticated*, a pejorative term meaning that efforts have been made to conceal any changes, whether by cleaning, rebinding, or *cannibalizing*—using parts of another book to replace any missing or inferior pages or illustrations.

Whether they sell primarily new or used books, or even valuable antiquarian editions, independents increasingly rely on the internet to advertise their stock to the greater world. The ability to reach out and find the right reader for the right book is one of the critical tools that enable independent booksellers to hold their own against the industry giants: the superstores and online merchants.

BOOKSTORE CHAINS

The large chain bookstores may lack the personal service and charm of independents, but for many readers those deficits are more than compensated for by a significantly larger inventory and consequent discounting. Although chains may have made their biggest impact on the book trade at the end of the twentieth century, they had been around for many decades beforehand. The earliest significant bookstore chain was founded in England by W.H. Smith in 1848. William Henry Smith (1825–91) and his brother inherited their father's stationery and news business in 1816, and by 1846 William's son was also part of the firm. When the railways began spreading across Britain and the rest of the world, Smith realized that travelers represented an enormous potential market. As railway travel became routine, it also became boring. To help travelers fill up the hours of ennui, Smith established stalls in and near railway stations, where he sold periodicals and other light reading. His first bookstall was opened in Euston Station in London in 1848, and by 1850, W.H. Smith was the largest newspaper distributor in the United Kingdom. The success of his venture can be gauged by the fact that most contemporary publishers quickly started producing inexpensive, one-volume reprint editions of novels and other lighter works in "railway library" series, often with garish covers that were intended to quickly draw the eye. (The popular name for railway novels was *yellowbacks*, after the covers on the books produced by Routledge.) W.H. Smith's continues to sell books and other materials in train stations, airports, and town centers around the United Kingdom and Europe, with subsidiaries around the globe, including in Canada (where it became known as SmithBooks).

The next bookstore chains to make a significant impact on bookselling emerged in the 1960s and 1970s. This was a period of great transition in retailing, with many stores of all kinds abandoning Main Streets and High Streets

GLORIOUS CHAIN STORES

Although many think "bookstore chain" means a predictable series of bland, uniform outlets, that is not necessarily so. Some chains have made the most of unique locales. For example, the Selexyz Boekhandels chain in the Netherlands purchased a thirteenth-century former Dominican church in the center of Maastricht for its Selexyz Dominicanen branch. The store opened in 2006 after extensive remodeling of the building, which had previously served, among other things, as a warehouse and as a bicycle parking lot. Selexyz Dominicanen features several stories of stacks that ascend high into the arches of the former nave, giving visitors a close-up view of the medieval frescoes. A café in the choir end includes a central cross-shaped table that houses current periodicals for browsing. The Selexyz branch in Arnhem is also housed in a historic building, a nineteenth-century post office that is now the city's *Boekenpaleis*, or palace of books.

Similarly, the bookstore described as "South America's most beautiful," El Ateneo Grand Splendid in Buenos Aires, is also part of an Argentinean bookstore chain, Ateneo. The store is located in the former Grand Splendid Theater, which still features frescoes painted to celebrate the end of World War I. Originally built as an opera house, the building became a movie palace in the 1920s and then a radio theatre. Throughout the twentieth century its use shifted back and forth between live performances and films, and the building was finally slated for demolition in the 1990s. It was rescued and converted to a bookstore in 2000, with an elegant café on the former stage and, appropriately, a strong collection of recorded music. The store estimates that it welcomes 3,000 visitors per day—many of whom come to marvel at the architecture and stay to make a purchase.

in favor of the new suburban shopping malls. Waldenbooks was launched in Connecticut in 1962, and B. Dalton in 1966 by the Dayton's department store chain (now Target Stores). At their peak in the early 1980s, both chains had stores in shopping malls across the United States. What made these chains distinctive is that they were expressly designed to cater to the new mall shoppers' habits. The stores featured wide, well-lit storefronts that invited customers in. In front, customers would find prominently displayed gift books and seasonal books, as well as discounted special purchases (often *overstocks*, or books for which publishers had overestimated the demand and which they were willing to sell at or below cost). Large signs clearly directed customers to other categories of books, primarily genre fiction, self-help and business books, and children's books (especially those with commercial tie-ins, such as stories based on television characters).

While many of these stores also carried some classics and other serious literature, their inventories emphasized new releases rather than backlist titles. In effect, the new chains sold books the way other mall stores sold athletic shoes or jellybeans: the latest items were heavily advertised and available in bulk. Although the chain stores' personnel might be knowledgeable about books in a particular sales category, their primary function was to help customers complete their purchases quickly and efficiently.

The chain store concept quickly spread around the globe, with some international players and many national or regional ones. For example, the two largest bookstore chains in Japan are currently Kinokuniya and Junkudo, and the top four chains account for approximately half of all Japanese book sales. In Sweden, the largest bookstore chains are Akademibokhandeln and Bokia. The Mexican publisher Fondo de Cultura Económica also operates a good-sized bookstore chain in Mexico and elsewhere in Latin America, while El Ateneo dominates in Argentina.

Book lovers who had been fortunate enough to live in areas with good independent bookstores may have found the experience of shopping in these new chains both aesthetically and intellectually underwhelming, but for millions of shoppers in towns not previously well served by bookstores, the chains were a godsend. The stores were convenient and unintimidating. There was little need to ask for assistance: not only were genre categories clearly labeled, but the books themselves were usually displayed face out, so the covers could be seen even from outside the store. No matter where you lived, you could still know which books were on the New York Times Best Sellers list and buy them at a discount. For the first time for many readers, a book could become an impulse purchase—a self-indulgence, a gift, or a reward for a child's good behavior.

A creative twist on the mall bookstore success story was made by Half Price Books, based in Dallas. Originally launched in 1972 in a converted laundromat, the Half Price Books chain sells a combination of new (usually overstock) and used books and other media. By actively purchasing used books and recorded items at all of their stores, Half Price Books keeps its stock fresh for repeat customers and provides a valuable recycling service to the neighborhoods it serves. The store's concept and organization has been very profitable: Half Price Books reported revenues of about $220 million in 2010, and it continues to open new outlets. Like many other bookstore chains, Half Price Books also works with local literacy groups and nonprofits to support and promote reading.

THE SUPERSTORES

The next major development in book retailing was the emergence of the *big-box stores* or *superstores*. Although there were some very large bookstores prior to

FOYLES: A LEGENDARY SUPERSTORE

Foyles, located in the traditional bookselling district of London on Charing Cross Road, was launched in 1903 by William (1885–1963) and Gilbert (1886–1971) Foyle. Having failed their civil service exams, the brothers took out an advertisement to sell their textbooks and soon discovered there was an untapped market for used educational books. They bought more books, resold them at a profit, and went into business. By 1906 they had set up what would be the first of several shops on Charing Cross Road, and by the end of World War I, they boasted a stock of over a million books. In the 1920s they expanded further, and William, sometimes described as the "Barnum of Bookselling," declared that the shop was now the world's largest bookshop. (According to the Foyles website, he later had this claim ratified by the *Guinness Book of Records*.)

The Foyles expanded their business further in the 1930s, opening branch shops around London and launching a subscription library service; they also invested in book clubs, music, and a library supply service. The Foyles also kept a wary eye on events in Europe, and when news came that the Nazis were burning books in Germany, one of the family reportedly telegrammed the Führer, offering to buy the books instead. When war broke out again, the brothers continued to thumb their noses at Hitler, threatening to protect their shop by covering the roof with copies of *Mein Kampf*. As it happens, they did end up using old, damaged books as sandbag filler to protect the store from bomb damage—a helpful precaution, since Charing Cross Road sustained a hit that destroyed the shop directly across the road from them.

The second generation took over Foyles after the war, with William's daughter Christina (1911–99) becoming the main proprietor after her brother's death in 1957. Her main innovation was a series of Foyles lunches, which brought together readers and writers. The idea reportedly sprang from an incident when Christina this—such as Foyles in London, which adopted the motto "largest bookshop in the world" and actually had that claim ratified by Guinness World Records, or Coles in Toronto, which began billing itself as "The World's Biggest Bookstore" in the 1940s—these tended to be individual stores, rather than chains, and they also tended to be in major cities, rather than in the suburban and provincial areas typically served by shopping malls.

By the 1980s, when the book-buying habit had really taken hold of ordinary suburban and small-town shoppers, the limited shelf space and shallow backlists of the average mall bookstores began to be a disadvantage. Following the example of a number of sporting goods and electronics store chains, some book retailers began to migrate from inside the malls to larger, stand-alone stores.

The largest and most successful of these big-box stores in the United States are Barnes & Noble, which was founded in 1977 and is now the largest

recommended John Galsworthy's (1867–1933) *The Forsyte Saga* (1906–21) to an elderly customer who wanted some reading for the train. The gentleman bought the book but shortly thereafter returned it to the store with an inscription—the customer had, in fact, been Galsworthy.

Like many businesses in Britain at the time, Foyles began to decline in the 1970s, and Christina's mercurial management style contributed to a long spell of rapid employee turnover that further eroded the store's stock and reputation. According to the company's website, even though it was likely that Foyles had the books a reader might want, neither customers nor the staff would be able to find them. A nearby competitor, Dillons, began running an advertising campaign with the slogan "Foyled Again?" to pick up disgruntled customers, and Foyles' windows became infamous for the dusty, curling—literally shopworn—volumes that languished there. Things got so bad that in the early 1980s, Christina is said to have offered the lease of the store to a young man who had recently opened a shop in the Kensington area of London: Tim Waterstone (b. 1939), founder of what is now the United Kingdom's largest superstore chain.

After Christina's death, the store passed into the hands of her nephew Christopher (b. 1943). He immediately began trying to set Foyles back on track, spending over £4 million pounds to renovate the flagship store on Charing Cross Road, modernizing the accounting systems, launching a website (which now accounts for 10 per cent of sales), and opening new branches. Under his management, Foyles' fall-off in trade was not only staunched (it had been losing as much as 20 per cent per year), but it returned to profitability. Aided both by modernization under Christopher and the demise of many other booksellers in the United Kingdom, Foyles has again become a major force in the book trade. In 2011 it opened its first branches outside of London in seventy years, and the following year it was named as UK National and Children's Bookseller of the Year.

combined bricks-and-mortar and online chain in the world; the recently defunct Borders, which was founded in 1971 and rapidly expanded after 1992, when it was purchased by Kmart; and Books-a-Million, originally founded in 1917, and now maintaining a significant presence in the southeastern United States. Another superstore giant, Crown Books, was founded in 1977 and became the third largest chain in the United States by the early 1990s, before collapsing into bankruptcy in 1997. In Canada, the main superstore is Chapters, which was founded in 1995 through a merger of Coles with SmithBooks, the Canadian-owned descendant of W.H. Smith, and which now also embraces the formerly independent major chain Indigo.

In the United Kingdom, the largest superstore chain is Waterstone's, which opened its first store in 1982 and whose Piccadilly branch is billed as the biggest bookshop in Europe. The Blackwell's chain, launched in Oxford in 1879 and rapidly expanded in the 1990s, is also a major player, although its offerings are aimed more at the academic and educational market. Blackwell's was the first UK bookseller to offer online sales.

Although their store designs, inventory, and development and sales strategies differed somewhat, the new book superstores shared a common goal: each wanted its outlets to be the destination bookstores in any given town or region. To achieve that goal, the superstore chains took some similar steps. First, they designed stores that were, in general, more upmarket than the typical mall or High Street bookstore. To attractively display the deeper range of books they carried, the superstores typically installed wooden bookcases. While taller banks of bookcases might range around the perimeter of the store, housing the extensive backlists, the central portions of the store were usually furnished with shorter cases, often featuring *endcaps*, extra shelves at the ends of the ranks that enabled the stores to display featured books face-out. The shorter bookcases kept the sightlines open. This not only enabled customers to readily see the different departments around the store (and, incidentally, allowed the sales staff to keep an eye on the customers), but it also meant that the lighting could be a bit more subdued and warmer than in a typical shopping-mall store.

To further create a relaxing ambience, many superstores placed upholstered furniture at key points around the store, and they also introduced the now ubiquitous in-store coffee shops. Where in the seventeenth and eighteenth centuries coffeehouses had incidentally made reading material available, now the bookstores incidentally made coffee available—and the outcome was much the same. These back-to-the-future innovations strongly encouraged customers to consider the superstores as leisure destinations: places to browse at will, then sit comfortably with a book and a hot drink. The inevitable result was that customers frequently left with bags of books, media, and stationery products.

The success of the superstores was extraordinary, but there were costs. Many independent bookstores that had withstood the onslaught of the mall bookstore chains were overwhelmed by the arrival of the superstores. They could not carry enough stock to compete with stores whose floor size could be ten or more times their own. They also found themselves at a pricing disadvantage. Not only did the superstores have the clout to negotiate fiercely with publishers on pricing strategies for high-volume purchases, but they were large enough that they could afford to take a loss on some books, particularly new releases and bestsellers.

However, independents gradually realized that they could leverage significant power if they worked together, and the trade associations that represented independents around the world soon stepped up to help their members develop websites and other communication and marketing tools. In addition, a variety of online marketplaces were created to help independent stores advertise their wares, among them Alibris, which was launched in 1997 as a partnership of independent booksellers, and Abebooks, which was launched in 1996, originally as a used booksellers' site, but soon incorporating new books as well. Furthermore, many stores that maintained their focus and a manageable size found they were able to weather the competition. Some industry analysts predict that in the wake of Borders's demise and that of a few other chains, these stores may even see an increase in sales and traffic. As one real estate consultant noted in a 2011 article in *Bloomberg Businessweek*, bookselling may be one of the only retail industries in history that will eventually "go full circle, back to the way it originally was."

As the superstores increasingly dominated bookselling, critics began to express concern about the effects the stores' buyers might have on the publishing industry more generally. When there were thousands of independents and a score of mall bookstores, wholesale book-buying remained relatively decentralized. There would always likely be a range of retail customers interested in the quirkier books in any given publisher's lists, and those books would continue to filter through to the end readers for whom their authors intended them. However, critics warned that with a significant portion of all bookstores in a given region (or even country) consolidated into just a few hands, decisions about which books would be purchased from publishers would almost certainly become more mainstream and less adventurous. Readers' options would eventually be restricted to the safest, most formulaic, most predictable genres, while experimental fiction, edgy reportage, and most poetry would fall out of view. Even the midlist, middlebrow fiction and nonfiction that had been most publishers' bread and butter for decades would go into decline if independent-minded buyers were no longer there to stand up for it.

Curiously, however, these predictions not only did not come to pass, but there was good evidence that midlist books were actually thriving under the superstores' domination. Some of this was due to the book-buying policies of the stores themselves, which turned out not to be as cynical or crassly philistine as critics had feared. And some of this was due to the concurrent rise of the television- and community-based book club movements. Television book club sponsors Oprah Winfrey in the United States and Richard Madeley and Judy Finnigan in the United Kingdom drove an unprecedented demand for exactly the kinds of midlist fiction that critics had been so worried about. And the superstores not only stocked these books in quantity and displayed them

BARNES & NOBLE

With the bankruptcy and closure of its nearest competitor, the Borders superstore chain, Barnes & Noble is now the world's largest big-box bookstore chain, selling approximately 300 million books per year, worldwide. Besides physical books, Barnes & Noble is also an industry leader in e-book sales, with about 27 per cent of the total e-book market.

Barnes & Noble sprang from an 1870s printing business launched in Illinois by Charles Barnes. His son William, along with partner G. Clifford Noble, started a bookstore in New York City in 1917. In 1971 the store was purchased by Leonard Riggio (b. 1941), who already had a successful small line of college bookstores. After he purchased the New York flagship store, Riggio quickly expanded the business by acquiring other stores and small chains. Soon Barnes & Noble was a national retailer, one of the first to use television advertising to sell books and also one of the first to offer standard discounts on New York Times Best Sellers. Returning to the business's printing roots, Riggio also launched a publishing branch, mostly offering out-of-copyright classics under the B & N imprint.

During the 1980s, Barnes & Noble experimented with a number of store footprints and sizes as it continued to grow. It purchased the B. Dalton mall store chain in 1987, which overnight made it the largest book retailer in the United States. Two years later it purchased the discount superstore chain BookStop, which gave it the necessary know-how and infrastructure to create what, in 1992, became the definitive bookselling superstore. The company describes their store concept as an "information piazza" that combines knowledgeable staff with comfortable surroundings—cafés, music offerings, upholstered chairs—and, of course, a vast stock of books.

Barnes & Noble was also an early adopter of the internet, shifting relatively smoothly from the catalogue-based mail-order sales system it had developed in the 1970s to a web-based one in the late 1990s. Barnesandnoble.com is now one of the largest online booksellers, with over 1 million new titles in stock and links to used and out-of-print stock through approved merchants as well. The bookseller has also aggressively pursued the e-reader market, releasing its first Nook in 2009 and beating the competition to the market with the first color e-reader the following year. Through all its rapid growth, and despite some bibliophiles' complaints about the homogenized shopping experience offered by Barnes & Noble and its competitors, the company has maintained an admirable record of customer satisfaction, regularly scoring high marks in independently conducted surveys.

prominently, but they also undertook to support the smaller indigenous book clubs in their communities. They stocked individual book clubs' selections and provided meeting space and other useful services, all of which helped to bring committed, book-buying readers into their stores on a regular basis. (Book clubs are discussed in more detail in Chapter 10.)

Another concern was that the superstores would leverage their purchasing power to try to drive down prices and cut into publishers' profits. This does seem to have happened, and all of the chains appear to have negotiated fiercely, even though the publishers are reluctant to complain about it on the record. For example, one publisher interviewed by the *Guardian* newspaper pointed out that one of his firm's novels sold 60 per cent of its run through Waterstone's. "So I'm not going to slag them off even though I hate what they're doing to bookselling in this country," he said testily. Until 1991 British booksellers had largely adhered to the Net Book Agreement, which stated that retailers would sell books at the prices recommended by the publishers. The agreement had been in place for nearly a century, since 1900, but Waterstone's was the first to break it and offer books at a discount. The agreement almost immediately collapsed (and it was ruled illegal in 1997), but so did many of the independent booksellers, who could not afford to meet or beat Waterstone's prices.

However, just as the ordinary mall bookstores would find themselves superseded by the big-box stores, the superstores themselves soon had a rival looming over them. The next big thing—the biggest thing so far in the history of bookselling—was just around the corner: internet-based book sales, led by the largest e-retailer of them all, Amazon.com.

ONLINE BOOKSELLERS

The internet first became a social force in the late 1980s and early 1990s. Early on, commercial providers such as CompuServe and AOL offered their clients some retail options, while governments, institutions of higher education, and some businesses began to build websites that provided goods and services to online customers. However, it was the launch of Amazon.com that set off the current age of e-commerce, and particularly online bookselling. Amazon's success prompted traditional bricks-and-mortar retailers to launch their own sales sites and inspired the creation of a large number of specialist online booksellers. Crucially, it also sparked the creation of a number of *aggregators*, who operate online marketplaces for booksellers, especially used book dealers. In addition to Alibris, Abebooks, and Amazon Marketplace, other important bookselling aggregators in the English-speaking world are the International League of Antiquarian Booksellers, UK Bookworld, and Bibliocom.

The Internet Superstore: Amazon.com

By 1994, if you had the right equipment, you could order a pizza online. But it wasn't until the following year, 1995, that the bookselling world would be fundamentally changed by a new venture that promised—eventually—to put all of the world's books within reach of any reader with just a few clicks of a mouse. Seattle entrepreneur Jeff Bezos (b. 1964) arguably had the grandest vision for the sales potential of the web. He realized that the internet could liberate both buyers and sellers from their particular locales: anyone, anywhere, could advertise on the web, and the advertised products could be shipped to anyone, anywhere. After its launch, Amazon.com quickly diversified from books into a vast range of other products, and it has since opened websites and distribution centers around the world.

Besides recognizing that the internet had real potential to become something more than a handy way to stay in touch with friends and family, Bezos's main insight was that a virtual bookseller would have some significant economic advantages over a traditional bricks-and-mortar store. In the first place, it would not need to invest in those bricks and mortar, nor maintain them—a significant, and immediate, reduction in retail overhead. Furthermore, a virtual bookseller would not need a flesh-and-blood sales staff to be on duty during opening hours, only technical and customer service staff to create and maintain the inventory and customer account databases. Opening hours? Those could be all day, every day, at no additional cost, and the technical and customer service employees could report for duty any time, from almost anywhere, as long as the work got done. Inventory itself was originally intended to be virtual: initially, Amazon placed orders directly with the publishers and had the books shipped directly to customers. When this proved not to work as efficiently as hoped, Amazon set up a large network of massive distribution centers and began filling orders directly.

From its relatively modest but ambitious start in Seattle, Amazon has grown to include sites in the United Kingdom, Germany, France, Japan, Canada, Italy, and China, and it now ships goods to nearly 200 countries. According to the company, Amazon's many distribution sites around the globe encompass more than 26 million square feet of merchandise, including not only books but electronics, sporting goods, and even jewelry. Amazon Marketplace, its third-party partnership program, has more than 2,000 members and constitutes about one-third of total sales. Amazon's proprietary e-book reader, the Kindle, was first launched in 2007. The Kindle comes in several styles and price points, which has helped to significantly boost its sales: Amazon sold 4 million of the devices in December 2011 alone. Sales of Kindle-format e-books overtook hardcover books by the middle of 2010 and paperbacks by the end of that year, and by mid-2011, Amazon reported that e-books for Kindle were outselling *all* printed books combined. (Free Kindle e-books are excluded from these sales figures.)

For many would-be book buyers, Amazon was even more exhilarating than the superstores had been, and it was not entirely hubristic for the company to begin billing itself as offering the "Earth's Biggest Selection." Nearly every book currently in print could be ordered from one source and delivered directly to the customer's doorstep. And those books were usually less expensive than the same titles at the local store (assuming there was a local store, and that it stocked them), both because Amazon passed along its savings in overhead and because it pursued a rather cutthroat pricing policy to build up a solid customer base. To keep those customers, Amazon enacted shipping policies that favored larger purchases (free shipping on orders over a total amount, special deals for customers in loyalty programs). As the online catalogue expanded and became ever easier to use, with recommendations, tie-ins, birthday reminders, and wish lists pushing titles before readers' eyes, Amazon's "one-click shopping" also became more seductive.

But for other book buyers, Amazon.com was a nightmare. Its enormous catalogue and alluring ease of use represented a real and ever-growing threat to bricks-and-mortar stores, whether independent, mall-based, or big-box. Smaller independent stores that had managed to stave off the threats from the chain stores by providing above-average customer service learned to their sorrow that special orders were no longer enough to keep their customers coming back. The remaining mall stores saw their comparative price advantage dissipate, and the big boxes lost on both price and backlists. As all of these local stores began to contract or even to close their doors, readers increasingly lost their ability to browse among real, physical books. The tactile relationship with the book that is so important to many readers—the ability to stroke the paper, to flex the spine, to smell the ink—was under siege. Bricks-and-mortar stores had long nurtured readers' desire to dip into the pages before deciding to commit to a book: those comfortable chairs and hot drinks encouraged readers to sit down and become better acquainted with a new discovery. Crucially, the real bookstores' ranks of full and enticing shelves had also enabled the serendipity of discovering a book never imagined but absolutely fit to purpose. If it was no longer possible to browse idly among a variety of physical books, how would such discoveries be made?

Perhaps not surprisingly, as it increased its share of the book market, Amazon also sought to replicate some of the experiences of real-life browsing. One result was the "look inside" or "search inside" feature now offered for a significant number of titles. By digitizing select portions of the books—typically most of the front and back matter, as well as some representative passages from the main content—Amazon has endeavored to make it possible for readers to virtually thumb through the pages, sampling the author's approach and at least theoretically making it possible to decide if the rest of the book would be worth reading. Increasingly sophisticated search engines have also made it easier to find, say, all titles on a particular subject or all books by a given author, thus approximating the experience of browsing along an actual bookshelf.

Although the truly physical aspects of book shopping—touch and smell—still elude e-commerce, a generous policy on returns means that readers who wish to inspect their books more closely can take a chance on ordering them.

Other Internet Booksellers

Although Amazon.com is by far the largest online bookseller, it has never been the only one. Perhaps ironically, one of the other early e-commerce ventures was intended in part to prevent the kind of hegemonic power over the book-buying public that Amazon has come to hold. Abebooks—created as Advanced Book Exchange—was originally intended to counter the pressure chain stores were exerting on independent booksellers. It was a searchable online database that combined the electronic catalogues of hundreds of independent booksellers, initially in the United States, but soon, with the acquisition of German and later Spanish sites, all over the world. At the outset, Abebooks was geared to the used book trade, but it quickly expanded into new books as well, and in 2008 it was acquired by Amazon.com, which now operates Abebooks as a stand-alone operation.

Another increasingly significant player in the online book market is eBay. Also founded in 1995, eBay—originally AuctionWeb—was created by computer programmer Pierre Omidyar (b. 1967) as a kind of experiment in internet sales. Since its creation, it has grown to embrace over 94 million users worldwide, with over $62 billion in gross volume sales. In 2002 the company acquired both the PayPal online payment system and the discount site Half.com to further support its business plan. eBay currently offers nine different categories of books, including e-books.

DISTRIBUTORS AND WHOLESALERS

Although this chapter has so far been concerned with retail book sales, most books do not go directly from the publishers to the retailers. Instead, they are channeled through distributors and wholesalers. Although the two words are sometimes used almost interchangeably and they provide similar services, distributors and wholesalers organize their businesses differently. *Distributors* work more closely with publishers: they provide physical warehousing for publishers' books and sell books to both wholesale and retail customers on terms dictated by the publishers. *Wholesalers* work more closely with retailers and libraries, and their terms are generally dictated by those end customers. According to American distributor Partners Publishers Group (PPG), wholesale discounts tend to run about 55 per cent off the retail price, while distributors' discounts run between 65 and 70 per cent. Wholesalers are also usually nonexclusive (they allow their customers to use multiple services), while distributors prefer exclusive contracts.

Like most of the other players in the contemporary publishing world, book distributors and wholesalers emerged in the nineteenth century, providing an invaluable service to publishers and booksellers. In an era of constantly expanding literacy and demand for books, publishers would have found it impossible to effectively advertise their publications to the myriad booksellers and libraries throughout their potential markets. And booksellers and libraries, especially smaller ones, would have found the task of surveying all the existing publishers' lists to find books they might like to stock similarly daunting. Distributors and wholesalers provided the essential linking services: they selected titles from publishers' catalogues that they thought they could sell on, acquired quantities of them at a reduced price for their warehouses, and aggregated the resulting lists. Bookstores and libraries could then contact their preferred distributors or wholesalers for information about new titles from a wide range of publishers, select the most promising ones, and arrange to have those particular titles shipped to them.

Some of the earliest wholesalers and distributors were W.H. Smith, which built on its own enormous purchasing power in the United Kingdom to create a wholesale business for other booksellers (its current wholesale descendant is Bertrams), and Simpkin, Marshall, a publisher founded in 1814 that ran a major centralized book distribution center from its headquarters in London from at least 1889 to 1940, when its premises were destroyed in the Blitz. Baker & Taylor in Charlotte, North Carolina, began as a publisher and binder in 1828, but later in the century it moved into distribution. It now claims to be the world's largest distributor of books and entertainment media, with over 1.5 million titles in stock and 36,000 customers in 120 countries. (The company earned the affection of many booklovers for its eponymous cat mascots, who took up residence in the early 1980s in a Baker & Taylor box in the Douglas County Public Library in Minden, Nevada.) Other important companies in the wholesale end of the publishing industry include Ingram Book Company, established in 1964 and based in Nashville, which claims to be the largest wholesaler in the world, with over 2 million titles and 71,000 retail and library customers; TBS (The Book Service Ltd.), the main distribution arm of Bertelsmann and now the United Kingdom's largest distributor, with over 100 million books distributed annually, and 9,000 customers worldwide; and Gardners Books, a UK distributor that claims to have the largest range of books and other media in stock.

Wholesalers and distributors typically purchase books from publishers at a discount, usually about 35 to 40 per cent. This discount covers their costs and also provides a margin for the booksellers' overhead and profits as well. Some of the larger booksellers, including some superstore chains like Barnes & Noble and especially online retailer Amazon, have enough outlets and potential sales that they purchase directly from publishers and provide their own distribution. Amazon, for example, now has multiple distribution centers around the globe to ensure that it can fulfill orders as quickly as possible. Some non-specialist big-box stores also buy direct from publishers. For example, an article in the *Wall Street Journal* reports that the American discount giant Costco sometimes purchases as much as 25 to 30 per cent of the print run for titles its book buyer, Pennie Ianniciello, thinks will do well in the stores. The stores stock a maximum of 200 titles in its typical no-nonsense, no-frills retailing style: the books are piled on large, 85-foot tables, offered at discounts as high as a whopping 40 per cent off, and if they don't sell quickly, they are pulled. It isn't an aesthetic experience, but classic and contemporary books that appear in the "Pennie's Picks" column of the store's online newsletter typically see a big boost in sales.

This overall system of distributing books has worked fairly effectively for the past century and more, but it has one drawback—a drawback that in most countries distinguishes books from other consumer goods. In order to make it economically viable for these companies to serve as warehouses and distributors for publishers, most arrange to take the books on a *sale-or-return* basis. In other words, they purchase the books on spec: if the books are not sold on to retail customers within a specified period of time, they can be returned to the publisher for a refund. Now, if this were the only link in the sales chain, the business model would be fairly straightforward, but the same sale-or-return terms are typically passed on by the wholesalers and distributors to their retail clients. This means, in effect, that when a bookstore purchases a quantity of books, the sale is only truly "final" if the books are bought by customers who don't return them. If the books either don't sell or are returned to the store, the store can return them to the distributor, the distributor can return them to the publisher, and everyone gets their money back—except for the publisher, who is left with a stock of what is evidently unsalable merchandise, destined to be remaindered or pulped, and the author, who can be left with the puzzle of a negative royalty statement. Books, in essence, are one of the only consumer items that can be *un*-sold.

BOOK FAIRS

Another long-established way of connecting publishers with booksellers are *book fairs*, publishing trade shows held at regular intervals around the world. Book fairs bring publishers, authors, agents, wholesalers, retailers, and others interested in the book trade together to share lists of forthcoming titles, develop new partnerships for translation and other subsidiary rights, celebrate recent achievements, and try to take the measure of emerging trends. Book fairs of various kinds have been in existence since the Middle Ages, and one of largest and most venerable is the Frankfurt Book Fair. Although the Frankfurt Fair predates the age of Gutenberg, it rose to its current importance in the first century of the print era. In addition to printers and publishers, early book fairs like Frankfurt's also attracted typefounders, engravers, translators, proof cor-

THE FRANKFURT BOOK FAIR

One of the largest and oldest book fairs in the world, the Frankfurt Book Fair grew in importance in the century after Gutenberg invented the printing press. By 1569, it was already one of the most important book fairs in Europe, attracting nearly a hundred printer-publishers from across Germany, Switzerland, France, Italy, and the Netherlands. In addition to providing meeting space for the attendees, the city also provided warehouse space, so that any unsold books could be held over for sale at the next Fair. Originally, the Frankfurt Fair convened twice a year, in both spring and fall; today, the Fair happens annually in mid-October.

Because of its long history and importance to the trade, information about the early centuries of the Frankfurt Fair is fairly easy to come by. Early print-er-publishers went to enormous pains to bring their works to Frankfurt. For example, in 1534, the Geneva printer Christoph Froschauer (c. 1490–1564) brought along for sale 2,000 copies of one of the first world atlases to include the Americas, Joachim Vadian's (1484–1551) *Epitome trium terrae partium*. By 1574, the French printer Henri Estienne (c. 1528–98) described the Frankfurt Fair as "la nouvelle Athènes" (the new Athens), a place where a prince could come to equip an army. Catalogues of books for sale at the Fair were printed from 1590 until the end of the eighteenth century, and the surviving copies provide a detailed survey of the range and variety of works printed in Europe during that time.

Frankfurt Book Fair Catalogue, 1551. (5496714). Copyright © Imagebroker RM/F1online.

Although the Frankfurt Book Fair has remained active for more than 500 years, it has suffered some setbacks. For example, although both Protestant and Catholic publications were circulated freely in the first century after Gutenberg, in 1579 the Holy Roman Emperor Rudolf II (1552–1612) began to censor which books could be exhibited, and many book dealers decamped to Leipzig.

In recent decades, the Frankfurt Book Fair has drawn as many as 300,000 visitors, who include not only book trade members but also persons involved in the film, multimedia, and other associated industries. According to the official website, the Fair annually brings together over 7,400 exhibitors from 100 countries. In addition to the displays and meetings among the various players, the Fair sponsors an educational program, the Frankfurt Academy, to help publishing professionals stay abreast of trends, and it also hosts a variety of online publishing resources. Other recent developments include the annual practice of featuring one country as a "Guest of Honor": in 2012, the Guest of Honor was New Zealand; in 2013 it is Brazil; and in 2014 it will be Finland. The featured country's book trades thereby receive an extra measure of visibility and promotion.

rectors, and authors, all of whom were seeking new information, techniques, and opportunities.

Other important book fairs include those in Leipzig, which held pride of place from the 1630s until after World War II; the Cairo Book Fair, the largest fair in the Arab world and the second-largest after Frankfurt, with as many as 2 million annual visitors; the Buenos Aires International Book Fair (*Feria Internacional del Libro de Buenos Aires*), which is not only one of the largest in Latin America but one of the largest in the world, with over 1 million visitors each April; and the Beijing International Book Fair, now considered one of the top four fairs in the world and growing annually. Book fairs are also held annually or biennially in many other cities, including Geneva, Prague, New York City (BookExpo America), Seoul, Tokyo, and Warsaw. Besides hosting trade and educational events, some book fairs also sponsor various literary prizes.

However, there are many smaller book fairs as well, designed to draw local and regional authors, readers, and sellers together, and some that bill themselves as "festivals" instead. One such event is the much-loved Hay Festival, held annually for the past quarter-century in Hay-on-Wye, the "Town of Books" in the Brecon Beacons of Wales, just near the English border. Although tiny (population 1,500), Hay is a bookselling mecca in the United Kingdom, with over thirty shops selling mostly secondhand books. The town draws upwards of a half-million visitors each year, many during the late spring Festival. The hilly streets in Hay are a wonderful mix of carefully tended specialist shops and what appear to be jumble sale leftovers. In his account of life in Hay-on-Wye, American-born writer Paul Collins describes the spillover from self-proclaimed "King of Hay" and Festival inaugurator Richard Booth's (b. 1938) bookshop:

> In a field at the bottom of the castle hill is a motley collection of rusted
> metal bookshelves and clapped-out old hardcover books, all left to
> sit in the open air. This is the end of the line for the printed word, the
> place where absolutely unsalable books from Booth's stock wind up....
> These unfortunate volumes are not brought inside at the end of the
> day; they just sit out in the wind and the rain until some buyer takes
> pity on them and drops a few pence into the unmanned box, or until
> the action of sun and moisture upon the paper decomposes the books
> into pulp.

Whether retail or wholesale, booksellers perform a vital function for authors and readers. They bridge the gulf between the one and the other, bringing an author's ideas and insights into contact with those for whom they are intended. Booksellers' efforts are complemented by the work of another key player in the book circuit, libraries, whose development is traced in the next chapter.

SELECTED BIBLIOGRAPHY

Abebooks. http://www.abebooks.com.

Amazon. http//www.amazon.com.

American Booksellers Association. http://bookweb.org.

Austen, Ben. "The End of Borders and the Future of Books." *Bloomberg Businessweek*, 10 November 2011.

Australian Bureau of Statistics. http://www.abs.gove.au/AUSSTATS.

Baker & Taylor. http://www.btol.com.

Barnes & Noble. http://www.barnesandnoble.com/.

Basbanes, Nicholas. *Patience and Fortitude*. New York: HarperCollins, 2001.

Bertrams. http://www.bertrams.com.

Book Industry Study Group (BISG). *Used-Book Sales: A Study of the Behavior, Structure, Size and Growth of the US Used-Book Market*. New York: BISG, 2006.

Booksellers Association. http://www.booksellers.org.uk.

Booksellers Association. Used Books: A Brief Overview. 2006. http://www.booksellers.org.uk/BookSellers/media/SiteMediaLibrary/News%26Industry/Used-Books-A-Brief-Overview.pdf.

Booksellers New Zealand. http://www.booksellers.co.nz.

Carter, John, and Nicolas Barker. *ABC for Book Collectors*. 8th ed. London: British Library, 2004.

Collins, Paul. *Sixpence House: Lost in a Town of Books*. London: Bloomsbury, 2003.

Eisenstein, Elizabeth L. *The Printing Revolution in Early Modern Europe*. Cambridge: Cambridge UP, 1983.

Fischer, Steven Roger. *A History of Reading*. London: Reaktion Books, 2003.

W&G Foyle Ltd. http://www.foyles.co.uk/about-foyles.

Frankfurt Book Fair. http://www.book-fair.com/en/.

Gardners Books. http://www.gardners.com.

Glaister, Geoffrey Ashall. *Encyclopedia of the Book*. 2nd ed. New Castle, DE: Oak Knoll, 1996.

Greco, Albert N., Clara E. Rodríguez, and Robert M. Wharton. *The Culture and Commerce of Publishing in the 21st Century*. Stanford: Stanford UP, 2007.

Higuchi, Siichi. "The Book Market of Japan." Presentation at Frankfurt Book Fair, October 2007.

Indigo Books and Music, Inc. Timeline and History of Canada's Bookstore; Company Fast Facts. http://www.chapters.indigo.ca/home.

Ingram Book Co. http://www.ingramcontent.com.

Jeffries, Stuart. "Sold Out." *The Guardian*, 10 November 2009.

Kaestle, Carl F.; and Janice A. Radway, eds. *A History of the Book in America, Volume 4. Motion: The Expansion of Publishing and Reading in the United States, 1880–1940*. Chapel Hill: U of North Carolina P, 2009.

Kaplan, Marcia. "Amazon Prime: 5 Million Members, 20 Percent." *Practical Ecommerce*, 16 September 2011. http://www.practicalcommerce.com/articles.

Khosravi, Shahram. "Disappearing Bookstores: A Letter from Sweden, Toronto, and Iran." *The Toronto Review of Books*, 17 April 2012. http://www.torontoreviewofbooks. com.

Lamonde, Yvan, Patricia Lockart Fleming, and Fiona A. Black. *History of the Book in Canada. Volume 2: 1840–1918*. Toronto: U of Toronto P, 2005.

Mandelbrote, Giles, ed. *Out of Print and Into Profit: A History of the Rare and Secondhand Book Trade in Britain in the Twentieth Century*. London: British Library and Oak Knoll, 2006.

Moeran, Brian. "The Field of Japanese Publishing." *Creative Encounters Working Paper 46*. Copenhagen: Creativity at Work, 2010.

Partners Publishers Group (PPG). http://partnerspublishersgroup.com.

Pepys, Samuel. *The Diary of Samuel Pepys: A Selection*. Ed. Robert Latham. London: Penguin, 1985.

Powell's Books. http://www.powells.com.

Rose, Matthew. "Selling Literature Like Dog Food Gives Club Buyer Real Bite." *Wall Street Journal*, 10 April 2002.

Rosen, Judith. "Used Books: On the Up and Up." *Publishers Weekly*, 9 August 2010.

WHSmith PLC. History of W.H. Smith. http://www.whsmithplc.co.uk/about_ whsmith/history_of_whsmith.

Strand Book Store. http://www.strandbooks.com/.

TBS. http://www.thebookservice.co.uk.

Teather, David. "Raconteur Who Wrestled to Keep Foyles in the Family." *The Guardian*, 1 November 2007.

Whitlock, Nathan. "Will the Last Bookstore Please Turn Out the Lights?" *Globe and Mail*, 17 July 2010.

CHAPTER NINE

LIBRARIES

Libraries are collections of books and other materials that are gathered for use but not for sale. For many readers, libraries are even more important resources than bookstores: they are the most powerful and widespread institutions dedicated to making book culture available to individuals of all ages, languages, and socioeconomic backgrounds. Located in population centers both large and small and often free, libraries expand readers' options in almost infinite directions. A private collection in an individual's home can provide hours of pleasure and a record of one's thoughts and encounters over the years. A school or neighborhood public library can open children's eyes to wonders previously unimagined. An academic library or specialist archive can bring together the world's wisdom in ways that bring a subject alive and prepare the soil for new discoveries in science and the arts. And a national library can serve as a living monument to the achievements and aspirations of a whole people, collecting and preserving the record of accomplishments (and failures) that provide light for future generations.

Libraries and *archives*, or collections of largely informational documents and other materials, appear to have been in existence since the earliest times. Historian Lionel Casson (1914–2009) explains that one of the oldest libraries or archives discovered by archaeologists dates from around 2300 BCE, in the ancient city of Ebla in Syria. The library consists of about 2,000 clay tablets, with subjects ranging from administrative records related to produce and trade to incantations and Sumerian myths. It also includes tablets that seem to have comprised the ancient library's reference section: lists of Sumerian words for various items, as well as translations of lists of Sumerian words into Eblaite. The earliest evidence of library catalogues are nearly as old, from about 2000 BCE. By the thirteenth century BCE, such catalogues had added useful innovations, such as bibliographic notes that identified titles, authors, and the general content of the tablets in the collection. The existence of such catalogues provide evidence that larger and more comprehensive libraries were being amassed, libraries that were large enough to require more than one individual's memory to keep them organized and useful.

However, although libraries have an ancient pedigree, ideas about how libraries should be organized and who should have access to them have changed significantly over the millennia. This chapter will look at the evolution of the modern library, from the late eighteenth and nineteenth centuries to the present day. Over the last 200-plus years, libraries around the globe have changed in response to improvements in literacy and expanded access to educational opportunities. Two important developments in the modern era have been the rise of the public library movement and the creation of national libraries. These changes have been accompanied by the professionalization of library care and management, or *library science*, and they have also spurred developments in academic and private libraries and archives. As their collections have grown and changed, librarians, archivists, and other collection curators have directed more attention to the preservation and conservation of the books and materials in their care. Most recently, the digitization of library collections has become one of the most exciting—and sometimes most controversial—topics related to the future of libraries.

THE EVOLUTION OF THE LIBRARY: ANCIENT GREECE TO THE RENAISSANCE

Many of the features of the modern library have their roots in Ancient Greece, one of the first cultures to support the relatively high literacy rates required to generate both enough texts and enough readers to give rise to libraries. In *Libraries of the Ancient World*, Lionel Casson suggests that the key components were in place by the fourth century BCE: numerous texts on a wide range of subjects were available, scriptoria were able to provide copies at reasonable prices, and people were beginning to collect them. Over the next couple of centuries, both personal and royal libraries began to be established, most notably the great library of Alexandria, in about 300 BCE. At its height, the library is believed to have contained nearly half a million scrolls and also some codices. The sheer size of the library's collections meant that it was necessarily an innovator in library science. To the library's directors over the years, we owe such helpful developments in bibliography as ordering collections alphabetically, sorting them by categories, developing catalogues and shelf lists, and developing labels. Scholars who worked at Alexandria also laid the groundwork for such literary fields as grammar, lexicography, commentaries, and textual criticism. Greek libraries such as those in Alexandria and in Pergamum also appear to have provided models for what are still familiar features of libraries: compact stacks complemented by well-lit areas in which readers can spread out their books.

The libraries at Alexandria and Pergamum were created and maintained by royal patrons, and they were presumably intended for the use of nobles and scholars. However, there is some evidence that Ancient Greece was also the origin of more publicly supported and accessed libraries. For example, inscriptions from Athens, Rhodes, Cos, and elsewhere list the names of individuals who contributed to the establishment of libraries: some donated books, and others gave money for the building and the collections. Some or all of these libraries may have been attached to the gymnasiums used for athletic and military training.

Officials and guests attend the opening of the new Library of Alexandria in Egypt, 16 October 2002. Patrick Kovarik/ AFP/Getty Images.

To a certain extent, the Romans followed the Greek model in libraries as they had in other aspects of culture. We have numerous accounts from letters and other documents of the contents of cultivated Romans' own libraries, and excavations at Herculaneum, which was buried along with Pompeii in CE 79 by the eruption of Vesuvius, reveal what a private citizen's library looked like. The library of the Villa of the Papyri consists of a small room whose walls were lined with eye-level shelves and which also had a large, free-standing, double-sided bookshelf in the middle of the room. The room contained about 1,800 papyrus rolls that could be removed to an adjacent colonnade where the light would be suitable for reading.

In addition to private libraries, the Romans also had public libraries. Rome itself had at least three between 39 BCE and CE 14 and several more afterwards, and there were also libraries in other locales. The remains of the library on the Palatine Hill, constructed by the emperor Augustus (63 BCE–CE 14) in 28 BCE, and of a nearby one constructed in about CE 112 by the emperor Trajan (53–117), provide valuable clues about the appearance and organization of Roman public libraries. Because the collections included both Greek and Latin works, which were customarily shelved separately, everything was duplicated: both libraries featured two large rooms containing statuary and featuring niches along the side walls for fitted wooden bookcases with closing doors, as well as central areas containing tables and chairs for readers. The scrolls would have been laid on shelves in the bookcases with their identifying tags out towards the readers, and the height of the niches suggests that there must have been movable wooden steps available to reach the highest shelves. Trajan's library also apparently contained metal screens between the supporting columns, so that the stacks could be closed off from the central public spaces after hours. The vast size of Trajan's library suggests that it likely held about 20,000 scrolls. In addition to these large purpose-built libraries, the Romans also constructed public libraries as part of other public complexes, particularly as part of the recreational and cultural facilities associated with public baths.

As discussed in Chapter 2, the decline of the Roman Empire brought about a decline in literacy and book culture in Europe. The libraries that survived were primarily associated with nobility or with monasteries, and the emphasis in most of the religious communities was on collecting Bibles and other important Christian texts. While many of these medieval monastic libraries seem to have contained few books, there were some notable exceptions. The scholar Cassiodorus (c. 485–585) founded a monastery in southern Italy that he called the Vivarium, founded in part on the principle that the study and copying of all kinds of texts was a high calling, not mere drudgework. Casson reports that the library at the Vivarium included not only all the important

THE VATICAN LIBRARY

Although there is evidence that the Roman Catholic Church was collecting books and archives as early as the fourth century, most of those items were dispersed in the first half of the thirteenth century. Therefore, the earliest of the vast collections that make up the modern Vatican Library in Rome, officially the Bibliotheca Apostolica Vaticana, date back only to the mid-fourteenth century. Pope Nicholas V (1397–1455) is credited with ordering that the manuscripts acquired by himself and his predecessors be organized and made available to scholars, and he established a single reading room to that end. Sixtus IV (1414–84) completed this work, nominating the first librarian and moving the collection into a building facing on the cortile del Belvedere. The new library building was divided into four rooms: the Bibliotheca Latina and Bibliotheca Graeca, for books and manuscripts in those languages; the Bibliotheca Secreta, for materials not directly available to readers (despite the name, neither this nor the Vatican Secret Archives are actually closed to consultation—they merely entail closed stacks); and the Bibliotheca Pontificia, for papal archives. Although most readers consulted the works on site, loans were also made.

The Vatican Library expanded greatly from the sixteenth to the eighteenth centuries, as succeeding librarians actively sought out purchases and bequests of major collections of works, both secular and sacred. The current building was authorized by Sixtus V (1520–90) and designed by Domenico Fontana (1543–1607), who was responsible for a number of buildings and renovations in the Vatican. Among the many large and valuable collections of books that were added in this expansive period were the Palatine library of Heidelberg, the library of the Dukes of

Christian works, but nearly all those of the major Latin and Greek pagan writers, as well. Cassiodorus's book of guidelines, the *Institutiones*, served as inspiration for many later monastic libraries, including those established by the Irish missionary Columbanus (540–615) and his followers.

It would be another thousand years before something like the Roman public libraries began to reappear in Europe. Historian Matthew Battles describes how Italian Renaissance princes and patrons like Cosimo de' Medici (1389–1464) began to amass books and build monuments to learning—and, not incidentally, to themselves. The Florentine scholar and bookseller Vespasiano da Bisticci (1421–98) served as a consultant to many who were building collections and libraries in fifteenth-century Italy, including the Medici family, the duke of Urbino, Federico da Montefeltro (1422–82), and Pope Nicholas V. His influence can be seen in some of the greatest Italian libraries, from the sumptuous San Marco and Laurentian libraries in Florence to the Vatican Library in Rome. In his *Lives of Illustrious Men of the XVth Century*, Vespasiano described what Battles calls the "appetite" for books that consumed his patrons. The duke of Urbino "had a mind to do what no one had done for a thousand years or

Urbino, the books of Queen Christina of Sweden (1626–89), and the Capponi and Ottoboni libraries. The acquisition of a significant number of objects during this period also led to the creation of two museums, the Museo Sacro, which featured Christian artifacts, and the Museo Profano, which featured secular ones. Efforts were also made in this period to produce a comprehensive catalogue of the collection, but only a partial version was actually published.

In the early nineteenth century, when Rome was annexed to the French Empire under Napoléon Bonaparte (1769–1821), the Vatican Library became a National Library, and the printed books collection was significantly expanded. Towards the end of the century, under the directions of Leo XIII (1810–1903), the library was reorganized so that it could accommodate more researchers, and a new Reading Room for Printed Books was opened up. Both card catalogues and printed catalogues were also prepared at this time and were continued until the electronic catalogue was completed at the turn of the twenty-first century.

The Vatican Library's collections expanded exponentially during the nineteenth century, when it became one of the largest libraries in the world, a standing it maintains today. To increase its utility to scholars around the world, many of the Vatican Library's manuscripts were microfilmed beginning in the 1950s, and the films are now housed at the Pius XII Memorial Library in St. Louis, Missouri. The library presently contains over 180,000 manuscripts, over 1.6 million printed books, including nearly 9,000 incunabula, as well as coins, medals, prints, drawings, and photographs. Library historian Matthew Battles calls it "one of the most delightful scholarly libraries in the world."

more; that is, to create the finest library since ancient times. He spared neither cost nor labour, and when he knew of a fine book, whether in Italy, or not, he would send for it." The duke pursued "the only way to make a fine library like this": he bought up all the Latin poets and the relevant commentaries on them, then moved on to the orators, grammarians, and historians, and finally added the Greek writers as well. These Renaissance cathedrals of learning weren't public in the sense that the Roman ones had been, or that future libraries would be, but they were self-contained storehouses of the world's wisdom that could be accessed by scholars. And the systematic, all-embracing collecting principles that Vespasiano urged on his patrons became the basis for grand libraries of later ages, most notably the great national libraries.

MODERN LIBRARIES

From the Renaissance to the eighteenth century, the number of libraries across Europe gradually increased, and libraries began to be built in the European colonies in North America as well. Many of these libraries were private collections or incorporated into religious and academic institutions. Others were subscription-based libraries. Subscription libraries might be organized by communities, trade guilds, or others who banded together to purchase a collection of books that could be accessed by members, either on the premises or perhaps on loan. Benjamin Franklin (1706–90) established such a library in 1731, made up primarily of the personal books owned by members of his literary club, the Junto. The resulting subscription library, the Philadelphia Library Company, inspired imitators throughout the North American colonies. In the nineteenth century, mechanics' institutes were important sites for subscription libraries that provided access to books for working-class people in Europe and elsewhere, although because they often privileged scientific, technical, and other "improving" works over entertaining ones, their offerings were sometimes a little dry.

Commercial libraries were also on the rise. By the late seventeenth century, many printers and booksellers organized *circulating libraries*, lending fiction and other popular literature by the volume for a nominal subscription fee. Although many of these were managed on a local basis and remained fairly modest in size, some were much larger ventures. The largest and most successful was Mudie's Select Library in London, which held the lion's share of the circulating-book business throughout the British Empire for nearly a century, from 1842 to 1937. Subscribers at Mudie's basic level could check out as many as three volumes at a time and exchange them whenever they were ready for a new one. In addition to individual and family subscriptions, Mudie's also offered packages for groups and institutions, enabling far-flung communities to maintain small but up-to-date libraries. The company's special boxes and trunks of reading materials could be ordered in person, by letter, or by telegraph and were promptly dispatched almost anywhere in the Empire.

There were also *traveling* or *itinerating libraries* during this period. One such library was created in 1817 by Samuel Brown of Haddington, Scotland. According to historian Richard Altick (1915–2008), Brown bought 200 volumes, divided them into four sets, and sent each set to a different village in East Lothian. After two years, the collection was replaced by another set and sent on to the next village. Within twenty years, Brown's itinerating library had grown to over 2,000 volumes and forty-seven circulating sets. This traveling library model was also used in Canada: for example, in the 1820s, the Edinburgh Ladies Association in Cape Breton created such a library to circulate religious literature and works in Gaelic among communities in Nova Scotia. And in 1837, there were reports that the explorer John Franklin (1786–1847) was planning to set up such a system in Van Diemen's Land, or what is now modern Tasmania.

In addition, some libraries during this period were created as public institutions. However, Altick warns that most of these were "public" in only a very limited sense. The founders seldom left money to maintain the buildings or the collections, and the collections themselves often consisted of theological and other scholarly works that were of little use or interest to ordinary readers. For example, Chetham's Library in Manchester, the oldest public library in Britain, was founded in 1653 by Humphrey Chetham, a successful cloth merchant who also endowed a school for underprivileged boys. Unlike many other library founders, Chetham had indeed endowed his library sufficiently. But nearly 200 years later, when the Public Libraries Committee of the House of Commons summoned Chetham's librarian to describe the library and its users, the librarian boasted about Chetham's antiquarian holdings (the library still contains one of the best collections of sixteenth-century books in existence) and complained that of the few readers who did apply for admission, many simply wanted access to the latest popular periodicals.

However unsatisfactory the Chetham librarian's 1849 parliamentary testimony may have been, the very fact that there was a Public Libraries Committee at that time, and that it was inquiring into the provision of public access to books, shows that there had been some significant changes in attitudes over the previous centuries about what ordinary people had to read. The democratic movements and socioeconomic reforms of the eighteenth and early nineteenth centuries had fostered new views about the importance of education, of which library access was one significant component. The era gave rise to three key developments in the history of libraries: the public library movement, the rise of national libraries, and the professionalization of librarianship.

THE PUBLIC LIBRARY MOVEMENT

The public library movement arose in Europe and North America in the nineteenth century, as a logical outgrowth of increasing state support for literacy and education. Most of the earliest examples of public libraries depended primarily on patrons and societies for support. By the early 1830s, political and cultural leaders in Great Britain began to discuss the idea of state-supported libraries in relation to other government reforms, but the idea was contentious; by 1845, what had originally been an act allowing taxation to create publicly funded libraries and museums was passed with only the museum levy in place. Thus, the honor of creating one of the first tax-supported public libraries in the English-speaking world fell instead to Peterborough, New Hampshire. The town library was founded in 1833 and is still operating today.

However, the supporters of public libraries in Britain continued to press their case, and the hearings before the Public Libraries Committee in 1848 and 1849 were a result of that pressure. In 1850, a new bill was proposed in Parliament to fund museums and libraries, and this time it was passed. The 1850 Public Libraries Act authorized boroughs in England and Wales that had at least 10,000 residents to raise a halfpenny on the pound for the construction of public library and museum buildings—but only if a sufficient number of

MUDIE'S SELECT LIBRARY

Of the many subscription circulating libraries in the nineteenth century, by far the greatest—in terms of books, members, and global reach—was Mudie's Select Library. Launched by Charles Edward Mudie (1818–90) in 1842, by 1852 it had moved into a splendid, custom-built building on New Oxford Street, and over the next decade it added nearly a million volumes to its collection, nearly half of which were fiction. The library also circulated periodicals. By the 1880s, Mudie's holdings included at least 6 million volumes. Subscribers at the basic rate of one guinea per year (half that of his biggest competitor) were entitled to borrow up to three volumes at a time. More expensive subscriptions were taken out by book clubs (at a minimum rate of 2 guineas per year) and libraries. For example, for a subscription of 200 guineas per year, an institution was entitled to borrow up to 20,000 volumes. An 1884 article in the *Pall Mall Gazette* reported that Mudie's circulated over 100,000 books per week. Subscribers in London could visit the flagship library or one of several branches around the city, and both Londoners and those further afield could submit their book requests by penny post or by telegraph. Mudie's not only maintained a fleet of vans for pickup and delivery of books, but it also managed a large export service that relied on trains and steamships to send books throughout the British Empire.

Mudie was a savvy entrepreneur, and many of his practices would be imitated by both libraries and booksellers in subsequent eras. He advertised extensively and also published a regular catalogue of offerings that noted which books were most in demand, thereby creating early bestseller lists. He also ordered books in large quantities—usually at least 500 copies, and sometimes whole printings of books that had proven popular in earlier serializations—which kept his costs down and ensured that the local rate-payers elected to do so in a referendum. The other catch was that those taxes could only be used for the buildings and staff, not for the books. In 1853, the law was amended to extend to Scotland as well. As Altick notes, the immediate effects of this legislation were unimpressive. Although the large industrial cities of Manchester and Liverpool both passed the necessary referenda and undertook building projects almost immediately, other towns repeatedly voted down the levies. By 1896, a full generation later, only 334 districts had approved library levies, while a number of major population centers had not—including most of London, where only two parishes had state-supported libraries.

In the United States, progress towards creating public libraries ebbed and flowed, depending on the state. The first state to authorize municipal libraries supported by taxation was Massachusetts, which passed the necessary legislation in 1848. The first library to be created with public funds was the Boston Public Library, which opened its doors in 1854. Among those who had

his subscribers could get their hands on the newest releases. Mudie also developed a smooth operation for selling off his overstock. As the demand to borrow certain works wore off, he sold most of the copies at used book rates—sometimes releasing his own extra copies into the market just as the publishers were releasing their own cheaper reprint editions. Mudie was also a shrewd assessor of his subscribers' needs and wants. The "select" in his library's title was no mistake: Mudie carefully scrutinized the works that he purchased to ensure that they would be appropriate for his mostly middle-class and female borrowers. Books bound in the library's distinctive covers with the Pegasus imprint could be safely left lying on a parlor table. They were unlikely to bring a blush to the cheek of an unsuspecting reader.

Mudie's flagship location on New Oxford Street was organized for maximum efficiency, but it was also designed to impress. The main gallery featured a high domed ceiling and ionic columns, surrounded by several tiers of bookshelves. Readers entered into the main gallery from the street and handed in their book requests at a central desk. Many of the books were shelved in stacks ranged around the main gallery or in adjoining passages and rooms, so that they could be quickly retrieved. If the desk staff could not reach a book, they used a special whistle to signal colleagues above. Other books, including all of the fiction, were in a labyrinth of iron stacks below the main floor that could be accessed by speaker tubes and runners; lifts brought books up from the lower levels. In addition to exchanging as many as 2,000 volumes in the main library itself, Mudie's also sent out some 700 boxes per week.

Although circulating libraries continued into the twentieth century, their heyday was over. Mudie's subscriber base declined in the 1920s, and the library moved from New Oxford Street to Kingsway in 1934. Mudie's finally closed its doors in 1937, and the flagship building stood empty until it was destroyed during the Blitz.

urged its founding were Edward Everett (1794–1865), a former governor and past president of Harvard University, and his colleague at Harvard, George Ticknor (1791–1871). Everett and Ticknor had envisioned a free, publicly supported library that would combine a solid collection of current works for reference and study with a collection of general literature that would help foster a love of reading. The Boston Public Library combined those two ideals, with non-circulating scholarly and reference works on the second floor, and circulating "pleasant literature of the day" on the first floor. (However, as in many other libraries of the day, there were constant debates about what the proper mix of these two kinds of books should be, with forces ever ready to reduce the amount dedicated to pleasure reading in order to increase the more academic and improving titles.)

CHETHAM'S LIBRARY

The oldest public library in Britain, Chetham's Library in Manchester was founded in 1653 by Humphrey Chetham (1580–1653), a wealthy textile merchant who directed in his will that the librarian was "to require nothing of any man that cometh into the library." The governors appointed to fulfill Chetham's will purchased and renovated a 1421 building that was originally part of Manchester's Collegiate Church to create the library and the school that surrounds it. Chetham's Library and School stands as one of the finer examples of medieval construction in the northwest of England. Originally dedicated to educating underprivileged boys, Chetham's School is now an internationally recognized school of music. In addition to the library that bears his name, Chetham also endowed five smaller regional libraries, which were designed to be chained and housed in portable chests that could also serve as reading desks. The libraries were to consist of "godly Englishe Bookes" that would tend towards "the edification of the common people."

When it opened, Chetham's Library was the only independent library facility in the north of England, and the governors wanted to furnish it with books and manuscripts comparable to those held at the universities of Oxford and Cambridge. The Library was housed above ground level to protect the books from damp. Large presses, or bookcases, were built radiating off two corridors that form an L, and all of the newly acquired books were chained to the bookcases, in accordance with contemporary practice and Chetham's will. The books were ordered by size, with smaller books on the shelves near the top and larger ones near the bottom. Small portable stools were provided so that scholars could move their seats to the required desk to consult the volumes.

In the early years, Chetham's Library mostly collected books that would be useful to the many clergymen, lawyers, and doctors in and around Manchester. By the eighteenth century, the collection had already outgrown its original space, so

Canada's first legislation to create public libraries came somewhat later. In Ontario, the 1882 Act to Provide for the Establishment of Free Libraries carved out a space for tax-supported public libraries in the province. As in the United Kingdom and the United States, local citizens could petition to establish a levy for the library. In 1895, the act was amended so that the province could re-designate some of the privately established libraries, such as those created by mechanics' institutes, as "public." The western provinces were next to adopt the necessary legislation: British Columbia in 1891, Manitoba in 1892, Saskatchewan in 1906, and Alberta in 1907. In the Maritimes and Quebec, where there were already a fair number of privately founded or church-sponsored libraries, the need for tax-supported public libraries was less acutely felt, so the pressure to create the laws to establish them was also less.

the book presses were heightened and the chains were largely abandoned. Instead, wooden gates were constructed at the end of each facing set of presses. From that point on, books were brought to readers in the Reading Room.

Knowing which book a reader might wish to consult was somewhat challenging, however, as no proper catalogue of the library's holdings was published until 1791, and then the books were listed only by subject and size, rather than by author and title. (They were also listed only in Latin.) But for those who did know what to ask for, Chetham's Library contained many riches: the library owns more than forty medieval manuscripts, as well as many later ones, many of which are related to the history of the northwest of England. The collection also contains over 120,000 volumes, most of them published before 1850. The library's endowment was generously tipped in favor of book and manuscript purchases. For example, the early governors authorized £20 for the purchase of a particularly desirable eight-volume Bible, but the first librarian was paid only £10 (plus room and board) for a year's wages. Because of the library's intended utility for local professionals, it is especially rich in early works of science and medicine.

The Reading Room is housed at the base of the library's L-shaped corridors to best catch the light. In addition to a number of large reading tables, the Reading Room also contains the chained book chests that were part of one of the smaller regional libraries established by Chetham. The Reading Room has drawn many distinguished scholars over the centuries, but perhaps the most famous are the political philosophers Friedrich Engels (1820–95) and Karl Marx (1818–83). Engels lived in Manchester from the 1840s through the 1860s while he managed his father's textile mill in adjoining Salford, and he and Marx are reported to have worked on the early drafts of the *Communist Manifesto* (1848) in an alcove of the Reading Room. Today, Chetham's Library remains an important rare book repository and center for historical study, and it continues to collect material related to regional history.

However, while it might appear from these dates that Canada was a little behind the curve in creating public libraries, it was not. Legislation passed elsewhere in the English-speaking world had not translated to a surge in library building. As noted above, by the end of the nineteenth century, Britain was still significantly under-served by public libraries, and there had been no widespread movement to build them in the United States, either. Laws allowed communities to establish levies for libraries, but many communities remained reluctant to do so. From one perspective, the projects seemed big and daunting: who would undertake them and keep them going? From another perspective, there was concern about the costs: could the local community really afford additional taxes? Others worried about the impact on volunteerism: if the state provided a service like a library, what would happen to the local impulses to philanthropy and public service? And finally, there was the ever-vexed problem of what kinds of books should be provided: improving or entertaining, bound volumes or periodicals, classics or contemporary works?

What was required was someone to jump-start the process by providing advice, plans, and—crucially—upfront funds for buildings and endowments. Fortunately, not one but two such individuals stepped forward, and the great era of public library building began.

The Library Builders: John Passmore Edwards and Andrew Carnegie

The two great library builders of the late nineteenth and early twentieth centuries were John Passmore Edwards (1823–1911) and Andrew Carnegie (1835–1919). Both were self-made men who rose from fairly impoverished childhoods to command great wealth, and some of that wealth derived from newspapers. (The two briefly held a joint interest in the same newspaper in the 1880s.) Carnegie, whose wealth mainly derived from railroads and steel, was able to practice munificence on a much grander scale than his contemporary, but the exponential increase in the number of public libraries constructed at the turn of the twentieth century compared to all previous eras rests on the two men's combined determination to invest in the betterment of those who wished to rise through self-improvement.

Passmore Edwards was born to a working-class family in Cornwall and was largely self-educated, mostly through cheap books he bought for himself. When he was twenty, he began a career as a clerk and later moved into journalism and lecturing on political reform. After a couple of business failures, in 1876 he purchased *The Echo*, a halfpenny newspaper that supported mostly Liberal politics. Passmore Edwards devoted the profits from the paper to philanthropic work, endowing hospitals, convalescent homes, orphanages, art galleries, museums, a public garden, an endowed scholarship at Oxford, countless public drinking fountains—and twenty-four libraries. Passmore Edwards had been a fervent campaigner for the Free Libraries Act, and when its passage failed to translate to the building of libraries, he determined to further the cause more practically. Many of the libraries he built were in the East End of London, an area that was crowded with some of the poorest inhabitants of the city, many of whom (especially towards the end of the century) were new immigrants.

In a short autobiographical pamphlet, *A Few Footprints*, which was privately printed in 1905, Passmore Edwards explained his motivations. More than fifty years after the Free Libraries Act had been passed, he complained, there were still "almost as many public libraries in a single State in America as we have altogether" in Britain. Public libraries were worth supporting, he declared, "because they are educative, recreative, and useful; because they bring the products of research and imagination, and the stored wisdom of ages and nations, within the easy reach of the poorest citizens; because they distribute without curtailing the intellectual wealth of the world; because they encourage seekers after technical knowledge, and thereby promote industrial improvement; because, being under the public eye, they are economically conducted; because they teach equality of citizenship, and are essentially democratic in spirit and action, in as much as they are maintained out of public rates and subject to public control." "All may not use them," he concluded, "but all may do so if they like; and as they are means of instructing and improving some, all are directly or indirectly benefited by them."

Most of the Passmore Edwards libraries were built between 1892 and 1903, and they differed widely in style and facilities. Some were attached to schools or galleries, while others were standalone buildings; some remain standing today and are still associated with their original purposes. One of the more interesting Passmore Edwards libraries was built in Camberwell in 1903 and included public baths and washhouses. An account in the *London Argus* at the time of the building's opening approvingly describes it as a striking example of artistry and practicality, "an embodiment of the modern public spirit, which is covering local London with institutions designed to minister to the comfort and welfare of the inhabitants." The main entrance led to a central hall, lighted from above, off of which were located a newspaper reading room, reference area, and lending library, all divided from one another with glazed screens. The bathing facilities included large first-class and second-class pools, as well as individual "slipper baths" and the necessary changing rooms and other accoutrements. The washhouse area included laundry facilities, mangles, and a small eatery. Although its architectural style was a fairly standard late-Victorian mock Tudor, by combining facilities for public hygiene and physical exercise with ones for exercising and enriching the mind, the Camberwell Passmore Edwards library seems to have looked back to Ancient Rome and the last great era of public library building.

Andrew Carnegie claimed that his decision to devote much of his vast wealth to the building of public libraries came from his childhood. Carnegie was born into an impoverished weaving family in Fife, Scotland. Economic conditions became so bad that the family emigrated to the United States, where Carnegie worked first in a cotton factory and later as a messenger for a telegraph company. He later said that it was the ability to borrow one book a week from a free library provided by his employer during his messenger days that led him to rank libraries as the highest possible object for philanthropy. (He also highly valued universities, as evidenced by his endowing what is now Carnegie Mellon University in Pittsburgh.) Carnegie was a hard, driven business owner, but he believed that those who were successful had an obligation to give back to the community, and he managed to give away about 90 per cent of his vast wealth before his death, much of it by endowing the Carnegie Corporation of New York and a similar institution in the United Kingdom, both of which were charged with supporting the "advancement and diffusion of knowledge." In all, Carnegie and the trusts he established founded nearly 3,000 free public libraries between 1883 and 1929. By far the largest number were in his adopted country, where Carnegie libraries were established in forty-six states—constituting nearly half of the 3,500 or so public libraries in the United States in 1919. But Carnegie libraries were also built in Britain, Ireland, and Canada, as well as a few in Australia, New Zealand, the Caribbean, and even Fiji.

In the early years of his philanthropy, Carnegie simply bestowed libraries on a few selected communities. He also built a number of libraries that were in multipurpose recreation centers, like many of those founded by Passmore Edwards. However, as Carnegie's philanthropic efforts became both more ambitious and more focused, he and his assistant James Bertram (1872–1934) devised what became known as the "Carnegie formula" to determine which communities should be supported in their quest for a new, purpose-built public library. Crucially, the Carnegie formula required that communities make a financial commitment to the project: the civic authorities had to guarantee that they would provide an annual 10 per cent of the library's construction costs to support ongoing operations and maintenance. Communities also had to demonstrate that there was a need for a public library—not difficult, when such libraries initially were so few and far between—and provide the building site. To demonstrate the need for a library, many towns and neighborhoods turned to the numerous women's clubs that were being formed during this period to promote educational, social, and political reforms. Organizing libraries was just one of the many projects these clubs undertook as newly educated and politically empowered women began turning their time and talents to community service. Finally, applicants for Carnegie library funds also had to ensure that free service was provided to all. The free service to all requirement created some special challenges in the southern United States, which was still strictly segregated at the time, but rather than making integration a sticking point, Carnegie simply funded a number of separate libraries for African Americans where they were requested.

Carnegie put no explicit restrictions on what libraries built with his funds had to contain or what they had to look like, and as a result, they were built in a wide variety of architectural styles that suited the particular towns in which they were sited. However, after 1907 his assistant Bertram did require that library plans—and the necessary building permits and proofs that the supporting taxes had been voted in—be submitted to him. After 1911, he provided all applicants with six different floor plans that showed how to achieve the best accommodations for the money.

All of the suggested plans feature one main story over a basement, where a central furnace and other service areas could be located. (The Carnegie Foundation discouraged the use of fireplaces, not so much because of the fire risk but because they took up a large amount of space that could be better devoted to books.) The plans also depict large reading rooms with high windows that let in a lot of light and also allow for bookshelves all around the walls. Unlike most earlier libraries, which typically had *closed stacks* that were only

THE TACOMA PUBLIC LIBRARY

The Main Library in Tacoma, Washington, dedicated in 1903, is representative of the many public libraries established with Carnegie funds. The first library in Tacoma was a subscription library, established in 1886 in the home of Grace R. Moore, a member of one of the women's clubs that were so instrumental in library creation in the late nineteenth century. Members of the club and their families paid 25 cents for the privilege of borrowing books, most of which were volumes from their own personal libraries. The library could also accommodate unmarried men who wished to read there—but they had to pay 50 cents. By 1893, the collection had outgrown Moore's sitting room, so the subscription library was moved to a room in City Hall.

The creation of a proper public library for the growing city happened almost by accident. In 1901, a local Presbyterian minister, Calvin Stewart, wanted funds to expand Whitworth College, so he contacted the Carnegie Foundation. After meeting Andrew Carnegie's assistant James Bertram, Stewart left without gaining any support for the college—but he did secure the necessary funds to build a public library. The first Carnegie library in the state of Washington, the Tacoma Library was built in a Renaissance revival style, with a grand marble staircase, copper-clad dome over the original reading room, high ceilings, and decorative murals and columns. The building was lovingly restored in the 1990s. (Fortunately, an ill-founded 1950s urban renewal project that threatened to dismantle the original building or cover its façade with bland Eisenhower-era glass-and-steel rectangles was abandoned because of cost.) Still part of the Main Library of the Tacoma Public Library system, the original Carnegie building now houses the library's rare books and historical collections, as well as meeting rooms. Grace Moore, the city's first library creator, is memorialized today by a branch library named in her honor.

accessible by library staff, Carnegie libraries featured *open stacks*, shelves that patrons could browse themselves. Librarians in such libraries filled the role of guide, rather than gatekeeper. Carnegie library plans also usually feature a staircase ascending to the main reading room, reportedly to evoke the idea of elevation through learning, and exterior lamps to suggest enlightenment. Contrary to some reports, it was not required to put Carnegie's name on the building, although many communities chose to do so out of gratitude.

Grand Public Libraries

Passmore Edwards and Carnegie were visionaries, and most of the libraries they erected a century ago have remained important, central institutions in the towns and neighborhoods where they were constructed. But while the two men were the most significant patrons of the public library movement, they certainly were not alone. Larger cities in North America, such as Chicago, New York, and Montreal, established their own library guilds and foundations and built some of the most beautiful and renowned public libraries.

Chicago's Public Library emerged from the ashes of the great Chicago Fire of 1871. Immediately after the fire, a number of prominent Londoners proposed to raise funds and donations to endow the city with a free public library. A gift of 8,000 volumes (some of which are still part of the collection) provided the necessary motivation for the state legislature to pass the Illinois Library Act of 1872, which authorized cities to create library levies. The elegant Central Library finally opened on Michigan Avenue facing Grant Park in 1897, nearly twenty-six years to the day that the city had burned to the ground. The building, which featured marble staircases, a grand dome, mosaics, and Tiffany glass, was designed to be virtually incombustible. The Chicago Public Library's collections and other services outgrew the building by the mid-twentieth century, and in 1991 a new main branch, the Harold Washington Library Center, was opened. Located a few blocks away, the new library evokes the architecture and spaces of the great library-building age of the previous century, but with all the modern conveniences and electronic resources that present-day libraries require.

The grand main branch of the New York Public Library on Fifth Avenue was built largely out of funds bequeathed to the city by former governor Samuel J. Tilden (1814–86), who dedicated over $2 million to creating a free public library. The Tilden bequest was creatively combined with the funds and collections of two preexisting libraries: the Astor Library, which had been founded by the then wealthiest man in America, John Jacob Astor (1763–1848), and the Lenox Library, a scholarly collection of rare books brought together by bibliophile James Lenox (1800–80). The Beaux Arts styled building, with its elegant columns and guardian lions "Patience" and "Fortitude," opened in 1911. The building was a modern temple to knowledge, featuring wide staircases leading to enormous reading rooms. The seven floors of closed stacks below

The New York Public Library entrance, c. 1915. Image courtesy of the Library of Congress.

the main reading room encompassed about seventy-five miles of shelves and over a million books. The library has just undergone its first major renovation, which has sought to undo some of the damage of a century's pollution and constant use.

The first true public library in greater Montreal was in Westmount. It was founded in 1897, in honor of Queen Victoria's Diamond Jubilee, and opened in 1899. For many years, Montreal's Francophone and Anglophone communities maintained mostly separate library facilities. Among the French-speaking residents, the Catholic Church played a significant role in book culture, and the church-sponsored *Oeuvre des bons livres*, or Institute for Circulating Good Books, remained an important source of approved reading materials from its founding in 1844 until the beginning of the twentieth century. Another significant church-sponsored library in Montreal was the Bibliothèque Saint-Sulpice, which opened in 1915 with 80,000 volumes. Thanks to a very active collecting strategy in its early years, Saint-Sulpice rapidly expanded and gained a national reputation as a research library; its collections are now part of the Grande Bibliothèque Nationale. The Westmount Public Library, by contrast, was intended to serve primarily the Anglophone community. Described by one historian as "a jewel in a park," the library featured a massive round tower, arched entryway, and large bay windows. Besides providing reading materials to the local area, Westmount also served as a model for tax-supported libraries in Quebec and beyond, not least because of its early adoption and implementation of professional librarianship.

Public Libraries Today

Once the public library movement caught hold, most communities found libraries to be an essential part of the landscape. In some regions, public libraries were intentionally sited in close proximity to public schools, so that their collections and outreach programs could be used to enhance the offerings at the schools. These interconnections can still be seen today, with public libraries frequently offering afterschool and summer reading programs that help to keep young people engaged with books throughout the year. For many, visits to public libraries are some of their earliest and fondest memories. In *The Library in America*, author Paul Dickson locates the origins of his lifelong passion for libraries in his childhood visits to the public library in Yonkers, New York (a Carnegie building), which he describes as having been to him "the most important and impressive place in town." In regions in which it is difficult for readers to get to a library, public library systems often devise means of bringing the library to the readers. Mobile libraries, or *bookmobiles*, visit areas not otherwise served by stand-alone library buildings, and they can also bring books to schools, convalescent homes, and other locations where residents may find it difficult to get out and about on their own. A visit from such a mobile library to Buckingham Palace serves as the plot-launching device for Alan Bennett's (b. 1934) novella *The Uncommon Reader* (2007).

Most modern library systems are concerned with meeting the evolving needs of their communities. In recent decades, this has meant adding media to the collections and installing computers and other necessary infrastructure to help readers access electronic information and entertainment. Modern libraries have also watched the bookselling industry carefully, adopting and adapting trends in merchandising that can help to make books and other items attractive and easy to access. Many public libraries now have "grab-and-go" sections of recent releases and popular fiction near the doors and checkout desks, so that patrons can pop in and out of the building quickly. Some have also experimented with self-service checkout stations, e-book downloads, and online reservation and dispatch services, while still others have invited coffee shops and other small food vendors to open outlets on or adjacent to their facilities. Libraries have also tried to increase their foot traffic by experimenting with new kinds of clubs and social outreach opportunities. A number have even experimented with speed-dating sessions, in which participants carry a book with them to each meet-up, an idea that seems to have its origins in Belgium, where it is called *bibdating*.

But however much they modernize in response to changes in book culture, public libraries still have roots in the past, and they still require the kinds of forward-looking philanthropic efforts that past sponsors undertook at the turn of the last century. Many public libraries have faced serious challenges in recent years as a result of the global economic downturn. As local tax bases have declined, governments have looked to eliminate nonessential services, and libraries have often been slated for diminished service or outright closure. However, readers and their librarian champions have frequently fought back against these measures, insisting that continued access to books and information are more, not less, important in difficult times. For example, Seattle opened a new Central Library in 2004 to critical and popular acclaim, but just six years later the Seattle Public Library system was threatened with drastic cuts due to a city budget crisis. The head librarian, Susan Hildreth, pointed out that the public library was "one of the key bastions of democracy," serving as an "equalizer" by providing much-needed computer access, references and job assistance, and 400 key programs, including English language classes and tutoring programs. Even reducing hours, one of the less drastic measures that can be taken, can have negative consequences. If libraries are closed on weekdays, schoolchildren can't visit them on field trips and become familiar with their environments and offerings. And if they are closed evenings and weekends, working people and their children can't get there.

In early 2011, the threatened closure of libraries across Britain prompted the creation of a national "Save Our Libraries Day." Philip Pullman (b. 1946), author of the popular *His Dark Materials* trilogy (1995–2000), was just one of many authors, librarians, educators, and ordinary readers who spoke up to defend their community libraries. In an impassioned speech on behalf of Oxfordshire libraries, nearly half of which were being slated for closure, Pullman noted that a public library reminds citizens that there are "things above profit," things "that stand for civic decency and public respect for imagination and knowledge and the value of simple delight." A year later, in early 2012, the results of such protests were mixed: public library closings in Somerset and Gloucestershire were halted by legal challenges, but in the borough of Brent in northwestern London, six libraries were closed, despite efforts that included twenty-four-hour vigils outside the Kensal Rise branch. Over 400 UK libraries remain in a perilous state of economic uncertainty.

A similar problem, but with a twist, faced the small American town of Gilmanton in 2008. Located in New Hampshire—the same state that gave birth to the first tax-supported public library—Gilmanton also needed a financial benefactor, not to protect its library from closure, but instead to cover the new library's operating expenses so that it could actually open. A volunteer group had secured, renovated, and furnished the building with books and computers, but the volunteers had fallen short of their goal to staff and maintain it. The library did eventually manage to secure the funds required to open, but their website suggests that they are still heavily dependent on volunteers and fund-raising to keep going.

NATIONAL LIBRARIES

National libraries, libraries that are formally established by the state, are another legacy of the eighteenth and nineteenth centuries. They are largely an outgrowth of romantic nationalism, originally conceived as monuments to the country's literary heritage. National libraries were intended to project a particular image of the national culture. Thus, when they were created by large and powerful nations—as in the case of some of the oldest national libraries, those of Britain, France, and the United States—they were necessarily conceived on a very impressive scale. Over the past two centuries, the number of national libraries has grown dramatically, so that now nearly every country in the world has a national library, as do some semiautonomous regions and districts. Especially since the end of World War II, when libraries were enshrined as one of the key concerns of UNESCO, the role of national libraries has also coalesced around a number of key functions. These functions include the preservation of national heritage and the production and maintenance of a *national bibliography*, or record of the works published in the country or region. National libraries also often serve as the official depositories for those works, and they sometimes also serve as the coordinating centers for all library services in the country.

Because of their importance to national self-image, national libraries have usually followed a different trajectory of growth and support than have other kinds of libraries. Even—or perhaps especially—in times of war or other adversity, national libraries have tended to be protected, both physically and economically. As historians Elmer Johnson and Michael Harris put it, the "collective success and survival" of national libraries "have meant much to the total history of libraries in the western world." It is largely because of this ongoing actual and emotional investment in national libraries that the book world is so shocked when they fall prey to natural disasters (floods and fires) or, especially, when they become the targets of intentional destruction, as described in Chapter 6.

THE FIRST NATIONAL LIBRARIES

The first national libraries were created in the great wave of romantic nationalism that began to sweep Europe in the eighteenth and early nineteenth centuries. The three largest and most influential of the early national libraries were the British Museum Library in London (now distinct from the museum, and known simply as the British Library), the Bibliothèque Nationale in Paris, and the Library of Congress in the United States. Although the histories and circumstances of their creation are somewhat different, all three of these libraries had the distinct benefit of being the main focus of their nations' library-building efforts in an era when the amalgamation and concentration of state power was seen as a good. They also benefited from staying mostly out of harm's way as natural disasters and, especially, wars swept across Europe and North America.

Other countries with long, respected library histories, such as Italy and Germany, unified their state power somewhat later, and their national libraries are still dispersed rather than centralized. Italy has two National Central Libraries, one in Florence and the other in Rome, as well as national/regional libraries in Milan, Venice, Turin, and Naples. Germany's National Library, Die Deutsche Nationalbibliothek, combines what were the official state libraries of the former West and East Germany, in Frankfurt-am-Main and Leipzig, respectively, with the Music Archives in Berlin. But the complicated history of Germany's divisions along political and religious lines means that there are also significant regional libraries, such as the Bavarian State Library in Munich and the Berlin State Library, which have major holdings and virtually equal status to the official national libraries. Russia has both a National Library in St. Petersburg and a Russian State Library in Moscow. The former contains the Russian imperial collection, dating back to Catherine the Great (1729–96). The latter was founded in 1862 as Russia's first free public library and has since become the official Russian depository library.

The British Library

The first national library to be designated as such was the British Museum Library (now the British Library), which was created in 1753 as part of the British Museum. The original collection of books and artifacts was a combination of gifts from wealthy benefactors, notably the physician Sir Hans Sloane (1660–1753), and two extraordinary groups of manuscripts that were purchased by Parliament: the Harleian Collection, assembled by Robert Harley (1661–1724), the first Earl of Oxford and Earl Mortimer, and his son Edward (1689–1741); and the Cotton Library, assembled by Robert Bruce Cotton (1571–1631), who gathered many of the rare and valuable manuscripts that were offered for sale after the 1530s dissolution of the monasteries.

The original holdings grew dramatically a few years later, when king George II (1683–1760) donated the Royal Library collection of over 9,000 volumes. The Royal Library collection also included many books still in unbound sheets, which had been deposited with the library by printers in accordance with the 1662 Press Licensing Act. Happily, when the Royal Library collection passed to the British Library, the deposit requirements were deemed to go with it. Thus, from 1757 on, the British Library was entitled to receive one copy of every work printed in the United Kingdom.

During its first century, the British Library grew substantially, but in a rather haphazard way. Most of the early staff were physicians and clergymen whose primary responsibilities were outside the institution, so the library's work was done in a dilettantish way, if at all. Squabbles broke out regularly, not

Interior of the British Library, 2004. Photograph by Andrew Dunn.

least about the best way to create and maintain a catalogue of the collections. (This would remain a perennial problem well into the twentieth century.) There were ongoing tensions between the Manuscripts department and the Printed Books department about funding, purchases, and even the possession of particular texts. And there were also serious problems with the physical spaces allotted to the library. For many years, the Reading Room was small, stuffy, and damp—so much so, that by 1774 the room's superintendent refused to occupy it for reasons of health. As the collections continued to grow, the floors were no longer able to support the weight of the books. Fears of theft and of dust (which contained soot, among other irritants) led to the introduction of metal grills over the shelves and necessitated regular closings for top-to-bottom cleaning. And there were also fire hazards—not only because of the proximity of fireplaces and candles to the paper books, but also because of gunpowder stored in the building on behalf of the local militia, who trained in the Museum's grounds.

By the 1830s, it was clear that something needed to be done, and Parliament set up a number of inquiries to look into the British Museum's organization and facilities. By this point, other European nations and even the United States had established national libraries, and one of the British Library's newer staff members, Antonio Panizzi (1797–1879), pointed out that many of these libraries were already significantly larger and better funded than Britain's—especially the national library of Britain's long-time rival, France. Panizzi argued that the British Library should aggressively develop its collection of rare and expensive books so that it would become a destination for scholars. But rare and antiquarian collecting should not be at the expense of the regular, contemporary acquisitions. Parliament was swayed by Panizzi's vision of a British Library that represented in scale and splendor the power and riches of the British Empire, and they rewarded him by appointing him Keeper of Printed Books, and later head Librarian.

Under Panizzi's direction, both the collections and the facilities of the British Library improved dramatically. Besides authorizing important purchases from book and manuscript dealers around the world, Panizzi also strenuously pursued printers and publishers throughout Britain and the empire to make sure that they were complying with deposit requirements. Books, periodicals, maps, and other materials poured in, in all languages. Panizzi also oversaw the efforts to rationalize and—crucially—speed up the cataloguing of the collections. From the beginning, efforts had been made to replace painstakingly handwritten ledgers with typeset volumes, but the rapid growth of the collections meant the volumes were out of date almost before they left the compositors' hands. Furthermore, because the original catalogues were compiled mainly by antiquarians, they were not always organized in ways that were useful to general readers. Panizzi insisted that the catalogues be alphabetically based and cross-referenced. To keep the catalogues reasonably up-to-date, a hybrid system of handwritten and typeset loose-leaf ledger volumes was developed, with three separate sets of volumes organized by author, title, and subject. (Duplicate sets were maintained for public and library staff use.) The loose-leaf solution meant new pages could be easily inserted into the catalogues, and the pages themselves could be cut apart and interleaved with lists of new accessions. When the volumes became too full, they would be subdivided into separate new volumes. The loose-leaf volumes remained in use until the turn of the twenty-first century, by which time they had increased in number to some 2,300 volumes. They were finally fully replaced by an electronic catalogue after the move to the new St. Pancras location. Although they were serviceable, the size of the catalogue volumes made using them a daunting task. The Irish poet William Butler Yeats (1865–1939) wrote that while reading in the British Library in 1880s, "I remember often putting off hour after hour consulting some necessary book because I shrank from lifting the heavy volumes of the catalogue."

Of all the developments in the British Library under Panizzi's direction, the most memorable and certainly the best-loved was the building of the great round Reading Room and Iron Library, which were designed by architect Sydney Smirke (1798–1877) and opened to great fanfare in 1857. The new Reading Room solved nearly all the problems of the previous spaces: it was vast, with accommodations for over 450 readers; the windows, located all around the base of the domed ceiling, just above the three levels of reference book stacks that surrounded the room, meant that natural light could flood in (when the notorious London smogs were not at their worst); well-positioned gaslights (replaced by electric lamps almost as soon as the technology was available) provided supplemental light; and the radiant heating and fresh air ventilation systems kept the room comfortable. The librarians' desk, where readers would place their book requests, was located at the center hub of the room, with the catalogues arranged in concentric rows of shelves immediately surrounding it. A private passage led from the librarians' desk to the stacks, so that runners could fill the orders. The long readers' desks were arranged like spokes between the catalogues and the outer walls. Each seat at the desks was numbered and had its own bookshelf immediately before it, providing both book storage and some privacy for study. Originally, a separate rank of desks was reserved for women. While the Reading Room's splendor and comfort was what most visitors noticed, perhaps the real wonder was the engineering.

THE PRIVATE CASE

One problem that has long vexed librarians is what to do with works that are deemed inappropriate for certain readers. In the early years, the staff and trustees of both public and subscription libraries worried that readers would prefer fiction and other light reading to more improving fare. Some libraries simply chose to stock fewer frivolous titles; others limited the number of such volumes that could be checked out. Even today, many school and public libraries have policies that limit access to certain books in their collections on the basis of age or parental consent. To ensure that these works do not accidentally get into the wrong hands, some items are kept in restricted areas in closed stacks, from which they are retrieved only by special request.

Although the British Library has always had closed stacks, it has also always had books that have been deemed too risqué for the general collection. Since at least the 1840s, these books were segregated in the "Private Case," which was initially housed in the Keeper's (head librarian's) office and eventually moved to a special basement storeroom. According to Paul Cross, formerly on the British Library staff, the books in the Private Case were all stamped, catalogued, and press-marked (labeled) like the other books in the collection, but from 1841 the catalogue entries and shelf list records were filed separately in the Keeper's office. Readers who wanted to see items in the Private Case had to make a special, personal application for them.

All kinds of rumors sprang up about what might be included in the Private Case, the most common being that it was a collection of erotica. However, the extant catalogues for the Private Case suggest that the books were not erotica per se, but simply works that the librarians and trustees of the library deemed obscene. Some of the books were gifts to the library, while others were purchased as "specimens of literature or as illustrative of manners," as a librarian testifying to the trustees put it in 1890. For much of the nineteenth century, many regarded French novels as too decadent for British tastes—as British Library historian P.R. Harris observes, "especially those containing illustrations"—so many of the earliest works

Smirke's design solved the age-old library problem of the weight of the books by making the bookcases of cast iron and part of the overall structural support of the dome. They also helped to reduce the risk of fire, as did iron doors separating portions of the stacks and a soon-added telegraph link directly to the nearest fire station.

By the mid-twentieth century, the British Library was again outgrowing its space, and after several decades of debate, planning, and more debate, the decision was taken to separate the Library from the British Museum. The 1972 British Library Act combined the former British Museum Library with the National Central Library and the National Lending Library for Science and

sent to the Private Case were indeed French. And those novels, including translations of the work of novelist Émile Zola (1840–1902), were also among the earliest works to be deselected in the 1890s and early 1900s, when tastes and morals had shifted. The number of books in the Private Case varied over that half-century, from twenty-seven in 1850 to several hundred in 1900, when the "case" actually consisted of about a dozen small cupboards. However, at the very moment that some books were being let out of the Private Case, the British Library librarians and trustees were somewhat confounded by a major bequest by Henry Spencer Ashbee (1834–1900), a well-traveled bibliophile who amassed significant collections of the works of Miguel de Cervantes (1547–1616)—and of erotica. Among other things, Ashbee is suspected of being the author of the anonymously published *My Secret Life* (1888–94), a multi-volume work about the sexual exploits of a Victorian gentleman. Of the 1,600 books he left to the British Library, 1,000 were deemed "of an erotic or obscene character" and consigned to the Private Case.

The existence of the Private Case was first made public in 1913, when *The Intermediate Sex* (1908) by author and early gay activist Edward Carpenter (1844–1929) was deselected. An article published shortly thereafter, entitled "The Taboos of the British Museum Library," provides early evidence of objections to the freedom of access and expression that the Private Case represented, and the following year more books were moved to the general collection. However, more works were still also being added to the Private Case. Cross's examination of later catalogues reveals that quite a few books by controversial but now largely canonical authors spent time in the Private Case, including Henry Miller's *Tropic of Capricorn* (1939), most early editions of the Earl of Rochester's works (they were removed in 1952 after the publication of a complete collection of his works), John Cleland's *Memoirs of a Woman of Pleasure*, also known as *Fanny Hill* (1748), and the Marquis de Sade's *Justine* (1791). The turning point came in the wake of court rulings on Penguin's 1960 publication of an edition of D.H. Lawrence's *Lady Chatterley's Lover* (1928), an event that changed obscenity guidelines. The British Library created a new pressmark for newly legalized works that dealt openly in sexual matters and added the books to the General Catalogue. Nearly all works are now accessible to readers.

Technology to create the new British Library; the British National Bibliography and the Office for Scientific and Technical Information were added to the institution a couple of years later. A new location for the library was secured near St. Pancras railway station, and a new, purpose-built library building was constructed. The St. Pancras location opened in 1998 and features three floors of well-lit reading rooms arranged around a central glass-enclosed column of bookshelves containing the books of the original Royal Library. There are also exhibit spaces and a conservation center. While many older readers still mourn the loss of the round Reading Room (which has been absorbed by the British Museum and is now mainly used as exhibition space), the St. Pancras location offers vastly more readers' desks, more onsite storage for books and periodicals, a fully integrated digital catalogue, and the necessary infrastructure for electronic devices for research and writing. The increased capacity also means that would-be readers no longer need to provide credentials and affidavits to obtain reader's tickets. Greater access has its drawbacks (more readers, especially younger ones, create more noise), but these drawbacks are balanced by the convenience of having most materials on-call electronically and available in the building, rather than having to submit requests in pencil and sometimes wait days for them to be retrieved from remote storage areas.

The Bibliothèque Nationale

Technically, the second major national library in the world was the Bibliothèque Nationale in Paris, created in 1789 when the Revolutionary government declared by edict that the Royal Library was now the National Library. The Royal Library's pedigree was of much greater antiquity, by some accounts dating as far back as Charles V (1338–80), who created a personal library in the Louvre in 1368. However, since Charles the Wise's library, like most other early personal libraries of that era, was broken up and dispersed upon his death, the French Royal Library is conventionally agreed to have its origins in the reign of Louis XI (1423–83). In the next century, Francis I (1494–1547), a great Renaissance patron of the arts and letters, came up with the idea of a depository requirement. In a 1537 decree, Francis required that all printers and booksellers deposit in the Royal Library at Blois one copy of every book printed or sold in France. This innovative acquisitions scheme (it could, of course, also be used to monitor what was being printed and distributed for political or religious reasons) would be adopted by virtually every other major library and enshrined with the concept of copyright. (For discussions of censorship and of copyright, see Chapter 6.)

Between its removal to Paris in the late sixteenth century and its redesignation as the National Library 200 years later, the Royal Library became one of the largest and most admired libraries in the world. In the early eighteenth century, librarian Abbé Jean-Paul Bignon (1662–1743) reorganized the collections into separate departments for Printed Books, Manuscripts, Prints, and so

Bibliothèque Nationale de France, rue de Richelieu site, 2012. Photograph by Vincent Desjardins.

forth, and he also pursued an aggressive acquisitions program, seeking books on all subjects. Bignon was also responsible for making the library's riches more widely available. Under his supervision, the Library was opened first to scholars, and then to the public as well, albeit only for very limited hours. The Revolution temporarily suspended the acquisition of books through deposit, but the now National Library was significantly enriched with books and manuscripts confiscated from the aristocracy and clergy or simply abandoned by those fleeing the revolutionary forces. The Bibliothèque Nationale estimates that as many as 250,000 books, 40,000 manuscripts, and 85,000 prints were acquired by these means. Additional books and artifacts brought back from around the world by the triumphant emperor Napoléon Bonaparte further swelled the collections.

By the middle of the nineteenth century, when the French political situation has stabilized sufficiently, it became clear that the library required both reorganization and a new building to house its vast collections. In 1858, a committee was convened under the direction of author Prosper Mérimée (1803–70) to make recommendations, and a new building was designed by Henri Labrouste (1801–75). Labrouste traveled to London in 1857 to see the newly opened Reading Room and Iron Library of the British Library, and he incorporated some of Smirke's engineering innovations, particularly the integrated iron stacks, in his design for the building on rue de Richelieu in Paris. The centerpiece of Labrouste's design, the Printed Books Reading Room, is a long oblong, with a roof supported by narrow iron columns between the tiers of bookshelves. The librarians' desk is located in a recess at one end of the room, which also gives access to the stacks. Medallion windows around the roof immediately above the top tier of stacks allow filtered daylight into the room, supplementing the lamps on the long reading tables. Not only was the new building a triumph, but the library's collections and prestige were further enhanced with the subsequent acquisition of the papers of Victor Hugo (1802–85), which inaugurated a series of bequests of the papers of important French authors.

The Bibliothèque Nationale grew larger in the twentieth century, expanding into new locales and also going underground for new stacks. By the 1970s, there was nowhere else to go, and in 1988, President François Mitterrand (1916–96) announced that France would undertake the construction of a new National Library, with the largest and most modern facilities available. Dubbed by some as the "TGB," or "Très Grande Bibliothèque"—a nod to the French high-speed TGV trains, which also presented challenges during construction due to their ambitious scale—the new reference library building on the Quai François-Mauriac was finally opened in 1996. Designed by Dominique Perrault (b. 1953), the Bibliothèque François-Mitterrand features four facing towers, meant to suggest four open books, which are organized around a central garden that evokes a medieval cloister. The library currently has more than 14 million volumes (10 million of which are in the new building), including approximately 12,000 early printed books (or *incunabula*) and approximately 250,000 manuscripts. Its collection expands by as many as 150,000 volumes per year, mainly due to copyright deposit requirements.

The Library of Congress

The third major national library established in the early era was the Library of Congress, created in 1800 by the second President of the United States, John Adams (1735–1826). Originally intended solely as a reference and research library for members of Congress, the Library was allocated a rather modest initial grant of $5,000, and the first 700 or so volumes arrived from London the following year. In 1802, President Thomas Jefferson (1743–1826), a noted bibliophile, created the post of Librarian of Congress, and he followed the progress of the Library carefully during and after his tenure. The Library's books were housed in the Capitol building until 1814, when they were destroyed by fires set by British troops. In a country—indeed, a continent—with only a nascent printing and publishing industry, the loss of such a collection of books was significant. Jefferson offered his own personal library to replace those lost in the fire, and in 1815 Congress approved the purchase of Jefferson's nearly 6,500 volumes for $24,000. The acquisition of Jefferson's books vastly expanded the scope of the library, as his collection included works on architecture, arts, science, literature, and geography, as well as texts in multiple languages.

Over the next half-century, the Library of Congress expanded slowly, but it began to face competition from the nearby Smithsonian Institution. Founded in 1836 from funds bequeathed by the British scientist James Smithson (c. 1765–1829), the Smithsonian was created as a center for scientific research, but it soon became the depository for a variety of collections, and by the 1850s there were moves to have it declared the main US library. Smithsonian librarian Charles Coffin Jewett (1816–68) even managed to get the Smithsonian declared a copyright deposit library, thereby expanding its holdings. The question of which library would prevail was complicated by a second devastating fire at the Library of Congress in 1851, which destroyed about two-thirds of the collection, including a large proportion of Jefferson's books. A new, fireproof room was opened in 1853, with elegant surrounding galleries. The outbreak of the American Civil War (1861–65) created further difficulties. However, infighting at the Smithsonian led to Jewett's resignation in 1858, and that, combined with the end of the war, helped to consolidate the position of the Library of Congress. In 1866 the Smithsonian transferred a significant portion of its books, approximately 40,000 volumes, to the Library of Congress, at once making its collection one of the largest in North America.

The Librarian of Congress after the war, Ainsworth Rand Spofford (1825–1908), was instrumental in putting the Library on a solid footing. Like his British contemporary Antonio Panizzi, Spofford was a modernizer. He professionalized the Library's budget, reorganized the collection management, and secured copyright deposit provisions for the Library. From 1870 on, two copies of all works published in the United States had to be submitted to the Library of Congress. As the country was rapidly evolving its printing and publishing trades, copyright deposit would prove an invaluable aid to expanding the collections. However, Spofford, like his contemporaries, also sought to increase the Library's holdings in other areas. For example, pointing to the British Library's efforts to collect more works specifically related to the history, culture, and topography of the British Isles, in 1867 Spofford urged that the Library of Congress should make a concerted effort to document and preserve the record of the young republic. Just as Panizzi had appealed to Parliament's inborn rivalry with France, Spofford needled Congress with a reference to Britain, urging them to release the funds required to purchase a collection of Americana that had just come on the market. "It is not creditable to our national spirit to have to admit the fact," he chided, "that the largest and most complete collection of books relating to America in the world is now gathered on the shelves of the British Museum." And as the Library's holdings grew, Spofford also successfully lobbied Congress for a new, dedicated building separate from the Capitol.

Opened in 1897, the new Library of Congress building on Capitol Hill was one of the most splendid buildings in America. (Since 1980, it is known as the Jefferson Building.) Built in an Italian Renaissance style popular during the Beaux Arts era, the Library featured four interior courtyards to let in light, arranged around a circular central reading room (like the Bibliothèque Nationale's building, also inspired by the British Museum Library), and capped with a 23-carat gold-plated dome topped by a Torch of Knowledge. Marble statuary and murals by American artists were distributed throughout the building, and visitors were shepherded into the grand interior spaces through massive bronze doors followed by an imposing marble staircase whose lavish decorations cleverly depict different aspects and trades of the history of the book. At the time of its opening, it was billed as the "largest, costliest, and safest" library building in the world. Yet despite its vast size, the rapid growth of the collections meant that more space was soon required. Another new building, the Adams Building, was constructed in 1928 and linked to the main building by underground tunnels, and three of the original four courtyards of the Jefferson Building were filled in, two with extra book stacks, and the third with an auditorium.

Today, the Library of Congress is one of the likeliest contenders for largest library in the world, with approximately 152 million items, including over 34 million books and other printed items, over 66 million manuscripts, and millions of recordings, photographs, and other materials. It contains over 800 miles of shelf space. The Library adds about 10,000 items to its catalogue each day, most of which come from copyright deposit. Additional items that are deposited but not added to the collection are generally exchanged with other national libraries, which are another important source of acquisitions. Building on Jefferson's legacy, the Library has continued to collect works in languages other than English, and its holdings now include items in approximately 470 languages, comprising about half of the Library's collection. It is also the largest rare books library in North America, with a particularly large collection of incunabula and a copy of the first extant book printed in America, *The Bay Psalm Book* (1640).

In addition to serving Congress and visitors to its Washington, DC, sites, the Library of Congress also serves readers throughout the country and around the world, through departments like the US Copyright Office, the Cataloguing in Publication program and Cataloging Distribution Service, the National Library for the Blind and Physically Handicapped, the Preservation Office, and the Children's Literature Center.

MODERN NATIONAL LIBRARIES

National libraries took on new roles in national and international relations after World War II. In addition to the devastating cost in lives, the war also exacted a terrible toll on the cultures and cultural legacies of many of the affected peoples, and libraries were seen as important players in reclaiming, documenting, and preserving those legacies. National libraries fell under the purview of UNESCO, the United Nations agency charged with promoting peace through education, science, and culture, and their modern functions were largely defined as a result of a late 1950s Symposium on National Libraries. According to the guidelines set out in the *UNESCO Bulletin for Libraries* in 1966, national libraries are understood to be the "outstanding and central collection of a nation's literature." National libraries should serve as depository libraries in their respective countries, but in addition to collecting their own nation's publications, they should also serve as the central point for collections of foreign literature. In addition, national libraries should assume responsibility for producing and maintaining the national bibliography and for providing bibliographic services to the rest of the country. In recent years, national libraries have also assumed greater roles guiding and maintaining public library systems (some countries have made their national libraries the central administration hubs for their public library systems) and for national preservation and conservation efforts.

After a long quiet period of mainly consolidation and maturation, the past couple of decades have seen a renaissance of national library building. The main cause for this has been the emergence of new nations in the postcolonial era. The priorities for some of these new nations have been to establish repositories for official archives, while others have wanted administrative centers for literacy and educational initiatives. These are some of the motivations behind the new national libraries that have been created on the African continent since the 1960s, and in parts of Eastern Europe since the 1990s. In other cases, ethnic and linguistic minorities have sought to establish (or reestablish) a cultural heritage that had been suppressed by the dominant culture. This is one explanation for a rising number of libraries that include "national" in their names, even though their collecting and outreach efforts appear to be more regional in focus.

One example of a national library with a regional flavor is the Bibliothèque Nationale du Québec. The National Library of Canada had only been established in Ottawa in 1953. (A Canadian Parliamentary library had been authorized as early as 1791, but until the National Library was created, the Ottawa library contained mostly law and history books.) When the idea of a "national" library in Quebec was floated some 10 years later, some critics thought it would be superfluous. Wouldn't a *bibliothèque provinciale*, or provincial library, be more appropriate? However, Jean-Noël Tremblay (b. 1926), Quebec's Minister of Cultural Affairs at the time, pointed to the examples of Catalonia, Scotland, and Wales, all of which were stateless nations that nevertheless had national libraries. He argued that if UNESCO's definition of a national library was one that would acquire and conserve the country's literary productions, then only a national library, properly so-called, would do. From its creation in Montreal in 1968, the Bibliothèque Nationale du Québec assumed the tasks of a national library, and after a period of negotiation with the National Library of Canada, the Quebec National Library gradually assumed more responsibility for specifically Quebec-published or Francophone collecting, while Ottawa continued to try to represent the totality of the Confederation. In 1978, the language distinction was formalized when the Quebec National Library secured the right to issue ISBNs for Francophone publishers from across Canada.

As with many national libraries, the success of the Bibliothèque Nationale du Québec has owed much to the efforts of active head librarians. The first director of the Library, Georges Cartier (1929–94), sent his staff around the world to study operations, collection development, and conservation, and he launched concerted efforts to acquire the manuscripts of distinguished Quebec authors, many of whom were reluctant to leave their literary papers to the National Library in Ottawa. By the turn of the twenty-first century, the literary manuscript collection had grown from fewer than 1,000 documents to over 10,000. Along with manuscripts, Cartier also sought out Quebec-related periodicals and older books, laying the groundwork for what would become one of the world's most complete collections of works related to French North America. Subsequent directors have continued to develop the collections as well as the Library's role in the community. Like many other national libraries at that time, in the 1990s the Bibliothèque Nationale's responsibilities were expanded so that it became not just a national archive and study center, but the administrative hub for the Quebec public libraries as well. The Grande Bibliothèque Nationale was created by the Quebec Assembly in 1998, and a new building commensurate with its name was opened in 2005 to great acclaim. The new Library in central Montreal encases the central archives and non-circulating rare books and reference center in a vast public space, with multiple floors of open-stack access to books and media, a large children's library, and ample study spaces, all wonderfully illuminated with quantities of natural light. The inaugural exposition of the Grande Bibliothèque declared to the community that *"Tous ces livres sont à toi!"*—"All these books are yours!" The high levels of foot traffic and positive responses to surveys in the first years since the Library's opening suggest that the combined national-public library model is working very well.

LIBRARIANSHIP

Another important modern development in the history of libraries has been the professionalization of librarianship. The rapid growth in size and number of libraries in the nineteenth and early twentieth centuries meant that there was a great need for individuals to staff them. Carnegie himself recognized the importance of librarians to the successful continuation of the many libraries he had built, and after 1919, all financial support from his Foundation was directed to library education and professional development, rather than to building. As they had been for millennia, nearly all the new libraries were initially managed and staffed by men, most of whom had scholarly backgrounds. For example, historian P.R. Harris reports that when a woman applied for a cataloguing position at the British Library in 1863, she was refused: at the time, the only positions for women were as maids and ladies' room attendants.

However, as women achieved higher educational qualifications and continued to move into the workforce, librarianship was one line of work that was increasingly open to them, and in 1895 the British Library hired its first woman to a professional post, to catalogue and organize a major bequest of postage stamps. Marian the Librarian, the character in *The Music Man* (1957) by American composer and playwright Meredith Wilson (1902–84), is thus a representative type. In 1912, the year in which the musical is set, many communities would have found themselves in a similar situation to the fictional town of River City, Iowa: needing someone to manage the collections and assist the readers in the new town library, and relying on an educated, single woman to fill that role.

Cataloguing Systems

Even as both men and women moved to fill the new positions created by the rapid expansion in the number of libraries, the structure and focus of those positions began to change in response to other factors related to the growth of the libraries' collections. In particular, the new librarians realized that it was incumbent on them to impose a better, more logically grounded system of organization on the libraries' holdings. Older libraries had often simply assigned a book a fixed spot on a shelf, and the next book acquired was set next to the previous one, sometimes regardless of author or topic. Every library had its own system, as well. This had worked while both the influx of books and the number of readers requiring access to them were relatively contained, and also while most stacks were closed. The staff at a particular library knew the idiosyncrasies of their locale's shelving and cataloguing system, and they could (usually) be relied on to find the needed books or manuscripts. However, as more materials poured in and as readers began to expect direct access to the shelves of certain kinds of libraries, it was clear that a better, more universal and infinitely expansive system of organization was required. Even such venerable libraries as the British Library undertook reform. Under Panizzi's guidance, by the 1850s all books in the library were assigned a distinctive *press-mark*, or cataloguing number, that incorporated the press (bookcase) number, the shelf number, and the book's actual position on the shelf. The pressmarks were written on the spines of every volume and also next to the book's entry in the catalogues. Although this was still a fixed location shelving system, it greatly facilitated the library staff's ability to retrieve and replace particular volumes quickly.

The key name in the history of library organization, however, is Melville (or Melvil) Dewey (1851–1931). As Matthew Battles recounts, Dewey was a life-long pursuant of efficiency, always seeking ways to save time and money. As a student, he worked in the library at Amherst College in Massachusetts, and he became frustrated with the illogicalities of its fixed location shelving system. He knew of the British Library's numerical classification system, and he also knew of other libraries that were divided according to branches of learning. Such systems had been used in various libraries going back to ancient times, and even the Vatican Library divided its collection into broad categories of sacred and profane. Dewey's innovation was to superimpose a decimal-based numerical system on broad classifications of knowledge: the *Dewey decimal system*. The Dewey decimal system, first published in 1876, organizes all knowledge into ten classes, which are further broken down into divisions and sections. Works are assigned a number based first on broad subject classification, and then on relationships within the subject, including place, time, and type of material. For example, *Literature* is in the eighth class, so all works related to literature begin with numbers in the 800s. The tens digit designates language or nationality: American literature is 810, British literature 820, German literature is 830, and so on. Within each language or national category, the ones digit signifies genre, from *poetry* (1) to *miscellaneous* (8), with the number 9 varying depending on the language or nationality. After the first three digits, a decimal is added, and the following digits designate time period and specific author.

So, for example, to find a copy of Shakespeare's *Romeo and Juliet* in a library organized on the Dewey decimal system, readers would search for 822 (English literature, drama), then 822.3 (Elizabethan period), then 822.33 (Shakespeare), and finally the proper letter from O to Z, which cover the individual works (letters A to N cover such texts as biographies, criticism, and complete editions in English or in translation). Shakespeare's tragedies are between S and Z, with *Romeo and Juliet* assigned the letter U. Primary texts of *Romeo and Juliet* begin with the number 822.33.U3, while secondary works (criticism and commentary about the play) begin with 822.33.U4.

The appeal of the Dewey decimal system was its logicality and expandability. Any book on any topic—and from any era—could be quickly assigned a unique number, and that number would be predictable from library to library. However, it wasn't just the rationality of Dewey's system that led to its rapid adoption in the United States and beyond, but also Dewey's other innovations in library science. As he did with his cataloguing system itself, Dewey had a knack for adapting, improving, and popularizing preexisting ideas. He adapted Harvard University's "slip catalogue"—cut up pieces of paper with book information on them—into a standardized *card catalogue*, a system of drawers filled with uniform-sized cards containing information about the books in the library (including their Dewey decimal numbers) and arranged by author, title, and subject headings. Card catalogues were much easier to update than the loose-leaf catalogue volumes used at the British Library and elsewhere: when new books were acquired, librarians could simply open the appropriate drawers and insert the new cards. Always entrepreneurial, Dewey formed a company, the Library Bureau, to sell the necessary cardstock and cabinets to accommodate his system, as well as other library furniture and accoutrements. (One not inexpensive item offered in an 1890 Library Bureau catalogue was an adjustable five-wheel Dewey classification number stamp, which promised to add "uniformity and legibility" to catalogue cards.) The card catalogues remained a prominent feature of nearly all libraries until the turn of the twenty-first century, when they were finally supplanted by electronic catalogues.

Dewey also was a founding member of the American Library Association (ALA), the oldest professional association of librarians. Created in Philadelphia in 1876 and now based in Chicago, the ALA is the largest library association in the world, with over 60,000 members. It has inspired the creation of similar organizations around the world, and it remains an important international advocate for literacy and freedom of information. He also helped establish the first professional journal for librarians, the *American Library Journal*, and in 1887 he founded the first library school at Columbia University in New York. The School of Library Economy was notable for admitting female students from the outset (although Dewey's assumption was that the women graduates would work under male library directors). All of these new institutions not only helped shape the emerging profession, but they also helped spread the use of Dewey's cataloguing system.

The major competitor for Dewey's cataloguing system is the subject headings system created for the Library of Congress in 1897. The *Library of Congress classification* system was devised by Herbert Putnam (1861–1955), who would soon after become the longest-serving Librarian of Congress. Up until 1897, the Library of Congress had used the fixed location system that had been set up by Thomas Jefferson. But as the Library was preparing for its move to the new building in 1897, Putnam realized that the move created an unprecedented opportunity to rationalize the collections and set them on a more systematic footing for the future. Like Dewey, he envisioned a cataloguing system that combined the orderliness of categories of knowledge with the expandability of numerals. The categories devised by Putnam were tailored to the actual holdings of the Library of Congress at the time, so they were essentially practical rather than theoretical. Although the Library of Congress subject headings proved so generally useful that they were quickly adopted by other libraries around the world, they have also garnered criticism from those who find them unduly America-centric.

The Library of Congress classification system begins with letters, rather than with numbers, starting from A, *General Works*, to Z, *Bibliography, Library Science, and General Information Resources*. A second letter designates additional subcategories within each class of books, and it is followed by a series of numbers, starting at 1 and continuing as required to provide subcategories under each heading. To use the example of Shakespeare's *Romeo and Juliet* again, under the Library of Congress system a reader would look first in Class P (Language and Literature), then in PR (English Literature), and finally in the range 2199 to 3195 (English Renaissance, 1500–1640). Within each period, the books are arranged alphabetically first by the primary authors' surnames, and then by title. Editions of *Romeo and Juliet* begin with PR2831 and are followed by a decimal point; the letter and number combinations after the decimal point are determined by such factors as the editors and the date of publication.

Specialization

Another outcome of the professionalization of library work was the development of a number of specialties within library science. For example, although many visitors to libraries interact mainly with librarians working in and around the circulation desks, most mid-sized to large libraries also employ staff who specialize in reference and acquisitions. Reference librarians have additional training that helps them direct patrons to the best information resources for their needs. Especially as electronic media have come to supplant print editions of essential reference works, such as encyclopedias, many readers have come to depend on reference librarians to help them identify and navigate the available databases. Collections managers and technical services staff, who do the physical work of ordering, cataloguing, and readying materials for library users (including attaching labels and anti-theft devices), usually work well out of the sight of most library visitors. However, without their efforts, the holdings of the library would be neither refreshed nor returned for other patrons' use.

Other library specialists include archivists and those who work in special collections. *Archives* are collections of documents, records, and other materials related to a particular subject, organization, or individual. Although they are often found in libraries, they can also be independent institutions or located within other kinds of organizations. For example, the Shakespeare Birthplace Trust in Stratford-upon-Avon manages a dedicated Library and Archive that brings together one of the largest collections of resources related to Shakespeare in the United Kingdom, including materials related to the Royal Shakespeare Company. The National Yiddish Book Center in Amherst, Massachusetts, was created to collect and preserve Yiddish books, many of which were simply being discarded as older Yiddish speakers died. Besides serving as an archive, the Yiddish Book Center also offers language classes and other educational programs and has helped to build Yiddish book collections in other libraries both large and small, and as far away as Australia, China, and Japan.

While both of these examples are stand-alone archives, the Labour History Archive and Study Centre in Manchester, England, is located within a larger institution, the People's History Museum. Consonant with the museum's focus on the history of working people and the industrial revolution, the Labour History Archive includes papers, periodicals, and pamphlets related to the British Labour Party and to the history of the trades union movement. Many university libraries include archives and special collections that feature rare, valuable, and focused books. Librarians who work in such archives and special collections are often accomplished, knowledgeable scholars in their own right, with a detailed knowledge of the contents, provenance, and interconnectedness of the collections under their management.

CONSERVATION AND PRESERVATION

One of the key roles of libraries today is the conservation and preservation of cultural history. Libraries are often described as the memory centers of human history: they are where the record of our thoughts and dreams are gathered together. When libraries are endangered, our heritage is at stake. When they are destroyed, they can take with them the fabric of an entire portion of humanity.

Because of the nature of their contents, libraries have always been particularly susceptible to the threats of flood and fire. As discussed in Chapter 6, war has often been a threat to libraries, but natural events can cause terrible destruction as well. The second half of the twentieth century witnessed a number of high-profile library disasters that prompted many libraries and professional associations to develop emergency preparedness plans. But more ordinary events, some virtually invisible, have also precipitated greater concern about library conservation and preservation. (Although the terms are frequently used synonymously in relation to librarianship, *conservation* entails the broader, ongoing program of stabilizing and protecting books and other materials, while *preservation* usually means the technical work of, say, repairing torn pages, damaged spines, or scratched surfaces.)

While libraries whose collections include many older and rare books have long been engaged in conservation and preservation efforts, in recent decades many more ordinary libraries have also had to expand their conservation programs, as it became clear that many of the items published in the late nineteenth and early twentieth century had been printed on chemically unstable, acidic paper. And another challenge has been the sheer proliferation of materials. Many libraries have run out of space for their collections, and hard decisions have had to be made about what to keep and what to discard in order to make room for new acquisitions.

Emergency Preparedness

One of the most important events driving emergency preparedness for libraries was the 1966 flood in Florence, Italy. The Arno River rose to its highest levels since the sixteenth century, and the water levels rose dramatically when fears that a critical dam would burst forced engineers to release additional water from the reservoir. In addition to the loss of over 100 lives and the displacement of thousands of people from their homes, many of the city's cultural treasures were destroyed or damaged. As one of the jewels of the Italian Renaissance, Florence was home to many architectural wonders, galleries, and numerous

libraries and archives. Among the most important—and most seriously affected—were the Biblioteca Nazionale Centrale di Firenze, or the National
Central Library of Florence, a copyright deposit library dating back to the
eighteenth century but containing books and manuscripts of all eras, and the
Biblioteca del Gabinetto Vieusseux, which contained an unprecedented collection of nineteenth-century European books and periodicals, especially those
having to do with the unification of Italy. Nearly one-third of the Biblioteca
Nazionale's holdings were damaged, and virtually all of the 250,000 volumes
of the Gabinetto Vieusseux. Relief workers in the Gabinetto Vieusseux found
pages had come loose from the books, floated upwards, and become stuck to
the ceilings. Another library disaster that riveted public attention was the burning of the Los Angeles Public Library in 1986. The fire was set by an arsonist in
the closed stacks, where a tightly packed system of vintage iron shelves created
a chimney for the flames and also made it almost impossible for firefighters
to get in and control the blaze. In addition to the 400,000 volumes destroyed
by the flames, as many as 1.2 million more were damaged by smoke and water.

Both of these disasters challenged the skills of the conservators. In disasters of this magnitude, preservation necessarily needs to be undertaken over
time, but books that have become wet must be dried quickly and in a controlled way to avoid the serious risk of mold. Since only a very limited number
of books could be attended to immediately, methods needed to be devised to
stabilize the others until they could be attended to. The solution was to freeze
the books, which would hold them until conservators could properly inspect
them and determine whether they could be restored. Once in the conservation
lab, the books would be carefully unbound, cleaned with distilled water, dried,
blocked, and rebound. However, because of the time and energy involved, only
the most important or valuable books could be restored; others would simply
have to be replaced.

In addition to providing crucial testing grounds for conservation methods, the disasters prompted many libraries to improve their facilities to defend
against such events and to develop emergency preparedness plans. For many
larger libraries, this has meant improving the climate control in stacks by stabilizing humidity and reducing exposure to sunlight, fluorescent lights, and
heat; installing fire doors and other barriers to isolate sections of the stacks and
reading rooms from one another; and installing smoke detection and sprinkler
systems. The emergency plans typically include schemes for removing materials from harm's way (if feasible) or making arrangements for additional offsite
storage space—and for the use of commercial freezers.

Brittle Books

The problem of *brittle books*, those printed on acidified paper and susceptible
to browning and crumbling, was first recognized as a major challenge to library collections in the 1960s. Books and periodicals published between the

1850s and 1980s—some 305 million volumes in the United States alone—had been printed on industrial wood-pulp paper (see Chapter 3). By the 1980s, the rhetoric in some circles about brittle books was bordering on hysterical. Books were described as disintegrating before one's very eyes, consuming themselves, as the title of a contemporary documentary put it, in *Slow Fires* (1987).

Although the condition of most acidic books and periodicals was nowhere near as dire as the alarmists made out, the idea that library collections large and small might simply self-destruct prompted a number of creative preservation efforts. The first plan was derived from earlier efforts to save space: microfilming. *Microfilm* (rolls) and *microfiche* (sheets) had been touted in the 1930s and 1940s as a solution to the proliferation of periodicals in library collections, especially newspapers. Proponents had argued that libraries could discard their bulky, unwieldy back files of newspapers and replace them with tidy, compact cabinets of microfilm, and most libraries went along with the scheme—ironically, as Nicholson Baker recounts in his 2001 jeremiad *Double Fold*, resulting in the destruction of so many archived copies that complete runs of the *New York World*, one of the most popular newspapers at the turn of the twentieth century, are now more rare than Gutenberg Bibles or Shakespeare First Folios. The "Microfix" advocates suggested doing for bound books what had already been done for periodicals. The problem was that in order to be microfilmed, the books, like the newspapers before them, would have to be unbound and cut apart. If they were indeed as fragile as feared, it would be impossible to rebind them and replace them on the shelves. In effect, the books would have to be destroyed to be saved.

The next set of solutions proposed to fight chemicals with chemicals. If the books were deteriorating because they were too acidic, then they should be deacidified: the paper should be treated so as to raise the pH to neutral (7.3+), stable levels. Two chemical treatments were attempted. The *DEZ process* employed diethyl zinc, a highly flammable chemical that was developed as a possible rocket fuel but rejected because it was too dangerous and unstable. DEZ binds to oxygen molecules to create zinc oxide, which is alkaline. The DEZ process entailed putting books on special racks in a vacuum chamber, subjecting them to high heat, impregnating them with the DEZ, and then cooling them down again. Testing showed that the process did reduce the acidity of the paper, but the chemicals, combined with the heat, also discolored the pages and their bindings. A major explosion and fire in 1985 ended the experiments.

Since a heat-based treatment had failed, more hope rested on the *Bookkeeper process*, which involved soaking books in a bath of alkaline magnesium oxide. When dried again, particles of the magnesium oxide would adhere to the pages through static electricity, reducing the acidity of the pages but leaving the surfaces with a strange dusty texture.

A better solution, digitization, developed in the 1990s and now looks like the path forward. Early digitization programs shared some of the limitations of microfilm: the scanned images were not always accurate or clear, and there was no good system for proofreading and correcting the digitized texts. However, second-generation digitization projects, including Google Books, seem to have resolved those issues, and they are also being conducted with greater care for the original books, or *leaf masters*. Digitization can make even the rarest and most fragile items accessible to readers anywhere, and the original can be returned to a safe, climate-controlled environment. (For more discussion of digitization projects, see Chapter 4.)

Space

More intractable for many libraries has been the challenge of space. As publications and other materials continue to pour in, libraries have either had to annex additional spaces or to thin their collections—a process formally called *deaccessioning*, but more colloquially known as *weeding*—to make room for them. As mentioned above, the need for more space is what initially motivated many microfilming efforts. It has also provided the rationale for a number of the major digitized databases that are now part of the essential collections of academic and larger public libraries, such as *JSTOR*.

Deciding what to remove from library shelves is a complicated process, but for more general collections usage is usually the most important factor. Many library systems operate ongoing usage surveys that count books that are actually checked out as well as ones that are removed from their place in the stacks. Such libraries often request that readers not re-shelve any books they remove, but instead place them on designated shelves or carts. Larger libraries and collections, especially those that support postgraduate research, sometimes shift infrequently used books to a remote storage site, rather than deaccessioning them altogether. That way, books that have fallen out of use can be retrieved again if requested. However, most libraries simply remove books that are no longer in regular demand. Formerly, such books formed the core of regular fund-raising book sales; now they tend to be more systematically disposed of through online sellers. Books in subjects that undergo rapid, regular transformation, such as those related to science and industry, tend to be weeded more quickly, while those in subjects like history or literature may remain indefinitely. Duplicates and earlier editions of works that have since been updated are also regularly deaccessioned.

All of these efforts to organize and preserve materials ultimately seek to serve one key constituency: readers. While both library staff and readers may joke about libraries that seem to discourage readers from touching the books—let alone removing them and reading them—without readers, books are literally just paperweights. The final chapter of this book will therefore turn its attention to the last component in the book publishing "communication circuit": readers.

SELECTED BIBLIOGRAPHY

Altick, Richard D. *The English Common Reader: A Social History of the Mass Reading Public, 1800–1900.* 2nd ed. Columbus: Ohio State UP, 1998.

American Library Association. http://www.ala.org.

Baker, Nicholson. *Double Fold: Libraries and the Assault on Paper.* New York: Random House, 2001.

Basbanes, Nicholas A. *Patience and Fortitude.* New York: HarperCollins, 2001.

Battles, Matthew. *Library: An Unquiet History.* New York: Norton, 2003.

Beason, Tyrone. "Branching into the Future." *Seattle Times,* 17 October 2010.

Bibliothèque Nationale de France. http://www.bnf.fr/fr/acc/x.accueil.html.

British Library. http://www.bl.uk.

Carnegie Libraries of California. http://www.carnegie-libraries.org.

Casper, Scott E., Jeffrey D. Groves, Stephen W. Nissenbaum, and Michael Winship, eds. *A History of the Book in America. Volume 3: The Industrial Book, 1840–1880.* Chapel Hill: U of North Carolina P, 2007.

Casson, Lionel. *Libraries in the Ancient World.* New Haven: Yale UP, 2001.

Chetham's Library. http://www.chethams.org.uk.

Chetham's Library: Three Centuries of the Written Word. London: Scala Publishers, 2008.

Chicago Public Library. http://www.chipublib.org/aboutcpl/history/index.php.

Cole, John Y. *Jefferson's Legacy: A Brief History of the Library of Congress.* 2006. http://www.loc.gov/loc/legacy.

Cross, Paul J. "The Private Case: A History." In *The Library of the British Museum: Retrospective Essays on the Department of Printed Books,* ed. P.R. Harris. London: British Library, 1991. 201–40.

Dickson, Paul. *The Library in America: A Celebration in Words and Pictures.* New York: Facts on File, 1986.

Esdaile, Arundell. *National Libraries of the World: Their History, Administration and Public Services.* 2nd ed. London: Library Association, 1957.

Fleming, Patrica Lockhart, Gilles Gallichan, and Yvan Lamonde, eds. *History of the Book in Canada. Volume One: Beginnings to 1840.* Toronto: U of Toronto P, 2004.

Goodnough, Abby. "Town Seeks a Library Benefactor to Ward Off Taxes." *New York Times,* 18 November 2008.

Griest, Guinivere L. *Mudie's Circulating Library and the Victorian Novel.* Bloomington: Indiana UP, 1970.

Harris, P.R. *A History of the British Museum Library, 1753–1973.* London: British Library, 1998.

Jefferson, G. *Libraries and Society.* Cambridge: James Clarke, 1969.

Johnson, Elmer D., and Michael H. Harris. *History of Libraries in the Western World.* 3rd ed. Metuchen, NJ: Scarecrow, 1976.

Lamonde, Yvan, Patricia Lockhart Fleming, and Fiona A. Black, eds. *History of the Book in Canada. Volume 2: 1840–1918.* Toronto: U of Toronto P, 2005.

Library of Congress. http://www.loc.gov.

Line, Maurice B., and Joyce Line, eds. *National Libraries*. 3 vols. London: Aslib, 1979–95.

MacLennan, Birdie. "The Library and Its Place in Cultural Memory: The Grande Bibliothèque due Québec in the Construction of Social and Cultural Identity." *Libraries and the Cultural Record* 42.4 (2007): 349–86.

Mearns, David C. *The Story Up to Now: The Library of Congress, 1800–1946*. Washington, DC: Library of Congress, 1947.

New York Public Library. http://www.nypl.org/help/about-nypl/history.

Page, Benedicte. "National Library Day Marks a Year of Protests Against Library Closures." *The Guardian*, 2 February 2012.

John Passmore Edwards. http://www.passmoreedwards.org.uk.

Petroski, Henry. *The Book on the Bookshelf*. New York: Knopf, 1999.

Pullman, Philip. "Leave the Libraries Alone. You Don't Understand Their Value." 20 January 2011. http://falseeconomy.org.uk/blog/save-oxfordshire-libraries-speech-philip-pullman.

Slow Fires: On the Preservation of the Human Record. Dir. Terry Sanders. American Film Foundation, 1987.

Stam, David H., ed. *International Dictionary of Library Histories*. 2 vols. Chicago: Fitzroy Dearborn, 2001.

Tacoma Public Library. http://www.tpl.lib.wa.us/page.aspx?hid=42.

Tolzmann, Don Heinrich, Alfred Hessel, and Reuben Peiss. *The Memory of Mankind: The Story of Libraries Since the Dawn of History*. New Castle, DE: Oak Knoll, 2001.

"Tous ces livres sont à toi!" De l'Oeuvre des bons livres à la Grande Bibliothèque (1844–2005). Montreal: Bibliothèque Nationale du Québec et Les Presses de l'Université Laval, 2005.

Vatican Library. http://www.vaticanlibrary.va/home.php?pag=storia.

Wollan, Malia. "One Way to Encourage Checking-Out at the Library." *New York Times*, 3 March 2011.

Yeats, William Butler. Chapter 12. *Four Years*. 1921. The Literature Network. http://www.online-literature.com/yeats/four-years/12/.

CHAPTER TEN

READERS

In an essay about the founding of the Reading Experience Database (RED), publishing historian Simon Eliot muses about the challenges of studying the history of reading. Just because we know that certain persons came into contact with, or even possessed, certain books, we can't necessarily know if they *read* them. The world is full of beautiful, well-stocked libraries used only for sleeping. Nearly everyone has a story of buying or borrowing a book that was acquired more to impress someone else than for actual consumption (or that they really intended to read but somehow never did). People regularly quote (or misquote) authors without having actually read them; most reading performed by people the world over is (and likely always has been) the kind of quick, ephemeral reading that seldom gets recorded: scanning posters, advertisements, news items, or even—although Eliot doesn't mention them—tweets and text messages. With the evidence of reading so hard to find and difficult to quantify, why even bother to search it out? Because, Eliot explains, if we want to understand the history of the book, we have no alternative: "To write the history of a product without also writing the history of its consumption is to have a cart without a horse.... the way books are read, who reads which books, determines the intellectual and cultural context in which the next generation of books will be read," as well as influencing the views and techniques of those who will write them.

Readers complete Robert Darnton's "book circuit," closing the loops that connect authors to publishers to distributors like stores and libraries to the people for whom the words were ultimately intended. For many authors, the belief in an ideal reader out there somewhere, the one who is waiting to hear their message, is what keeps the words flowing. Opportunities to interact with their readers, through readings and lecture tours, book signings, or chat rooms, blogs, and tweets, can be as gratifying to the authors as meeting the authors can be to their fans. Similarly, readers enjoy interacting with one another, sharing their enthusiasms or dislikes, and becoming bound together through their common journey through a given text. But they also enjoy simply losing themselves in the author's world or in the pure experience of reading itself. Mexican writer Gabriel Zaid (b. 1934) says that reading's essential pleasure is that it "liberates the reader and transports him from his book to a reading of himself and all of life."

Those who study the history and theory of reading tend to follow particular methodological approaches. As literary historian Bonnie Gunzenhauser explains, some scholars take a mostly empirical approach, gathering detailed statistics in order to answer questions about what was being read and by whom in a particular time and place. Others take a more theoretical approach, asking how the meaning of given texts, and of the era and environment in which they exist, is shaped by those who read them. Still others focus on the neurological and pedagogical aspects of reading, seeking to understand how we coordinate the complex tasks that enable us to decipher the various systems used to render speech into visual (or tactile) symbols and how best to teach those skills to children and others who have not yet acquired them.

This chapter will explore several facets of reading. It will first explore the different kinds and purposes of reading, as well as the trends in who reads and why. Along with *literacy* and *illiteracy*—the ability and lack of ability to read and write—this section will also explore the phenomenon of *aliteracy*, the choice *not* to read by those who have the skills to do so. The chapter will also look at some of the tools developed to aid reading, from spectacles and book rests to the latest innovations in e-readers. The chapter will also consider how a sense of community can shape the experience of reading, and it will conclude with a look at some of the most popular kinds of books, in order to better understand how readers' decisions about what they read for pleasure can both complement and challenge reading for other purposes.

LITERACY

A Saharan proverb says "Praise God for the one who brought us the pens that spared us from having to use our feet and replaced the need for speech with words." Writing and reading bring the world closer. Because of the power of the written word, *literacy*, or the ability to read and write, is now highly valued in most cultures. Literacy not only fundamentally improves most individuals' chances for bettering themselves socially and economically, but it also plays a critical role in ethical, moral, and religious education. Thus, religious and state institutions have been at the forefront in efforts to teach children and adults how to read, and many countries and organizations track literacy rates as an important indicator of progress. According to UNESCO, the global adult literacy rate in 2010 was 84.1 per cent, with male literacy (88.6 per cent) almost 10 per cent higher than female literacy (79.7 per cent). The regions with the highest levels of illiteracy are mainly in the developing world, especially in Southern Asia and sub-Saharan Africa. Women have made some gains in recent years, but they still make up the largest numbers of those who cannot read, comprising 64.1 per cent of the total. By contrast, in the developed world, literacy rates tend to be quite high, usually 99 to 100 per cent, with male and female literacy rates much more closely aligned.

Because literacy is so crucial to many aspects of modern life, being unable to read is a real disadvantage. According to the National Coalition for Literacy, for example, in the United States those who live in poverty or who are imprisoned are much more likely than the general population to be illiterate. The UK National Literacy Trust observes that not just illiteracy but poor literacy skills also hold people back: 63 per cent of men and 74 per cent of women with poor skills never receive employment promotions. Many who cannot read are ashamed of the fact, and they may develop elaborate strategies to prevent anyone from realizing their predicament. Claiming not to have one's glasses is a common ploy, as is simply following someone else's lead. Such individuals may not reveal their secret until much later in life. In 2012, ninety-eight-year-old James Arruda Henry made international news for revealing his lifelong illiteracy. He had managed to conceal the fact by employing a number of stratagems, including asking people to repeat written information for him and sending his wife to secretarial training so she could handle the family's household accounts. However, at age ninety-two he heard of another older man's rise from illiteracy: George Dawson, the grandson of

GEORGE DAWSON: LATE-LIFE LITERACY

George Dawson (1898–2001), sometimes referred to as a "poster child for literacy," was the grandson of former slaves who finally learned to read and write at the age of ninety-eight. Born in Marshall, Texas, Dawson grew up in the difficult era of segregation and Jim Crow laws, and one of his earliest memories was of the lynching of a black boy. The eldest of five children, Dawson, like his parents before him, was never schooled, although his younger siblings were. Instead, from the age of eight he worked in a variety of manual labor jobs to help support the family, progressing over the years from sawmill worker to road repair to dairyman.

Although Dawson had been interested in the idea of education and reading when he was a child, he simply never had the time or opportunity to learn to read. His wife was literate and handled most of the family business that required reading skills. It wasn't until he was in his nineties that both time and opportunity came to him: a literacy volunteer in Dallas stopped at his door, and after talking to the volunteer for a while, and learning that he had worked with other adult learners, Dawson decided to learn to read.

Over the next few years, Dawson learned to read and began to study for his General Education Degree, or GED. When he turned 100 in 1998, his fellow students threw him a surprise birthday party, and for the first time in his life, he was able to read his cards on his own. Dawson next worked with Richard Glaubman to write a memoir, *Life Is So Good* (2000). The poignancy and optimism of Dawson's memoir garnered much media attention, and in 2001 he was invited to appear on the *Oprah Winfrey Show*.

former slaves who finally learned to read and write at the age of ninety-eight. Dawson's memoir *Life Is So Good* (2000) won him an appearance on the *Oprah* television show, and he was also dubbed a "poster child for literacy." Henry decided that if Dawson could do it, so could he, so at age ninety-two he began teaching himself to read. His wife's death set back his efforts, but he eventually tried again, and with the help of a literacy tutor he not only learned to read but also wrote his own memoir, *In a Fisherman's Language* (2012).

Until fairly recently, the mechanisms by which the brain learns to read were not terribly well understood, and those who failed to learn to read were often unfairly branded as insufficiently motivated or less mentally equipped. However, contemporary research on *dyslexia*, the inability to process the inputs and information required to read and write, has shown that individuals with the condition (also known as *developmental reading disorder*, or *DRD*) generally have average or even above-average intelligence levels. Certain physical conditions, which often run in families, interfere with the brain's language processing capabilities, and this makes it difficult for dyslexics to coordinate the various physiological and mental processes necessary for reading. For example, it is difficult for many dyslexics to come up with rhyming words or to separate the component sounds (*phonemes*) that make up spoken words. This in turn interferes with their ability to recognize individual words or words combined in sentences. However, as the underlying causes of dyslexia have become better understood, scientists and educators have been able to devise systems to help many dyslexics to work around their particular challenges and learn to read and write.

Another rare brain-based problem is *alexia*, the inability to read after one has already learned to do so. The neurologist and popular science writer Oliver Sacks (b. 1933) has described the case of Howard Engel (b. 1931), a Canadian detective fiction writer, who as a result of a stroke in 2001 lost his ability to read. His first realization that there was a problem was when he picked up his morning paper and thought that it had been printed in not just another language, but another writing system—Cyrillic or Korean, perhaps. Engel's stroke had affected the part of the brain associated with recognizing visual word forms, a process that combines information from auditory and speech areas, as well as from intellectual, executive, memory, and emotion areas. Fortunately for Engel, however, his form of alexia turned out to be *alexia sine agraphia*: the inability to read *without* the inability to write. Through slow experimentation, Engel discovered he could still write fairly fluently, although he could not read what he had just written. And gradually, as he continued writing and trying to read, his condition improved sufficiently that he could make out letters and words. He eventually began work on another novel in his Benny Cooperman series, in which the detective is afflicted with the same condition from which the author was suffering. Engel employed a range of typographical strategies (larger and bolder fonts, special indenting systems) so that he could read portions of his own drafts, and he also relied on his editor to read the completed draft aloud to him, so that he could fix the structure in his mind. The novel, entitled *Memory Book*, was published in 2005.

Aliteracy

Socioeconomic, educational, and neuro-physiological disadvantages may all create barriers to literacy. But there are other challenges to reading, as well. In recent years, many individuals and institutions in the book world have turned their attention to the phenomenon of *aliteracy*, the refusal to read even though one can. As many aspects of modern culture have become more visual, more and more people have chosen not to read, especially not to read books. A 2001 article in the *Washington Post* noted the increase in aliteracy in the West, especially in the United States, and cited reading specialists who pointed out that most of the reading done in the contemporary world is *efferent*, or purposeful (as in reading for information), rather than *aesthetic*, or pleasurable. Those who do not read for pleasure do not benefit from books' ability to stretch and flex the imagination, and they thus miss out on important opportunities to improve their own quality of life. But what concerned some experts even more was that those who regularly avoided reading now were less likely to pass the habits of literacy along to the next generation. Parents are the most important reading role models for children. Their failure to read could ultimately result in a reduced quality of life for others, as well.

These concerns have prompted a number of studies to assess who is and isn't reading. In the United Kingdom, organizations such as the National Literacy Trust regularly assess reading levels and survey individuals to determine what and how often they are reading. A 2012 report notes that reading drops off significantly from childhood to teen years, with 30 per cent of five- to eight-year-olds but only 17 per cent of fifteen- to seventeen-year-olds reading from a book every day. (Teenagers do read other materials.) The Public Lending Right (PLR), an organization that has tracked library usage since the early 1980s, primarily to ensure that author royalties are accurately assessed, also reports that adult borrowing from libraries has dropped in recent decades. In particular, adult borrowing of fiction—a key component of pleasure reading—has dropped significantly.

The drop-off in general reading rates caused a frustrated Missouri bookstore owner to burn his overstock in 2007, when he could not find any libraries or thrift stores to take the books. Tom Wayne cited a downturn in customer traffic and an overall decrease in reading rates as his reason for lighting a pyre outside of Prospero's Books in Kansas City. The store's website now claims this was a piece of performance art, akin to the more recent "Book Burning Party" campaign in Troy, Michigan, which sought to overcome resistance to a public library levy by threatening instead to simply close the library and have a book-burning party. The save-the-library campaign not only garnered unprecedented support for the levy, but it also won an advertising award.

In the United States, the National Endowment for the Arts (NEA) has conducted a number of studies to determine why and how American reading habits have changed. The 2004 and 2007 NEA studies, *Reading at Risk* and *To Read or Not to Read*, provided sobering evidence that not only were Americans reading less, but they were also participating less in many aspects of civic and cultural life. As in the United Kingdom, reading rates dropped off in the teen years, but book-reading among college graduates also declined. According to the 2004 study, only about half of adults in the United States reported reading any kind of book outside of those required for work or school, and fewer than half of those surveyed reported reading a "literary" book. Both studies reported that those who read less also attended fewer cultural and sporting events, volunteered less in their communities, and voted less frequently. While the 2007 study cautioned that correlation did not mean causation, the documented decline in engagement with others—whether mediated through books or not—warranted attention.

Happily, the most recent NEA study, from 2009, provides a bit of hope. *Reading on the Rise: A New Chapter in American Literacy* reports the first marked increase in adult literary reading in the United States in more than two decades, with improvements in all categories (men, women, and all ethnic or racial groups). In his preface, Dana Gioia, the Chairman of the NEA, notes with particular satisfaction the significant increase in literary reading among young adults aged eighteen to twenty-four, who reversed a 20 per cent decline in reading in 2002 to a 21 per cent increase in 2008. He credits this dramatic reversal to the concerted literacy efforts launched in the wake of the earlier, alarming reports.

There have been many efforts at all levels of society to combat both illiteracy and aliteracy. Many communities support literacy initiatives of one sort or another, including extra tutoring in schools, adult education outreach programs, parenting classes, and various kinds of community reading networks. Some of these programs and reading communities are discussed later in this chapter.

TOOLS FOR READING

In *A History of Reading* (1996), Argentine-born writer Alberto Manguel (b. 1948) describes a series of gestures familiar to many readers:

> pulling the glasses out of a case, cleaning them with a tissue or the hem of the blouse or the tip of the tie, perching them on the nose and steadying them behind the ears before peering at the now lucid page held in front of us. Then pushing them up or sliding them down the glistening bridge of the nose in order to bring the letters into focus

and, after a while, lifting them off and rubbing the skin between the eyebrows, screwing the eyelids shut to keep out the siren text.

The invention of eyeglasses is just one of many synergistic developments in the history of the book. Without the development of these various tools, reading would not only be more uncomfortable and inconvenient, but in some instances it would be virtually impossible. *Presbyopia*, a condition in which the lens of the eye loses its ability to focus on closer-in items, gets its name from the Greek for "old man" (*presby*). It tends to afflict individuals in their forties, just at the age when many scholars are reaching their most productive years. Without better light sources, spectacles, and other aids to reading, the world of books would be closed to those most likely to contribute further riches to it.

Aids to Vision

Readers have always sought better light to help them extend their hours—and years—of reading. As discussed in earlier chapters, libraries and scriptoria through the ages have been carefully sited to make maximum use of natural light. Larger windows with better glass contributed greatly to the productivity and ease with which readers could scan a page or copy a text. The development of different kinds of lamps, candles, screens, and shades have also been crucial to extending the reading and writing life. In earlier eras, glass surrounds or *chimneys* not only helped prevent drafts from blowing out candle and lamp flames, but they also helped to magnify the light, making it easier to see. They could also be used to isolate candles from flammable items like bed linens, thereby allowing centuries of readers to read in the comfort of bed. *Snuffers* helped remove excess wax and straighten the wicks of candles so that the flames would burn more cleanly, just as adjustable wicks allowed lamps to be turned up or down to better illuminate a page or to reduce glare. Various systems and sizes of screens could be used to protect readers' eyes from the glare of a candle or fire while at the same time directing more light on the page.

   In the nineteenth century, gaslights extended both work and leisure hours by bringing safe, comparatively bright light into public buildings and private homes, and by the end of the century it was being augmented and then replaced by electric lights. Lampshades made of green glass, as well as special visors made of green-tinted leather or fabric (the proverbial *green eyeshades*), were devised to protect the eyes from the unaccustomed glare of these artificial lights. In the twentieth and twenty-first centuries, manufacturers have experimented with different kinds of lightbulbs that not only save energy but better reproduce the full-spectrum light of the sun, making it easier to see the page without eyestrain. And the latest generation of e-readers now allows readers to read in bed from gently backlit screens.

   Most readers in the developed world probably take bright, reliable lighting for granted, but elsewhere in the world it can be difficult to come by. In

Guinea, one of the poorest nations in the world, only about one-fifth of the population has access to electricity, and even then it is subject to frequent power cuts. As a result, as dusk settles, students of all ages gravitate to the few sites with reliable electric lighting: the parking lots at Gbessia International Airport and at petrol stations, and sometimes in the faint pools of light cast just outside the windows of wealthier Guineans. A 2007 article described children and young adults reading peaceably at the airport, often in age-related clusters under the arc of the lights. One university student said living near the airport gave him an edge: his reading days could be extended beyond those of Guineans in other parts of the country.

Spectacles have a surprisingly long history. Before custom-made lenses were devised, readers used a variety of devices to magnify the texts they were studying. Among the tools used in the ancient world were tubes of reed or paper (which would help the eye to focus on a particular spot), various kinds of clear crystals or lumps of polished glass, and glass bowls filled with water. No one knows who invented the first set of purpose-made reading lenses, but they were probably devised by a craftsman in the region of Pisa, Italy. They were already in fairly wide use by the thirteenth century. According to Manguel, by 1268 the English scientist Roger Bacon (c. 1214–92) was describing magnifying lenses in a way that appears to be from experience, rather than from hearsay, and in 1306, a priest in Florence told his congregation that he had met the inventor of spectacles. Italian author Umberto Eco's (b. 1932) historical novel *The Name of the Rose* (1980), set in the early fourteenth century, features a mystery-solving English monk, William of Baskerville, who, among other things, wears spectacles. The Guild of Venetian Crystal Workers already had official rules governing the procedure for making eyeglasses as early as 1301. We have illustrations of some of the earliest models of spectacles, and also some physical evidence of what they looked like. For example, a scholar working in the Rare Books Room at the Harry Ransom Center in Texas recently discovered the impression of a pair of medieval spectacles in the endpapers of one of the Center's early printed books. The design of the glasses suggests that they were made in the late 1400s or early 1500s. The owner of the glasses had evidently left them inside the back cover when he closed the book. Other early books have been found with space for spectacles hollowed out of their wooden covers.

Glasses remained fairly rare and expensive until the fifteenth century, when the proliferation of print increased the demand and made it more economical to produce them. According to Steven Fischer, the eyeglass styles changed gradually over the ensuing centuries. The earliest pairs were designed to clip on just above the bridge of the nose; the earliest known depiction of this kind of spectacles is in a 1352 portrait of Cardinal Hugh of Saint-Cher (c. 1200–63) in Provence. Later iterations included *lorgnettes*, spectacles mounted on a handle and popular in the eighteenth century; single-lens *monocles*, which became popular in the nineteenth century; and eyeglasses with hooked arms that fastened over the ears, also a nineteenth-century innovation. Bifocals,

a	b	c	d	e	f	g	h	i	j	k

l	m	n	o	p	q	r	s	t	u	v

w	x	y	z

Braille alphabet.

trifocals, tinted lenses, and many other variants came along as lens-making technology improved, and the twentieth century ushered in the era of contact lenses and refined surgical correction. All of these have significantly extended the number of years and greater ease with which readers can read.

Other strategies have been required to make book culture available to those whose vision is more severely impaired. For generations, most individuals who could not read for themselves for whatever reason—age, illiteracy, lack of visual acuity—relied on having words read to them. Reading aloud remains a powerful force for instilling a love for books: many committed readers have fond memories of being read to by family members or of attending organized story times in libraries and schools. However, in the eighteenth and nineteenth centuries, special measures began to be taken to make books immediately accessible to visually impaired readers.

One of the most renowned innovators was Louis Braille (1809–52). Blinded as the result of a childhood accident, Braille attended one of the first schools in the world especially for the blind, the National Institute for Blind Children in Paris. In order to teach the children to read, the school initially relied on specially printed books whose words were embossed in large type on heavy paper and traced by the children's fingers; in order to write, the children learned to trace leather cutouts of letters. The books produced in this way were necessarily rather cumbersome, and they did not contain a great deal of information. One of Braille's dreams was to devise a more flexible system that could open up the entire world of books to the visually impaired. In the 1820s, Braille learned of a special military code that consisted entirely of raised bumps and dashes. The code was meant to be read solely by the fingers, so that soldiers would not need to strike a light on the battlefield and risk giving away their positions. By 1824, Braille had refined the system to just six raised dots that could be combined to create any letter and could be read with just one touch of the finger. Later innovations included a device with a sliding frame affixed to a slate, so that blind students could use a stylus to write in legibly straight lines, and a Braille typewriter. Although Braille's writing system was adopted by his school only after his death, in the next generation it gradually spread throughout Europe and the world.

By the early twentieth century, most countries had schools for the blind, produced Braille books through both private and governmental programs, and were also using sound recording technology to produce "talking books." In the late twentieth century, the (re)discovery that many sighted readers also enjoyed listening to books helped expand the market for audiobooks, and at about the same time computers provided invaluable additional tools for improving visually impaired persons' access to print culture.

Devices for Readers

From the earliest days, readers and writers have sought tools that would make their activities easier and more comfortable. As discussed in Chapter 3, one theory behind the success of the codex over the scroll was that the codex was easier to flip through and to transport. With the help of a sturdy paperweight (or perhaps just another volume) and a few bookmarks, readers could lay a codex-format book flat and move back and forth between selected pages, taking notes or making annotations as necessary. But there are many other practical devices that have been developed over the millennia to make readers' work easier. For example, the *lectern* (also sometimes called a *bookstand* or *copy stand*): depicted in some of the earliest illustrations of book reading and writing, lecterns hold books at a slight angle for greater ease in reading. The most useful have adjustable bars or arms that will hold the books open, leaving both of the reader's hands free for note-taking.

But what if you have more than one book that you wish to consult? Alberto Manguel describes a number of early, ingenious devices that provided readers with easy access to multiple books. For example, a fourteenth-century engraving depicts an octagonal desk that enables a scholar to work at one position, then swivel the desk and read the books from any of the other seven positions. A sixteenth-century engraving in a book on useful machines shows a wonderful large vertical, wheel-shaped desk. The reader would load the books into the machine, then sit and turn the wheel up or down to access the desired volume. In the early nineteenth century, US President and book lover Thomas Jefferson (1743–1826) devised a revolving bookstand at his home in Monticello. The stand could hold as many as five books at a time, all in adjustable book rests, and it folded down into a tidy cube for storage purposes.

Bookshelves, although often taken for granted, also have a venerable history. In *The Book on the Bookshelf* (1999), engineer and cultural historian Henry Petroski (b. 1942) traces the innovations in bookcase design and materials from the jars, baskets, and bins used for storing scrolls to the various kinds of shelves that now store codices. As anyone who has purchased inexpensive particle-board bookcases has learned to their sorrow, bookcases have to be sturdy enough to support the weight of the books. Thus, as collections of books burgeoned in the nineteenth and twentieth centuries, one of the engineering challenges was to find materials and shelf layouts that could satisfactorily support vast quantities of books. Iron was the first modern innovation: it was used in the 1857 British Library Reading Room and other libraries to provide both shelf space and structural support for the library building (see Chapter 9). Iron was eventually replaced by steel and other lighter, stronger metals.

The introduction of electricity at the turn of the twentieth century meant that book stacks no longer needed to let in natural light, so the shelves could be taller and placed closer together. Movable bookcases had been in existence for centuries—for example, in grand private libraries, where shelves were hinged on doors so that when they were closed, the inhabitants would see an uninterrupted, complete wall of books. In the early twentieth century, however, shelves were devised that could be rolled together when the books on them did not need to be consulted, thereby enabling even more shelves to be fitted into the same floor space. Contemporary versions of such *compact shelving* typically involve two fixed (immovable) ranges, with three or four sliding ranks between them. Turning a crank slides one or more ranks of shelves forward or backward on rails embedded in the floor, enabling one aisle to be opened at a time.

Other reading devices can be much smaller and more modest. Many readers use bookmarks, whether they are custom-made or merely a torn scrap of paper. For many book lovers, either option is far preferable to *dog-earing* (turning over a corner of the page) or simply leaving the book face down on a table. In an essay in her 1998 book *Ex Libris*, American author Anne Fadiman (b. 1953) recalls a hotel maid leaving a stern note for her brother, who had left his book face down. "Never do that to a book!" the maid admonished, having inserted a bookmark at the appropriate place and left the book neatly closed on the nightstand. Fadiman uses the essay to distinguish between what she calls "courtly" and "carnal" readers of books. Courtly readers observe the niceties of proper bookmarks, and they protect the covers and spines of their books from damage or even signs of use. Carnal readers, by contrast, leave books any which way and are as happy marking pages with feathers and dead bugs as with dog-ears. Cheerfully describing her own book-loving family as determinedly "carnal," Fadiman notes with wonder friends and colleagues who actually buy two copies of every book, one for reading, and the other to be preserved, pristine and smooth, on the shelf.

Other book devices include erasable pens and pencils that allow for note-taking and highlighting without permanent consequences, custom-made adhesive flags and other removable markers that can be used to indicate key passages, padded lap desks and pillows to facilitate reading while reclining, detachable lights for reading in the dark, mini-projectors for beaming a book's pages on to the ceiling or wall, and a plethora of covers, carriers, and other gear to make transporting and protecting books easier and more attractive. Nearly all of the items devised for printed books have their e-book analogues. All of these tools, added to the standard furniture of desks and chairs, testify to the importance of the act of reading.

READING COMMUNITIES

Although many think of reading as a fundamentally solitary occupation—the reader alone, lost in a book—reading can also be an important social activity. A recent study by the Pew Research Center, for example, shows that many readers are still deeply committed to reading to children and sharing their reading experiences with others. (Those who read with children also overwhelmingly prefer print books to e-books for that purpose.) In the modern era, readers have often joined together in reading communities such as book societies or clubs to share topics of research, to discuss their own writing, to provide a direction for future investigations, or simply to talk about what they have read. Some of these communities have been fairly informal: spontaneous or semi-regular gatherings at coffeehouses or taverns, for example, or encounters at literary evenings or salons. Others have been very formal, with official memberships and scheduled presentations of lectures and discussions. Some groups have been centered on the notion of mutual self-improvement, while others have focused on pleasure reading and the simpler joys of sharing a book.

Historians have been actively engaged in collecting and publishing information about reading communities in various times and places, and also about how such communities can bridge geographic distance and distinctions of class and origin. One important international effort to gather evidence about reading practices is the Reading Experience Database (RED), which has initiatives in the United Kingdom, Australia, New Zealand, Canada, and the Netherlands. Launched in 1996 and covering the period of 1450 to 1945, the RED already contains over 30,000 records and is growing daily; the public is cordially invited to contribute additional records. In other projects, historians have documented, for example, the importance of reading communities to the Enlightenment. From the seventeenth century, various groups of professional and amateur scholars across Europe met and corresponded regularly to discuss new discoveries and theories. Some of these groups eventually achieved official status in their respective countries, like the Académie Française, begun in 1635 to formalize rules for the French language, or the Royal Society, founded in 1660 in London to further scientific study and experimentation. Others were more informal but nevertheless influential associations, such as the Lunar Society of Birmingham. The "Lunar men" were a group of manufacturers and professional men in the British Midlands who began meeting in the 1760s and went on to become some of the founding fathers of the industrial revolution.

Readership studies have also examined reading communities created to serve particular groups of readers, whether they were formed on the basis of gender, race, or economic status. Communal reading has long played an important role in women's lives, both before and after women began to have access to better educational opportunities. Scholars have brought to light the importance of shared reading to women religious in the Middle Ages; to those participating in more formal literary societies, from the Blue Stockings Society of 1750s England to the many Shakespeare clubs that arose in the rural United States in the late nineteenth century; and to women in contemporary Iran. As Persian writer Azar Nafisi's (b. 1947) *Reading Lolita in Tehran* (2003) reveals, such groups have provided women readers with active, supportive forums in which they can engage seriously with what they are reading. Studies have also revealed the importance of reading societies for minority groups within the culture, such as the "Negro Literary Societies" created in the United States in the nineteenth century, and of those serving poorer and working-class readers, such as the many mechanics' institutes created in the industrial age. Children's reading has also become a distinct subdiscipline of literary and historical study over the past generation, with scholars exploring how the emergence of a distinct body of books intended for children has shaped the reading habits and world views of both younger and older readers.

Readership studies of particular periodicals have also yielded fascinating accounts of how the readers and writers involved with those publications conceive of themselves as an interconnected, interactive community. And anyone who has written or followed a blog or a *cellphone novel* (a narrative written completely in text screens and usually accessed from a website, first popularized in Japan), or who has engaged with such contemporary phenomena as *fan fiction* or *fanfic* (stories written by fans about the characters and settings created by authors), knows that such communities of readers and writers can be completely absorbing.

In the past century, a couple of especially influential reading communities have included the first major mass-market book club and the more recent "book clubs of the air." The Book-of-the-Month Club, Oprah Winfrey's book club in North America, and the on-air club founded in the United Kingdom by Richard Madeley and Judy Finnigan, have all involved millions of readers. Although each of these clubs has been criticized for the kinds and the quality of literature that they have advocated, and also for their approaches to reading and culture, what makes them stand out is the incredible reach each club has had during its heyday. Because of their great popularity, they offer some valuable insights into prevailing ideas about reading and readers in the twentieth and twenty-first centuries.

The Book-of-the-Month Club

Although literary societies in North America date at least as far back as the Junto, founded by Benjamin Franklin (1706–90) in Philadelphia in 1726, they began to proliferate at the turn of the twentieth century. Most of the literary societies and clubs were local and thus relatively small. This changed with the creation of the Book-of-the-Month Club (BOMC), the brainchild of a Manhattan advertising copywriter, Harry Scherman (1887–1969). After an abortive university career (despite being an engaged scholar and gifted linguist, he dropped out of university twice), Scherman moved to New York City and worked as a critic and playwright. According to cultural historian Janice Radway (b. 1949), Scherman initially turned to copywriting as a sideline to support his more serious literary endeavors. However, he discovered he had a knack for writing catalogue copy, especially ads for mail-order books.

Scherman's first success in selling complete lines of books involved the Little Leather Library, a set of tiny editions (3 1/4 x 4 inches) of Shakespeare and other classic works. Published in the early 1920s, the collection grew to include about 100 books that were sold first in dime stores and then by mail. Although the books sold very well—sales estimates are between 30 and 40 million individual volumes—Scherman realized early on that their potential was limited: by definition, there were only a certain number of "classic" works. If he wanted customers to continue purchasing books, he would need to expand the texts that were available, and that meant selling new books. But new books were risky: how could readers know that they would like them and, more importantly, be impelled to buy more? Scherman's solution was to market not particular books but the "book habit." Subscribers to his new venture would receive a regular infusion of new reading materials, selected by experts, that would keep them on a steady diet of solid and pleasurable fare.

The Book-of-the-Month Club was launched in 1926. It incorporated a number of distinctive features that contributed to its success. First, it promised to send readers the "best" books published each month, books that were billed as classics in the making. These books were selected by a panel of judges whose decisions were guided by what they felt would have a broad appeal to the tastes and aspirations of BOMC members. Since most of the BOMC's subscribers were thought to be teachers, professionals, and managers—knowledge workers of various kinds—the books were selected with their interests and concerns in mind. Moreover, although literary books were frequently included in the lists, reflecting the belief that BOMC's readers wanted to know which new books were gathering critical bouquets, literary works were not the only ones selected, nor were they even the majority of offerings.

As Radway explains it, the books under consideration for the BOMC were divided into categories, such as "serious fiction" or "hammock literature," "sea sagas" or "woman's novels," "literary biographies" or "nature books." Each category was assessed within its own set or "plane" of expectations and on its own merits. The goal was to select the best representatives of each type of book. If a reader liked mysteries, then BOMC's detective fiction offerings could be trusted to offer a good read; if a reader preferred popular history, then the titles in that category would likely prove interesting. In many respects, the selection committee's choices were surprisingly broad-minded, and a number of BOMC selections went on to become bestsellers—indeed, are now considered classics. But the judges also tended to avoid certain kinds of books. For example, they steered clear of much literary fiction that was deemed too challenging, including many works of high Modernism, and they also avoided books that strayed too far from what were perceived to be their white, middle-class subscribers' interests. Although minority authors and books that presented more diverse or multicultural experiences were few and far between, African American novelist Richard Wright's (1908–60) *Native Son* (1941) was a surprise exception to this rule, as was novelist Kamala Markandaya's (1924–2004) bleak depiction of life on the margins in India, *Nectar in a Sieve* (1954).

However, BOMC's success was not all due to its carefully sifted and organized lists of offerings. Scherman also introduced a savvy technique that helped ensure that book sales would be sustained at a high level: the negative option. Rather than relying on subscribers to request that particular books be sent to them, BOMC automatically mailed each month's selection. Subscribers not wishing that month's offering either had to return a card in advance, refusing the book, or had to return the book itself. Scherman rightly counted on psychology and laziness to ensure that most subscribers would simply accept and pay for the books that were sent to them. If the handsome hardcover volumes began to accumulate unread on the shelves, so be it: at least their presence attested to the owners' desire for the kind of cultural capital the titles represented. A BOMC package on the front step or resting on the hall table signaled that the house's inhabitants were sophisticated readers who wanted the real thing, not abridged editions offered by such organizations as Reader's Digest, whose Condensed Books series, containing several works in each volume, was published quarterly from 1950 to 1997.

Scherman's formula for the Book-of-the-Month Club proved wildly successful. Its membership jumped to 95,000 in just two years, and to more than half a million in its first decade. During its first four decades, BOMC sold over 200 million books. Since bookstores were not that common in much of North America at that time, BOMC and its many imitators offered a vital service for readers. The club's popularity finally began to wane in the 1960s, when inexpensive paperbacks became more widely available and mall stores began to fan out across the continent. However, BOMC responded by adding a paperback club (Quality Paperback Books) that reenergized its member base. The company also dramatically expanded its range of specialty book clubs to include everything from children's books to cookbooks to military history. Now available online under the umbrella organization Bookspan, BOMC continues to be a major player among the commercial book clubs that still serve upwards of 20 million members in the United States alone.

Book Clubs of the Air

The concept of the book club took a new turn in 1996, when American television personality Oprah Winfrey (b. 1954) launched the "Oprah's Book Club" segment on her long-running daytime program, the *Oprah Winfrey Show*. Featured fairly regularly on the program from 1996 to 2002, and subsequently relaunched in less frequent and different iterations (classic books from 2003 to about 2007, Book Club 2.0 in 2012), Oprah's Book Club took the original book club concept, in which small groups of readers would meet regularly together to discuss a book of their choosing, and turned it on its head. Oprah's club embraced all of her millions of viewers, and she chose the books herself. Unlike many book clubs, however, Oprah's did not seek to publish or directly profit from the club's endorsement. Initially, Oprah would simply announce the title, and her audience members would be invited to read the book over the next month and tune in to a special discussion of it, often with the author present as a special guest on the show. It wasn't even necessary to actually read the book, Oprah assured her readers: anyone could benefit just from listening in on a conversation about books.

Initially, many scoffed at the notion of Oprah's Book Club, especially professional readers such as critics and academics. Oprah's selections were middlebrow—even lowbrow—novels, they complained. The plots typically featured middle- and lower-middle-class women, and they hinged on melodramatic plots of family disintegration. The *Wall Street Journal* complained that the themes and vocabulary levels in most of Oprah's selected novels were insufficiently challenging for adult readers. Even some authors were nonplussed by being selected, most famously Jonathan Franzen (b. 1959), who was afraid that the critical reputation of his 2001 novel *The Corrections* would be sullied by joining the ranks of novels bearing their distinctive Oprah's Book Club sticker. (Franzen needn't have worried: his novel went on to win a National Book Award and was a finalist for several other highly regarded literary prizes, including the Pulitzer Prize for Fiction.)

However, publishers and booksellers quickly discovered that Oprah's imprimatur was the publishing equivalent of winning the lottery. According to the *New York Times*, in its first three years alone, Oprah's Book Club was responsible for twenty-eight consecutive bestsellers, comprising more than 20 million volumes sold and over $175 million in revenue. In fact, Oprah-related sales alone catapulted many of the selected authors into the ranks of millionaires. The desperate scramble for copies of Oprah's selections at bookstores and libraries meant that her organization soon had to begin giving publishers advance warning that one of their books had been selected, so that they could arrange to reprint and distribute copies to meet the anticipated demand. And as the club continued, it rebutted many of the charges of its critics. A 2011 survey by the Nielsen Company compiled sales data for bestselling Oprah selections over the previous decade. At the very top of the list was German-born Canadian author Eckhart Tolle's *A New Earth* (2005), a metaphysical essay about the power of thought, with over 3.3 million copies sold; this was followed by James Frey's semi-autobiographical *A Million Little Pieces* (2003) and Elie Wiesel's Holocaust memoir *Night* (1960), with over 2 million copies each; and in fifth place came Cormac McCarthy's dystopian fantasy, *The Road* (2006), with about 1.3 million copies sold. Not only are the sales figures quite striking, but the titles themselves show how Oprah's selections for her book club had become much more diversified—and also more intellectually challenging—over the years.

Partly because of the sheer numbers of books sold and titles discussed, Oprah's Book Club gradually became a subject of academic study, and some of the more sympathetic investigators pointed to Oprah's importance as a "literacy sponsor." By repeatedly urging that her viewers take up a book, identify with the characters' plights, try to apply the life lessons to their own experiences, or simply tune in and absorb how other readers tried to engage with texts that required staying power and were sometimes difficult to comprehend, Oprah modeled how reading could be a part of everyday life. One of the appeals for her audience was that these were books Oprah had read and been moved by. Not only did she vouch for the books as good reads, but there was an implicit promise that reading them would enable her viewers to share something with the woman herself, something felt to be more intimate than simply buying the brands of cookware or sleepwear or even automobiles that she also endorsed.

While Oprah exercised her greatest influence over audiences in North America, other regions also had their book clubs of the air. In the United Kingdom, the biggest book club was sponsored by daytime television personalities Richard Madeley (b. 1956) and Judy Finnigan (b. 1948), a married couple who hosted the eponymous *Richard & Judy* daytime chat show from 2001 to 2008. (In 2009, the program was briefly revived in an evening slot on a digital-only channel.) The Richard & Judy Book Club segment began in 2004 and featured ten books a year, seasonally adjusted to allow more serious winter reading and lighter "summer reads." Richard and Judy's influence on book sales was similar to Oprah's: books by authors that typically experienced sales only in the range of 5,000 to 20,000 copies jumped to as many as 100 times that number after they were selected for the on-air club. One of the first novels to experience the exciting spike in sales due to Richard and Judy's endorsement was the historical novel *Star of the Sea* (2004), by Irish writer Joseph O'Connor (b. 1963). According to *Prospect* magazine, the novel's sales were at about 4,400 copies in the week before the show aired. In the following week, sales quadrupled to over 18,000, finally totaling about 600,000. Total sales revenue for Richard and Judy–endorsed books in the first two years alone were estimated to be nearly £44 million, amounting to one in every fifty books sold in the United Kingdom.

Unlike Oprah's Book Club, however, decisions about which books to select for the Richard & Judy Book Club were not made by the hosts themselves. Instead, the show's producer, Amanda Ross, selected the books. The intention behind having a third-party selector was to open up the range of responses to the books. Whereas Oprah's choices were personal to her and always championed by her, Richard and Judy were more neutral about the titles chosen for their shows. One host often liked a particular book more than the other, which led to more natural, unforced debate about what was good or not in the texts. However, like the selections in the older Book-of-the-Month Club, viewers trusted that the books selected for *Richard & Judy* would be good reads. The fact that a number of books chosen for the program were also shortlisted for the prestigious Man Booker literary prize also illustrated that popular reads and literary reads did not have to be different books: prestigious prize winners could be purchased at Tesco's along with the week's groceries.

SPECIAL BOOKS FOR SPECIAL READERS

As the discussion of book clubs suggests, one of the questions that readership studies frequently engage is which kinds of books are best suited for which kinds of readers. This question can take a variety of forms. For instance, the question might be framed prescriptively: which books *should* a particular group of readers read? Throughout history, certain readers have been encouraged to read certain kinds of works and discouraged—or outright prohibited—from reading others.

Gender is one long-standing dividing line affecting which books should or should not be read. In classical Japan, for example, men and women learned and used different scripts, thereby reinforcing that certain kinds of reading and writing were more appropriate to one or the other. One of the earliest novels in world literature, the eleventh-century *Tale of Genji* by a woman of the Japanese court now known as Murasaki Shikibu (c. 978–1014), was written in a form of *hiragana* script then used exclusively by women. This is not necessarily a historically remote problem, either. In his autobiography *Punjabi Century, 1857–1947* (1968), Indian business leader Prakash Tandon (1911–2004) relates how his parents could not write to one another when his father was away on engineering projects, because they did not share a common written language. Literary historian Kate Flint notes that women's reading in the West was contested ground well into the twentieth century, with both men and women acutely aware that reading was one way in which individual identity was shaped or confirmed. It was long a matter of serious concern that girls and women be shaped by their reading in ways considered appropriate to their intended roles in society.

Not just girls' but children's reading generally has also been an area of interest. The emergence of a distinct body of literature written for children is a fairly recent development. Although there were a number of books directed towards young readers in the eighteenth and early nineteenth centuries, the real age of children's publishing is generally considered to have begun in the 1890s. As childhood began to be understood as a distinctly different stage of development from adulthood, children were increasingly channeled into their own communities, activities, and reading materials. Publishers began to produce and then to specialize in didactic and pleasure reading for children, and awards such as the Newbery Medal, created in 1922, began to be given for excellence in children's books. School and public libraries were charged with building collections appropriate for budding readers, and more attention was paid to the content, structure, and style of books intended for children. (Chapter 7 discusses educational publishing for children.) By the turn of the twenty-first century, books for children had become one of the largest and most rapidly growing publishing categories of all times, due in large part to the unprecedented popularity of the *Harry Potter* series by English author J.K. Rowling (b. 1965). Published between 1997 and 2007, the seven books were huge international bestsellers, with the last four breaking all previously existing records for first print runs and first-day sales for *any* category of book, not just children's literature.

Another issue that lies behind the question of what books are best for what readers is the matter of reader choice. Given the freedom to pick for themselves, what do certain readers *choose* to read? Publishers have been trying to answer this question since the beginning of the industry. Historian William St. Clair notes that this question seriously perplexed publishers in England in the 1780s, when a large number of works first went out of copyright and the publishers could decide which ones to put back into print. The publishers knew that scholars were already deciding which of those books were the "best" ones, but what relationship did that judgment bear to which books would sell? Many publishers fell back on standard improving titles, but some took their chances with the newer, if more morally dubious, novels. Within only a generation, fiction proved to be the genre of choice for most general readers.

Publishing historian Jonathan Rose (b. 1952) has attempted to get to the heart of what working-class readers in the nineteenth and twentieth centuries actually chose to read, rather than what they were offered to read, by scouring a variety of documents, including autobiographies, library archives, opinion polls, and periodicals. Perhaps not surprisingly, the overwhelming majority of working-class readers preferred the fiction of Daniel Defoe, John Bunyan, and Charles Dickens. The coal miners of the South Wales valleys were renowned for their political engagement and strong union activism, but even they seem to have far preferred popular fiction to works of political thought or political biographies for their leisure reading.

This section will look briefly at some of the kinds of books that people most frequently choose for themselves. By far the most popular categories of books in the modern era are genre fiction. *Genre fiction* is distinguished from *literary fiction* by being more plot- than theme-driven, and by containing plots that are somewhat more formulaic and characters who are somewhat more stereotypic than their literary cousins. Genre fiction also tends to be lighter in tone than literary fiction: it is usually meant primarily to be entertaining

J.K. ROWLING: THE MAGIC OF HARRY POTTER

One of the world's most popular contemporary authors, Joanne (J.K.) Rowling (b. 1965) studied literature and languages in university and taught English in Portugal before returning to the United Kingdom in the 1990s. The idea for a story about a boy wizard had come to her some years earlier, but she finally began to write it in 1994. At the time, she was an unemployed single mother, living in Edinburgh and studying to earn a Scottish teaching certificate. Much of her first book's manuscript was written in a café with her daughter asleep in the pram by her side. Having finished the story, Rowling sent it to the Christopher Little literary agency, who enthusiastically began shopping it around to publishers—all of whom rejected it. Finally, a fairly small press, Bloomsbury Books in London, accepted Rowling's manuscript and offered her a very modest £1,500 advance against royalties.

Life was about to change. *Harry Potter and the Philosopher's Stone* was published in 1997 with a typically small print run for a first book for children: just 1,000 copies, about half of which were slated for distribution to libraries. However, the library sales proved fortunate, as librarians loved the novel and eagerly recommended it to readers. Over the next year, the book won a few children's literature awards and was also picked up for US publication by Scholastic Books, who in 1998 issued it under the title *Harry Potter and the Sorcerer's Stone*. The same year, the sequel, *Harry Potter and the Chamber of Secrets*, was also published.

Initial critical response to the books was mixed, and the paranormal subject matter led to bannings by some libraries and school districts—but readers loved them. Harry Potter's world of magic and Muggles (the wizarding world's name for ordinary humans) entranced readers young and old, and Rowling's often humorous recasting of archetypal tales of heroes and villains, good and evil, life and death drew a growing audience—literally. As more volumes in the series were produced, both the characters and the complexity (and darkness) of the works were increased to suit the ages of their intended readers. The last volumes were immense, serious tomes, with the final one, *Harry Potter and the Deathly Hallows* (2007), topping out at over 600 pages.

rather than intellectually and aesthetically challenging. Although genre fiction is often scorned by professional readers and academics, its overwhelming and enduring popularity makes it the major category in the contemporary publishing world, and its authors and publishers are often far better known, better remunerated, and even better loved by their readers than some of their more high-minded colleagues.

If the books had followed the trajectory of many other children's and young adult novels, building a steady readership over generations, Rowling's story would not be particularly noteworthy. However, the *Harry Potter* books proved to be a publishing phenomenon. Each of the last four books in the series broke all previous records for largest initial print runs and first-day sales. Released simultaneously in the United Kingdom and United States, *Harry Potter and the Goblet of Fire* (2000) sold over 3 million copies on the first day, an all-time record. *Harry Potter and the Order of the Phoenix* (2003) smashed that record: the book sold over 7 million copies of its unprecedented 8.5-million-copy print run on the first day. But *Harry Potter and the Half-Blood Prince* (2005) sold 9 million copies on the first day, and the final volume, whose initial print run was a whopping 12 million copies, sold 11 million on the first day. Paperback and audiobook editions, complete sets, and other versions have all added up to over 400 million copies worldwide, in more than sixty languages.

Rowling's series not only broke all sales records for all kinds of books, but it prompted changes in the way bestselling books were registered and recorded. By 2000, the first three *Harry Potter* books had been on the New York Times Best Sellers list for seventy-nine weeks, prompting complaints from other authors, especially those who were writing more literary fiction for adults. To better accommodate those authors, and to indicate that children's and young adults' books had come of age, the *New York Times* launched a new Children's Best Sellers list in 2000, shortly before the scheduled release of the fourth volume in the series. Rowling's books remained on that list through to the end of the series, aided not only by their own inventiveness but also by the release of movie versions of each of the volumes.

Not without reason, Rowling's story has been described as one of rags to riches, akin to that of Charles Dickens in the nineteenth century. From an unemployed single mother struggling to make ends meet, she has been catapulted into the ranks of the rich and famous. She received the Order of the British Empire (OBE) in 2000 for her contributions to literature and the arts. Instantly recognized almost anywhere she goes, Rowling has also become one of the wealthiest women in the United Kingdom, by some accounts commanding more wealth even than the Queen, and she is actively involved in a number of philanthropic endeavors, especially related to children, poverty, and multiple sclerosis. She has also begun writing for adults, publishing novels in 2012 and 2013.

Romance

By far the largest category of fiction publishing is romance fiction. *Romances* are stories that center around a plot in which two individuals fall in love and try to make their relationship work. Traditional romances feature conventional male-female couples in either contemporary or reality-based historical settings, but recent decades have seen a proliferation of variants: gay couples, paranormal or science-fiction settings, plots that center on questions of spirituality or religion, or plots that import elements of mystery or suspense. What ties all of these variants together is that the novels end in an emotionally satisfying and optimistic manner: the couple are firmly united, and perhaps on their way to marriage and family. "Happily ever after" is a defining characteristic of the form.

According to the Romance Writers of America, which regularly tracks and publishes statistics about the romance industry, romance is the largest single category of the consumer books market, regularly making up over 13 per cent of all books sold and comprising over $1 billion in sales annually. In recent years, it has also become one of the top-selling categories in e-books. Romance fiction's nearest competitors are the relatively new category of religious/inspirational fiction, which sold about $759 million worth of books in 2010, and mysteries, which sold about $682 million. By comparison, literary fiction only earns about $455 million annually in sales. Romance novels also regularly top out most of the bestseller lists, with the only important challenger being books with movie tie-ins. While women are the primary consumers of romance fiction, purchasing over 90 per cent of all romance books, men also read them, sometimes comprising as much as 13 per cent of the market. (More men read romance fiction in Latin America, a fact played to great comic effect in the 1984 film *Romancing the Stone*, about a romance novelist trying to rescue her sister from kidnappers in Colombia, and in its 1985 sequel *The Jewel of the Nile*.) What many non-romance readers may not know is that romance readers tend to be older (in their thirties to fifties) and also fairly well educated (42 per cent with a college degree or higher). These factors seriously challenge stereotypical notions of impressionable young women devouring romance novels because they don't know any better. Such novels actually offer more to their fans than non-romance readers suspect.

According to the contributors to *Dangerous Men and Adventurous Women* (1992), a volume on the appeal of romance, most readers of the genre are drawn to precisely those elements that non-romance readers tend to criticize. For example, the novels' repetitive elements and stereotypical characters are intended to tap into readers' experiences and expectations, while the sometimes overwrought language is intended to heighten the drama of these archetypal encounters. Furthermore, most romance readers delve into the novels not to withdraw from the real world, but simply to provide themselves with a brief respite from their ordinary roles and responsibilities. The plots' predictability means that romance novels can be quickly picked up and put down. While some readers may identify with the heroines, not all do. The perennial popularity of romance set in exotic settings and the growing popularity of suspense and paranormal variants of the genre suggest that many readers like the remoteness and impossibility of the novels: they are escapist fantasies. And romance readers also like knowing that they will always get a happy ending: no matter what travails the heroine experiences along the way, all will be well by the last page of the book. In some respects, then, romance reading is pleasure reading at its most elemental.

NORA ROBERTS: QUEEN OF ROMANCE

The pen name of Eleanor Marie Robertson (b. 1950), Nora Roberts is one of the all-time bestselling romance novelists. She also publishes mysteries under the pseudonym J.D. Robb, and other books under the names Jill March and Sarah Hardesty. Born in Maryland, Roberts worked briefly as a legal secretary and then stayed home while her children were young. Snowbound during a particularly fierce blizzard, she began writing, and several manuscripts and rejections later, she published her first novel, *Irish Thoroughbred*, in 1981 with the new romance imprint Silhouette. She hit her stride a few novels later, with the first in what would become a very successful saga about the MacGregor family, *Playing the Odds* (1985).

Over the past thirty-plus years, Roberts has written more than 200 novels, and there are more than 400 million copies of her works in print. That kind of productivity requires a great deal of discipline: Roberts reports that she writes eight hours a day, every day. She usually begins with a character or plot situation and fleshes out the work from there. One of the keys to her success has been sequels: many of her works are conceived as trilogies, and she writes all three books in quick succession, to sustain the plot lines and character consistency. Readers who pick up one of the books are almost certain to read the others. Roberts has also been an innovative and driving force in the romance genre, helping to shift its parameters from predictable young-heroine-and-swarthy-hero stories to tales that incorporate suspense and paranormal elements. She was in the forefront of creating heroines who were much more independent and less passive than many of the traditional romance heroines had been. These factors combine to explain why she has drawn in many who were not ordinarily romance readers, including many male readers.

Roberts's works have been regular and sometimes spectacular bestsellers, often crossing out of the romance category to appear in the more general *New York Times* and *Publishers Weekly* bestseller lists, even though her works are rarely reviewed by mainstream literary critics. She was also the first author named to the Romance Writers of America Hall of Fame.

Action/Adventure and Suspense

Another popular category of genre fiction is *action/adventure* novels. Action novels make up only about 9 per cent of consumer book sales. However, when combined with *suspense* fiction—a category that can include many kinds of thrillers, mysteries, and detective stories, and that makes up about 8 per cent of fiction sales—the combined categories compare favorably with romance fiction. They also provide a kind of gender balance in popular fiction reading, as males make up a significantly higher percentage of readers of these kinds of novels. (However, women still read more, in virtually all categories of literature, than do men.) Because trends in action and suspense writing tend to respond to geopolitical developments, the subgenres most popular at any given time can differ greatly. For example, in the early to mid-twentieth century, the *western* was a popular genre, with novelists such as Louis L'Amour (1908–88) commanding huge readerships. Spy novels were especially popular during the Cold War (1947–91), and a particular kind of hard-edged, guerilla warfare–style fiction was published in great quantities during and in the wake of the Vietnam War (1955–75). All of these subgenres tend to have their analogues on the big screen as well, so that trends in movie-making can affect tastes in popular fiction and vice versa. The adventures of super agent James Bond, created in the 1950s by English novelist and former Naval Intelligence officer Ian Fleming (1906–64), took on a new life after the character's screen portrayals in the 1960s and 1970s. The Bond films are the longest-running, most successful film franchise in the world (helping to continually reintroduce generations of readers to the original Fleming novels), and nearly everyone in the world recognizes the numbers "007."

The impact of real-life events on these subgenres could be seen after the terrorist attacks of September 2001. In the wake of the attacks, some New York publishers especially hesitated to release certain kinds of action novel. For example, a representative of Penguin Putnam told reporter Martin Arnold of the *New York Times* that she wanted to steer clear of novels featuring chemical or biological terror for awhile, instead focusing on more traditional fare, such as police procedurals and plots revolving around serial killers. Similarly, a publisher with St. Martin's Press predicted that writers and readers would be returning to fiction featuring CIA and MI5 characters. Even novelists themselves said that writers were likely to turn, at least temporarily, to plots and characters that were less likely to fray contemporary readers' still raw nerves. Author Nelson DeMille (b. 1943), for example, thought that there would be an upsurge in nostalgia, an attempt to retreat to the presumably simpler times of Arthur Conan Doyle (1859–1930), when Sherlock Holmes solved mysteries in London and beyond. Arnold himself wistfully suggested a revival of John le Carré's (pen name of David Cornwell, b. 1931) Cold War spy thrillers. That all of these works have since been revived on both page and screen suggests how closely publishers and writers can gauge popular tastes.

Detective fiction has one of the longest and most distinguished literary legacies, dating back to French, American, and English traditions in the nineteenth century. Its real popularity, however, can be dated to the invention of Sherlock Holmes in the 1880s, and the subsequent creations of English writer Agatha Christie (1890–1976), whose Belgian detective Hercule Poirot, first introduced in 1920, and whose amateur, elderly detective Miss Marple, first introduced in 1927, are perennial favorites. Christie was a prolific writer, with more than sixty novels, a host of short stories, and a few plays to her name. She is regarded by some as the bestselling novelist of all time, with more than

SCANDINAVIAN CRIME SUCCESS: STIEG LARSSON

Swedish journalist and novelist Stieg Larsson (1954–2004) was one of the rising tide of internationally popular Scandinavian crime writers. A successful investigative journalist who was instrumental in exposing right-wing and racist political parties in Sweden, Larsson initially turned to science fiction writing in the 1970s, authoring and editing a number of fanzines in that period. He began writing the crime series for which he is renowned, the *Millennium Series*, sometime in the 1990s, although he made no effort to publish the volumes until just before his death in 2004.

The *Millennium Series* centers on the efforts of Larsson's alter-ego, crusading journalist Mikael Blomkvist, and his edgy anti-heroine associate, Lisbeth Salander, the eponymous "girl with the dragon tattoo." The three published novels (there are reportedly fragments of at least one more) evoke a dark, ugly world of misogyny, neo-Nazis, and cruelty. First published in Swedish and then in English translations, the series includes *The Girl with the Dragon Tattoo* (2008), originally published under the title *Män Som Hatar Kvinnor*, or "Men Who Hate Women," *The Girl Who Played with Fire* (2009), and *The Girl Who Kicked the Hornets' Nest* (2009). Larsson was a voracious reader not just of Scandinavian crime fiction, but also of American detective novels. But he also claimed to have been strongly influenced in the creation of Lisbeth Salander by the popular Swedish children's stories about Pippi Longstocking, written by Astrid Lindgren (1907–2002). One of Mikael Blomkvist's more mocking nicknames is "Kalle Blomkvist," a character created by Lindgren.

Larsson died suddenly of a heart attack in 2004, leaving a confusing literary estate behind him. His family and his long-time partner, author and architect Eva Gabrielsson (b. 1953), have disagreed about what to do with the remaining partial manuscript (or manuscripts) that might continue his popular series. Readers around the world would certainly be eager to read more about Blomkvist and Salander: the series has already sold 65 million copies worldwide, and the filmed versions of the books (both the original Swedish and the more recent English-language versions) have also been major hits.

4 billion copies of her works in circulation in over 100 languages. Although Christie mostly wrote in the tradition of Doyle, with detectives who relied on brain rather than brawn to resolve mysteries, other detective writers, particularly in America, went for a more muscular form of fiction. *Hard-boiled* detective fiction was especially popular in the 1920s to 1940s, where it could be found in the pages of cheap magazines like the *Black Mask*—the so-called *pulps*—and on the screen in film noir. According to historian Erin Smith, hard-boiled detective fiction drew as many as 10 million regular readers in its heyday, especially urban working-class men, who found in it both a reflection and an escape from the mean streets in which they lived and worked. Among some of the best-known and most widely respected writers of hard-boiled detective fiction were Dashiell Hammett (1894–1941), creator of detective Sam Spade and of the nameless private investigator, the Continental Op, and Raymond Chandler (1888–1959), creator of detective Philip Marlowe. Many of Hammett's, Chandler's, and others' characters also came alive on the silver screen, portrayed by some of the finest actors of the era, such as Humphrey Bogart.

In recent years, one surprisingly popular trend has been the global appetite for Scandinavian crime fiction. Swedish writer Stieg Larsson has dominated the international bestseller lists with his dark, posthumously published *Millennium Series*, but he is far from the only Scandinavian writer whose work has caught the public's imagination. Other notables include Norwegian author Jo Nesbo (b. 1960) and Swedish writer Henning Mankell (b. 1948), whose detective Kurt Wallander has become an international favorite in both Swedish- and English-language television productions.

In his 2007 novella *The Uncommon Reader*, English author and playwright Alan Bennett imagines the Queen as someone who has come late to the habit of reading. Drawn to select a book from a visiting bookmobile at Buckingham Palace by a desire not to seem impolite, the Queen graduates from a grudging, dutiful approach to reading—"Once I start a book I finish it…. Books, bread and butter, mashed potato—one finishes what's on one's plate"—to a fierce desire to read more. Unlike ordinary ("common") readers, who are often imagined as being elevated by their reading, the uncommon reader in Bennett's fantasy is leveled into a fellow feeling with her subjects that her position as queen has precluded. "Books did not care who was reading them…. All readers were equal," she muses, finding that the act of reading is exhilaratingly "anonymous," "shared"—"common."

Reading enables us to enter into the thoughts of people far remote from us in time and space, to imagine ourselves as better (or worse) than we can ever be, to have adventures in places that are long gone or will never exist. Ultimately, as the Queen in Bennett's book comes to realize, a full and deep engagement in the world of books is one of the most humanizing pleasures available to us.

SELECTED BIBLIOGRAPHY

Arnold, Martin. "In a Spot: The Bad Guys." *New York Times*, 4 October 2001.

Bennett, Alan. *The Uncommon Reader*. New York: Farrar, Straus and Giroux, 2007.

Bloom, Clive. *Bestsellers: Popular Fiction Since 1900*. 2nd ed. Houndmills, Palgrave Macmillan, 2008.

Bookspan. http://www.booksonline.com.

Callimachi, Rukmini. "When the Lights Go Out, Students Take Off to Airport." *Guardian*, 20 July 2007.

Christoffersen, John. "At 98, Once-Illiterate Lobsterman Is an Author." *Guardian*, 29 March 2012.

Crossen, Cynthia. "Read Them and Weep." *Wall Street Journal*, 13 July 2001.

Eliot, Simon. "The Reading Experience Database; or, What Are We to Do About the History of Reading?" 1995. http://www.open.ac.uk/Arts/RED/redback.htm.

Erwin, Micah. "Early Printed Book Contains Rare Evidence of Medieval Spectacles." *Cultural Compass*. Harry Ransom Center, 17 April 2012. http://www.utexas.edu/opa/blogs/culturalcompass/2012/04/17/medieval-spectacles.

Fadiman, Anne. *Ex Libris: Confessions of a Common Reader*. New York: Farrar, Straus and Giroux, 1998.

Fischer, Steven Roger. *A History of Reading*. London: Reaktion Books, 2003.

Flint, Kate. *The Woman Reader, 1837–1914*. Oxford: Clarendon, 1993.

Gunzenhauser, Bonnie. Introduction to *Reading in History: New Methodologies from the Anglo-American Tradition*. London: Pickering & Chatto, 2010.

Hall, L. Mark. "The 'Oprahfication' of Literacy: Reading 'Oprah's Book Club.'" *College English* 65.6 (2003): 646–67.

Krentz, Jayne Ann, ed. *Dangerous Men and Adventurous Women: Romance Writers on the Appeal of Romance*. Philadelphia: U of Pennsylvania P, 1992.

Lamb, Mary R. "The 'Talking Life' of Books: Women Readers in Oprah's Book Club." In *Reading Women: Literary Figures and Cultural Icons from the Victorian Age to the Present*, ed. Janet Badia and Jennifer Phegley. Toronto: U of Toronto P, 2005. 255–80.

Lappin, Elena. "Reading Richard and Judy." *Prospect*, February 2006.

Manguel, Alberto. *A History of Reading*. New York: Viking, 1996.

Max, D.T. "The Oprah Effect." *New York Times Magazine*, 26 December 1999.

McDowell, Kathleen. "Toward a History of Children as Readers, 1890–1930." *Book History* 12 (2009): 240–65.

National Coalition for Literacy (NCL). Adult Literacy Fact Sheet 2009. http://www.ncladvocacy.org/HealthLiteracyFactst2009/AdultLiteracyFacts2009.pdf.

National Endowment for the Arts (NEA). *Reading at Risk: A Survey of Literary Reading in America*. Washington, DC: NEA, 2004.

National Endowment for the Arts (NEA). *Reading on the Rise: A New Chapter in American Literacy*. Washington, DC: NEA, 2009.

National Endowment for the Arts (NEA). *To Read or Not to Read: A Question of National Consequence*. Washington, DC: NEA, 2007.

National Literacy Trust. *Literacy: State of the Nation.* January 2012. http://www. literacytrust.org.uk/assets/0001/2847/Literacy_State_of_the_Nation_-_2_Aug_2011. pdf.

Pew Research Center. *The Rise of e-Reading.* 5 April 2012. http://libraries.pewinternet. org/2012/04/04/the-rise-of-e-reading.

Prospero's Books. http://prosperosbookstore.com/?page=Home.

Radway, Janice A. *A Feeling for Books: The Book-of-the-Month Club, Literary Taste, and Middle-Class Desire.* Chapel Hill: U of North Carolina P, 1977.

Reading Experience Database (RED). http://www.open.ac.uk/Arts/reading/index.php.

Nora Roberts. http://www.noraroberts.com.

Rohrer, Finlo. "How Richard and Judy Changed What We Read." *BBC News Magazine,* 1 July 2009. http://news.bbc.co.uk/2/hi/uk_news/magazine/8128436.stm.

Romance Writers of America (RWA). Romance Literature Statistics. http://www.rwa. org/cs/the_romance_genre/romance_literature_statistics.

Rose, Jonathan. *The Intellectual Life of the British Working Classes.* New Haven: Yale UP, 2001.

J.K. Rowling. http://www.jkrowling.com.

Sacks, Oliver. "A Man of Letters." *New Yorker,* 28 June 2010.

St. Clair, William. *The Reading Nation in the Romantic Period.* Cambridge: Cambridge UP, 2004.

Smith, Erin A. *Hard-Boiled: Working-Class Readers and Pulp Magazines.* Philadelphia: Temple UP, 2000.

Tan, Teri. "A Land of Avid Readers." *Publishers Weekly,* 18 September 2006.

Tompkins, Jane. *West of Everything: The Inner Life of Westerns.* New York: Oxford UP, 1992.

Twiddy, David. "Fed-Up Store Owner Torches Books." *Tacoma News Tribune,* 29 May 2007.

UNESCO Institute for Statistics. "Adult and Youth Literacy." *UIS Fact Sheet* No. 20, September 2012. http://www.uis.unesco.org/FactSheets/Documents/fs20-literacy-day-2012-en-v3.pdf.

Weeks, Linton. "Aliteracy: Read All About It, or Maybe Not." *Washington Post,* 14 May 2001.

Zaid, Gabriel. *So Many Books: Reading and Publishing in an Age of Abundance.* Philadelphia: Paul Dry, 2003.

ACTIVITIES

Author Study: Critical Biography

What do you know about your favorite authors, contemporary or classic? A *critical biography* is an account of an individual's life that focuses on a particular theme in that person's life as a way of shaping the information about him or her. Rather than simply presenting a timeline of *where* and *when*, a critical biography tries to get at the *why* and *how* of an individual's life and work. For understandable reasons, most critical biographies of authors use their writing lives as the focus, seeking to explain something about how the author-as-person shapes his or her choices about genres, topics, or themes.

Write a brief critical biography of an author of your choosing. In addition to the basic chronological details about the author's life, discuss how you think the author as an individual is expressed in, complemented by, or complicated by the author's works. To research your topic, you might read a representative sample of the author's works and look at biographical and autobiographical material, as well as at other critical assessments of the author's literary output. Many living authors now maintain websites, blogs, and Twitter and Facebook accounts to keep readers apprised of their publications and other activities. In addition, many literary societies, individual scholars, and ordinary readers have created websites and other resources dedicated to particular authors, both living and dead.

Meet the Author

Many authors regularly give readings or sign books at bookstores and libraries, provide interviews on local radio and television stations, and lecture on campuses and in other community forums. Some even conduct writing workshops with students and others, sharing insights and techniques that can help them improve their own writing skills. Meeting an author whose work one has admired can be very exciting—and for many authors, meeting readers who have been genuinely moved by their writing is equally thrilling.

Find out which authors will be reading, lecturing, or signing in your area over the next weeks or months, and make arrangements to attend an author event. (If you have the resources to support such an event, you may even wish to organize an author visit to your own institution.) In preparation for the author's visit, read a representative sample of his or her work and learn all you can about the author's most recent publications or ongoing projects. If the forum will be one in which questions and discussion are allowed, prepare a question or two that you might ask if you have the opportunity.

Access to Book Culture

A number of countries and international organizations sponsor regular events to call attention to the importance of access to book culture. For example, the American Library Association (ALA) sponsors an annual Banned Books Week at the end of September. International organizations such as PEN and Amnesty International also participate in Banned Books Week, helping to call attention to banned and challenged books, as well as to the difficulties faced by writers and would-be readers in many parts of the world. In addition, UNESCO sponsors World Book and Copyright Day (also known as the International Day of the Book) every year on April 23, the traditional date of death for two giants of world literature, Miguel de Cervantes and William Shakespeare. The United Kingdom celebrates UK World Book Day on March 1.

Organize an event on your campus or in your community to recognize either of these annual events, or create your own book culture celebration. Possible activities might include a book sale or book exchange; readings of banned or challenged books; special exhibits in the library and other public spaces; a speaker forum on issues of freedom of the press; a read-a-thon; a screening of films or documentaries related to issues of access, such as *Fahrenheit 451*, the 1966 film adaptation of Ray Bradbury's classic science fiction novel; or collecting books or monetary donations for a local or international literacy program.

Publishing Trends and Publicity

One of the continuing challenges for the publishing industry is gauging which books are likely to capture readers' imaginations and then getting information about those titles out to the reading audience. In addition to traditional strategies for reaching readers, including print advertising and special displays in bookstores, publishers have increasingly embraced various kinds of new media marketing techniques, from Twitter and Facebook to YouTube "book trailers" to pre-publication cataloguing and book galley releases on websites such as Edelweiss and NetGalley.

Assess a range of publicity avenues to investigate what kinds of titles are currently on offer or in the pipeline from publishers. What do the current publishing trends seem to be, and which seem most promising? Which kinds of books seem to be on the rise, and which ones are declining? How are publishers reaching out to different audiences? Are certain kinds of books marketed more heavily in one form of publicity than in another? Which avenues for reaching readers seem most effective or least effective?

Judging Books by Their Covers

A book's cover design and cover copy—the preview of a book that usually appears on the back cover or in the front flap—are often overseen by a publisher's marketing department, rather than by the editors or the author. The goal is to make the book instantly appealing to its intended readers. Sometimes the same book can be issued with distinctly different covers and copy for different formats (hardcover versus paperback, or editions intended for younger or older readers). For example, once it became clear that adults were reading J.K. Rowling's *Harry Potter* books, the volumes were reissued in editions with more adult-themed covers.

Look at a range of books and assess their cover designs and copy. Who is the intended audience? How can you tell? How well do you think the images or typography on the cover catch the tone or intention of the book? How well does the back cover or flap copy prepare readers for the actual content of the book? Once you have a feel for the general rules of cover design and copy writing, select a classic or contemporary book and try designing your own cover or writing your own cover copy, targeting that book to a particular readership. For example, you might try to repackage a classic horror story, such as Robert Louis Stevenson's *The Strange Case of Dr Jekyll and Mr Hyde* (1886), for readers of contemporary paranormal young adult fiction (such as Stephanie Meyer's *Twilight* series [2005–08]).

Book Trailer

One newer development in book promotion is the *book trailer*, a video advertisement for a book that works along the same lines as a movie trailer does for a film. Book trailers may enact portions of a text (with either live action or animation) or simply evoke the book's tone or mood with slide-show style images and a soundtrack. Book trailers are easy to find on YouTube; a number of other websites also aggregate trailers, including Book Screening and Book Trailer Central.

Create a book trailer for a classic or contemporary book of your choosing. Which elements of the book best lend themselves to a short video presentation? What style of treatment might best convey the book's essence to potential readers? How might you most effectively whet a reader's appetite without giving away too much of the plot (or the ending)?

Book Collecting

A number of college and university libraries sponsor book collecting awards for students. In the United States, there is even a national award, the National Collegiate Book Collecting Contest. Unlike those of professional book collectors, student collections generally are not judged on the value or rarity of the items they contain, but on their owners' rationales or goals in bringing the books together. Such collections do not have to be particularly extensive, either: typically, student book collections contain as few as twenty or twenty-five books. To qualify for most such contests, the collections must be owned by the students themselves, and they must be accompanied by a statement of why and how the items were brought together, and how the collection fulfills the collector's goals.

If your institution already sponsors a book collecting contest, submit your collection to it. If not, work with your campus library to establish a class-based or university-wide collection competition. Determine what the criteria will be and the prizes (if any). Arrange to display representative samples of finalists' collections, in order to inspire other students to share their book habit.

The Books on the Shelves

In *The Library at Night* (2006), Argentine-born writer Alberto Manguel muses on the various ways that he has organized his own personal library of books. As a boy, he arranged them by size; later, he arranged them by subject; still later, he experimented with organizing the books by language, by color, or by how much he liked them. Since the turn of the twentieth century, large, professional libraries have usually organized their books according to either the Dewey decimal or the Library of Congress (LOC) cataloguing systems; older libraries often still have their own unique methods of sorting the books in their collections, sometimes now supplemented by more modern cataloguing systems.

Study the similarities and differences between the Dewey decimal and LOC systems. What are their relative merits for organizing large collections used by diverse readers? Which system (or which characteristics of either system) do you think is more efficient and user-friendly?

Now consider how you organize your own collection of books. What are your sorting criteria? Can you quickly lay your hands on the particular volume that you need, or do you regularly have to search for it? If you have experimented with different ways of organizing your shelves, which methods have been most useful or least satisfactory? If you have e-books, how do you organize them on your e-reader or other electronic devices? Compare your rationales for organizing your collection with someone else. If you had to merge your two libraries, how would you arrange them?

Bookstore or Library Ethnography

An *ethnography* is a systematic detailing of a particular community, based on close study. For this activity, visit a bookstore or library in order to analyze how it goes about the business of bringing published texts and readers together. You might simply arrange to spend time there, observing who comes in to browse the shelves and whether they come away with books. Or you might arrange to interview the librarians or store employees, or perhaps even some of the patrons. Your goal is to write a short ethnography of the library or bookstore, including a brief description of it (name, location, niche, clientele), as well as an analysis of how it positions itself and its wares to its customers.

Based on the general reading you have done and visits to other bookstores and libraries, you should be able to gather a great deal of information about your chosen site simply from spending some time there. For example, you should be able to see fairly quickly whether the store or library caters to general readers or specialized ones, and how successful it seems to be in serving its particular clientele. A shelf check should give you a pretty good idea of the breadth and depth of the holdings, and keeping track of how many potential customers come in during a given period of time and whether they leave with books or other items should give you an idea of how successful the store or library is in pitching its books to readers.

Reading Experience Database (RED)

The Reading Experience Database (RED) is an international effort to collect evidence of individual readers' interactions with texts, from 1450 until the end of World War II (1945). Some of the national sites are still in very early phases, but a couple, notably the UK and Canadian sites, are not only searchable but also encourage contributions from the public.

Search the RED for information about particular kinds of readers or reading material. For example, you might want to find evidence of children's reading at the turn of the twentieth century, or evidence of readers interacting with new scientific discoveries. What kinds of experiences are included in the RED? What do you learn about different readers' motivations for reading, or their emotional or intellectual responses to what they read? If you look at evidence from different time periods, how do readers' accounts of their reading experiences differ? Are there any aspects of reading that seem to remain fairly constant across time and space? What conclusions can you draw from examining such evidence of reading?

Reviewing

Although book reviewing was once mainly the province of professional readers, the web has created a multitude of opportunities for citizen reviewers. Blogs and other sites, often organized around particular genres or authors, provide multiple forums for commentary about different kinds of books. In addition, the major online retailers (such as Amazon, Barnes & Noble, Waterstone's, and W.H. Smith) all invite reader reviews and commentary about the books they offer for sale. The most helpful reviews, whether written by professionals or amateurs, tend to be those that reveal enough (but not too much!) of the book's content so that potential readers can get a feel for it, and that offer thoughtful, text-based rationales for why the work meets—or fails to meet—reader expectations.

Select a book you have read recently, and review it. You might simply share your review with others in your class, or you might upload it to an existing book review forum. You also might consider creating a class or campus-wide blog for book reviews, to keep others in your community informed about what is being read in your area.

Community Reads

A number of communities large and small now sponsor "Everyone Reads" or "One City One Book" programs, in which a whole city, neighborhood, or school commit to reading the same book during a particular period of time. The first such initiative was launched in Seattle in 1998, and it has been much imitated, with local and national initiatives in the United States, United Kingdom, Canada, and Australia. If your community already participates in such an initiative, find out when it is held and what the next title will be, and join in. If your community doesn't already have such a program, launch one. (You might start with just a campus-based program.) Choose a book that you think might have broad appeal, and organize publicity through bookstores, libraries, and schools to build interest in a shared reading experience.

"Literature" versus "Fiction"

Although most of the novels assigned and discussed in university settings tend to be literary texts, most of the novels readers choose to read on their own time tend to be popular genres, including romance, thrillers, science fiction or fantasy, manga, and graphic novels. Most bookstores and libraries mark this distinction between the kinds of books they stock by organizing their offerings into the broad categories of "literature" and "fiction," and they may devote substantial shelf space to particular subgenres of popular fiction.

Lovers of literature can usually explain why they find literary fiction to be more stimulating and rewarding if they are looking for a substantial read. But even fans of particular subgenres sometimes find it difficult to articulate to a non-fan why they so enjoy a certain kind of text. While more and more analytical accounts are being written of the pleasures to be found in a well-crafted comic book or a finely honed detective story, some nonreaders of those genres remain skeptical and refuse to sample popular fare outside their comfort zones.

For this activity, read a work in a popular fiction genre with the goal of better understanding what enthusiasts of that genre find satisfying about it. You may choose a work in a genre with which you are already familiar (even if you wouldn't ordinarily confess to being a reader of that kind of book), or you may choose a work in a genre that you have never encountered before. You might choose your book at random, or you might find out which authors and titles are particularly recommended by fans of the genre, and what informed critics have to say about them. After you have read your book, analyze it. How did your particular book work? What aspects of the character and plotting were conventional—even predictable—and where were the surprises? To what extent did your book's genre mirror some of the expectations you might have for more literary fiction, and to what extent did it diverge from those expectations? After reading the book, do you have a better understanding of why fans of that genre are enthusiastic about it? Are you tempted to read more of that kind of fiction?

RESOURCES RELATED TO BOOK CIRCUITS

The following organizations may prove useful in analyzing and participating in book circuits. In addition, most individual libraries and booksellers have websites that may provide additional links.

Authorship

American Society of Journalists and Authors. http://www.asja.org.
Association of Authors' Agents (AAA). http://www.agentsassoc.co.uk/index. php.
Association of Authors' Representatives (AAR). http://aaronline.org.
Authors Guild. http://www.authorsguild.org.
Canadian Authors Association. http://www.canauthors.org.
Fellowship of Australian Writers. http://www.writers.asn.au.
PEN International. http://www.pen-international.org.
Society of Authors. http://www.societyofauthors.org.

Bookselling

Abebooks. http://www.abebooks.com.
American Booksellers Association. http://www.bookweb.org.
Baker & Taylor. http://www.btol.com.
Booksellers Association. http://www.booksellers.org.uk.
Booksellers New Zealand. http://www.booksellers.co.nz.

Libraries, Literacy, and Reading Initiatives

American Library Association (ALA). http://www.ala.org/.

Australian Library and Information Association (ALIA). http://www.alia.org.
au/.
Canadian Library Association (CLA). http://www.cla.ca/.
Canadian Literacy and Learning Network. http://www.literacy.ca/.
Chartered Institute of Library and Information Professionals (CILIP). http://
www.cilip.org.uk/.
Library and Information Association of New Zealand Aotearoa (LIANZA).
http://www.lianza.org.nz/.
Library of Congress (LOC). Local/Community Resources. http://www.read.
gov/resources/.
National Collegiate Book Collecting Contest. http://hq.abaa.org/books/
antiquarian/abaapages/contest.
National Year of Reading (Australia). http://www.love2read.org.au/index.cfm.
Reading Experience Database (RED). http://www.open.ac.uk/Arts/reading/.
UNESCO. http://www.unesco.org/new/en/education/themes/education-
building-blocks/literacy/.
United Kingdom Literary Association (UKLA). http://www.ukla.org/.
World Literacy Canada. http://www.worldlit.ca/.

abecedary: alphabet table

acquisitions: process of securing an author or manuscript for publication, often performed by an *acquisitions editor*

advance: payment to author in advance of royalties on sales, usually issued in parts on signing of contract and after submission of a completed manuscript

aesthetic reading: reading for pleasure; compare *efferent reading*

agent: artistic and business representative for authors; usually receives a percentage of an author's earnings in return for advising on manuscripts, pitching works to publishers, and negotiating financial terms

alexia: loss of ability to read, often due to a medical condition; compare *dyslexia*

aliteracy: choice not to read, even though one is able to; compare *literacy, illiteracy*

amanuensis: secretary or literary assistant who writes from dictation

antiquarian booksellers: booksellers who deal in old and rare books and manuscripts

apocrypha: books other than those deemed authoritative or canonical, especially as related to scripture

archive: collection of documents and sometimes other materials, often for informational purposes; also, the act of collecting and recording such materials

ascender: part of a letter that rises above the *e*-level; compare *descender*

author: someone who creates or originates with words and whose writings are usually intended for circulation

back matter: all material that follows the main body of a book's text, including indexes, appendixes, glossaries, and bibliographies; compare *front matter*

bibliography: history, identification, and description of books

bifolium: book made up of sheets folded one time, to create two leaves or four pages; also called a *folio*

big-box store: large bookseller with centralized ordering and distribution networks; also called *superstore*

black letter: family of scripts and typefaces popular in the medieval period, characterized by angularity and height; also called *Gothic*

bleed: text or other matter printed so as to run off the edge of the page when the page is trimmed

blurb: short quote or other publicity notice meant to promote a book, often printed on a book cover or jacket; also, the act of generating such a notice

boards: rigid parts of a clothbound book cover, traditionally made of wood and now usually of heavy cardboard

book challenge: form of censorship, or attempt at censorship, in which an entity charges that a book is inappropriate for a particular readership

book fair: publishing trade show

boustrophedon: accordion-folded book; also, zigzag or back-and-forth pattern of reading

brittle books: books made of acidic, wood-pulp paper, and susceptible to browning and crumbling

broadsheet: sizable sheet of paper printed on one side; also called a *broadside*

butterfly: form of bookbinding in which sheets are folded with printing to the inside, and the folded ends of the sheets are glued to one another

calligraphy: handwriting or lettering

canon: authoritative list of books, as in those accepted as scriptural or as the authentic works of a particular author

canvassing book: sample book, usually a partial prototype, used by door-to-door sales representatives to solicit subscriptions for a forthcoming title

catchword: word set at the bottom of the last page in a gathering or quire that indicates the first word in the next gathering

CD-ROM: compact disc with read-only memory that cannot be altered by the user

censorship: process of preventing particular texts or images from being read; see also *book challenge*

chapbook: small booklet, usually of less than forty pages, typically containing poems, tales, or tracts

character: sign or symbol used in writing or printing

chase: frame in which text and illustrations are locked up for relief printing

CIP (Cataloguing in Publication) data: information for a library catalogue entry, including author's name, title, publisher information, subject headings under which the book can be searched, and Dewey decimal classification number

circulating library: library that lends books to readers; also called *subscription library*

closed stacks: in a library, shelves that can only be accessed by library personnel; compare *open stacks*

cloth binding, clothbound: book binding in which pages are stitched or glued to a cover made of stiff boards and covered with cloth; also called *hardbound* or *casebound*

codex, codices: paged book, made of folded and sewn- or glued-together sheets

colophon: inscription at the end of a book or text with information about its production; also, an identifying emblem or device used by a printer or publisher

common press: wooden-frame press used in the West from the fifteenth to the nineteenth century

composing stick: wooden or metal shelf that fits in the hand and is used for setting type by hand

compositor: typesetter

concertina: bookbinding method in which pages are bound together at outside edges, so that the book can be folded in a zigzag fashion; also called a *sutra* or *scripture* binding

conservation: stabilization and protection of books and other materials; compare *preservation*

copyediting: detailed, word-by-word editing of spelling, punctuation, grammar, usage, and structure of a manuscript, usually performed by a *copyeditor*; also called *line editing* or *subediting*

copyleft: philosophy that creative works should be made available for free, through open access; compare *copyright*

copyright: legal right to reproduce and distribute a creative work; copyright may be granted or licensed by the creator of the work to another individual or institution

cuneiform: wedge-shaped script used in ancient Mesopotamia

deaccessioning: removing an item from a library's collection; also called *weeding*

descender: part of a letter that extends below the type baseline; compare *ascender*

desktop publishing: process of using personal computers and inkjet or laser printers or the internet to publish a work; may be used by publishers or by authors who self-publish; see also *print on demand*, *self-publishing*

determinative: symbol that provides clues about the function or meaning of other symbols in a writing system

developmental editing: process of making certain that a manuscript conforms to the publisher's guidelines for content, presentation, and organization, often performed by a *developmental editor*

diacritic: mark, such as a dot or line, used to indicate a phonetic change to a character

distributor: in bookselling, an entity that provides warehouse space to publishers and sells books on to wholesale and retail customers; compare *wholesaler*

dust jacket: paper cover for a book; also called *book jacket* or *wrapper*

dyslexia: inability to process the inputs and information required to read and write; also called *developmental reading disorder (DRD)*; compare *alexia*

e-book: digital version of a book, usually read on an electronic device like an e-reader

efferent reading: reading for a purpose, as in reading for information; compare *aesthetic reading*

endcap: extra shelves at the end of a rank of shelves that enable stores or libraries to display featured books face-out

endpapers: protective sheets at the front and back of a book that cover the boards and affix a book's cover to its body; see also *flyleaf*

ephemera: printed paper items intended for short-term use

epigraph: quotation at the beginning of a text or of a section of the text that suggests the theme

e-reader: dedicated electronic device for reading digital books

exemplar: original text used for copying

fair use: legal reproduction of a portion of a copyright item, subject to restrictions related to purpose of use, the nature of the original work, the portion of the original to be used, and the effect on the original

fee-for-service: one-time payment to an author from a publisher, in lieu of royalties; compare *royalty*

flap: part of a book jacket that folds inside the book's cover; often used for promotional copy

flyleaf: the part of the endpapers at the front and back of a book that is not glued to the cover

folio: term that has several meanings in publishing contexts, including: a page (or leaf) number in a book or other document; a sheet of paper folded once, to create two leaves or four pages; a book format made up of single-fold sheets (also sometimes called a *bifolium*)

font: complete set of type characters, including upper and lower case, numerals, punctuation, and any special characters; also, a complete set of matrices in a composing machine

form, forme: secured assembly of all type and illustrations from which an impression will be printed

frisket: hinged bracket or frame on a press that keeps the paper in place on the *tympan*

front matter: all material that precedes the main body of a book's text, including title page, copyright page, table of contents, acknowledgments, dedication, preface, or foreword; usually assigned roman page numbers; compare *back matter*

galley: tray used for depositing lines of composed type; also, first proofs made from a typeset text; see also *page proof*

gathering: collection of sheets folded together to make up section of an unbound book; also called *quire* or *signature*

glyph: sign or symbol that conveys information nonverbally

gutter: space between pages on a two-page spread or between columns in a multi-column text block; compare *margins*

hard copy: paper version of text, as distinguished from photographic or electronic copies

hardcover: book whose pages are stitched or glued to a cover made of stiff boards and covered with cloth; also called *casebound* or *clothbound*

hieroglyph, hieroglyphic: system of ancient Egyptian picture writing

history of the book: study of the history of reading, writing, printing, and publishing; also called *history of print culture* and *publishing studies*

hot metal: method of mechanical typesetting, in which the typecasting and typesetting are combined to produce a complete line of composed type

icon: pictorial image that conveys information nonverbally

ideogram: sign or symbol that depicts that item being represented; an "idea sign"

illiteracy: inability to read and write; compare *literacy, aliteracy*

illumination: illustration in a manuscript; also, the process of illustration

imposition: arrangement of type in the form, so that when the printed sheet is folded into pages, the pages appear in the correct order

imprint: name under which a publishing house issues books

incipit: enlarged initial capital letter, used to mark beginning of an important passage in a manuscript

incunabulum, incunabula: book printed before 1500

ink-stone: impermeable surface, typically stone, spread with ink and used to transfer the ink to other media for printing

intaglio: printing done from an image that is below the surface of the printing plate, as in etching or line engraving; compare *letterpress*

ISBN (International Standard Book Number): 13-digit code that identifies the specific edition and format of a book, the language or region of publication, and the publisher; serial publications are issued with *ISSNs (International Standard Serial Numbers)* and printed music with *ISMNs (International Standard Music Numbers)*

italic: type style inspired by cursive scripts and featuring a curve or slant to the right

justify: spacing text so that it is aligned on both ends with other lines of text

lead, leading: long, thin strip of metal inserted between lines of hand-set type to provide space between the lines

leaf, leaves: single sheet of paper that contains a page on each side

leaf master: original, printed or handwritten copy of a text that has been digitized

letterpress: printing done from raised type or blocks, also known as *relief* printing; also used to describe contemporary craft or artisanal printing, as distinguished from larger-scale industrial printing; compare *intaglio*

lexigraphic: writing system based on words

library: collection of books and other materials gathered for use, rather than for sale

library science: professional study and management of libraries, including collecting, organizing, preserving, and disseminating information

ligature: frequent letter combination, such as *fi* or *st*, that is combined in one piece of type

lingua franca: common language used between people of diverse native tongues

literacy: ability to read and write; compare *illiteracy, aliteracy*

logogram: word-sign

logography, logographic: writing system in which the component signs or symbols are based primarily on words, rather than on sounds

logophonetic: writing systems that combine word-signs and sound-signs

majuscule: capital letter

manuscript: text written or prepared by hand, as opposed to being printed by mechanical means; also, the pre-publication version of a text

marginalia: marginal notes in a book or other text; sometimes examined to glean clues about a text's production or previous owners

margins: the three outside edges of a page, surrounding the text block; compare *gutter*

markup codes: codes or symbols inserted into a manuscript to indicate different textual elements, such as basic text or head levels; used by designers, typesetters, and programmers to specify which fonts should be used for each element; also called *type codes*

matrix, matrices: mold used to cast metal type

microfiche: reduced photographic record of printed materials, produced in sheets; compare *microfilm*

microfilm: reduced photographic record of printed materials, produced in rolls; also, the process of producing microfilm or microfiche; compare *microfiche*

miniature: manuscript book illustration; can be of any size

miniscule: small letter

movable type: type that can be assembled, disassembled, and reassembled in a frame to print different documents

national bibliography: record of the works published by a country or nation

national library: library formally established by a state to perform official functions for the country, including preserving the national heritage, producing a record of works published in the country, and often serving as the official depository for those works

obscenity: material regarded as abhorrent or taboo, usually because of sexual or violent content

octavo: sheet of paper folded three times, to create eight leaves or sixteen pages; also, book made up of triple-folded sheets

open access: philosophy that creative works should be made available for free; also, the process of making those works available; see also *copyleft*

open stacks: in a library, stacks that can be accessed and browsed by all readers; compare *closed stacks*

orphan book: book whose copyright status cannot be determined

orthography: spelling

page proof: typeset page that shows all text and illustrations in place, preparatory to printing; see also *galley*

pamphlet: short, unbound publication, typically with no cover or with a paper cover

paper: writing material made of plant or cloth fibers mixed with water, sieved, and dried

paperback: book covered with heavy paper or cardboard, usually with a glued spine

papyrus: writing material made from the pith of the papyrus reed

parchment: writing material made from the skins of animals, especially goats, sheep, or calves

patronage: financial sponsorship of an author by individuals or institutions; compare *subscription*

pecia, peciae: gathering, or portion of an unbound book, consisting of a folded sheet of eight pages

perfect binding, perfect-bound: book in which the pages and cover are held together at the spine by an adhesive

phonetics: system of speech sounds in a language; also, the study of those speech sounds

piracy: theft of another's work by producing unauthorized copies; compare *plagiarism*

plagiarism: theft of another's work by passing all or a portion of it off as one's own; compare *piracy*

plate: prepared surface from which printing is done; traditionally composed of stone or metal, most plates are now made of glass or plastic and coated with a photosensitive emulsion; also, a page in a printed text that contains illustrations, especially if printed on a different kind of paper than the rest of the text

platen: flat wooden or metal plate in a printing press that exerts pressure on the printing surface; also, the roller in a typewriter and some kinds of printers against which the impression is struck

pothi: form of bookbinding in which narrow, slat-like leaves are tied together at two points with string and then rolled up or stacked zigzag fashion

prepress: elements of print production that precede the printing itself, including typesetting, design, and layout

preservation: repair and maintenance of books and other materials; compare *conservation*

pressmark: in a library, a cataloguing number

primary rights: in relation to copyright, the right to produce print and electronic versions of a work; compare *subsidiary rights*

print culture: culture in which books are primarily produced by mechanical means; compare *scribal culture*

print on demand (POD): form of digital publishing in which individual copies of books are printed and bound upon order

printer's devil: apprentice in a printshop

printing: process of making an impression of an image from inked blocks, type, plates, or cylinders; see *letterpress, intaglio, xylography*

process colors: the four ink colors—black, cyan, magenta, yellow—from which other colors and shades of ink can be blended

production: all physical work done to transform a manuscript into a physical or electronic book, including copyediting, design and illustration, layout, typesetting, proofreading, indexing, and either printing and binding or coding for electronic release; often overseen by a *production editor*

production house: service that handles design, production, and sometimes editorial and marketing work for publishers

proof: copy of printed material used for checking accuracy

proofreader: one who reads and corrects proofs

proofreader's marks: set of symbols and systems of underlining that indicate how an edited manuscript should be rendered in type, used by *copyeditors, proofreaders,* and *typesetters*

propaganda: words and images designed to persuade, especially in the service of an authority or a cause

provenance: record of ownership or possession of a book

pseudonym: fictitious name adopted by an author; also called *pen name*

public domain: status of works that are not under copyright; they can be reproduced and circulated without restriction

publisher's reader: advisor employed by publishers in the nineteenth century to read and recommend manuscripts for publication; also called *manuscript reader*

publishing house: entity that acquires, produces, issues, and promotes books and other publications; see also *imprint*

pulp: magazine or book printed on cheap paper and often containing sensational material; compare *slick*

quarto: sheet of paper folded twice, to create four leaves or eight pages; also, book made up of double-folded sheets

quipu: system of knotted strings used by Incans for recording information; possibly a form of three-dimensional writing

quire: collection of sheets folded together to make up one section of an unbound book; also called *gathering* or *signature*

readability level: reading level at which a particular text is aimed, arrived at by formulas that consider vocabulary, as well as fonts, size of type, and amount of white space

rebus: graphic symbol representing a recognizable speech sound

register: in printing of two or more colors, the precise superimposition of images; also, in printing on two sides of a sheet, the precise alignment of the text block on both sides

relief printing: printing done from raised type or blocks, also known as *letterpress* printing; compare *intaglio*

roman: type style inspired by inscriptions on Roman monuments and featuring serifs

royalty: payment to an author from a publisher calculated as a percentage of sales; compare *fee-for-service*

rubric: red-letter text, often used to mark beginnings of text sections or important words or names

rubrication: process of adding red-letter text to a manuscript

ruling: process of scoring a sheet of parchment or paper to prepare it for writing; also called *lining*

running heads, running feet: repeated text at the top (*head*) or bottom (*foot*) of a page that provides information about the author and title; may also include the page number or *folio*

sans serif: letter or typeface with no short lines extending from the upper and lower ends; compare *serif*

scribal culture: culture in which books are primarily produced by hand; compare *print culture*

scriptorium, scriptoria: workshop for the production of hand-copied books

scrivener: scribe, or copier

scroll: rolled book, often made from papyrus or parchment

self-publishing: process of producing, copying, and distributing one's works on one's own, without the aid of a publisher; see also *desktop publishing*, *print on demand*

semasiographic: writing system based on concepts and not tied to any specific spoken language, as in musical notation

serif: short lines extending from the upper and lower ends of a letter; also, letter or typeface that includes those lines; compare *sans serif*

shared profits system: publishing agreement in which authors agree to receive a share of the profit on any book copies sold beyond the number needed to recoup the printing expenses; also called *half-profits system*

signature: collection of sheets folded together to make up one section of an unbound book; also called *gathering* or *quire*

size, sizing: substance, such as a glaze or additive in the paper pulp, used to smooth and seal a writing surface to control absorbency and ensure the ink does not bleed; also, the process of preparing the surface

slick: magazine published on glossy paper; compare *pulp*

slug: line of type created by a hot metal mechanical typesetting machine

sort: specific character (letter, punctuation, numeral) in a font

stereotype: full-sized metal duplicate of a typeset form, made by taking a plaster mold of the form and then casting it in metal

subscription: system of paying for book production with funds collected from potential readers; compare *patronage*

subsidiary rights: in copyright, rights such as serialization, audiobooks, translation, or film or television adaptation; compare *primary rights*

subsidy: allowance or payment to help defray publication costs

syndicator: organization that sells columns, serialized fiction, comics, and other works to newspapers

tilia: Roman writing tablets made of thin slices of folded wood

tympan: frame on a press on which the sheet to be printed is secured; often padded to regulate pressure on the area to be printed; see also *frisket*

typescript: original version of a document made through the use of a typewriter; compare *manuscript*

typesetter: one who sets type or composes graphics for printing; also called *compositor*

uncial: writing system that combines capital and small letters

variorum: edition of a work containing variant versions of the text, often with notes by more than one editor

vellum: particularly fine grade of parchment, typically made from the skin of lambs, kids, or calves

vernacular: local language

web: paper manufactured in a continuous roll, rather than in individual sheets

whirlwind: form of bookbinding in which a stack of pages of gradually increasing length are pasted together at one edge, with the longest sheet at the bottom and shortest on top, then reinforced with a rod on the glued edge

white space: areas of a page without text or illustrations

wholesaler: in bookselling, an entity that sells books from publishers to retail and library customers; compare *distributor*

wiki: collaborative website on which contributors can add, edit, or delete content

wrapped back: form of bookbinding in which printed sheets are folded with printing to the outside, the leaves are bound together at the open (spine) edge with paper screws, and the spine is covered with a glued protective cover

xerography: photocopying; also referred to as *photoreproduction*

xylography: woodblock printing

LANDMARKS IN THE HISTORY OF THE BOOK

3700–3400 BCE	Egyptian hieroglyphic writing
3400–3000	Akkadian cuneiform writing
c. 2700	*Epic of Gilgamesh*
c. 2400	Earliest texts of *Book of the Dead*
c. 2300	Earliest known library at Ebla in Syria
2100–2000	Classical Egyptian hieroglyphic script developed; Semitic alphabetic writing systems
c. 1750	Code of Hammurabi
c. 1200	Chinese oracle-bone inscriptions
c. 1000	Mesoamerican glyphic writing; Aramaic script; earliest known abecedary created (Tel Zayit in Israel)
c. 900	Greek alphabet
c. 759	*Iliad*
c. 725	*Odyssey*
c. 650	Demotic Egyptian script
403	Athens adopts 24-letter Greek Ionic alphabet
c. 300	Library at Alexandria founded
c. 200	Small seal Chinese script; square Hebrew script; earliest known Mayan texts; Roman 23-letter Latin alphabet adopted
c. 100	Parchment "invented" in Pergamum
	Dead Sea Scrolls; development of the codex
CE c. 100	Coptic script; paper described by Cài Lún; Vindolanda tablets; earliest known fragments of Christian Bible
c. 300	Arabic script
383	Vulgate Bible commissioned
c. 500	Library at monastery of Vivarium founded
653	First authorized edition of the Qur'an
c. 700	Buddhist "great spell" printed by Chinese Empress Wu
751	Papermaking spreads to Middle East
c. 760	Pagoda prayers printed by Japanese Empress Shōtoku
c. 770	Papermaking spreads to Japan
c. 800	*Book of Kells*

868	*Diamond Sutra*
900s	Fatimid library and university founded in Egypt; Bi Shēng invents movable type in China
1000s	First European universities founded
1030s	First account of recycled paper in Japan
1100s–1600s	The Renaissance
1200s	Book of Hours; *Biblia Pauperum;* first spectacles
1300s	Vatican Library founded
1400–1440s	King Sejong develops Korean Hangul characters and commissions movable type
1440s	Gutenberg invents printing and movable type in Germany
1450s	Frankfurt Book Fair founded
1456	Gutenberg Bible printed
1460s	Roman and italic typefaces
1469	First printing patents granted in Venice
1470s–1500s	Printing spreads throughout Europe; age of incunabula
1515	Pope Leo X issues first official Roman Catholic censorship decrees
1517	The Reformation begins with Luther's 95 Theses
1520s–1530s	Tyndale's English translations of Bible printed
1534	Luther's German translation of Bible printed
1537	Francis I issues first library depository decree in France
1539	First books printed in North America by Juan Pablos in Mexico
1540s	Garamond typefaces created
1555	Officina Plantiniana founded in Antwerp
1557	Stationers' Company incorporated in London
1559	*Index Librorum Prohibitorum* first enforced internationally
1562	Inquisition destroys Mesoamerican codices
1568–73	Antwerp Polyglot Bible printed
1611	King James Bible printed
1623	Shakespeare's *First Folio* printed
1635	Académie Française established in France
1644	Milton's *Areopagitica* defends free press
1653	First public library in Britain founded (Chetham's Library in Manchester)

1660	Royal Society established in Britain
1687	The Enlightenment begins with publication of Newton's *Principia Mathematica*
1700s	Caslon typefaces created
1710	Copyright Act enacted in Britain
1750s	Baskerville typefaces created
1750–80	*L'Encylopédie* published in France
1753	British Museum Library founded
1755	Johnson's *Dictionary of the English Language* published
1787	First Amendment of the US Constitution guarantees freedom of the press
1789	Declaration of the Rights of Man affirms freedom of thought and opinion in France; Bibliothèque Nationale founded
1790	US Copyright Act enacted; Royal Literary Fund founded in London
1793	Chénier Act affirms authors' economic rights in France
1800	Stanhope iron press invented; wood-pulp paper; US Library of Congress created
1800s	Bodoni typefaces created
1822	Champollion announces translation of the Rosetta Stone
1824	Braille system created
1842	British Copyright Act extended throughout the Empire; Mudie's Select Library established
1847	Canadian Customs Act bans obscenity
1848	First bookstore chain, W.H. Smith's, founded
1860s	First typewriters invented
1866	Officina Plantiniana prints its last book
1870s	Literary agents
1873	Comstock Act forbids use of US postal service to send "obscene" materials
1876	Dewey decimal system created
1884	Society of Authors founded in London
1886	Linotype invented
1887	Berne Convention establishes first international copyright agreement
1891	US Chace Act acknowledges copyright of foreign authors

1895	Roycroft Press founded in New York
1896	*Kelmscott Chaucer* published
1897	Monotype invented; Library of Congress (LOC) cataloguing system created
1900s	Gill typefaces created
1921	PEN International founded
1926	Book-of-the-Month Club founded
1930s–1940s	Paperback revolution; microfilming
1933	Nazi book burnings in Germany
1948	UN General Assembly passes Universal Declaration of Human Rights, affirming freedom of thought and expression
1952	Universal Copyright Convention
1953	National Library of Canada established
1954	Comics Code Authority established in US
1957	*Code de la propriété intellectuelle* passed in France, affirming authors' moral rights in their work
1959–62	*Lady Chatterley's Lover* trials strike down obscenity laws in Britain and North America
1960s	Modernization of Chinese characters in People's Republic of China
1960s–1970s	Rise of modern bookstore chains
1966	*Index Librorum Prohibitorum* ceases publication
1966–76	Cultural Revolution in People's Republic of China
1968	Bibliothèque Nationale du Québec established
1970s–1980s	Rise of international publishing conglomerates; rise of book superstores
1971	Project Gutenberg launched
1980s	Internet and digital revolution begin
1988	*Oxford English Dictionary* published on CD-ROM
1989	US joins Berne Convention
1990s	Resurgence of ethnic and religious violence leads to increased destruction of libraries and other cultural objects
1994	Agreement on Trade-Related Aspects of Intellectual Property Rights (TRIPS)
1995	Amazon.com launched
1996	Reading Experience Database (RED) launched; Oprah's Book Club begins
2000s	First commercially successful e-readers created

2001	*Wikipedia* launched
2004	Google Books launched; Richard & Judy Book Club begins
2005	Danish cartoons controversy
2011	Comics Code Authority abandoned in US
2012	*Encyclopedia Britannica* ceases publication of paper edition

Abbott, C.S., 140
Abebooks, 259, 264
Abu Bakr (caliph), 58
academic publishing,
    226–29
Académie Française, 102,
    103, 104, 164, 324
Acereda, Alberto, 169
acidified paper, 308–10
acquisitions, 230–31
action/adventure, 336–38
Adams, John, 298
adaptions, 169, 172, 336
advances, 160, 220
advertising industry, 119–20
Aeschylus, 205
Afghanistan, 192
aggregators, 261
Aiken, Paul, 155
Aitken, William Maxwell,
    206
al-Dhahabi, 59
al-Hakam II (caliph), 59
al-Hakim (caliph), 59
Albatross Books, 122
alexia, 316
Alibris, 259
aliteracy, 317–18
Altick, Richard, 180, 277,
    279
Amazon.com
    about, 261–64
    copyright, 202
    customer base, 245
    distribution centers, 265
    Kindle, 133, 171, 226, 262
    textbook leasing, 226
    See also online book-
        sellers
American Brat, An (Sidhwa),
    172
American Library
    Association (ALA),
    182, 305, 342

American Society of
    Journalists and
    Authors (ASJA), 157
Amis, Martin, 220
Anabaptists, 94
ancillary materials, 222–23
Anglican church, 94, 95–96,
    187
animal skins. See parchment
Anna Karenina (Tolstoy), 168
anonymous publishing,
    149–54
antiquarian booksellers,
    250–53, 259, 261
Antwerp Polyglot (Bible),
    98
Apocrypha, 64
Apple products, 133, 202
Arabic script, 33, 59
archives. See libraries
Areopagitica (Milton), 193
Arias Montano, Benito, 98
Arnold, Martin, 336
Arouet, François-Marie. See
    Voltaire
Arpanet, 127–28
Ars Moriendi, 82
Art of Racing in the Rain, The
    (Stein), 169
art program, 239
artist's books, 137
Ashbee, Henry Spencer, 295
Association of Authors'
    Agents (AAA), 164
Association of Authors'
    Representatives
    (AAR), 164
Astor, John Jacob, 286
Ateneo, 254, 255
Athanasius, 63
Atlantic, The, 163
audiobooks, 170
Augustus (emperor), 273
Aurelius, Marcus, 52
Aurora Floyd (Braddon), 213

Authorized Version (Bible),
    96
authorship
    about, 145–46
    anonymous publishing,
        149–54
    associations, 164–67
    Authors Guild, 164, 165
    Authors League Fund,
        156, 157
    bibliography, 140
    collaboration, 146
    columnists, 215
    economic support,
        156–57, 165, 195
    freedom of expression,
        165–67
    literary agents, 162–64,
        230
    literary estates, 162, 195
    marketing, 233
    modern idea of, 146–49,
        228
    new journalism, 215
    open access, 204
    patronage system, 147–48
    profession of, 145, 155–59,
        165
    pseudonyms and pen
        names, 146, 149–54, 190
    readers, 313
    Royal Literary Fund,
        156–57
    study of authors, 341–42
    transmission, 146
    See also copyright
Avrin, Leila, 56, 57

B. Dalton, 245, 255
Bacon, Francis, 151
Bacon, Roger, 320
Báez, Fernando, 190
Bakaršic, Kemal, 192
Baker & Taylor, 265

Baker, Nicholson, 107, 126, 309
Baldacci, David, 170
Ballantine, Betty, 123
Ballantine, Ian, 123
Bambi and Me (Tremblay), 169
Banned Books Week, 182
Barker, Robert, 96
Barnes & Noble, 115, 133, 171, 245, 257–58, 260
Barnes, Charles, 260
Barnes, William, 260
Barrett, T.H., 79
Basbanes, Nicholas, 192, 247, 248–49
Bashō, 153
Baskerville, John, 87
Bass, Benjamin, 248
Bass, Fred, 248–49
Battles, Matthew, 275, 303
Bay Psalm Book, The, 300
Bell, Acton, 154. *See* Brontë, Anne
Bell, Currer. *See* Brontë, Charlotte
Bell, Ellis. *See* Brontë, Emily
Beloved (Morrison), 182
Benedict XIV (pope), 97
Bennett, Alan, 288, 338
Benny Cooperman series (Engel), 316
Bentley, Richard, 213
Benton, Megan, 111
Berne Convention, 198–99
Bertram, James, 284, 285
Besant, Walter, 164
Beyle, Marie-Henri. *See* Stendhal
Bezos, Jeff, 262
Bi Shēng, 78–79
Bible. *See* Christian Bible; Hebrew Bible; religious writing
Biblia Pauperum, 82, 83
bibliography, 16, 140–41, 290
Biblioteca Nazionale Centrale di Firenze, 308
Bibliothèque Nationale (France), 290, 296–98

Bibliothèque Nationale du Québec, 287, 301–02
Bibliothèque Saint-Sulpice, 287
big books, 220
big box stores, 115, 245, 256–61, 263, 265–66
Bignon, Abbé Jean-Paul, 296–97
Bill, John, 96
bindings, 240, 242–43
  artist's books, 137
  techniques, 77–78, 105–06
  value, 140–41
biography, 341
black letter fonts, 86
blacklisting, 190–91
Blackwell's, 258
Blair, Eric. *See* Orwell, George
Bloomsbury Group, 171
Blume, Judy, 170
blurbs, 240
Boccaccio, Giovanni, 70
bodice rippers, 241
Bodley, Thomas, 185
Bodoni, Giambattista, 87
body text, 238
Boleyn, Anne, 94
Bond, James, 336
Book-It Repertory Company, 169
Book of Kells, 65–66, 130
Book of the Dead, 26–27, 130
Book-of-the-Month Club (BOMC), 245, 325, 326–28
Book on the Bookshelf, The (Petroski), 322–23
Book Revolution, The (Escarpit), 16–17
books
  book arts, 139
  book burnings, 188–90
  book challenges, 182
  book circuit, 135
  book collections, 343–44
  book trailers, 343
  bookmarks, 323
  bookmobiles, 288
  bookshelves, 322–23

defined, 15–17
  development of, 15
  history of, 16
Book of Hours, 66, 130
Books-a-Million, 258
Bookseller of Kabul, The (Seierstad), 192
booksellers
  author interests, 155
  big box stores, 115, 245, 256–61, 263, 265–66
  book trade fairs, 246, 266–68
  bookstore chains, 245, 253–56
  censorship, 192
  control of titles, 155
  distributors, 264–66
  e-books, 133–34
  ethnography, 344–45
  history of, 245
  independents, 115, 245, 246–53, 259, 263, 317
  Islamic world, 60, 192
  mail-order catalogues, 245, 260
  modern age, 245–46
  online sales, 252, 257, 258, 259, 260
  price of books, 261
  Renaissance, 246
  Roman empire, 52–53, 246
  sale-or-return, 266
  state involvement, 177
  stationers' guilds, 180–81
  superstores, 115, 245, 256–61, 263, 265–66
  used and antiquarian booksellers, 250–53, 259, 261
  wholesale trade, 245, 259, 264–66
  See also online booksellers
Booth, Richard, 268
Borders, 115, 245, 258, 259
Boston Public Library, 279–80
Boswell, James, 103
boustrophedons, 41, 42, 49–50

Bowdler, Thomas, 237
bowdlerization, 237
Braddon, Mary Elizabeth, 213, 214
Bradley, Katherine Harris, 154
Braille, 170, 321–22
Braille, Louis, 321–22
Brecht, Bertolt, 165, 190
breviaries, 66
Bride, The (Sidhwa), 172
Brink, Jean, 148
British Library, 201, 290, 291–96, 297, 299–300, 303
brittle books, 308–10
Brontë, Anne, 154
Brontë, Charlotte, 154, 212
Brontë, Emily, 154
Brooke, Rupert, 156
Brown, Albert Curtis, 164
Brown, Dan, 160
Brown, John, 158
Brown, Samuel, 277
Brown, Spencer Curtis, 164
Buddhism, 79–80
Budge, E.A. Wallis, 27
Bunyan, John, 331
Burgess, Hugh, 107
Burne-Jones, Edward, 112
Burney, Fanny, 152, 158
Business of Books, The (Schiffrin), 221
butterfly binding, 77–78

Caesar, Julius, 61
Cài Lún, 39
Calvin, John, 93–94
Camilla (Burney), 158
Canadian Authors Association (CAA), 165
Canadian National Institute for the Blind (CNIB), 170
Canadian Writers' Foundation, 165
Canterbury Tales (Chaucer), 68–69, 70
canvassing books, 159
card catalogues, 304–05
Carefoote, Pearce, 185
Carlos III (king), 99, 185

Carnegie, Andrew, 282, 283–86, 302
Carpenter, Edward, 295
Carroll, Lewis, 153
Cartier, Georges, 302
cartoons, 194, 236
Caslon, William, 87
Cassiodorus, 274–75
Casson, Lionel, 271, 272, 274–75
Cat in the Hat, The (Seuss), 225
Cataloguing in Publication (CIP) data, 232–33
cataloguing systems, 141, 293, 303–06, 344
Catcher in the Rye, The (Salinger), 182
Catherine of Aragon (queen), 94
Catholic Church
 censorship, 41, 96–97, 183–85
 Encyclopédie, 101
 propaganda, 204
 public libraries, 287–88
 regulating print, 178–79
 Vatican Library, 274–75
Caxton, William, 181
Cecilia (Burney), 158
censorship
 about, 177–78, 181, 183
 blacklisting, 190–91
 book burnings, 188–90
 book challenges, 182
 book culture, 342
 bowdlerization, 237
 Catholic Church, 41, 96–97, 183–85
 Comics Code Authority (CCA), 188
 ethnic cleansing, 188–90, 191–92
 Frankfurt Book Fair, 267
 Harry Potter series, 332
 Islam, 167
 modern era, 190–92
 obscenity, 188
 pornography, 186–88
 Private Case, 294–95
 self-publishing, 170–73
 state censorship, 185–88

Third Reich, 166, 188–90, 256
 World War II, 207
 See also regulating print
Cervantes, Miguel de, 185
Champollion, Jean-François, 24–26
Chandler, Raymond, 124, 338
Chapman, John, 214
Chapters, 115, 245, 258
Charing Cross Road, 247
Charles V (king), 296
Chateaubriand, François-René de, 156
Chaucer, Geoffrey, 68–69, 70, 112
Chetham, Humphrey, 277, 280
Chetham's Library, 280–81
Chicago Public Library, 286
children's books, 331
China
 bookbinding, 77–78
 censorship, 191
 Cultural Revolution, 191
 movable type, 78–79
 multicolor printing, 78
 oracle-bones, 36–37
 paper, 39–40
 scribal culture, 79
 woodblock printing, 76–81
 writing systems, 21–22, 35–38, 38
Chomsky, Noam, 206
Christian Bible
 Antwerp Polyglot, 98
 Apocrypha, 64
 Authorized Version (Bible), 96
 Biblia Pauperum, 82, 83
 Biblia Regia, 98
 codex form, 61–62
 development of, 62–64
 Gutenberg Bible, 86, 90–91, 95
 King James Bible, 96
 Septuagint, 63, 64
 vernacular translations, 95–96
 Vulgate (Bible), 63–64

See also religious writing
Christianity
  Anglican church, 94, 95–96
  Catholic Church, 96–97, 101
  codex, 61–62
  indulgences, 93
  Protestantism, 93–94
  Reformation, 93–94, 94–96
  regulating print, 178–79
  state censorship, 187
Christie, Agatha, 123, 124, 337, 338
Churchill, Charles, 158
Churchill, William, 104
Cicero, 52
CIP. *See* Cataloguing in Publication data
circulating libraries, 120–21, 213, 240, 276, 278–79
Clair, Colin, 178
Clark, Giles, 162
class
  reading choices, 331
  regulating print, 180
classroom sets, 222
clay tablets, 29, 30
Cleland, John, 295
Clemens, Samuel Langhorne. *See* Twain, Mark
Clement VII (pope), 94
Clement VIII (pope), 64
Clifford, Margaret, 148
climate controls, 308
Clinton, Bill, 220
Clinton, Hillary Rodham, 220
cloth-based paper, 112
cloth bindings, 240, 243
codex
  Christian Bible, 62–64
  Christianity, 61–62
  colophons, 69
  defined, 34
  emergence of, 49–50, 58–62
  exemplars, 67
  Islamic bookmaking, 59–61

Mayan, 41–43
parchment, 34
Qur'an, 58–59
religious writing, 50
Roman Empire, 61, 62
rubricators, 67
Semitic writings, 56–57
structure of, 50
  See also print formats
Codex Dresdensis, 42
Codex Peresianus, 42
Codex Tro-Cortesianus, 42
Cold War, 190–91, 207
Coleridge, Samuel Taylor, 156
collaborative publications, 203–04
Collins, Paul, 268
Collins, Wilkie, 213
colophons
  cuneiform tablets, 29
  defined, 29, 69
  Diamond Sutra, 79–80
  first printed colophon, 90
  medieval Jewish books, 57
  scribal culture, 69
color printing
  China, 78
  publishing process, 242
  two-color printing, 90, 91
Color Purple, The (Walker), 182
Columbanus, 275
columnists, 215
Comics Code Authority (CCA), 188
commissioned texts, 230
common press, 75–76, 88–93
Common Sense (Paine), 205
communication circuit, 17, 135
Communist Manifesto (Marx and Engels), 281
composing sticks, 84
Compton's Multimedia, 126
computer printers, 125
concertina binding, 78
Concise Oxford Dictionary, 227
Condell, Henry, 150

conductors, 214
Congregation of the Index, 97
Conrad, Joseph, 164
conservation, 307–10
Constable, Archibald, 152
contracts, 160–65, 231
cookbooks, 241
Cooper, Edith Emma, 154
Copper Canyon Press, 221
copyediting, 235–37
copyright
  author's warranty, 160
  contracts, 160–61
  copyleft, 203–04
  copyright clearing-houses, 200
  copyright depositories, 201–02
  defined, 155
  digitization projects, 165
  droit d'auteur, 197
  droits patrimoniaux, 197–98
  electronic copies, 202
  fair use, 200–01
  Google Books, 131
  grant of rights, 160–61
  grants and patents, 178, 181
  international copyright protections, 198–99
  manufacturing clause, 199
  modern law, 201–02
  open access, 203–04
  origins of, 155–56, 195–98
  orphan books, 131
  piracy, 202
  plagiarism, 202
  public domain, 196
  Society of Authors, 164
  See also authorship
Cornwell, David, 336
Corrections, The (Franzen), 328
correctors, 67
Cortés, Hernán, 42
Costco, 266
Cotton, Bruce, 291
Council of Trent, 64
cover design, 239–41, 343

Cracking India (Sidhwa), 172
Creative Commons, 203
Creel, George, 206
critical biography, 341
Cromwell, Oliver, 187
Cross, Paul, 294
Crow Eaters, The (Sidhwa),
    172, 173
crowd-sourcing, 129
Crown Books, 258
cultural artifacts, 16
Cultural Revolution, 191
cuneiform, 21, 28–31
Cunningham, Michael, 168
Cunningham, Ward, 126
Curtis Brown agency, 164
Curtis, Cyrus H.K., 119
cylinder press, 105, 107
cylinder seals, 75

d'Abbeville, Gérard, 72
da Montefeltro, Federico,
    275
Da Vinci Code, The (Brown),
    160
Dale-Chall readability
    formula, 224
d'Alembert, Jean le Rond,
    101
Damasus I (pope), 63
*Dangerous Men and
    Adventurous Women*
    (Krentz), 334–35
Dante Alighieri, 70
Darío, Rubén, 169
Darnton, Robert, 17, 135,
    145, 313
Davies, Robertson, 164
Dawkins, Richard, 227
Dawson, George, 315–16
de Graff, Robert F., 122
de Landa, Diego, 41, 97
de Nave, Francine, 99
de Sade, Marquis, 295
de Vere, Edward, 151
Dead Sea Scrolls, 34–35, 130
Defoe, Daniel, 331
DeMille, Nelson, 336
Derrida, Jacques, 168
Derusha, Will, 169

"Description of Cooke-
    ham, The" (Lanier),
    148
design, 238–41
desktop publishing, 116, 171
detective novels, 124, 336–38
determinatives, 26
developmental editing,
    233–35
Dewey decimal system,
    304–05, 344
Dewey, Melville, 303
diacritics, 33
Dialogue with Death
    (Koestler), 167
Diamond Sutra, 79–80, 130
Diaspora, 55–56
Dickens, Charles, 198, 214,
    331
Dickson, Paul, 288
dictionaries
    Académie Française, 102,
        103, 104
    CD-ROM format, 126
    Chinese, 37
    *Dictionary of the English
        Language* (Johnson),
        102–03, 104
    Oxford English Dictionary,
        103, 126
    subscription publication,
        158
    university presses, 227
    See also spelling
*Dictionary of the English
    Language* (Johnson),
    102–03, 104
*Dictionary of National
    Biography*, 164
Diderot, Denis, 101
digitization projects
    about, 129–31, 137–38
    brittle books, 309–10
    copyright, 165
    print culture, 134–35
digitized books. *See* e-books
Dink, Hrant, 167
discrimination, 56
distributors, 264–66
Divine Comedy, The (Dante),
    70
Dixon, Franklin W., 154

Dodgson, Charles. *See*
    Carroll, Lewis
Dōkyō, 39
Don Quixote (Cervantes),
    185
Donatus, Aelius, 52, 82
Double Fold (Baker), 126, 309
Doyle, Arthur Conan, 124,
    336, 338
Dresden Codex, 42
droit d'auteur, 197
droits patrimoniaux, 197–98
Dryden, John, 168
du Maurier, Daphne, 164
*Ductor in Linguas, The
    Guide into Tongues*
    (Minsheu), 158
Dupin, Amandine Lucille
    Aurore. *See* Sand,
    George
dust jackets, 239–40
dyslexia, 316

e-books
    Barnes & Noble, 260
    booksellers, 133–34
    digitization projects,
        129–31, 134–35, 137–38
    e-readers, 131–34, 260
    ePub format, 131
    Open eBook (OeB)
        format, 131
    Project Gutenberg, 116,
        129
    sales figures, 116
    textbook leasing, 226
    See also electronic infor-
        mation
Earth (film), 172
East Lynne (Price), 213
eBay, 264
Echo, The, 282
Eco, Umberto, 320
editors
    editorial division, 230
    magazine conductors,
        214
    manuscript readers,
        212–13
    multinationals, 218, 220
    production houses, 218

publisher's readers,
212–13
See also publishers
education
Ancient Greek, 45, 51–52
fair use, 200
Frankfurt Book Fair, 267
literacy, 116–17
nineteenth century, 113
paperback sales, 122
primers, 66
public libraries, 289
Roman Empire, 51–52
state involvement, 177
universities, 71–72
woodblock printing, 82
educational publishing
ancillary materials,
222–23
classroom sets, 222
educational presses,
219–21
readability levels, 223,
224–25
textbook publishing,
222–26, 233
university presses,
226–29
used textbooks, 250
Edward VI (king), 95
Egyptian hieroglyphic, 21,
24–28
84, Charing Cross Road
(Hanff), 246, 247
Eisenstein, Elizabeth, 16, 72,
94–95, 246
electronic information
CD-ROMs, 126–27
crowd-sourcing, 129
developmental editing,
233
digitization projects,
129–31, 134–35, 137–38,
309–10
fair use, 200
Google Books, 130–31
Internet, 127–31
music file sharing, 202
Public Library of Science
(PLoS), 203
Wikipedia, 127–28

See also e-books; print
formats
Eliot, George, 154, 159–60,
214
Eliot, Simon, 313
Elizabeth I (queen), 94, 95,
148, 151, 186
emergency preparedness,
307–08
Emerson, Ralph Waldo, 214
emoticons, 23
Encarta, 126
Encyclopedia Britannica,
126–27
encyclopedias, 100–01,
126–27
Encyclopédie, 100–01
endcaps, 258
endowments, 227
Engel, Howard, 316
Engels, Friedrich, 281
Enlightenment, the, 99–100,
146, 193
Enuma Anu Ellil, 30
ephemera, 92, 120
Epic of Gilgamesh, 30
Epitome trium terrae partium
(Vadian), 267
Escarpit, Robert, 16–17
Estienne, Henri, 267
ethnic cleansing, 191–92
ethnography, 344–45
Evangeline (Longfellow), 159
Evanovich, Janet, 170
Evans, Mary Anne. *See* Eliot,
George
Evelina (Burney), 158
Everett, Edward, 280
Ex Libris (Fadiman), 323
exemplars, 67
experimental writers, 171

fact checking, 236
Fadiman, Anne, 323
Faerie Queene, The (Spenser),
148
fair use, 200–01
Family Shakespeare, The
(Bowdler), 237
Fanny Hill (Cleland), 295
fanzines, 203–04, 325

Farewell to Arms, A
(Hemingway), 234
Fast, Howard, 171
Fatimid library, 59
Faulkner, William, 164
fee-for-service, 230
Fellowship of Australian
Writers, 165
Female Quixote, The
(Lennox), 148
Few Footprints, A (Passmore
Edwards), 283
Field, Michael, 154
Finnigan, Judy, 260, 325, 329
fire, 308
Fischer, Steven, 30, 41, 81,
246, 320
Fischman, Sheila, 169
Fitzgerald, F. Scott, 182, 234
Fleming, Ian, 336
Flesch Reading Ease system,
224
Flint, Kate, 330
flooding, 307–08
flyleaves, 243
folios, 92
Fontaine, T.A., 187
Fontana, Domenico, 274
fonts, 81, 84, 86–88
Forever Amber (Winsor), 220
Forsyte Saga, The
(Galsworthy), 257
Foucault, Michel, 145
Fourdrinier machine, 108
forty-two-line Bible, 91
Foyle, Christina, 256–57
Foyle, Christopher, 257
Foyle, Gilbert, 256
Foyle, William, 256
Foyles, 256–57
France
censorship, 186
droit d'auteur, 197
droits patrimoniaux,
197–98
educational system, 117
freedom of expression,
193, 195
lettres de permission, 179
See also Bibliothèque
Nationale (France)
Francis I (king), 296

Frankfurt Book Fair, 266–67
Franklin, Benjamin, 87, 119, 276, 326
Franklin, John, 277
Franzen, Jonathan, 328
Frederick II (king), 147–48
freedom of expression
  about, 192–95
  Cold War, 191, 207
  PEN International, 165–67
  state censorship, 187–88
  state involvement, 177
  Third Reich, 188–90
Freud, Sigmund, 190
Frey, James, 329
Froschauer, Christoph, 267
Fry readability formula, 224–25
Fukuyama, Francis, 191
Fuller, Margaret, 214
Füssel, Stephen, 91
Fust, Johann, 93, 178
future trends, 134–35

Gabrielsson, Eva, 337
Galileo Galilei, 97
galleys, 84
Galsworthy, John, 257
Garamond, Claude, 86–87
Gardners Books, 265
Garnett, Constance, 168
Garnett, Edward, 212
gatherings, 92
Geisel, Theodor Seuss. See Seuss, Dr.
genre fiction
  about, 332–33
  action/adventure, 336–38
  compared to literary fiction, 346–47
  romance, 334–35
  suspense, 336–38
George II (king), 291
George IV (king), 156
Germany
  Bible translation, 95
  black letter fonts, 86
  educational system, 117
  national libraries, 291
  Third Reich, 165–66, 188–90, 207, 256

See also Frankfurt Book Fair; Gutenberg, Johannes; Luther, Martin
Gernsback, Hugo, 124
Gill, Eric, 113
Gioia, Dana, 318
Girl Who Kicked the Hornets' Nest, The (Larsson), 337
Girl Who Played with Fire, The (Larsson), 337
Girl with the Dragon Tattoo, The (Larsson), 337
glasses, 320–21
Glaubman, Richard, 315
GNU Project, 203
Goebbels, Joseph, 189, 207
Golding, William, 182
Gone with the Wind (Mitchell), 201
Google Books project, 130–31, 165
grammar, 103–04
Grande Bibliothèque Nationale, 287, 301–02
grant of rights, 160–61
Grapes of Wrath, The (Steinbeck), 182
Great Gatsby, The (Fitzgerald), 182, 234
Great Library of Alexandria, 272–73
Greece, Ancient, 21, 44–46, 272–73
Greenblatt, Stephen, 152
Gregory XV (pope), 204
Griffin, Dustin, 148
Grolier Codex, 42
Gulliver's Travels (Swift), 147
Gunzenhauser, Bonnie, 313
Gutenberg Bible, 86, 90–91, 95, 130
Gutenberg, Johannes, 75, 78–79, 82–88
Gutenberg press, 75–76. See also common press
gutter, 239

Haggadah, 57
Hale, Sarah Josepha, 214
Half Price Books, 255–56

half-profits system, 159
Halley, Edmond, 100
Hammett, Dashiell, 124, 338
Hammurabi's Code, 30–31
Handler, Daniel. See Snicket, Lemony
Hanff, Helene, 246–47
Hangul writing system, 81
hanji, 35, 38
hardcover books, 122, 243
Hardesty, Sarah, 335
Hardy Boys books, 154
Harlequin, 124, 221–22
Harley, Edward, 291
Harley, Robert, 291
Harmsworth, Alfred, 206
Harris, Michael, 290
Harris, P.R., 294, 302
Harry Potter series (Rowling), 154, 160, 331, 332–33, 343
Hart, Michael, 129
Harvard University Press, 227
Haven Foundation, 157
Hay Festival, 268
Hearst, William Randolph, 215
Hebrew Bible
  Dead Sea Scrolls, 34–35
  Talmud, 55
  Torah, 31–33, 56–57
  See also religious writing
height-to-paper, 84
Heminges, John, 150
Hemingway, Ernest, 123, 234
Henry, James Arruda, 315
Henry VIII (king), 94, 95
Herodian, 53
hieroglyphic, 21, 24–28
Hildreth, Susan, 289
His Dark Materials (Pullman), 289
History of Reading, A (Fischer), 246
History of Reading, A (Manguel), 318–19
Hitler, Adolf, 188, 207, 256
Hocking, Amanda, 173
Hogarth Press, 171
Holmes, Sherlock, 337
Homer, 45, 53

Horace, 246
Horror Writers Association, 165
Horton, Sarah, 227
hot metal composing, 110, 125
"How Should One Read a Book?" (Woolf), 16
Howsam, Leslie, 16
Hubbard, Elbert, 112
Hugo, Victor, 298
humor, 200–01, 236

Ianniciello, Pennie, 266
Ibarra, Joaquín, 185
ibn Abbad, Al-Sahib, 60
ibn Affan, Uthman (caliph), 59
ibn Hayyan, Jabir, 59
Ibn Khaldun, 60
Ibn Killis, 60
icons, 23
ideograms, 24
ideology, 207
Iliad (Homer), 45
illustration and illumination
    art programs, 239
    artist's books, 137
    Biblia Pauperum, 82, 83
    Book Arts Revival, 111–13
    book design, 238, 239
    Book of Hours, 65–66
    Book of Kells, 65–66
    digitization projects, 130
    Haggadah, 57
    illuminations defined, 67
    incipits, 67
    Islamic law, 192, 194
    Lindisfarne Gospels, 66
    miniatures, 60–61, 67, 83
    Muslim books, 57, 60–61
    rubricators, 67
    Saturday Evening Post, 119
    woodblock printing, 82
imprints, 218
In a Fisherman's Language (Henry), 316
incipits, 67
incunabula, 92

independent booksellers, 115, 245, 246–53, 259, 263
Index Librorum Prohibitorum, 96–97, 184–85
indexes, 241–42
Indiana (Sand), 154
Indigo, 258
indulgences, 93
industrial revolution, 104–06
Information, The (Amis), 220
Ingram Book Company, 265
ink, 75, 88
Innocents Abroad (Twain), 107
Inquisition, 41, 56, 97, 183
Intermediate Sex, The (Carpenter), 295
Internet, 127–31
Introduction to Bibliographical and Textual Studies (Williams and Abbott), 140
Invention by Design (Petroski), 227
iPad, 133
Irish Thoroughbred (Roberts), 335
ISBNs, 232
Islam
    censorship, 192
    prohibition of images, 192, 194
    Qur'an, 33, 50, 57–59
    Prophet Muhammad, 57–58
    Satanic Verses (Rushdie), 167
Islamic world
    bookmaking, 59–61
    illustration and illumination, 57
    libraries, 59–60
    literacy, 58–59
    Moorish regions, 55–56
    paper, 61
    scribal culture, 57–60
italic typefaces, 86
itinerating libraries, 277
iTunes, 202

James, Henry, 234
James I (king), 96
James II (king), 149
Jane Eyre (Brontë), 212
Japan
    booksellers, 247, 255
    paper, 39
    printing, 81
    writing systems, 35, 38, 330
Jefferson, Thomas, 117, 196, 298–99, 305, 322
Jehovah's Witnesses, 216
Jenkins, Jerry B., 222
Jenson, Nicholas, 86
Jerome, 63–64
Jewel of the Nile, The (film), 334
Jewett, Charles Coffin, 299
Jewsbury, Geraldine Endsor, 212–13
Johnson, Elmer, 290
Johnson, John H., 216
Johnson, Samuel, 102–03, 104, 148
Johnston, Edward, 113
Joy of Cooking, The (Rombauer), 173
Joyce, James, 182, 229
JSTOR (Journal Storage), 129
Judaism. *See* Hebrew Bible; Semitic writings
Julius Caesar, 61
justification, 84
Justine (de Sade), 295
Jyllands-Posten, 194

kanji, 35
katakana, 38
Keene, Carolyn, 154
Kefer, Heinrich, 93
Kelmscott Press, 112
Kernan, Alvin, 103
khipus. *See* quipus
Kilgour, Frank, 60
Kindle, 133, 262
    Kindle Direct Publishing (KDP), 171
    textbook leasing, 226
    See also Amazon.com; e-books; e-readers

King James Bible, 96
King, Stephen, 132, 157
King's Books, 247
Kipling, Rudyard, 162
Klein, Joe, 153
Knorosov, Yuri, 41
Koestler, Arthur, 167
Korea
    printing, 78, 81–82
    writing systems, 35, 38, 81
Krätli, Graziano, 60
Kreyling, Michael, 163
Kristin Lavransdatter
    (Undset), 168–69

Labour History Archive
    and Study Centre, 306
Labrouste, Henri, 297–98
Lady Audley's Secret
    (Braddon), 213
Lady Chatterley's Lover
    (Lawrence), 186–87,
    188, 295
LaHaye, Tim, 222
L'Amour, Louis, 336
Lane, Allen, 122, 123
Lanier, Emilia, 148
Lanston, Tolbert, 111
Larsson, Stieg, 337, 338
Lawrence, D.H., 186–87,
    188, 295
Lay of the Last Minstrel, The
    (Scott), 152
le Carré, John, 336
leads, 84
Lee, Harper, 182
Left Behind (LaHaye and
    Jenkins), 222
Lennox, Charlotte, 148
Lenox, James, 286
Leo X (pope), 183
Leo XIII (pope), 275
Les vues animées (Tremblay),
    169
Lessing, Doris, 153
letterpress printing, 75. *See
    also* common press
lettres de permission, 179. *See
    also* copyright
Lewes, George H., 154
lexigraphic systems, 23,
    29–30

librarianship
    cataloguing systems, 141,
        293, 303–06, 344
    Library Bureau, 304–05
    professionalization of,
        272, 302–03
    specialization, 306–07
    women, 302–03, 305
libraries
    about, 271–72
    archives, 306–07
    book challenges, 182
    circulating libraries,
        120–21, 213, 240, 276,
        278–79
    collection of Greek
        works, 45
    conservation and preser-
        vation, 307–10
    Cultural Revolution, 191
    digitization projects,
        129–31
    emergency preparedness,
        307–08
    ethnography, 344–45
    evolution of, 271–76
    Islamic libraries, 59–60
    modern libraries, 276–77
    the Renaissance, 71–72,
        275–76
    space concerns, 310
    traveling libraries, 277
    universities, 71–72
    Vatican Library, 274–75
    See also national librar-
        ies; public libraries
Libraries of the Ancient World
    (Casson), 272
Library at Night, The
    (Manguel), 343
Library in America, The
    (Dickson), 288
Library of Congress, 170,
    201, 290, 298–300,
    305–06, 344
Life Is So Good (Dawson),
    315–16
lighting, 319–20
Lindgren, Astrid, 337
Lindisfarne Gospels, 66
Linotype, 110
Lippmann, Walter, 206

list price, 161
literacy
    about, 314–17
    alexia, 316
    aliteracy, 317–18
    booksellers, 256
    defined, 116
    dyslexia, 316
    education, 116–17
    the Enlightenment, 100
    illustrated books, 65,
        66, 82
    Islam, 58–59
    Mayans, 41
    nineteenth century, 113
    Oprah Winfrey, 329
    phonetics, 21
    Reformation, 95
    Roman Empire, 51
    See also reading
literary agents, 162–64, 230
literary estates, 162, 195
Literary Fund, 156–57
literature
    Ancient Greece, 44–46,
        52–53
    compared to genre
        fiction, 346–47
    the Renaissance, 70
    Roman Empire, 52–53
    scribal culture, 70
    Sumerian texts, 30
Little Leather Library, 326
*Lives of Illustrious Men of
    the XVth Century*
    (Vespasiano), 275
Living History (Clinton),
    220
Locke, John, 149
Lodge, David, 164
logographic writing sys-
    tems, 22
Lolita (Nabokov), 182
Longfellow, Henry
    Wadsworth, 159
Longstocking, Pippi, 337
Look Homeward, Angel
    (Wolfe), 234
Lord of the Flies, The
    (Golding), 182
Lorimer, George Horace, 119

Los Angeles Public Library, 308
Losing Battles (Welty), 163
Louis XI (king), 296
Louis XIV (king), 179
lower case, 84
Lufft, Hans, 95
Lumley, Savile, 206
Lunar Society, 324–25
Luther, Martin, 93, 95
Lydon, Ghislaine, 60
Lynch, Patrick, 227

MacCarthy, Fiona, 112
MacLaren, Eli, 16
MacMahon, Kathleen, 160
Madeley, Richard, 260, 325, 329
Madrid Codex, 42
mail-order catalogues, 192, 245, 260
Maimonides, Moses, 55
Manguel, Alberto, 318–19, 320, 322, 344
Mankell, Henning, 338
Mann, Thomas, 189
Manual for Writers of Research Papers, Theses, and Dissertations (Turabian), 227
manufacturing clause, 199
Manufacturing Consent (Chomsky), 206
manuscript books, 228
manuscript readers, 212–13
Manutius, Aldus, 86
Mao Zedong, 191
March, Jill, 335
Marcus Aurelius, 52
Margaret of Cleves, 83
margins, 239
Marian the Librarian (character), 303
Markandaya, Kamala, 327
marketing, 231, 233, 240, 343
Marple, Miss, 337
Martial, 61
Marx, Karl, 281
Mary I (queen), 94, 95, 181
Masoretes, 56

mathematical notation, 22–23
Matsuo Kinsaku, 153
Mayan peoples, 40–41, 97
Mazarin Bible, 91
Mazarin, Jules, 91
McCarthy, Cormac, 329
McClung, Nellie, 160
mechanized typesetting, 108–11
Medici, Cosimo de', 275
Mehta, Deepa, 172
Mein Kampf (Hitler), 207, 256
Memoirs of a Woman of Pleasure (Cleland), 295
Memory Book (Engel), 317
Meredith, George, 212
Mergenthaler, Ottmar, 110
Mérimée, Prosper, 297
Mesoamerica, 40–41, 75
Mesopotamia, 21, 22, 75
Meyer, Michael, 220
microfilming, 126, 309
Middle Ages
   monastic scriptorium, 65–69
   scribal culture, 64–65
   wax tablets, 30
Middlemarch (Eliot), 154
Millennium Series (Larsson), 337, 338
Miller, Arthur, 167
Miller, Henry, 295
Million Little Pieces, A (Frey), 329
Mills & Boon, 124
Milne, A.A., 156, 164
Milton, John, 193
miniatures, 60–61, 67, 83
Minsheu, John, 158
minuscules, 84
miscellanies, 119
Mitchell, Margaret, 201
MobileReference, 202
mock-ups, 239
Modernist writers, 171
"Modest Proposal, A" (Swift), 147
Monotype, 111
Monroe, Marilyn, 167
Moore, Grace, 285

Moretus, Balthasar, 99
Moretus, Edward, 99
Moretus, Jan, 99
Morley, John, 212
Morris, William, 111–12
Morrison, Toni, 182
movable type, 78–79, 81–88
Mudie, Charles Edward, 278–79
Mudie's Select Library, 120–21, 213, 240, 276, 278–79
Muhammad (prophet), 57–58, 167, 193, 194
Murasaki Shikibu, 330
music file sharing, 202
Music Man, The (Wilson), 303
music players, 133, 170
musical notation, 22, 23
Muslims. *See* Islam; Islamic world
My Life (Clinton), 220
My Secret Life (Ashbee), 295

Nabokov, Vladimir, 182
Nafisi, Azar, 325
Name of the Rose, The (Eco), 320
Nancy Drew books, 154
Napster, 202
Nashe, Thomas, 148
National and University Library of Bosnia and Herzegovina, 191–92
National Institutes of Health (NIH), 203
national libraries
   about, 290
   Biblioteca Nazionale Centrale di Firenze, 308
   Bibliothèque François-Mitterrand, 298
   Bibliothèque Nationale, 290, 296–98
   Bibliothèque Nationale du Québec, 287, 301–02
   British Library, 201, 290, 291–96, 297, 299–300, 303

Cataloguing in Publication (CIP) data, 233
censorship, 191–92
copyright depositories, 201–02
evolution of, 290–91
Library of Congress, 170, 201, 290, 298–300, 305–06
modern era, 300–02
national bibliography, 290
National Library of Canada, 301–02
UNESCO definition, 300–01
Vatican Library, 274–75, 304
See also libraries
National Library Service for the Blind and Physically Handicapped (NLS), 170
Native Son (Wright), 327
Naturalis historia (Pliny the Elder), 28, 101
Nazi Germany, 188–90, 207, 256
Nectar in a Sieve (Markandaya), 327
Nesbo, Jo, 338
New American Library (NAL), 122–23
New Earth, A (Tolle), 329
new journalism, 215
New Press, 220–21
New Yorker, 236
newspapers, 180
Newton, Isaac, 99–100
Nicholas V (pope), 274, 275
Nicholls, David, 169
Night (Wiesel), 329
1984 (Orwell), 182, 202
Noble, C. Clifford, 260
Nook, 133, 171, 260. See also Barnes & Noble; e-books; e-readers
Norton, Bonham, 96
Norton, Scott, 233
Nunnally, Tiina, 168–69

Nupedia, 128

obscenity, 188
O'Connor, Joseph, 329
octavo, 92
Odyssey (Homer), 45
Of Mice and Men (Steinbeck), 182
Old Man and the Sea, The (Hemingway), 234
Oliphant, Margaret, 214
Olmecs, 40
Omidyar, Pierre, 264
One Day (Nicholls), 169
online booksellers
Abebooks, 264
about, 261
aggregators, 261
brick-and-mortar booksellers, 252, 257, 258, 259, 260
eBay, 264
See also Amazon.com; booksellers
open access, 203–04
Open eBook (OeB) format, 131
optical character reader (OCR), 129
oracle-bones, 36–37
orthography. See spelling
Orwell, George, 153, 202
outsourcing, 218
Oxford English Dictionary, 103
Oxford University Press, 227

Pablos, Juan, 97–98
page proofs, 241
Paine, Thomas, 205
Panckoucke, Charles-Joseph, 101
Panizzi, Antonio, 292–93, 299, 303
paper
brittle books, 308–10
cloth-based paper, 106–07
invention of, 39–40
Islamic bookmaking, 61
paper prayers, 81
papermaking, 61, 106–08

publishing process, 242
wood-pulp paper, 106–08
paperbacks
Book-of-the-Month Club, 327
cost of, 115
history of, 121–23
mass market vs. trade, 124–25
New American Library (NAL), 122–23
Penguin Books, 122, 123
Pocket Books, 122
popular genres, 124
publishing process, 242–43
See also print formats
papyrus, 26–28, 53
parchment, 32, 33–35, 67–68
Paris Codex, 42
parodies, 200–01
Parsons, Louella, 215
Passmore Edwards, John, 282–84
patents, 181. See also copyright
Patience and Fortitude (Basbanes), 248–49
patriotism, 158
patronage system, 147–48
Paul IV (pope), 184
Pearson, 219
Pelham-Holles, Thomas, 148
PEN International, 165–67
pen names, 146, 149–54, 190
Pencil, The (Petroski), 227
Penguin Books, 122, 123, 219
Pennsylvania Gazette, 119
Pepys, Samuel, 240, 246
perfect-bound books. See paperbacks
periodicals
about, 118–20, 124, 215
fact checking, 236
microfilm preservation, 126
Philosophical Transactions, 100
printing, 98, 232
publishers, 214

reading communities,
325
Saturday Evening Post, 119
as time capsules, 138–39
See also print formats
Perkins, William Maxwell,
234
Perrault, Dominique, 298
Perrin, Noel, 237
Petrarch, 70
Petroski, Henry, 227, 322–23
Pevear, Richard, 168
Philip II (king), 98, 181
Philosophical Transactions, 100
phonetics
Ancient Greek alphabet,
21
Chinese characters, 35–36
Egyptian hieroglyphs,
25–26
Hangul system, 38
logophonetic systems,
40–41
photocopying, 125, 200
physical condition, 251, 253
Pinker, James Brand, 163–64
piracy, 198, 202
plagiarizing, 202
Plantin, Christopher, 98–99
platen, 76, 89, 105, 109, 125
Platt, Myra, 169
Plautus, Titus Maccius, 152
Playing the Odds (Roberts),
335
Pliny the Elder, 28, 101
Pliny the Younger, 246
Plotnik, Arthur, 238
Poe, Edgar Allan, 159, 214
Poirot, Hercule, 337
political activism, 165–67
Politics and Prose, 247
Politkovskaya, Anna, 167
Pomponius Porphyrio, 52
Ponder Heart, The (Welty),
163
Pope, Alexander, 100
pornography, 186–88
Porphyrio, 52
pothi-bound books, 77
Powell, Walter, 252
Powell's Books, 250, 252

*Précis du système hiérogly-
phique* (Champollion),
26
Prenshaw, Peggy, 163
presbyopia, 319
preservation, 307–10
pressmarks, 303
Primary Colors (Klein), 153
primary rights, 161
primers, 66
Prince and the Pauper, The
(Twain), 199
Principia Mathematica
(Newton), 99–100
print culture
digitization, 134–35
expansion of, 97–99
history of, 16
See also scribal culture
print formats
artist's books, 137
bindings, 77–78, 105–06
boustrophedons, 41, 42,
49–50
canvassing books, 159
early printing industry,
92–93
ephemera, 92, 120
folios, 92
miscellanies, 119
octavo, 92
pulp fiction, 124
quarto, 92
scrolls, 24–25, 26–28,
49–50, 62
See also codex; electronic
information; paper-
backs; periodicals
printing
advantages of, 85, 88
Book Arts Revival, 111–13
Catholic Church, 96–97
compared to copying,
85, 91
Diamond Sutra, 79–80
the Enlightenment,
99–100
first printed books, 92
Gutenberg Bible, 86,
90–91, 91
Gutenberg, Johannes,
82–88

industrial revolution,
104–05
Japan, 81
Korea, 81–82
Mesoamerica, 75
Mesopotamia, 75
origins of, 75–76
periodicals, 98
prepress work, 125
print on demand, 126,
139, 242, 252
proofreading, 85, 88
publishing process,
241–43
Reformation, 93–94,
94–96
regulation of, 178–80
printing industry
Authorized Version
(Bible), 96
ephemera, 92
freedom of the press, 177,
193–95
Gutenberg Bible, 92
Officina Plantiniana,
98–99
production houses, 218
regulation of, 178–81
Renaissance printers, 92
See also censorship;
copyright
printing techniques
bookbinding, 77–78,
105–06
book arts, 139
Book Arts Revival, 111–13
color printing, 78, 90,
91, 242
common press, 75–76,
88–93
cylinder press, 105, 107
cylinder seals, 75
early printing industry,
92–93
Fourdrinier machine, 108
frisket, 89
industrial revolution,
105–06
letterpress printing, 75
Linotype, 110
Monotype, 111

movable type, 78–79, 82–88
rollers, 89–90
screw-press, 76, 88–89
Stanhope press, 105
steam-powered production, 105
stereotyping, 108–09
stitching, 106
typesetting, 78–79, 84–87, 108–11, 125
typewriters, 109–10, 125
woodblock printing (xylography), 76–81, 82, 88
See also production techniques
print on demand (POD), 126, 139, 242, 252
Priscian, 52
Private Case, 294–95
production, 235–43
production techniques
bibliography, 16
cuneiform tablets, 29–30
Dictionary of the English Language (Johnson), 103
Islamic bookmaking, 59–61
Mayan codices, 41, 42
medieval Jewish books, 57
monastic scriptorium, 67–69
movable type, 38
paper, 39, 61
papyrus, 28
parchment, 33, 35, 67–68
Qur'an, 33
Torah scrolls, 32, 33
university texts, 71–72
Vindolanda tablets, 53–54
See also printing techniques
production technology
computer printers, 125
desktop publishing, 116, 171
format changes, 134–35
microfilming, 126, 309

optical character reader (OCR), 129
paper-making process, 61, 106–08
photocopying, 125, 200
print on demand, 126
societal effects of, 16
Project Gutenberg, 116, 129
Prologus Galeatus (Jerome), 64
proofreading
correctors, 67
page proofs, 241
printing, 85, 88
proofreader's marks, 235–36
stereotyping, 109
propaganda, 204–07
Prophet Muhammad, 57–58, 167, 193
Prospero's Books, 317
Protestantism, 93–94, 178–79
Prussia, 117
pseudonyms, 146, 149–54, 190
public domain, 196
public libraries
Bibliothèque Saint-Sulpice, 287
bookmobiles, 288
Boston Public Library, 279–80
Carnegie libraries, 282, 283–86, 302–03
Chetham's Library, 280–81
Chicago Public Library, 286
library usage, 317
Los Angeles Public Library, 308
modern era, 288–90
New York Public Library, 286–87
Passmore Edwards libraries, 282–84
public library movement, 115, 117–18, 277–82
Public Library of Science (PLoS), 203

Roman Empire, 273–75
Seattle Public Library, 289
support for, 289
Tacoma Public Library, 285
Westmount Public Library, 287
See also libraries
Public Opinion (Lippmann), 206
publishers
circulating libraries, 121
communication circuit, 17, 135
copyright, 155–56
educational presses, 219, 221
growth of, 215–17
imprints, 218
micro-publishers, 221
multinationals, 217–21
orphan books, 131
paperbacks, 122–23
professionalization of, 212–15
publishing houses, 211
publishing trends, 342
Roman Empire, 52–53
specialization of, 211, 214, 216–17, 219, 220–22
star system, 220
superstores, 261
syndicators, 162
textbook publishing, 222–26
university presses, 226–29
See also editors; names of individual publishers
publishing arrangements
advances, 160, 220
agreement to publish, 161
commissioned texts, 230
contracts, 160–65, 231
fee-for-service, 230
half-profits system, 159
mail-order catalogues, 245
print on demand (POD), 126, 139, 242, 252
reprinting works, 161

royalties, 159–60, 161
self-publishing, 170–73
shared profits system, 159
subscription publication, 157–59
textbook leasing, 226
publishing process
about, 229–30
acquisitions, 230–31
art program, 239
binding, 242–43
book reviews, 345–46
book trailers, 343
bowdlerization, 237
Cataloguing in Publication (CIP) data, 232–33
copyediting, 235–37
cover design, 239–41, 343
design, 238–41
developmental editing, 233–35
dust jackets, 239–40
editorial division, 230
fact checking, 236
hardcover books, 243
indexes, 241–42
ISBNs, 232–33
marketing, 231, 233, 240, 343
mock-ups, 239
paperbacks, 242–43
printing, 241–43
production, 235–43
proofreading, 241–42
querying, 237
sample pages, 239
typesetting, 241
wrappers, 239–40
PubMed, 130
Pulitzer, Joseph, 215
Pullman, Philip, 289
pulp fiction, 124
Punjabi Century, 1857–1947 (Tandon), 330
Putnam, Herbert, 305

Qín Shǐ Huángdì, 37
quarto, 92
querying, 237
Quintilian, 52
quipus, 43–44

quires, 92
Qur'an
codex form, 50, 58
literacy, 59
memorization, 58–59
Prophet Muhammad, 57–58
scripts used, 33
See also Islam; Islamic world; religious writing
QWERTY keyboard, 109–10

radicals, 35–36
Radway, Janice, 326
railway novels, 253–54
Rais, Muhammad, 192
Randall, Alice, 201
Ransome, Arthur, 156
Rape of Lucrece, The (Shakespeare), 150, 152
Rashid, Ahmed, 227
Rasmussen, Eric, 150
Rawlings, Marjorie Kinnan, 234
readability levels, 223, 224–25
readers
action/adventure and suspense, 336–38
book circuit, 313
book collections, 343–44
book culture, 342
book ownership, 121
book reviews, 345–46
bookmarks, 323
bookshelves, 322–23
Braille, 170, 321–22
desks and stands, 322
devices for, 322–24
genre fiction, 332
glasses, 320–21
history of, 313
interaction with books, 16
libraries, 310
lighting, 319–20
literature vs. fiction, 346–47
Mayan codices, 42

Reading Experience Database (RED), 313, 324, 345
specialized books, 330–33
tools for reading, 318–24
vision aids, 318–22
visually impaired readers, 170
See also genre fiction; literacy
Reading at Risk (NEA), 318
reading communities
about, 324–25
book clubs, 259–60, 266
Book-of-the-Month Club, 245, 325, 326–28, 327
community reads, 346
television book clubs, 259–60, 328–30
Reading Lolita in Tehran (Nafisi), 325
Reading on the Rise (NEA), 318
Reformation, 93–94, 94–96, 146
regulating print
about, 178–80
lettres de permission, 179
licensing, 193
trade associations, 180–81
See also censorship
religious writing
Ancient Greek, 45
Ars Moriendi, 82
Book of the Dead, 26–27
Book of Hours, 66
breviaries, 66
Buddhist spells and calendars, 79
Catholic Church, 96–97
codex form, 50
Diamond Sutra, 79–80
Gutenberg Bible, 90–91
modern era, 334
oracle-bones, 36–37
paper prayers, 81
regulation of, 56
specialized publishers, 216, 222
woodblock printing, 82

See also Christian Bible; Hebrew Bible; Qur'an
Remarque, Erich Maria, 189
Renaissance, 69–72, 92
Richelieu, Armand-Jean du Plessis (cardinal), 103
Riding the Bullet (King), 132
Riggio, Leonard, 260
rights. *See* copyright
Road, The (McCarthy), 329
Robb, J.D. *See* Roberts, Nora
Robert, Nicholas-Louis, 108
Roberts, Nora, 153, 335
Robertson, Eleanor Marie, 335
Robinson, James, 17
Rockwell, Norman, 119
rollers, 89–90
Roman Empire, 51–55, 61, 62, 246, 273–75
roman typefaces, 86
romance
    about, 124, 221–22, 334–35
    cover design, 241
    Nora Roberts, 335
    Romance Writers of America (RWA), 165, 334
    See also readers
Romancing the Stone (film), 334
Rombauer, Irma, 173
Romola (Eliot), 160
Room of One's Own, A (Woolf), 149
Rose, Jonathan, 331
Rosetta Stone, 25–26
Ross, Amanda, 330
Rowling, J.K., 154, 160, 331, 332–33, 343
Royal Literary Fund, 156–57
Royal Society, 100, 324
royalties, 159–60, 161
Roycroft Press, 112
Roycroft, Samuel, 112
Roycroft, Thomas, 112
rubricators, 67
Rudolf II (emperor), 267
Ruppel, Berthold, 93
Rushdie, Salman, 167

Ruskin, John, 111–12
Russell, Diarmuid, 163

Sacks, Oliver, 316
Sackville, Lionel, 148
sale-or-return, 266
Salinger, J.D., 182
Saller, Carol Fisher, 238
sample pages, 239
Sand, George, 154
Sandeau, Jules, 154
Sanger, Lawrence, 128
sans serif typefaces, 86
Sarajevo, 191–92
Saro-Wiwa, Ken, 167
Satanic Verses, The (Rushdie), 167
satire, 200–01
Saturday Evening Post, 119
Scenes of Clerical Life (Eliot), 154
Scherman, Harry, 326, 327
Schiffrin, André, 220–21
scholarly editions, 228–29
scholarly presses, 226–29
Scott, Walter, 152
screen adaptations, 169, 172, 336
screw-press, 76, 88–89
scribal culture
    about, 50
    Ancient Greece, 272–73
    China, 79
    error prevention, 56
    income, 57
    Islam, 57–60
    Jewish diaspora, 55–56
    Masoretes, 56
    Middle Ages, 64–65
    monastic scriptorium, 65–69
    regulating print, 178
    the Renaissance, 69–70
    Roman Empire, 51–55
    See also print culture
scripture binding, 78
scrolls, 24–25, 26–28, 49–50, 62, 78–80
Seattle Public Library, 289
Second Chance, The (McClung), 160
seditious texts, 185–86

Seduction of the Innocent (Wertham), 188
Seierstad, Åsne, 192
Sejong the Great (king), 38, 81–82
Selexyz Bookhandels, 254
self-publishing, 170–73
Selfish Gene, The (Dawkins), 227
semasiographic writing systems, 23
Semitic writings
    Ashkenazim communities, 56
    codex form, 50, 56–57
    Dead Sea Scrolls, 34–35
    Haggadah, 57
    parchment, 34
    scribal culture, 55–56
    Sephardic communities, 55–56
    Talmud, 32, 55
    Torah, 32, 50, 56
    writing systems, 31–33
    See also Hebrew Bible; religious writing
Septuagint, 63, 64
Series of Unfortunate Events, A (Snicket), 153
Seuss, Dr., 225
Shakespeare, William, 150–52, 158, 229, 237, 305
Shapiro, James, 155
shared profits system, 159
Shōtoku (empress), 39, 81
Sidhwa, Bapsi, 172, 173
Sièyes, Emmanuel Joseph, 205
Silas Marner (Eliot), 159
Sisters in Crime, 165
Sixtus IV (pope), 274
Sixtus V (pope), 64, 274
Sloane, Hans, 291
slush piles, 231, 234
smart phones, 133
Smirke, Sydney, 293, 295, 297
Smith, Erin, 338
Smith, William Henry, 253
Smithson, James, 299

Smithsonian Institution, 299
Snicket, Lemony, 153
So This Is How It Ends (MacMahon), 160
Society of Authors, 164–65
Sock 'em with Honey (Sidhwa), 172
solicited manuscripts, 230
Somers, Jane, 153
Sound and the Fury, The (Faulkner), 182
Soyinka, Wole, 167
space concerns, 310
Sparks, Nicholas, 170
Spartacus (Fast), 171
speech sounds. *See* phonetics
spelling, 35, 100, 102–04
  See also dictionaries
Spenser, Edmund, 148
Spofford, Ainsworth Rand, 299
square Hebrew script, 31–33
St. Clair, William, 331
stage adaptations, 169, 172
Stamp Act, 180
Stanhope, Charles, 105
Star of the Sea (O'Connor), 329
star system, 220
Starter for Ten (Nicholls), 169
stationers' guilds, 180–81
steam-powered production, 105
Stein, Garth, 169
Steinbeck, John, 164, 182
Stendhal, 153
stereotyping, 108–09
Stewart, Calvin, 285
Stewart, Potter, 186
stitching, 106
stone inscriptions, 29, 31
Strahan, William, 104
Strand Book Store, 248–49
Stratemeyer syndicate, 154
subediting, 235–37
subscription publication, 157–59
subsidiary rights, 161
subsidies, 227

Subversive Copy Editor, The (Saller), 238
Sun Also Rises, The (Hemingway), 234
superstores, 115, 245, 256–61, 263, 265–66
suspense, 336–38
sutra binding, 78
Swan, Annie S., 214
Swift, Jonathan, 147
Sydenham, Floyer, 156
Sylvae (Dryden), 168
syndicators, 162

T. Eaton and Company, 245
Tacoma Public Library, 285
Tale of Genji (Murasaki), 330
Taliban, 192
Taliban (Rashid), 227
Talmud, 32, 50, 55
Tandon, Prakash, 330
Tanguts, 79
Tauchnitz, Bernhard, 121–22
taxes on knowledge, 180
TBS (The Book Service Ltd.), 265
television book clubs, 259–60
Temple, William, 147
termination clause, 161
textbook leasing, 226
textbook publishing, 222–26
textual criticism, 228
textual elements, 29
Thackeray, William, 214
Third Reich, 165–66, 188–90, 207, 256
This Side of Paradise (Fitzgerald), 234
Thorpe, Thomas, 150
Ticknor, George, 280
Tilden, Samuel J., 286
Tilghman, Benjamin C., 107
tilia, 53–55
To Engineer Is Human (Petroski), 227
To Kill a Mockingbird (Lee), 182
To Read or Not to Read (NEA), 318

Tolle, Eckhart, 329
Tolstoy, Leo, 168
Tom Sawyer (Twain), 199
Torah, 32, 50, 56
trade associations, 180–81
trade fairs, 246, 266–68
Trajan (emperor), 273
translation
  about, 168–69
  Ancient Greek, 59
  Antwerp Polyglot (Bible), 98
  Arabic translations, 59
  Christian Bible, 95–96
  katakana, 38
  poetry, 169
  Qur'an, 58
  Rosetta Stone, 25–26
travel writing, 216
traveling libraries, 277
treasonous texts, 185–86
Tremblay, Jean-Noël, 301
Tremblay, Michel, 169
Tropic of Capricorn (Miller), 295
Trylle Trilogy (Hocking), 173
Turabian, Kate, 227
Turow, Scott, 155
Twain, Mark, 107, 152, 199
Two Treatises of Government (Locke), 149
tympan, 89
Tyndale, William, 95
type
  design of books, 238
  mechanized typesetting, 108–11
  type design, 86–88, 112
  typesetting, 241
  typewriters, 109–10, 125

Uighur people, 79
Ulysses (Joyce), 182, 229
uncial, 45
Uncommon Reader, The (Bennett), 288, 338
Undset, Sigrid, 168–69
Universal Copyright Convention (UCC), 199
university presses, 226–29

unsolicited manuscripts, 230–31
upper case, 84
Urton, Gary, 43–44
used booksellers, 250–53, 259, 261

Vadian, Joachim, 267
van Pelt, Frederick, 187
variorum editions, 229
Vatican Library, 274–75, 275, 304
vellum, 34, 112
Venus and Adonis (Shakespeare), 150, 151–52
Vespasiano da Bisticci, 246, 275–76
Vindolanda tablets, 53–55
Virgil, 52, 53
vision aids, 318–22
visually impaired readers, 170
Vivarium, 274–75
Volokhonsky, Larissa, 168
Voltaire, 147–48
vowel sounds, 44
Vulgate (Bible), 63–64

Waldenbooks, 245, 255
Wales, Jimmy, 128
Walker, Alice, 182
Walker, Emery, 111
Wáng Yiróng, 37
war, 205–07
War and Peace (Tolstoy), 168
warranty, 160
Water (film), 172
Waterstone, Tim, 257
Waterstone's, 115, 245, 258, 261
Watson, Peter, 81
Watt, A.P., 162–64
Watt, Charles, 107
Waverley (Scott), 152
wax tablets, 30, 53
Wayne, Tom, 317
Web Style Guide (Lynch and Horton), 227
Wells, H.G., 163
Welty, Eudora, 163
Wertham, Fredric, 188
Westminister Books, 247

W.H. Smith, 245, 253–54, 258, 265
Wharton, Edith, 234
"What Is the History of Books?" (Darnton), 145
What Is the Third Estate? (Sièyes), 205
Wheeler, Maureen, 217
Wheeler, Tony, 217
whirlwind binding, 78
white space, 239
wholesale trade, 245, 259, 264–66
Wiesel, Elie, 329
wiki
  defined, 139
  open access movement, 203–04
Wikipedia, 128, 203–04
Wilde, Oscar, 214
Will in the World (Greenblatt), 152
William of Orange, 149
Williams, David, 156
Williams, W.P., 140
Williams, W.S., 212
Wilson, Meredith, 303
Winchell, Walter, 215
Wind Done Gone, The (Randall), 201
Winfrey, Oprah, 260, 315, 316, 325, 328–29
Winsor, Kathleen, 220
Wolfe, Thomas, 234
women
  anonymous and pseudonymous publishing, 149, 152, 153–54
  librarianship, 302–03, 305
  patronage, 148
  reading, 118, 325, 330
  Women & Children First, 248
  women's clubs, 284
  writing systems, 330
woodblock printing, 76–81, 82, 88
Wood, Ellen Price, 213
Woods, Christopher, 29
Woolf, Leonard, 171

Woolf, Virginia, 16, 149, 171
word-based writing systems, 22, 23
Works of Geoffrey Chaucer (Morris), 112
World War I, 205–06
World War II, 166, 206–07, 256, 300–01
wrapped back binding, 78
wrappers, 239–40
Wright, Richard, 327
Wriothesley, Henry, 152
Writers Emergency Assistance Fund, 157
writing media
  bamboo, 37
  bark, 41
  clay tablets, 29, 30
  palm leaves, 77
  paper, 39–40, 106–08, 112
  papyrus, 26–28, 53
  parchment, 32, 33–35
  shells and bones, 36–37
  stone, 29, 31
  string, 43–44
  tilia, 53–55
  vellum, 34, 112
  wax tablets, 30, 53
  wood, 39, 53–55, 77
writing systems
  about, 22–23
  Ancient Greece, 21, 44–46
  Arabic script, 33
  Braille, 170
  China, 21–22, 35–38, 38
  cuneiform, 21, 28–31
  determinatives, 26
  diacritics, 33
  Egyptian hieroglyphic, 21, 24–28
  emoticons, 23
  Hangul, 38, 81
  icons, 23
  ideograms, 24
  Japan, 35, 38, 330
  Korea, 35, 38, 81
  lexigraphic, 23, 29–30
  logographic, 22, 35–36
  logophonetic, 40–41
  mathematical notation, 22–23

Mesoamerica, 40–41,
  43–44
Mesopotamia, 21, 22,
  28–31
musical notation, 22, 23
Old Roman cursive, 54
origin of, 21–22
quipus, 43–44
phonetics, 21, 25–26, 38
radicals, 35–36
Roman Empire, 51
semasiographic, 23

Semitic writings, 31–33
  square Hebrew script,
    31–33
  uncial, 45
  vowel sounds, 44
Wǔ Zétiān (empress), 79
Wycliffe, John, 95
Wyden, Nancy Bass, 248

xylography, 76–81, 82

Yakubu Gowon, 167

Yale University Press, 227
Yearling, The (Rawlings), 234
Yeats, William Butler, 293
yellow journalism, 215
Yiddish Book Center, 306
You've Got Mail (film), 247
Yugoslavia, 191–92

Zaid, Gabriel, 313
Zapotecs, 40
Zola, Émile, 295

from the publisher

A name never says it all, but the word "broadview" expresses a good deal of the philosophy behind our company. We are open to a broad range of academic approaches and political viewpoints. We pay attention to the broad impact book publishing and book printing has in the wider world; we began using recycled stock more than a decade ago, and for some years now we have used 100% recycled paper for most titles. As a Canadian-based company we naturally publish a number of titles with a Canadian emphasis, but our publishing program overall is internationally oriented and broad-ranging. Our individual titles often appeal to a broad readership too; many are of interest as much to general readers as to academics and students.

Founded in 1985, Broadview remains a fully independent company owned by its shareholders—not an imprint or subsidiary of a larger multinational.

If you would like to find out more about Broadview and about the books we publish, please visit us at **www.broadviewpress.com**. And if you'd like to place an order through the site, we'd like to show our appreciation by extending a special discount to you: by entering the code below you will receive a 20% discount on purchases made through the Broadview website.

Discount code: **broadview20%**

Thank you for choosing Broadview.

Please note: this offer applies only to sales of bound books within the United States or Canada.